HARVARD EAST ASIAN SERIES, 33

THE BUDDHIST REVIVAL IN CHINA

The East Asian Research Center at Harvard University administers research projects designed to further scholarly understanding of China, Korea, Japan, and adjacent areas.

HOLMES WELCH

THE BUDDHIST
REVIVAL IN CHINA

with a section of photographs by

HENRI CARTIER-BRESSON

HARVARD UNIVERSITY PRESS

Cambridge, Massachusetts, 1968

Preface

This is the second in a series of three volumes on Buddhism in modern China. Whereas the first dealt with its system and institutions, this deals with its history, focusing on its rapid evolution in the three decades prior to the Communist victory of 1949. The third volume will take up what has happened (both institutionally and historically) under the Communist regime.

One problem in producing a series is how much to repeat. Should each volume be independent? Or may the author refer to explanations he has given earlier? As might be expected, I have chosen a middle course. Whatever is essential for understanding has, I hope, been included between these covers; but the reader will often be referred to my *Practice of Chinese Buddhism* (Harvard University Press, 1967) for amplification and incidental intelligence. Although the preface of the latter serves the present volume as well, two points bear repetition. First, the following account of the Buddhist revival in China focuses on men, organizations, and events, and deals only incidentally with doctrinal developments and intellectual history. Second, it is not exhaustive. It would have taken more time than was available to me (another two or three years) to complete the exploitation of even the basic source materials—hence the refrain in the notes that "more investigation is needed." It may also be worth noting that, whereas about a third of the data in the preceding volume came exclusively from interviews, the proportion is somewhat less in the pages that follow; and a larger proportion of such interview data comes from single informants rather than from the collation of interviews with several.

For active assistance in gathering material, reading parts of the manuscript, and suggesting improvements I want to thank Robert N. Bellah, Martin Bernal, Paul A. Cohen, Winston Hsieh, P. Y. Hsing, Sidney Liu, Shigeru Matsumoto, Masatoshi Naga-tomi, David Roy, Vincent C. T. Shui, Ernest Young, Mrs. John Quirk, and Mrs. Noriko Tamada. Mrs. John Mitchell read over the whole manuscript, as she had its predecessor, without being thanked until now. I am particularly indebted to Mr. Zunvair Yue (Yü Ching-yü), who went over each page with expert care and found many errors. The generosity of the Reverend Henry P. King made it possible to include the photographic essay by Henri Cartier-Bresson.

Although during most of the preparation of this volume I was on the staff of the East Asian Research Center at Harvard University, some of the material had been collected during the three previous years, when I was receiving a grant from the Joint Committee on Contemporary China. I take this opportunity to express my gratitude to both institutions. ·

I owe the greatest debt to the Chinese Buddhist monks and laymen whose kindness to a stranger and whose patience in answering his questions have well exemplified the bodhisattva path they follow.

Mrs. S. C. Chiu has once again proved herself the best typist in the Far East, while my wife is still my favorite editor.

HOLMES WELCH

Concord, Massachusetts
October 1967

Contents

Illustrations

A BUDDHIST FESTIVAL,
Photographed by
HENRI CARTIER-BRESSON

following page 131

THE BUDDHIST
REVIVAL IN CHINA

Chapter I

THE BEGINNINGS
OF THE REVIVAL

THE history of a religious revival might be expected to start with the decline and decay that preceded it. Yet it is questionable whether Chinese Buddhism was in a state of decay when the revival began. Indeed the very term "revival" may turn out to be inappropriate, and it is used in this book simply because it is the most convenient and customary way of referring to the varied developments that took place in Chinese Buddhism during the second half of the nineteenth century and the first half of the twentieth.

What were these developments? New publishing houses and bookshops were founded to give Buddhist literature a wider circulation. Schools were set up to provide a better education for monks and to train them how to spread the doctrine. Laymen organized Buddhist clubs, partly for social and charitable purposes (like a YMCA), and partly to hold sermons and worship (like a church). Ecumenical contact began with Buddhists abroad. At the same time, monks were trying to unite all the Buddhists of China in a single, national association. Certainly these developments sound like a revival but, as their details are examined in the ensuing chapters, a different significance may emerge.

The man often called the father of the revival is Yang Wen-hui.[1] If he was not its father, at least he exemplified its early phases and offers an appropriate point of departure. Since he came from an eminent family of Confucian literati, it may seem strange that he would have taken any interest in Buddhism at all. But such an interest was not really so strange—certainly much less so than the facade of Confucianism might lead us to believe. In any case he turned to Buddhism because of a series of misfortunes in his personal life, to the details of which we now turn.

YANG WEN-HUI

Yang was born in Anhwei in 1837—two years before the outbreak of the Opium War. In 1838 his father passed the metropolitan examinations, and they moved to Peking. There, when the boy was three years old, he became engaged to a girl of nine.[2] The Chinese view was that a fiancée so much older would be better able to take care of him and help him in case of family quarrels. Six years later she caught smallpox, which left her face so badly disfigured that the parents on both sides suggested breaking the engagement. Yang, by now ten years old, refused. He pointed out that the engagement antedated the smallpox and said: "If I won't have her, who will?" After five years they were married. Although the marriage seemed a happy one, his parents were unable to bear the thought that their only son was saddled forever with an ugly and domineering wife. They bought a couple of maid-servants and urged him to take them as concubines. Again he refused. He wished to avoid trouble in the household and, he said, if he took another wife, he wanted her to be a person he had chosen for himself on the basis of love and congeniality. When the Taiping Rebellion broke out, the family moved from Peking to Hangchow. There he did find such a person. He proposed to take her as a second wife with status equal to his first. But his first wife had just given birth to a son, and she would not agree to it.

Unable to marry the woman he really loved, Yang became depressed. He used to take long walks along the shore of the West

Lake. Browsing there in a bookshop one day, he noticed a copy
of *Ta-ch'eng ch'i-hsin lun* (The Awakening of Faith in the
Mahayana). Although until then he had felt no special attraction
to Buddhism, he bought the book and took it home. It made an
enormous impression on him. "He could not put it down," his
grand-daughter writes. "Suddenly he realized that love, family,
and country held no interest for him. From then on he began
searching for sutras in all the bookshops, monasteries, and temples, and got his friends to search on his behalf. Whenever he
heard that there was some important sutra tucked away somewhere, he would not rest until he had gotten hold of it. He went
everywhere discussing scriptures with eminent monks"—to the
point that when he saw an interesting-looking monk on the street,
he would follow him back to his temple.[3]

Members of his family began to worry about this absorption
in Buddhism but said nothing. In 1863, however, when his father
fell mortally ill, his mother asked him about the family's future.
Who would support them? He assured her that he would fulfill
his responsibilities: he was not going to become a monk. But he
had resolved to study Buddhist sutras and, in the future, to promote their circulation. In order to support his family, he accepted
a series of appointments from Tseng Kuo-fan, Li Hung-chang,
and others. Tseng Kuo-fan, the great viceroy, had received his
chin-shih degree in 1838, the same year as Yang's father. Yang
was put in charge of engineering and construction projects, such
as the building of new government offices in Nanking, where in
1866 he settled permanently. By this time he had found friends
who shared his interest in Buddhism. They were scattered through
central and south China—Kiangsu, Kiangsi, Hunan, and Kwangtung. With them he exchanged visits and ideas. "They considered
that the only hope for this age of the dharma in decay was the
circulation of sutras to save all sentient beings. The Lung-tsang
scriptures in the north were a dead letter. The Shuang-ching library had been burned by marauding troops. Therefore they resolved to cut printing blocks for the Tripitaka [the Buddhist
canon] in order to give it a wider circulation. They drafted by-
laws and over ten of the comrades took on the task of collecting
subscriptions."[4]

Apparently this was in 1866.[5] Then or soon afterwards they began to call themselves the Chin-ling Scriptural Press (Chin-ling K'e-ching Ch'u), Chin-ling being an old name for Nanking.[6] Yang Wen-hui, though busy with his engineering work during the day, would spend the evenings on Buddhism, collating texts for publication. He also engaged in religious practice, chanting the scriptures, reciting buddha's name,[7] and sitting in meditation. In 1874 he put up a building on the Pei-chi Ko, a hillock in Nanking, to store the wooden printing blocks that had been cut so far. Thereafter, though Yang himself was away for long periods, the cutting and printing never halted.

In 1878 he was invited to go to England with the new Chinese ambassador, who was Tseng Kuo-fan's son. He accepted the invitation and for the next three years served as a counselor in the London embassy. Because the latter also handled relations with France and Germany, he enjoyed the opportunity to investigate science and scholarship in different parts of Europe. He took a special interest in astronomy, geography, and optics; he bought a globe, a telescope, and a microscope to take back with him "in order to promote the sciences when he returned home." He also met Professor Max Müller, the giant of oriental scholarship, who was then supervising the translation of the *Sacred Books of the East* in fifty volumes, among them many works on Buddhism. A Japanese pupil of Müller, Nanjio Bunyiu, was preparing a catalogue of the Chinese Tripitaka. He and Yang became friends. According to one source, Yang helped him with the catalogue.[8] Nanjio told him that many Buddhist texts unobtainable in China were still preserved in Japan.

After a three-year tour Yang returned to Nanking and again devoted himself to publishing. When the illustrious Baptist missionary, Timothy Richard, called on him in 1884, he found him hard at work at his press and learned that he was the prime mover behind two other presses, one in Soochow and one in Hangchow.[9] The cost of some of the books they printed was defrayed entirely by lay donors, who assigned the merit arising therefrom to various causes, such as an early rebirth for their parents or a peaceful life for themselves. (The production of assignable merit—good karma—was a common reason for subsidiz-

1 Yang Wen-hui and his son with some of the instruments
brought back from Europe.

ing Buddhist art or literature.) In other cases it appears that
Yang paid for the printing out of his own pocket and, though it
amounted to only forty or fifty Chinese dollars* a book, it eventually exhausted his savings. Therefore in 1886 he went to London
for a second tour in the embassy. This time he studied English,
politics, and industry, and was so impressed with the importance
of what he learned that he urged the Manchu government to
send more of his compatriots abroad for study. When his advice
went unheeded, he resolved to quit government service for good
and to devote the rest of his life to Buddhism. This resolve he
kept. In 1890, two years after his return to Nanking, it happened
that a kinsman of his wife's was appointed to the Chinese embassy in Japan. Yang enlisted his help in collecting Buddhist books
there and wrote to Nanjio. Eventually the kinsman returned to
China with two or three hundred volumes that were not in the

---

* Here and below all sums are given in Chinese currency unless otherwise
specified. The value of a Chinese silver dollar varied widely, but it was usually
worth from a quarter to half as much as a U.S. dollar.

Chinese Tripitaka and that Nanjio had helped him to find.[10] Yang printed the best of them. When he ran through his savings again, he began to raise money by selling the scientific instruments that he had brought back from Europe or by manufacturing copies of them.[11] But he cannot have been altogether indigent, for in 1898 he bought a large estate in the middle of Nanking and put up an elaborate set of buildings into which he moved his family and the press the following year.

This, however, is getting ahead of the story. In 1893 something had occurred that must have broadened Yang's horizons. 1893 was the year of the Parliament of Religions in Chicago. Among those attending it was the same Reverend Timothy Richard who had visited Yang nine years earlier. There was also a lay devotee from Ceylon, the Anagarika Dharmapala, who had founded the Maha Bodhi Society in 1891 with the goal of restoring the Buddhist places of pilgrimage in India and promoting a revival of Buddhism. Dharmapala was a young man (only twenty-nine) of great enthusiasm. On the way back to his country, he stopped at Shanghai in the hope of winning the support of Buddhists in China. Since he could not speak Chinese, he asked for help from the Reverend Joseph Edkins whose *Chinese Buddhism,* completed in 1879, had made him the leading Western authority of the time. Rather naturally Edkins took him to the oldest and largest monastery in the Shanghai area, the Lung-hua Ssu.[12] On this first visit, little was accomplished. But a date was set for the following week, when Dharmapala would return, hold a discussion with the senior monks, and join them in performing devotions.

On the appointed day, December 28, 1893, Dharmapala was accompanied not by Edkins, but by Timothy Richard and Otto Franke, then of the German consular service. When he got to the monastery, he found that no preparation whatever had been made for the joint devotions. Nothing daunted, he unpacked a leaf of the Bodhi Tree and a three-foot stone image of the Buddha from Bodhgaya. He explained that it was eighteen hundred years old. The monks seemed unimpressed. Finally he asked Franke to translate a long appeal for Chinese help in protecting Buddhist holy places in India. It ended:

It is our object to restore the sacred rites, to station bhikkhus from all Buddhist countries in these places, to train them as Buddhist missionaries to preach Buddhism to the people of India, to retranslate Buddhist scriptures into Indian languages from Chinese; and to carry out this scheme, we have formed a great Buddhist society, called the Maha Bodhi Society, on an international basis. All the Buddhist countries, viz., Japan, Siam, Burma, Tibet, Ceylon, Chittagong and Arakan, have joined us in our work, and now I make this appeal to the Buddhists of China.

During the discussion that followed, the monks kept asking how Chinese Buddhists would be able to get to India and what was the position of the Indian government; but in the end they appeared to give in, promising to publish the text of Dharmapala's appeal. He left the monastery with a sense that he had won them over. The next day, however, they came to see him and begged to be released from their promise on the grounds that, if it were carried out, "difficulties" would ensue. Instead they proposed to let people hear about the Dharmapala's appeal by word of mouth.

Franke, who later wrote an account of the incident, was of the opinion that the monks changed their minds because Dharmapala had approached them on behalf of a religious *society*. De Groot, the eminent Dutch Sinologist, agreed and cited Franke's account to support his view that in China "a dread of everything in any way resembling association weighs most heavily on the State and its whole officialism . . . All societies, therefore, except those of fellow-clans people, have to be exterminated, like the sects, with strangulation, flogging, and banishment."[13] If involvement in an indigenous Chinese society was dangerous, it was much more so to get involved with a foreign society, especially one in India, a country that had been conquered by the same red-faced foreigners who were now threatening to conquer China—and whose representatives had accompanied Dharmapala to help him make his first contact. No wonder the monks at the Lung-hua Ssu refused to have anything to do with him.

Timothy Richard, always a benevolent soul, did not like to see Dharmapala disappointed. He remembered Yang Wen-hui in Nanking, who, unlike the monks, would be neither afraid of foreigners (since he had lived abroad for six years) nor afraid of the Chinese government (since he had high official connections). Yang was called to Shanghai to meet Dharmapala. The details of their conversation are not recorded, so far as I know. But we are told that Yang was moved by the earnestness with which Dharmapala urged the need to restore Buddhism in India and to spread it westward.[14] Nonetheless he felt constrained to reply that "it was out of the question for Chinese Buddhists to go to India; and he recommended rather that Indians be sent to China so that they might study the language and then translate into their mother tongue, with the help of native [Chinese] monks, as many sacred writings as the [Maha Bodhi] Society wished."[15]

Despite this rather inconclusive first contact, it seems probable that Yang and Dharmapala corresponded in the ensuing years. I have found no mention of it before 1908, when Yang received a letter from Dharmapala "agreeing that they should make a common effort to revive Buddhism in order to spread it throughout the world,"[16] but this agreement was probably the end product of a gradual change in Yang's point of view. There is evidence of such a change as early as 1894, when he collaborated with Timothy Richard on an English translation of the *Awakening of Faith*. Yang entered this collaborative venture "so that Buddhism might eventually spread westward."[17]

In 1896 the Japanese Higashi-Honganji sect established a branch temple in Nanking, not only to serve the growing number of Japanese Buddhists who lived there, but also to attract Chinese converts. In 1898 came the abortive Hundred Days of political reform, in which persons close to Yang were involved. In 1901, after China's fourth defeat at the hands of Westerners, reforms were started by the very conservatives who had cut them short three years earlier; barriers against intercourse with the outside world began to fall. In 1905 the civil-service examination system gave way to a program of modern schools.

All this must have had its effect on Yang's thinking. Whereas in 1893 he had rejected Dharmapala's proposal that Chinese Buddhists be sent to India, now he edited a textbook[18] and set up a school for the express purpose of training Chinese monks for missionary work abroad. There is some uncertainty as to when he began to prepare the ground for these steps, but the preface of the textbook is dated 1906 and classes began at the school in 1908. There is also some uncertainty about the role of Dharmapala, but the consensus seems to be that the school was originally his suggestion.[19]

It was located in Yang's mansion in Nanking (which also housed the Scriptural Press) and was called the Jetavana Hermitage (Chih-huan Ching-she). The twenty-four students enrolled (twelve monks and twelve laymen) were taught Buddhism by Yang himself, while other teachers (all laymen) gave the courses in English and Chinese literature. The only monk on the faculty, Ti-hsien, was dean of students (hsüeh-chien).[20] In Buddhist studies particular emphasis was given to the Dharmalaksana school, which Yang now felt to be the most compatible with science.[21]

This appears to have been the first time in Chinese history that monks studied Buddhist texts under a lay teacher, and it was a harbinger of things to come, not only in China but in all of Asia. Unfortunately Yang's personal resources proved unequal to the expense of housing, feeding, and teaching so many students; nor was he able to raise sufficient funds elsewhere. Laymen had long been accustomed to the idea of gaining merit through the support of publication, but they were not sure how much merit would accrue from financing a school. Hence it was forced to close down after one academic year. In 1909, the year it closed,[22] Yang founded the Association for Research on the Buddhist Religion (Fo-chiao Yen-chiu Hui) and served as its president and principal lecturer. Lectures on the sutras were given once a week, presumably to audiences composed largely of laymen. This was to be his last innovation. He had long been in poor health and died in 1911 at the age of seventy-five.

Although Yang Wen-hui is widely regarded as the father of Buddhist revival, his was not the first scriptural press, nor the first school for monks, nor the first Buddhist association. Scriptural presses had long been operated by certain large monasteries. In Kiangsu and Chekiang during the 1860's and 1870's, the monk Miao-k'ung set up five new ones which published some three thousand volumes of the Tripitaka. The best known of these five was the North Kiangsu Scriptural Press (Chiang-pei K'o-ching Ch'u) at the Fa-tsang Ssu in Yangchow. Although I have not ascertained the exact chronology of Miao-k'ung's activities, they began when he was still a layman (his lay name was Cheng Hsüeh-ch'uan) and are said to have antedated the efforts of Yang Wen-hui, indeed to have been the inspiration for them.[23] As for Buddhist schools, the first, as we shall see, was set up in 1904, three years before the Jetavana Hermitage, which was at least the third. The Buddhist textbook that Yang edited had already been edited and published by a Pure Land monk, Yin-kuang, only a short time before. As for Buddhist associations, we hear of one as early as 1900.[24]

The importance of Yang Wen-hui, then, lies not so much in the earliness of his efforts as in their influence. His scriptural press turned out over a million copies of Buddhist books. His disciples included some of the leading Buddhist monks and lay-men of the next generation. He started the revival of interest in the Dharmalaksana school. Most important of all, he was the first Chinese Buddhist to go to Europe, to become acquainted with European science, and to think of Buddhism as a world religion in a scientific world.

MODERN EDUCATION FOR MONKS

Mention has just been made of the Buddhist schools that preceded Yang Wen-hui's. The first of these was set up in 1904 at Changsha, the capital of Hunan. Its purpose was not so much to promote the education of monks as to protect Buddhist property. To understand how this could be, we must go back to the year 1898, when the young Kuang-hsü Emperor came under the influence of the group of reformers led by K'ang Yu-wei. Included in one of K'ang's memorials to the throne was a proposal that Buddhist and Taoist temples be converted into modern schools.

This was by no means a new proposal. It had been made as early as 1662 by Huang Tsung-hsi. Huang, one of the most renowned Ch'ing intellectuals, was no friend of the clergy. In his view, "the biggest Buddhist and Taoist monasteries, nunneries, and temples should be changed into academies to be directed by teachers of the classics and the smaller ones into elementary schools to be directed by primary teachers." Income from temple estates, he said, should be used for school upkeep.[25]

A month or so after K'ang Yu-wei echoed Huang's proposal, it was endorsed by an even more powerful voice. Chang Chih-tung suggested that, in order to provide premises for the schools that he too was advocating, 70 percent of the temples in China should be confiscated. Accordingly the emperor issued an edict on July 10, 1898, instructing the local authorities to convert into class-rooms those temples that were not used for ancestral rites. This was done with dispatch in a few areas, especially in Hunan where Chang Chih-tung himself was governor-general.[26]

The Hundred Days of reform were soon over. When the Empress Dowager resumed power in September 1898, she annulled almost all the edicts that had been issued at the instigation of the reformers, including the authority to confiscate temples.[27] But the reaction was short-lived: after the Boxer Rebellion she had to come to terms with the times. Throughout the country the existing academies were ordered to become primary schools, middle schools, and universities, and, where there were no acad-emies, new schools were ordered set up. But where were build-ings and money to be found? The central government was impoverished. Again eyes turned to Buddhist monasteries, which in many localities were the largest and emptiest buildings and which enjoyed a landed income that could be seized with less outcry than the gentry's. So about 1904 the government "issued a general order to use temple property wherever available for the establishment of schools."[28]

This marked the end of an epoch for Chinese Buddhism. De-spite their official Confucian commitment, most of the Ch'ing emperors had been patrons of the *sangha* (the Buddhist clergy), and the government had protected monasteries. Now it suddenly became the sponsor of their liquidation. It is not hard to imagine the dismay in Buddhist circles. What were they to do? A solution was provided by two Japanese priests, Mizuno Baigyo and Ito Kendo, who arrived in China at this very time (1904). They

pointed out that, if monastic property was being seized to promote modern education, the obvious countermeasure would be
for the monasteries to promote modern education themselves.
Since seizures of property were again particularly widespread in
Hunan,[29] Mizuno and Ito went to Changsha, the provincial capital, and set up the Hunan Sangha School (Hu-nan Seng Hsüeh-
t'ang) at the K'ai-fu Ssu. According to a Buddhist source, it was
established in order "to resist the occupation of monasteries and
the seizure of their property by officials and the gentry. This was
when the Chinese sangha began operating schools to protect its
property."[30] Although the Hunan Sangha School was operated
"on a very small scale," the idea was timely and similar institutions were soon established elsewhere.

It is difficult to place these developments in perspective. We
do not know how many Buddhist monks and monasteries there
were in the China of 1904. The numbers may have been lower or
higher than those reported in the first reliable survey, made a
quarter century afterwards: 738,000 monks and nuns living in
233,000 temples (by far the largest professional establishment
among China's religions).[31] Nor do we know how many Buddhist
temples were actually confiscated. The sources I have read do
not cite any outstanding examples; so it seems likely that now,
as later, most of those confiscated were small temples of no great
renown. Yet their fate served as warning to the large, famous temples and, as confiscations continued, monks became willing to
accept even further suggestions from Mizuno. He now urged that
they place themselves under the wing of the Higashi-Honganji
temple in Kyoto, the headquarters of the Japanese Buddhist sect
that had been carrying on missionary work in China since 1876
(not without political motives). Toward the end of 1904 some
thirty-five Chekiang monasteries became its affiliates, thirteen in
Hangchow alone, and the movement began to spread to other
provinces. Whenever any one of these monasteries was threatened
with confiscation, it could go to the Japanese consulate for protection.[32] This jolted Chinese officialdom, which must have had
visions of all the monasteries in China acquiring a kind of extraterritoriality. Soon a deputation of eminent monks arrived in the
capital from Shanghai. It was led by the famous "Eight Fingers,"

the abbot of the largest Ningpo monastery, whose peculiar name came from the fact that in his youth he had burned off two fingers as an offering to the Buddha.[33] With the help of Buddhist devotees at court, including Prince Su Shan-ch'i, an able and high-ranking Manchu, they presented a memorial to the throne, asking for the protection of monastic property. On April 12, 1905, they were rewarded by an imperial edict that deplored the harm done to the monastic establishment in the course of setting up schools and factories in various provinces. It ordered officials to protect all monasteries, large and small, "and not to permit evil gentry and rapacious underlings to make forced levies on monastic property on the excuse that this was in conformity with government policy"—phrasing from which we may infer that such levies *had* been in conformity with government policy until then. In any case the wave of confiscations in many provinces subsided.[34]

On September 1, 1905, an imperial edict abolished the examination system. Now instead of looking to examinations as the only ladder for official employment, people had to put their hopes in the schools that in most localities had yet to be established. Pressure for the confiscation of monastic property again increased. Almost immediately a progressive monk, Wen-hsi, opened the Sangha Middle School (Seng-li P'u-t'ung Chung-hsüeh) at the T'ien-ning Ssu, Yangchow. It operated for about two years and then was closed down by the authorities, who suspected that it might be a center for revolutionary activities. Wen-hsi was arrested. To take its place, the Sangha Normal School (Seng Shih-fan Hsüeh-t'ang) was established in Nanking in the autumn of 1910. Ti-hsien was placed in charge, but he soon resigned in favor of Yüeh-hsia. The Sangha Normal School operated only for one academic year and in 1911, according to one source, was "destroyed by the revolutionary army of the Republic."[35]

A history of all the early schools would prove repetitive.[36] None lasted long enough to be important in itself, but some of the monks who studied or taught in them were to establish successor institutions that were far more permanent. Ti-hsien, Yüeh-hsia, Yüan-ying, T'ai-hsü, Chih-kuang—these are men whose names we shall meet again and again. Chih-kuang enrolled in the Sangha Middle School when it opened in 1905, then in Yang

Wen-hui's Jetavana Hermitage in 1907, and then in the Sangha
Normal School in 1910. In other words he attended the three
most important of the early seminaries. All of them, he has told
me, were operated under a permit from the authorities. The curriculum had to be the same as that in the new lay schools, and
the instructors were laymen. Courses in Buddhism, taught by
monks except at the Jetavana Hermitage, were supplementary.
"The purpose of all these schools," in Chih-kuang's words, "was to
revive Buddhism (*hsing-chiao*), because for many years the clergy
had emphasized religious cultivation, not lecturing and exegesis,
and so monks did not have a deep enough understanding of the
scriptures."

It is true that many monks did not understand the scriptures,
and those who did seldom expounded them in public. The sangha's
educational activities were limited. Hence, as the educated public became more and more concerned with the improvement of
education, it became increasingly critical of the sangha—and
perhaps its criticism was exacerbated by the contrast with the
Christian missionaries, whose educational activities were so conspicuous. This was partly why Buddhist temples were among the
first buildings to be confiscated for the new lay schools. By starting schools of its own, the sangha hoped not only to "get the
jump" on the confiscators, but to counter the basis of their criticism. To give monks a modern education and train them how to
lecture in public would improve the sangha's public image. Furthermore, it would give the monks a firmer grasp of secular affairs
so that they could better defend their property by legal action.

This concern for property may seem surprisingly materialistic
and inappropriate. Actually it was no more inappropriate than,
say, the concern of a university's trustees for protecting its endowment.[37] Just as unearned income is necessary in Western
universities for teaching and research, so it was necessary in
Chinese monasticism to provide the leisure for study, meditation,
and other religious activities. The alternative was for monks to
support themselves by performing rites for the dead—beating a
"wooden fish" for a dollar a day—which, in fact, was the unedify-
ing occupation of the majority of the Chinese sangha.

This is as far as the history of Buddhist schools will be traced

for the present. Chapter Six will be entirely devoted to their proliferation and development and to the role they played in the
Buddhist revival. Now we shall take up a different thread in the
early pattern of the revival: revolutionary monks.

REVOLUTIONARY MONKS

One of the pupils at the Yang Wen-hui's school was T'ai-hsü.
Just as Yang's career exemplifies the early phases of the Buddhist
revival, its middle and later phases can be seen through the career of T'ai-hsü. He was born on January 8, 1890, in Hai-ning
hsien, Chekiang. He became a monk, as he says himself, because
of his "longing for the paranormal powers of immortals and
buddhas . . . between whom I made no distinction."[38] It was only
in 1906, two years after he was ordained, that he came to realize
that Taoist and Buddhist divinities were not the same. He studied
the Tripitaka and practiced meditation under the guidance of
Eight Fingers, who had presided at his ordination. He worked
on an enigmatic question[39] and had his nose tweaked. He wrote
on his first photograph: "You! I know you! You are you. You are
inscribing this for yourself." In the winter of 1907–08, as he read
a *prajna* sutra, he underwent a spiritual awakening in which he
had a sensation of radiance, timelessness, certainty, and so on. In
other words, his early career was conventional.

In the spring of 1908, however, he met a monk named Hua-
shan who, as T'ai-hsü's biographer puts it, "was the first person
to start modernizing the sangha."[40] Hua-shan told his young
friend about new trends at home and abroad, and said that
Buddhism could accomplish nothing unless it quickly mended its
ways and promoted education for the sangha. These were strange
ideas to T'ai-hsü, and the two of them argued for more than ten
days. Finally Hua-shan gave him certain books to read, a veritable library of political reform: K'ang Yu-wei's *Ta-t'ung shu*, Liang
Ch'i-ch'ao's *Hsin-min shuo*, Yen Fu's *T'ien-yen lun*, and T'an Ssu-
t'ung's *Jen-hsüeh*. By the time he had finished reading them, the
young man was completely won over. "His orientation shifted
from the absolute to the world of men," and he resolved that the
world should be saved through Buddhism.

In the summer of 1908 T'ai-hsü made friends with a monk who was not just a reformer, but a revolutionary. His name was Ch'i-yün and he came from Hunan (like Mao Tse-tung). He too had been a disciple of Eight Fingers in his youth, but then had gone to study in Japan where he had joined the T'ung-meng Hui, the revolutionary society that Sun Yat-sen organized in 1905. He returned to China with Hsü Hsi-lin and Ch'iu Chin, "to plot secretly for revolution."[41] It was Hsü and Ch'iu who engineered the unsuccessful uprising at Anking in July 1907. Most of the time Ch'i-yün wore Western clothes and leather shoes but, whenever it became advisable, he would put on his monastic gown and hide in a monastery. Presumably he was in hiding when T'ai-hsü first met him at the Smaller Chiu-hua Ssu in southern Chekiang. The young monk, probably still a little giddy with the new ideas he had imbibed from Hua-shan, was now introduced to an even stronger brew. Ch'i-yün loaned him such revolutionary literature as the *People's Tribune* and Tsou Jung's *Revolutionary Army*.[42] T'ai-hsü soon became an enthusiastic radical. In 1910 he moved to Kwangtung Province, where he became intimate with revolutionaries of every hue, particularly the socialists and the anarchists; attended many of their secret meetings; and even "learned their free and easy ways."[43] He read Bakunin, Proudhon, Kropotkin, and Marx. Ch'i-yün, who had been imprisoned in 1908 on the suspicion of revolutionary activities, was arrested again in May 1911 after the unsuccessful uprising in Canton. Among his papers was found a eulogy for its martyrs which had been written by T'ai-hsü. Soldiers were dispatched to arrest him too, but he escaped. When the revolution finally broke out in October 1911, he was staying with Tsung-yang in Shanghai.

Tsung-yang, then fifty years old, was one of the most remarkable monks in China. His career, like T'ai-hsü's, had begun conventionally, except for the fact that between his tonsure and his ordination he is said to have studied Sanskrit, Japanese, and English. He was ordained in 1880 at the Chin Shan monastery, a famous meditation center, and was among those slated to become its abbot.[44] People respected him not only for his ecclesiastical eminence, but also as a poet and painter. Among his disciples was Mrs. Silas Hardoon, the Chinese wife of a Baghdad millionaire in Shanghai. After he gave her the lay initiation in 1892,[45] he left Chin Shan, where his term as abbot still lay far in the future, and settled in Hardoon Gardens, her enormous estate in the French Concession. There he became interested in the new political movements and began to have contact with their leaders. It was his view that the only road to national salvation lay through better schooling for the nation's youth. Therefore in 1902 he joined a group of like-minded persons in setting up the Chinese Education Society, of which he was elected president. At first the aim was to prepare and distribute more modern and better textbooks. Soon, however, they joined with a group of radical students in setting up a new school, known as the Patriotic Society (Ai-kuo Hsüeh-she), funds for which were provided by Mrs. Hardoon. All went well for a time, but in June 1903 the students decided to sever relations with the Education Society, which was trying to interest them more in study than in political discussion and which they therefore regarded as too conservative. Tsung-yang accepted the break in a letter published in *Su-pao* on June 25th. Evidently he did not at this time share all the students' revolutionary ideas.

Su-pao, to which he was an occasional contributor, reflected a broad spectrum of anti-government opinion. Operating in the International Settlement in Shanghai, it could speak out boldly, since it seemed to be beyond the reach of the Manchu government that it was trying to overthrow. But now at the end of June 1903 the Chinese authorities were finally able to get their counterparts in the International Settlement to suppress both *Su-pao* and the Patriotic Society. Two of the leaders were arrested; the rest fled. Mrs. Hardoon helped Tsung-yang to make his escape to Japan. There for the first time he met Sun Yat-sen. They became friends and "together made plans for revolution." From that time on, when Sun needed money, Tsung-yang was often able to collect it for him from Buddhist devotees among the rich overseas Chinese. In the autumn of 1903, for example, he paid Sun's fare to Hawaii.[46]

After five years in Japan, Tsung-yang went back to Shanghai and to Hardoon Gardens. His first undertaking was to start the Patriotic Girls' School. His next was to edit and reprint the entire

Buddhist Tripitaka, a gigantic task that he began in 1909 and finished in 1913. Thirty monks and scholars, working under his direction, compiled the Pin-chia Hermitage edition in 414 stitched volumes at the cost of $150,000, much of which was supplied by Mrs. Hardoon.[47]

Thus he was in the midst of this great scholarly enterprise when T'ai-hsü met him in Hardoon Gardens on the eve of the Chinese revolution. For many years Tsung-yang had worn lay clothes and used a lay name (Huang Chung-yang). After the revolution was betrayed by Yüan Shih-k'ai, he became disillusioned and for the second time turned his back on the world. But when he returned to Chin Shan he did not receive the abbotship · to which he was entitled. His brother monks felt that it would be improper to hand the monastery over to someone who had lived as a layman and taken part in revolutionary politics. In 1916, excluded from the succession, he shut himself up at Chin Shan for three years' reflection. Only in 1919 did he emerge, to spend the last two years of his life in restoring the Ch'i-hsia Ssu, a famous monastery near Nanking.

Tsung-yang, Ch'i-yün, and T'ai-hsü were not the only revolutionary monks of the era. Another was Man-shu (1884–1918), a Cantonese born and brought up in Japan. There is no need to recount his career in any detail: it alternated between the dharma and revolution, monk's robes and Western dress. Like Tsung-yang he often used his lay surname, so that he was usually known as Su Man-shu. Most of the time he was not in a monastery at all, but out earning his living as a journalist and teacher. It was he who taught English at Yang Wen-hui's Jetavana Hermitage.[48]

Although Yang Wen-hui was not a revolutionary in the same sense, he too had opposed the Ch'ing dynasty all his life. When he was but eleven years old, Tseng Kuo-fan asked why he had not taken his preliminary civil-service examinations. Yang replied: "Why should I try to make my name under foreigners?"—meaning the Manchus. He never did take the examinations and always held government posts on a temporary basis and only because he needed the income. Revolutionaries like T'ai-hsü, Man-shu, and Ti-hsien were to be found at his school; his son became indirectly linked with the Hundred Days in 1898; and one of his pupils turned out to be its most famous martyr, T'an Ssu-t'ung. In 1896 the young T'an went to Nanking to await his civil-service appointment. Instead of keeping in touch with official circles, he devoted himself to the study of Buddhism under Yang Wen-hui. These Buddhist studies provided part of the basis for his one book, *Jen-hsüeh,* which with its brilliant and iconoclastic ideas on morals and government "had no equal throughout the Ch'ing period."[49] In 1898 when the Dowager Empress crushed the reform movement, he let himself be arrested and executed so that the movement would have a martyr. Buddhists might ask: was his martyrdom inspired partly by the bodhisattva ideal of self-sacrifice?

There were other lay Buddhists involved in reform and revolution. Chang Ping-lin (Chang T'ai-yen) was one of those arrested in the *Su-pao* case. He had already become immersed in the study of Buddhism and, while he was serving his three-year sentence in Shanghai, he "devoted himself single-mindedly to the work of Maitreya and Vasubandhu."[50] He expounded Buddhist scriptures to his fellow prisoner, Tsou Jung. "If you can understand these books," he told him, "then you can spend three years in prison without any feeling of misery."[51] Tai Chi-t'ao, another important figure in the activities that led up to the 1911 revolution, was not at that time a Buddhist, but became one after an attempt at suicide in 1922.[52] Liang Ch'i-ch'ao, the most illustrious leader of the reformers, had a lifelong interest in Buddhist philosophy.

Not only these eminent monks and laymen but many Buddhists who remain anonymous became involved in the political struggle of the times. For example, when the revolution broke out in 1911, the monks in some areas organized "sangha troops" (*seng-chün*). This happened in Shanghai, where Ch'üeh-fei of the Jade Buddha Monastery was the prime mover. The Shanghai monks are said to have joined in the battle for Nanking (December 2, 1911). Several hundred sangha troops were organized in Shaosing by the Venerable T'ien-yen of the K'ai-yüan Ssu: "He used monastic property to supply troops" and placed Ti-hsien, then abbot of the Chieh-chu Ssu, at their head.[53] In Wuhan, sangha troops were formed not at their own initiative, but on the orders of the commander-in-chief of the new Republican army. At least one monk, Yüeh-hsia, went to Shanghai to avoid getting involved.[54] As soon as the revolution was over, the troops disbanded.

These episodes, about which we know much too little, suggest that there might have been hundreds of revolutionary monks in China on the eve of the Republican era. But there is a danger of inflating the connection between Buddhism and the Chinese revolution. Many of the lay revolutionaries were anti-Buddhist and heartily supported the plan to take over monasteries for schools. As for the sangha, probably most of its members, then as always, considered that political activity was dangerous and contrary to their vows. They saw no reason to change the imperial system, since Chinese emperors had been patrons and protectors of Buddhism. Some of the most eminent monks, like Eight Fingers and Hsü-yün, were on good terms with members of the imperial family and high officials. They were conservatives not only ecclesiastically, but politically.

The developments described in this chapter—publishing houses, monastic schools, foreign contacts, and political action— cannot be attributed to the spontaneous initiative of this conservative majority of monks, or, indeed, of any other group of Buddhists. Rather, these developments came in reaction to a series of external events, each of which affected different categories of Buddhists in different ways and for different reasons. For example, the reason that Yang Wen-hui and his friends started their scriptural press in the 1860's was that so many of the Buddhist libraries around them had gone up in flames in the 1850's. This is not mere conjecture. When Timothy Richard inquired in 1884 why Yang was reprinting Buddhist books, he was told that it was "in order to replace those destroyed during the Taiping Rebellion."[55] This is partly why the reprinting began in central China, where the rebels made their headquarters. There and at that time, monastic Buddhism was flourishing. What motivated Yang was not the sight of monasteries in decay (because many of those he saw were just being rebuilt), but the traditional wish to gain merit by filling the shortage of Buddhist books.

But if Yang and his friends had little reason to consider Buddhism decaying, they must have become increasingly aware of the contrast offered by Christianity, more and more of whose evangelists they could see about them after the treaties of 1858 and 1860. It is a significant coincidence that 1866, the year Yang began his printing venture, was also the year when the first party of the China Inland Mission took advantage of the newly won right of Europeans to live in the interior rather than in the treaty ports. Letter-perfect in the gospel, they expounded it not intramurally to other clerics, but on street corners to audiences of common people. How many Buddhist monks knew their scripture so well? And of the few that did, how many were expounding it to lay audiences? Yet one of their traditional obligations was to spread the dharma among all sentient beings. Such thoughts must have reinforced Yang's determination to make the scriptures available.

When he went to England in 1878, Yang learned of the advanced state of Buddhist studies in Europe and Japan. It is safe to assume that he felt a twinge of national pride. Did China lag behind even in the study of her own books? In 1893 he came in contact with Dharmapala, who suggested to him the possibilities for Buddhist missionary work abroad, for converting India and the West. At first he appears to have been unimpressed by the idea, but two years later came China's defeat by Japan. Like many of his compatriots, Yang must have been disheartened by his country's backwardness. It was quite natural for him to ask himself: at least in respect to *Buddhism* can China play the role of the teacher, not the pupil, of other nations? But this would require specially trained personnel. Therefore he started his school to prepare monks for missionary work abroad.

The monks acted from different motives. In 1904, when they established the first monastic school, it was not to prepare for missionary work, but to prevent confiscation of their property. It is difficult to guess whether or not they would have eventually started monastic schools on their own initiative in order to spread the dharma for its own sake, but it seems fairly clear that when they did start them, it was because they were forced to. That is why such schools dated only from the confiscation of monasteries and then proliferated only as the threat of confiscation increased. The same applies to the Buddhist associations that the monks set up after 1912. Government protection for Buddhist property was urgently needed, and only by joining forces could it be secured. These facts do not mean that self-preservation was the sole reason why the clergy took part in the Buddhist revival. From the beginning there were a few monks who thought that this or that innovation was good in itself and, as the revival developed, more and more monks came to think likewise, so that one aspect of the revival became voluntary and deliberate modernization. But this did not provide the initial impetus.

Chapter II

THE STRUGGLE
FOR NATIONAL
LEADERSHIP

Yang Wen-hui died on October 8, 1911, just two days before the Republican revolution broke out in Wuhan. Whatever dwindling protection Buddhism had been given by the Ch'ing government now disappeared. All its earlier enemies—Confucians, Christians, modernizers, predatory officials, and bandits (the categories are obviously not exclusive)—swarmed in to carry out what one source describes as "a wave of expulsion of monks and destruction of monasteries in many provinces"[1] followed close behind by new enemies—warlords, Japanese, and Communists. Each group coveted Buddhist monastery buildings and land for its own special purposes. The buildings could be turned into spacious schoolrooms by the modernizers who were trying to promote mass education; into offices by the bureaucrats who had to house new organs of administration; into barracks by warlords, Nationalists, and Japanese; and into public hospitals, orphanages, and homes for the aged. The income from monastery farmland could be sequestered to operate the new schools, or the land could be confiscated outright to inaugurate programs of land reform, whether Nation-

2 The Ch'ung-en Pagoda, Sungkiang, Kiangsu, as it looked after its post-Taiping reconstruction (about 1900).

3   The Ch'ung-en Pagoda occupied by troops in the 1930's. Note how the
lattice work has been broken in the first-story railing; and how many
finials and windbells are missing from the eaves. On the temple building
in the rear, the ridge coping has fallen off the whole right end of the roof.

alist or Communist. Confiscation of any monastic property was grist to the mills of the antireligion movement of the early 1920's, the antisuperstition movement of the late 1920's, and the Marxist movement from first to last.

The sangha had been prepared for the earthquake of the revolution by the tremors of the previous decade. They had understood that it was necessary to shore up their position by improving their public image and by getting the active support of a far larger number of influential laymen. To this end, as we have seen, the first faltering efforts had been made in monastic education. In the next four decades these were to be enormously expanded. But more than education was necessary to meet the immediate danger. Parties and people's organizations, which had been forbidden under the Ch'ing, were springing up everywhere, each dedicated to advancing the interests of the segment of the population it represented. Buddhist monks followed suit. Even as the revolution was erupting, they began organizing to petition for laws that would protect their property, to protest laws that threatened it, and to intervene with the administrative authorities wherever necessary. From 1912 to 1929 they launched no less than eighteen separate Chinese Buddhist associations, all of which evaporated, some at once, some after achieving a modicum of their goals. Since many of their names are confusingly similar, particularly in translation, they will be distinguished below by the place and date of their establishment. Thus the reader will be able to tell that the Chinese Buddhist Association (Nanking, 1912) was not the same as the Chinese Buddhist Association (Shanghai, 1929).

What may have contributed more to the defense of Buddhist property than any national association of the sangha were the local groups of Buddhist laymen that sprang up in the larger cities, beginning about 1920. The sangha encouraged and supported them. Indeed it could be argued that few of them would have been started if the monks had not been working more actively to spread the dharma among the laity in the preceding decade. But, whatever their origin, these groups fostered devotion and gave laymen a more active role than ever before. Also, because of their charitable and educational activities, they were "up to date" and could be compared with pride to corresponding Christian groups. Laymen flocked to join, many of them influential and willing to use their influence to protect the sangha. As so often in China, protection by men was more effective than protection by law.

The Republican period, then, saw Buddhism build up three lines of defense against its enemies. First, there was the series of national Buddhist associations which served as a kind of lobby for the sangha. Second, there was the broadly based lay movement to which the sangha could look for support and protection. Third, there was the new educational system designed to train monks how to spread the faith, not only in order to fortify this lay Buddhist movement, but also to persuade the public at large that Buddhism was a component of Chinese culture worth preserving.

We shall deal with these developments here and in the chapters that follow. One of the difficulties is that so many of the organizations involved—associations, clubs, seminaries—were ephemeral or, if not ephemeral, in constant change. In some cases we know only their names, and not even when they were established or where. Another difficulty lies in distinguishing between plans and execution, rules and practice. K. L. Reichelt, a sympathetic observer, was right when he wrote: "Chinese in general and Buddhists in particular have a great love for detailed regulations. Each branch of activity has minutely worked out rules and each room has its little notice on the door stating what the room shall be used for . . . Unfortunately it is generally implied that when one has finished hanging up all these rules and notices, the most important thing has been done and the observance of the regulations is merely of secondary importance."[2] J. B. Pratt offers the following account of the Buddhist New Youth Society in Peking.

Its headquarters were in one of the rooms of the Kuan-yin Ssu, near the Parliament Building, and its equipment at the time of both my visits consisted of a set of tea cups . . . On my first visit to the headquarters I was told that they had two hundred members; on my second that they had five hundred. I do not think the membership really more than doubled during my absence. I think both answers were prompted by hope rather than by statistics, and that at my second visit hope had more than redoubled. For hopes should be mentioned along with tea cups as a part of the really very useful equipment of the association. The officers of the association, I was told, planned to have several schools, a Buddhist university, and many preaching places. Already, they assured me, the association conducted regular preaching services at the Kuan-yin Ssu once or twice a week (they were a little vague as to whether it was once or twice), and they published a journal which was supported in part by the emperor [P'u-i] and which counted many Japanese among its subscribers. These two were the only activities, they said, which were really started, but they hoped to open some of their schools in the spring. On taking my leave I unfortunately inquired as to the size of the audience at their bi-weekly preaching service, and was told that in the spring they hoped to have a large attendance; but that as a fact just at that time they hadn't any preaching services at all. Since my visit (I am informed) the association has been temporarily disbanded.[3]

Another visitor to China at about this same time was Mizuno Baigyo, the Japanese monk who had suggested in 1904 that monasteries protect themselves from confiscation by starting schools. In the early 1920's he appears to have gone from one Buddhist group to another, collecting from each a copy of its charter, a list of its officers, and a description of its activities and achievements. Unfortunately he tells us little of what he saw with his own eyes, so that there is no way of knowing how much there was in the real world that corresponded to these impressive documents. Equally important documentary sources are the biography of T'ai-hsü and *Hai-ch'ao yin*, the journal he published from 1920 on. But these tend to present a biased version of the many episodes in which he played a leading role, as we shall now see.

THE INVASION OF CHIN SHAN

In August and September 1911, "because of the spread of local autonomy there was a rapidly growing trend towards the occupation of monasteries and the seizure of their property. People from different places met in Shanghai and decided to dispatch Eight Fingers to Peking with a petition."[4] This was the beginning of eight critical months, in the course of which Buddhists struggled with one another for central authority to defend their religion.

As he reflected on the difficulties of his impending mission to Peking, Eight Fingers thought of his knowledgeable and energetic disciple, T'ai-hsü. He summoned him to the T'ien-t'ung Ssu and had him draw up a petition for the protection and reform of Buddhism. However, because of the deepening political crisis over railroad nationalization, they did not go to the capital after all. As the reader may recall, the eve of the revolution found T'ai-hsü in Shanghai, staying at Hardoon Gardens. During the last two months of 1911 he wandered from temple to temple in Chekiang, watching the spread of Republicanism and considering what his role should be. On January 1, 1912 Sun Yat-sen took office as provisional president. Within a few days T'ai-hsü arrived in Nanking and started organizing the Association for the Advancement of Buddhism (Fo-chiao Hsieh-chin Hui). Through the intercession of a friend in the Socialist Party, he secured the approval of the president's office and set up headquarters in the P'i-lu Ssu, which was to be the seat of many successor organizations that came and went in the decades that followed. At this point an old acquaintance, Jen-shan, turned up. He and T'ai-hsü had been fellow students at Yang Wen-hui's Jetavana Hermitage three years earlier. He had come to submit a startling proposal to the Ministry of Education: to transform the Chin Shan monastery into a modern school for monks (seng hsüeh-t'ang).

Chin Shan was the monastery that would not allow Tsung-yang to succeed to the post of abbot because he had worn lay dress and taken part in political activities. No institution in China was stricter in enforcing the monastic rules. With three to four hundred monks in residence, with an ample income from its large landholdings, with an orthodox meditation hall where collective meditation was carried on seven to fifteen hours a day for nine months of the year,[5] this was the acknowledged model for all the monasteries in China (which may be why Jen-shan made it his target). Its vast buildings, newly reconstructed, stood on a hillock by the Yangtze River just outside the city of Chen-chiang (between Shanghai and Nanking). Properly known as the

4 Chin Shan. The Kuan-yin Ko stands on the terrace just below the crest of
the hill, behind the long, many-windowed library of the Chiang-t'ien Ssu,
to which all the other buildings belong. The ragged peasant family in the
foreground has been gathering faggots from the monastery's land.

Chiang-t'ien Ssu, it did not have this hillock entirely to itself.[6]
There were other institutions adjoining it, over which it had no
jurisdiction. One was the Kuan-yin Ko, a hereditary temple[7]
that was above and behind it and could only be reached through
the monastery's main gate. Jen-shan had entered the clergy at
the Kuan-yin Ko. He and its other disciples, according to their
version of the story, had been insulted and oppressed by the
monks of the Chiang-t'ien Ssu. This seems to have been more
than a personal feud. It had to do with a "very big conflict"

between monks enrolled at the Sangha Normal School and the senior officers of the large monasteries of Yangchow and Chen-chiang, presumably over the students' progressive ideas on the reform of the sangha.

T'ai-hsü told Jen-shan that he had just founded the Association for the Advancement of Buddhism and described its program for "a new Buddhism in a new China." One feature of this program was the establishment of modern schools for monks. Jen-shan was delighted to find that their aims coincided. He proposed that the inaugural conference of the association be held at the Chiang-t'ien Ssu, with whose senior officers he was apparently on good terms now—otherwise it would be hard to explain what happened next. He and T'ai-hsü went there and told the officers about the plan for the conference, though not, presumably, about the plan to turn the monastery into a school. The officers offered their cooperation and agreed to play host. Moving into the Kuan-yin Ko, Jen-shan and T'ai-hsü sent out invitations to monks in Nanking, Shanghai, and Yangchow and to laymen as well as monks in Chen-chiang, where Chin Shan was located. On the day the conference opened, two to three hundred monks and three to four hundred lay guests were present. It may be significant that among the latter a majority belonged to the Socialist Party in Chen-chiang. Members of this party were the people to whom T'ai-hsü "felt closest" at this time.[8] Rather naturally he was nominated chairman, and read out the program and the by-laws that he had drawn up. As he wrote in his autobiography,

everything seemed to have been going smoothly. But after Jen-shan made a speech, the Yangchow monk Chi-shan immediately mounted the rostrum and delivered a strongly critical reply.[9] This angered Jen-shan, who went back up to the rostrum and launched into an account of the tyrannies of Ch'ing-ch'üan [the abbot of Chin Shan], Chi-shan, and others. He ended by proposing that the Chin Shan monastery be used to start a modern school and that all its property should be allocated to pay the school expenses. There was a lot of clapping from the [lay] guests in favor of the suggestion. Chi-shan shouted in a loud voice to the monks and the crowd became excited. Jen-shan's proposal was passed, and Jen-shan and I were elected to take over the Chin Shan monastery as the heaquarters of the Association [for the Advancement of Buddhism] and to make the necessary preparations to start a school for monks there . . . That evening Jen-shan led some twenty or more of his schoolmates into the monastery and set aside rooms for the headquarters of the Association, which went into operation next morning. They entered the business office (*k'u-fang*) to have a look at the monastery ledgers and went to the meditation hall to announce that a school was being started.

I myself went off to Nanking, leaving matters in Chen-chiang for Jen-shan to manage. One night (between February 7 and 17, 1912) Shuang-t'ing [the guest perfect of the Chiang-t'ien Ssu and later its abbot] and some other monks led several dozen of the monastery workmen to the headquarters of the Association and fought their way in. Jen-shan and many of the rest were wounded with knives and clubs [and driven out]. Later they started a lawsuit and, after a month or so, Ch'ing-chüan, Shuang-t'ing, and five or six of those who had been with them were imprisoned for terms ranging from several months to several years.[10]

In Buddhist eyes it was bad enough when monasteries—even second-rank monasteries—were taken over by unfriendly officials. Now, however, the greatest center of Chinese monasticism had been invaded, not by crass outsiders, but by those who owed it protection and respect. It was simply too much to be borne, and T'ai-hsü found himself in disgrace. Later his disciples tried to put the blame on the shoulders of Jen-shan who, they said, was really in charge of the fiasco. They pointed out that T'ai-hsü left for Nanking as soon as he saw the crudeness of the methods being employed. But he may also have left because he had anticipated the crudeness of the response—the sticks and knives.

The fracas scarcely exemplifies the loftiest in Buddhist ethical ideals, but it may be understood, though perhaps not excused, as an act of righteous indignation. The senior monks of the Chiang-t'ien Ssu must have felt tricked and betrayed. They had obviously not been told the real purpose of the meeting to which they were asked to play host. They were under the impression that the Buddhist association being inaugurated would work to prevent the seizure of monasteries, little dreaming that its first act would be to seize their own. Nor had they been told that T'ai-hsü would pack the meeting with his friends from the Socialist Party, thus ensuring a majority for whatever measures he proposed. Probably they could not even conceive of the possibility that invited guests would dare to vote away the property of the host monastery—property that belonged to the whole Buddhist sangha. Their indignation must have been fierce and it lives on in their disciples, who even today do not give the invaders credit for good intentions. T'ai-hsü, though he came to admit that their methods had been hasty and crude, always insisted that their intention had been a worthy one: to provide schooling for monks. The dharma disciples of Chin Shan dismiss this as a pretext: the real reason for the invasion, they say, was that Jen-shan wanted to strike the winning blow in his old feud with their monastery and to get hold of its buildings and land. If he had simply wanted to start a school, why could he not have done so with some other monastery that had a lot of empty rooms and no program of meditation to be disturbed?

Whatever the motives of its perpetrators, the "invasion of Chin Shan" (*ta-nao Chin Shan*) epitomizes the shock with which the Republican era burst upon the Buddhist establishment. It dramatically foreshadowed the long conflict ahead between conservatives and radicals in the sangha. It caused as much of a scandal as if, let us say, the editors of *Commonweal* occupied the office of the Roman Curia and announced that they were turning it into a school for worker-priests.

RIVAL BUDDHIST ASSOCIATIONS

Another conflict of the Republican era, this time between the sangha and the laity, came to light before six weeks were up. It was far less dramatic, but it also involved the establishment of a new Buddhist group. We have seen that among the disciples of Yang Wen-hui was Ou-yang Ching-wu (Ou-yang Chien), whom Yang on his deathbed had left in charge of the collation of texts at the Chin-ling Scriptural Press. Ou-yang was then forty years old. One of his Buddhist friends was Li I-cho who had been a fellow teacher at the Jetavana Hermitage. At some point during the first two months of 1912, they and five others decided to establish the Chinese Buddhist Association (Chung-kuo Fo-chiao Hui[11]) in Nanking. They drew up a charter and submitted it to President Sun Yat-sen for approval. It was a comprehensive document that first set forth general objectives and then laid claim to certain rights of supervision over the whole Buddhist establishment in China. The general aims were laudable enough: spreading the dharma, especially in factories, prisons, and hospitals; starting schools and study groups; and relief work. But the rights it laid claim to were astonishing:

The Association shall have the right to superintend all properties belonging to all Buddhist organizations.

The Association shall have the right to reorganize and promote all Buddhist business affairs.

The Association shall have the right to arbitrate disputes that may arise between Buddhists and to maintain order among them.

The Association shall have the right to require the assistance of the National Government in carrying out all the social, missionary, and philanthropic works stated above.

All activities of the Association within the scope of the law shall not be interfered with by the Government.

The National Government is requested to insert a special article in the Constitution to protect the Association after it has been acknowledged as a lawful organization.[12]

Here was something far more dangerous than the invasion of Chin Shan—a plan to place the whole Buddhist establishment in the hands of men who despised the sangha. For such was the attitude of Ou-yang and his friends. "They specialized in reviling monks and nuns and starting arguments between clergy and laity," we are told by the biographer of T'ai-hsü.[13] It is a measure of the confusion in government at the time that this charter was ratified by President Sun (presumably before Yüan Shih-k'ai took office on March 10), and the new association was formally inaugurated on March 20.[14] What happened next is unclear. Either now or earlier, the provisions of the charter provoked angry protests from other Buddhist circles. The Venerable Hsü-yün was summoned by telegram and he came all the way from Yünnan to confer with Eight Fingers in Shanghai, whereupon the two of them went to see Sun Yat-sen about getting the charter revised. There is no indication of whether or not they were successful.[15] We are only told that, after a new union of Buddhist groups was established in Shanghai on April 1,

Ou-yang's association in Nanking "dissolved of its own accord."[16]

For all its ambitious plans, it appears that Ou-yang's association never had more than ten members. On the other hand, the new union set up on April 1—the Chinese General Buddhist Association (Chung-hua Fo-chiao Tsung-hui)—had a much broader base and may be fairly described as the first national Buddhist organization in Chinese history. The immediate reason for its founding is said to have been the invasion of Chin Shan. "When Eight Fingers heard what had happened at Chin Shan, he was furious at the brashness of the progressives. Therefore he went to Shanghai and got together with monks from seventeen provinces to lay the groundwork for the establishment of the Chinese General Buddhist Association."[17] After several weeks of preparation they met at Liu-yün Ssu, a large Shanghai monastery, elected Eight Fingers as president, and approved a charter. According to one source, they also pledged a contribution to the government's military budget in return for official protection of monastic property.[18]

Eight Fingers, then in his sixty-first year, with a scraggly beard and a finger burned off either hand, was as imposing as he was eccentric. He had been orphaned as a boy in Hunan and entered the sangha at the age of seventeen without ever having received a proper education. Therefore, although he had no small reputation as a poet, he was sometimes unable to write down all the characters in the poems he composed. He was skilled in contemplative practices, but is said to have been so patriotic that, when the French attacked Formosa in 1884, he wanted to go and fight them with his bare hands. In a word, even though conservative, he seems to have been no less fiery than his progressive disciple, T'ai-hsü.[19] He was elected president of the association not only because he had organized the conference, but because he had friends in high places and had already displayed his talent for getting their help in protecting Buddhism (see p. 13). He also enjoyed the prestige that came from having served as abbot of three famous monasteries: the Shang-feng Ssu, the Ch'i-t'a Ssu, and the T'ien-t'ung Ssu.

One can sense his presence, perhaps, in the vigorous provisions of the charter of the new Buddhist association, which gave it

5   Eight Fingers.

many of the powers once exercised by the Board of Rites and the sangha officials under the Ch'ing dynasty. Without the association's approval, for example, monastic property was not to be sold, nor could a new abbot be selected; and if any abbot in office was guilty of misconduct, it could intervene and replace him. It reserved the right to screen candidates for ordination anywhere in the country, to refuse those whose background or motives were questionable, and to issue all ordination certificates. Monks and nuns throughout China were required to join and to abide by its regulations.

The charter also provided not only for controls but for the establishment of new institutions. There were to be seminaries modeled on Buddhist schools in Japan; centers for research into the doctrines of all sects, Hinayana as well as Mahayana, and centers for preaching these doctrines; orphanages, clinics, and workshops for the poor; programs of missionary work in the army, prisons, hospitals, and foreign countries.[20]

The intention was obviously to raise the quality of human material entering the sangha and, through a new educational system, to create from it a corps of Buddhists whose preaching and social-welfare work would disarm those critics who called monks lazy and ignorant in order to justify the confiscation of monasteries. It is important to note that this program of reform had not been launched by young radicals, but by respected conservatives from the great monasteries of Chekiang and Kiangsu.

Soon after the inaugural meeting, Eight Fingers and some of his fellow abbots sent off the charter to be ratified in Peking by the new government of Yüan Shih-k'ai. This would give them the legal status necessary to intercede with officials when monastic property was threatened. The year wore on and ratification did not come. Encroachment continued to be a problem in many places, particularly in Hunan, the native province of Eight Fingers. The monasteries there asked him to intercede with the Ministry of the Interior, and so on their behalf, as well as to get the charter ratified, he went to Peking. Unfortunately the man in charge of religious affairs at the Ministry of the Interior, Tu Kuan, not only favored the confiscation of monastic property, but had just had a survey made in order to carry it out more systematically. He turned a deaf ear to every argument that Eight Fingers put forth. Worse than that, he ridiculed and insulted the old man, who became so angry that when he got back to the Fa-yüan Ssu, where he was staying, he could not eat supper. Tears kept coming to his eyes as he thought of the future of Buddhism. The abbot, Tao-chieh (one of his disciples), tried to comfort him and took him to the house of a Hunanese friend, who talked poetry with him until midnight. The diversion proved temporary. When he returned to the Fa-yüan Ssu, he could not sleep, still indignant at Tu's attitude toward the fate of monastic property in Hunan. He tossed and turned and then lay still. When Tao-chieh walked over, he found that the old monk was dead—the Republic's first martyr to the Buddhist cause. This was on November 10, 1912.[21] Yang Tu, Hsiung Hsi-lin (soon to be premier), and other friends of Eight Fingers told Yüan

Shih-k'ai what had happened. The charter was quickly passed and promulgated by the cabinet. "Buddhist monasteries and their property enjoyed a little more security."[22]

A new president, the Venerable Yeh-k'ai, was elected at the first annual conference of the Chinese General Buddhist Association on March 31, 1913. Yeh-k'ai had only recently retired as abbot of the T'ien-ning Ssu in Changchow, which had been totally destroyed during the Taiping Rebellion and which he had helped to rebuild into one of the largest monasteries in China. By this time the association had nineteen branches at the provincial level and well over a hundred at the local level. An able staff had been appointed to carry on administrative work at the headquarters in the Ching-an Ssu (the Bubbling Well Monastery) in Shanghai.[23] The monthly house organ they published[24] shows that they were active in sending instructions and receiving reports from the branches, often with regard to the infringement of property rights and sometimes with regard to local reforms.[25] The scope of these activities was not confined to Buddhism. Taoist monks and laymen joined some of the branches, and protection was extended to Taoist monasteries and even to temples of the popular religion.

For reasons that have yet to be explained—but perhaps because the threat of encroachment receded[26]—these activities lost momentum during 1913. The house organ suspended publication, and many of the branches ceased operating. The charter's provisions for control and reform of the sangha were no longer implemented as vigorously as they had been at the beginning of the year. By 1914 the association had become dormant, and it remained so until it was revived to deal with another crisis.

This crisis came in the autumn of 1915, when Parliament began to consider a bill entitled "Regulations for the Control of Monasteries and Temples." It sharply increased government control—over ordination, public speaking, and reception of guests—and even provided for government dismissal of abbots who violated monastic rules. It gave unscrupulous local officials various means to threaten monks who resisted attempts at confiscation.[27] Faced with this new danger, the association got busy again. Setting up a kind of a lobby in a monastery near the

Parliament building, it tried to influence the voting. This angered Yüan Shih-k'ai, who ordered it to be dissolved. The bill was then passed and promulgated on October 29, 1915, but before it was put into effect, Yüan abdicated (March 22, 1916) and it became a dead letter.

The seesawing resumed when two monks, Chang-chia and Ch'ing-hai, applied to the Ministry of the Interior for permission to revive the association—that is, the Chinese General Buddhist Association (Shanghai, 1912)—with an amended charter. Ch'ing-hai, a Chinese monk, had been general manager of its house organ. Chang-chia was a Mongolian Living Buddha who was to play an increasingly important role in Buddhist affairs over the next thirty years.[28] The two of them won the approval of the ministry and established the Chinese Buddhist Association (Chung-hua Fo-chiao Hui). But two years later, in June 1919, the Peking Police Bureau announced that the Regulations for the Control of Monasteries would be brought into force. At about the same time, the Ministry of the Interior looked into its files and found that the Chinese Buddhist Association (Peking, 1917) had been set up contrary to law. It was ordered to dissolve.

One curious feature of these developments was the role of the Venerable Ti-hsien, a leader of the association in 1912. T'ai-hsü's biographer asserts that the offensive bill of 1915 had originally been drawn up for Yüan Shih-k'ai on the basis of a draft plan that Ti-hsien had submitted. When he returned to Peking in 1918 to lecture on the sutras and learned that the bill was no longer enforced, he talked to "important people in the Communications Clique."[29] It was because of their intervention that the Peking Police Bureau came to take action in June 1919. This in turn stirred up the Buddhists in Chekiang. T'ai-hsü and another monk came north to protest. After a month of lobbying they were unable to get the regulations rescinded, as had been their original goal, but the enforcement thereof was again allowed to lapse.[30]

Behind these events there was obviously factionalism and competition for authority, at the real nature of which we can only guess. Ti-hsien was called a "traitor to Buddhism" by a monk friendly to T'ai-hsü. T'ai-hsü's biographer asserts that Ti-hsien got the Ministry of the Interior to agree that ordination certifi-

cates and sangha registration forms would be purchasable only
from the Kuan-tsung Ssu, of which he was abbot.[31] This would
have been a move to acquire central authority over the sangha,
since its effect would have been that no one in China could have
become a monk without Ti-hsien's approval. But was he seeking
authority for his own sake, or only because he feared that otherwise it would fall into the hands of dangerous radicals like
T'ai-hsü? Probably almost all of the monks involved in this un-
edifying factionalism were honestly trying to advance what they
conceived of as the Buddhist cause.

The dissolution of the Chinese Buddhist Association (Peking,
1917) ended the fourth unsuccessful attempt to organize the
Buddhists of China—or at any rate the fourth attempt on which
I have found enough information to give an account of it.[32] At
least eleven other Buddhist associations came and went in these
early years, and some of them were national in scope.[33] Three
more that were intended, at any rate, to be national in scope
were soon to be set up by T'ai-hsü, whose organizing activities
will be the subject of the next chapter. None survived. It was
not until 1929 that a viable national association came into being,
and, as before, it was in response to a threat to monastic property.
Indeed its birth was almost a "retake" of the 1912 scenario, with
the role of Eight Fingers being played by Yüan-ying, an able
and much-revered monk who was one of his pupils.

THE CHINESE BUDDHIST ASSOCIATION (SHANGHAI, 1929)

Yüan-ying was a Fukienese, born in 1878. Ordained in 1897 at
the largest Fukien monastery, Ku Shan, he had practiced meditation under the leading Ch'an masters, including Eight Fingers.
In the 1920's and 1930's he served as abbot of one famous temple
after another in Fukien and Chekiang.

Throughout eastern Chekiang in 1927, there began a wave of
confiscation of temple property, probably connected with the
Nationalists' accession to power. Yüan-ying, who then headed
the Chi'i-t'a Ssu in Ningpo, protested, but to no avail. Soon came
a more serious development. In May 1928 a national conference
on education was convened in Nanking. It was attended by

seventy-seven delegates, nearly two thirds of whom had studied abroad—never an experience that fortified respect for native religion. Among them was Professor T'ai Shuang-ch'iu of National Central University, who had recently returned from the United States with a degree in education from Columbia. He proposed that first the property of large monasteries and then the property of small temples be confiscated and the income therefrom be allocated to the support of education. The proposal was adopted by the conference and found favor with Hsüeh Tu-pi, the Minister of the Interior, who began considering ways to carry it out. Word of this soon reached the Buddhists. Thoroughly alarmed, Yüan-ying set up the Kiangsu-Chekiang Buddhist Federation (Chiang-Che Fo-chiao Lien-ho-hui) and went to Nanking as its representative to protest against Professor T'ai's proposal.[34] This time he was more successful. At any rate, whether because of his efforts or others', the proposal was shelved.[35]

Buddhist leaders regarded this as nothing but a reprieve. They felt uneasy about the future. In order to "assume their share of social responsibility" and thereby to forestall new moves at general confiscation, they began to set up Buddhist children's homes and training workshops; opened additional seminaries; and undertook "work in agriculture and forestry that would make them more self-supporting."[36] The most important countermeasure, however, was to establish a body that could take quick action as soon as confiscation was threatened and try in the meantime to secure the repeal of a restrictive new set of regulations for the control of monasteries, passed in January 1929.[37] On April 12, 1929, the Chinese Buddhist Association (Chung-kuo Fo-chiao Hui) was founded in Shanghai. Delegates from seventeen provinces met at the headquarters of the Pure Karma Association (Fo-chiao Ching-yeh She) in the Enlightenment Garden, which was to remain the national center of Buddhist activities for several years. Yüan-ying, the guiding spirit, was elected its first president. T'ai-hsü was abroad, having left for a world tour on August 11, 1928, and took no part in setting up what he had so often tried to create himself.[38]

Although the association had lay members, the monks were

firmly in control. They submitted its charter[39] to the Ministry
of the Interior and also asked that the regulations of January
1929 be formally rescinded. Yüan-ying went to Nanking to plead
for this with the Legislative Yüan, which took up the question
in May. T'ai-hsü, who had returned on April 25, 1929, also submitted his views. The charter was approved on June 3, and a
more satisfactory set of "Regulations for the Supervision of
Monasteries and Temples" was drawn up and promulgated at
the end of the year (see p. 138). Branches were organized in
Kiangsu, Chekiang, Hupeh, Szechwan, and many other places.[40]
Things seemed to be going smoothly.

It was not to be for long. T'ai-hsü was elected to the standing
committee of the new association on June 3. He began at once
to squabble with the conservatives, led by Yüan-ying, who were
unwilling to support his grandiose plans for the reorganization
of the sangha. By November he had decided to resign from the
committee and to devote his time entirely to his own
little group in Nanking. But he did remain an ordinary member.
When the third national conference opened on April 10, 1931, he
was ready for a new assault, which he began with a blistering
speech in his best style. Now that the threat of monastery confiscation was removed, he said, people had lost all interest in
reform. Ever since 1929, finances and personnel had been going
from bad to worse. The charter had been violated in that persons
not properly accredited were allowed to attend meetings of the
standing committee. The office staff at the national headquarters
did not include a single monk or "truly devout" layman. Therefore the standing committee and the headquarters should be
reorganized. Monks and laymen of proper caliber should be
taken on, and semimonthly reports of their work should be dis-
seminated. A budget of at least $30,000 a year should be pro-
vided for publication work and for training monks to staff branch
associations at all levels. Otherwise, T'ai-hsü concluded, the
association, instead of promoting Buddhism, would make matters
worse and it would be better to dissolve it then and there.

Elections were immediately held for the executive committee
(chih-hsing wei-yüan-hui). The Shanghai-Hangchow group, despite its "manipulations," was defeated and the T'ai-hsü group

was victorious. "There was now an open split between the old and new parties." On April 11, when the new executive committee held its first meeting, the leading posts were taken over by T'ai-hsü and his supporters: Jen-shan, Wang I-t'ing, and Hsieh Chu-chen. They moved its headquarters to the P'i-lu Ssu in Nanking.

Their victory, however was Pyrrhic. As one of their journals recounts, "when T'ai-hsü proposed that the religious reforms voted at the National Conference should really be carried out, all the rotten senior monks got into a panic and began creating every sort of obstacle. Soon they egged on the evil gentry to go about and start rumors in order to sow suspicion and sabotage the plans. Secretly they got together and agreed not to pay in the contributions they had pledged [to the association]. At the same time, they incited the monks on the executive and supervisory committees to resign in a body." To make things worse a leading lay Buddhist published the accusation that the elections had been illegal and proposed that the headquarters be returned to Shanghai. Even Wang I-t'ing, who had been T'ai-hsü's friend and supporter since 1915, appears to have gone over to the opposition. T'ai-hsü, seeing that it would be impossible to carry on, resigned. In a bitter announcement run in the Shanghai newspaper *Shen-pao* on June 3, he castigated his former colleagues as the enemies of the reform of Buddhism, interested only in protecting monastic property. "There is no call for me to waste any more of my energy on the Chinese Buddhist Association," he concluded.[41]

On June 14 a second meeting of the executive council reappointed the conservatives to their former positions and moved the headquarters back to the Enlightenment Garden. T'ai-hsü, perhaps as a sop, was asked to take charge of the branch office that had been operating in Nanking. "Thus T'ai-hsü's work with the Buddhist Association was completely destroyed because Yüan-ying had been supported by the monasteries of Kiangsu and Chekiang and by prominent lay devotees in opposing the reform of Buddhism. The break between T'ai-hsü and Yüan-ying was irreparable."[42] It was the end of a long friendship. The two monks had signed a pact of brotherhood in 1906, and in T'ai-hsü's early years it was Yüan-ying, eleven years his senior, who had inspired him to seek a better education.

For the benefit of the outside world, appearances were preserved. T'ai-hsü was still listed next to Yüan-ying among the leaders of the association. But in the pages of his journal, *Hai-ch'ao yin*, his followers sniped at it as "an empty show, in the charge of 'dead wood,' who have ignored their responsibilities."[43] He could afford to bide his time. He was continuing to mold students to his own viewpoint at his seminaries in Wuchang and Amoy, and late in 1931 he opened another seminary near Chungking.[44] He would be able to count on many more supporters in the next generation. For its part, the Chinese Buddhist Association devoted itself to the protection of the Buddhist establishment. Though T'ai-hsü had told the third national conference that the threat of confiscation was over, that same year (1931) a new threat appeared. Professor T'ai and his colleagues at National Central University, undeterred by their failure in 1929, now set up the Society to Expedite the Promotion of Education with Temple Property. It had the same old plan: to confiscate monasteries throughout China. Yüan-ying, now a veteran in handling such attacks, vigorously protested as president of the Chinese Buddhist Association. He pointed out that under the Provisional Constitution there could be no discrimination based on religion or class and that all citizens had freedom of religious belief and the right to hold property inviolate. The new threat gradually subsided.[45] A presidential instruction of August 1, 1931, reiterated the guarantees to monastic property issued earlier. So far as I know, this was the last time that any serious attempt was made to confiscate all the monasteries in China.[46]

In the summer of 1932 the association asked the Kuomintang to issue licenses (*hsü-k'o cheng-shu*) to people's organizations. The association itself received license number one, and thus "Buddhism was preserved intact."[47] Buddhists from all over the country met to hold a fourth national conference, which reelected Yüan-ying as president.

The fifth national conference in 1933 was marked by a new internal crisis, the nature of which is unclear. "Jealous people made false and slanderous statements, but Yüan-ying handled them calmly, so that no damage was done to the standing of the association, and he was re-elected."[48] According to one informant, this refers to the fact that the provincial branches objected to having local chapters taken from under their jurisdiction and placed directly under the jurisdiction of the national head-quarters.[49]

In all there were eight national conferences. At the last, held in November 1936, the charter was amended to bring the association tightly under party and government control and to fore-stall T'ai-hsü's efforts to get control of it.[50] By this time it claimed over five hundred branches and chapters that reported to its national headquarters in Shanghai.[51] After the Japanese attack in 1937, it became inactive. Contrary to what we read in some sources,[52] it did not move to Chungking along with the government. It had an office in Chungking, which presumably adminis-tered the local branches, but was not recognized by the government as having jurisdiction over Buddhist groups else-where in unoccupied China. Both the seal and the president remained in Shanghai. This was not because Yüan-ying was a collaborationist, as some of his detractors have asserted. As early as 1931 he had appealed to Buddhists to mobilize against the Japanese. In 1937 he organized a sangha ambulance corps to assist wounded Chinese soldiers and civilians. In 1939, after he returned from a tour of Southeast Asia to raise relief funds for China, the Japanese arrested him. According to one version of the story, an informer had told the Japanese that some of the money he had raised went not to relief but to the war effort. According to another version, the Japanese had pressed him to accept the presidency of a new Sino-Japanese Buddhist associa-tion. He had refused and then been imprisoned.[53] Although he was released in less than a month, from that time on he stayed quietly at his preaching hall in Shanghai, the Yüan-ming Chiang-t'ang, going out on occasional lecture tours but avoiding the complications involved in an active presidency of the Chinese Buddhist Association.[54]

In the meantime T'ai-hsü was laying the groundwork for a new effort to take over national leadership. In 1938 he followed the government to Chungking, where his talents as a lobbyist

found even greater scope than before. This was partly because
his opponents in the great monasteries of Kiangsu and Chekiang
could not exert the same influence here in China's west as they
had in Nanking; and partly because the government needed help
and was readier to cooperate with anyone who could give it,
regardless of their credentials. T'ai-hsü proposed that he be sent
abroad on a "goodwill mission" to win support for China's war
effort. The government agreed and provided the money. When
he returned from the tour, he tried to use his credit with officialdom to increase his power in the Buddhist community: in 1941
he applied for permission to set up a Committee for the Reorganization of the Chinese Buddhist Association. Unfortunately
for him, the Ministry of the Interior wanted to continue taking
over monastic property unchallenged, and it refused to go into
the matter with the Ministry of Social Affairs.[55] He had to content himself with helping to found the Fellowship of Chinese
Religious Believers.[56]

Once the war was over, the government's need for freedom of
confiscation diminished. In December 1945 the Ministry of the
Interior and the Ministry of Social Affairs jointly ordered the
establishment of the committee that T'ai-hsü had asked for in
1941. Instead of being called a committee to reorganize the
Buddhist association, it was the Committee for the Reorganization of Chinese *Buddhism* (Chung-kuo Fo-chiao Cheng-li Wei-
yüan-hui), and its scope was correspondingly wider. This time
T'ai-hsü was in control at last. Although Yüan-ying and other
conservatives were members, T'ai-hsü and his lay disciple Li Tzu-
k'uan were in a majority on the standing committee of three, the
third member being the Living Buddha Chang-chia, whom we
last took note of when he had tried to revive the Chinese
Buddhist Association (Peking, 1917).[57]

After two years of preparatory work, during which the association resumed full-scale operation, a national conference
opened at Nanking on May 26, 1947. A new charter, approved
in advance by the Ministry of the Interior, was adopted by
seventy delegates from all parts of the country. Alas, T'ai-hsü
was not there to assume the presidency (as had been planned)

and thus to realize his life-long ambition of leading the Buddhists of China. He had died on March 17, 1947, less than three months before the conference opened. The cause of his death is said to have been a stroke brought on by high blood pressure, an illness consistent with his temperament. Chang-chia was chosen president in his place, partly because of the importance the government then attached to consolidating relations with Tibet.

The Chinese Buddhist Association (Chung-kuo Fo-chiao Hui) that emerged from the national conference of 1947 was not a new creation. It was a revival of, rather than a successor to, the

6 Li Tzu-k'uan at eighty-two. The old revolutionary and lay Buddhist leader stands in the garden of Chin Shan's sub-temple in Taiwan.

Chinese Buddhist Association (Shanghai, 1929). In its own literature it claimed an even earlier origin, identifying itself with the Chinese General Buddhist Association (Shanghai, 1912), although in fact there is little to justify this claim. In any case, it represented the highest stage of organizational development that Chinese Buddhism reached before the Communist victory. In considering its achievements, we may say that, although they fell short of its plans, they were still an advance over the past.

The national headquarters were moved from Shanghai to the P'i-lu Ssu in Nanking (as T'ai-hsü had briefly moved them fifteen years earlier). There a small permanent staff, responsible to an executive committee of thirty-one and a supervisory committee of eleven, worked to implement the sweeping provisions of the charter.[58] There was a branch association (fen-hui) in every province and metropolis, and a chapter (chih-hui) in every district (hsien) that had a sizable Buddhist population. The district chapters were subordinate to the provincial branches, through which they received instructions from national headquarters and sent back their own reports and requests. Much of this traffic was in connection with actions by the government, for which the Buddhist association was, as before, the principal intermediary with the sangha. If a decree was issued that would affect monasteries and temples, it was brought to their attention by the chapter to which they belonged. If they in turn had some complaint of encroachment by local officials, they referred it to the chapter, which took it as high as might be necessary to try to get satisfaction. The association was also responsible for seeing to it that religious subversion, that ancient bugaboo of Chinese rulers, was never allowed to sprout in its shade. The first duty enjoined upon the members was "not to contravene the existing programs or decrees of the government."[59] The association had more positive duties as well. Its branches and chapters were supposed to organize relief work by member monasteries, to set up schools and orphanages, and to promote the preaching of the dharma.

Every member of a branch or chapter was considered to be a member of the parent association, which on that basis claimed a total enrollment of 4,620,000. There were three categories:

monks and nuns; lay devotees; and group members (monasteries, temples, and lay clubs). Dues varied from a few dollars a year for the individual member to a percentage of income for the group.[60]

All of this may sound very businesslike. On paper, at least, the Chinese Buddhist Association was an impressive undertaking. But, as usual, there was a gap between paper and practice. Branches were supposed to carry out any orders received from national headquarters, but in fact they often ignored them. Chapters were supposed to remit four tenths of their membership dues to the branches, and the branches were supposed to remit half of these four tenths to the national headquarters. In practice such remittances were exceptional. Therefore, the association "was constantly in financial difficulties and asking for money from the provincial branches," as the head of one provincial branch tells us.[61] According to its regulations, only lay people who had taken the Three Refuges were eligible for membership. In fact, 15 to 20 percent had not done so. According to its regulations, any member was to be expelled for a violation of the law, insanity, or drug addiction. In fact, few were. According to its regulations, all of the monks and nuns in China were supposed to join. In fact, many did not. Of course, if they did not join, they were ineligible to turn to it for help and protection. The large number of abstentions is evidence, perhaps, that its help and protection were not as effective as they were supposed to be.[62]

Thus, even at its highest stage of development, the Chinese Buddhist Association did not become a tight, effective organization that could play even a minor role in deciding China's destiny. It was never comparable to the Soka Gakkai in Japan, or even to the National Council of Churches in the United States. The times were too chaotic, and Buddhists lacked the experience and perhaps the motivation to organize effectively. This was disappointing to people like T'ai-hsü. But, from another point of view, it may have been just as well. It is questionable how much a truly efficient association would have contributed to truly Buddhist goals (leaving aside the protection of monastic property). Since Buddhist goals in China did not include political action, they were better served, perhaps, by smaller groups operating at the local level, which were free to give less attention to bureaucratic mechanics and more to the substance of the work in hand.

Chapter **III**

T'AI-HSÜ

T'AI-HSÜ is widely regarded as the most important figure in the history of modern Chinese Buddhism. But where does his importance lie? For most of his life he was the leader of a small, dissident faction. Until just before he died, his ideas and activities had had little effect on the great majority of monks and devotees; and the effect they might have had was excluded by the Communist victory. The chief importance of T'ai-hsü lies in what he personified: one answer to the problem of modernization and one extreme in the Chinese Buddhist response to the West.

It is not easy to arrive at a balanced judgment of his virtues and shortcomings. He was certainly intelligent. He had personal charm and endless enthusiasm. On the other hand, he had a flair for manipulation and promotion—particularly for self-promotion. A more serious failing was that he does not seem to have pondered deeply enough on whether, if Chinese Buddhism was reformed in the manner he proposed, it would still be Buddhist or even Chinese. In my first two chapters T'ai-hsü has been one among many dramatis personae. Now we shall go back to the beginning of his career and run through those scenes where he took the center of the stage.

After the failure of the invasion of Chin Shan, T'ai-hsü found himself in disgrace with his elders and with many of his contemporaries in the sangha. In October 1914 he went into three years' sealed confinement (*pi-kuan*) on the sacred island of P'u-t'o Shan, some say to ponder on the error of his ways but in any case to read and think about Buddhist doctrine.[1] His later achievements as a scholar and teacher are often attributed to the research he now carried on. Nonetheless he kept in touch with the outside world. When the Monastery Control Regulations were passed in 1915, it stirred him to formulate his own plan for the control and reform of monasteries, entitled "The Reorganization of the Sangha System."[2] This was his first full-scale treatment of a subject that was to occupy his attention intermittently for decades. Between 1915 and 1947 he produced seven more versions, each representing an evolution over the last.[3] None was ever put into practice: they were, in fact, so impracticable and so grandiose that it is hard to see how they could have been taken seriously. Rather as if he were a child deploying regiments of toy soldiers, T'ai-hsü divided up the sangha into departments, each with its own specialty. For example, according to one of his later schemes, China was to have ten thousand scholar monks, who earned academic degrees in four grades according to the number of years they spent at study. The highest grade would consist of eight hundred monks with the Ph.D., each of whom had studied for nine years. Twenty-five thousand monks were to engage in good works (nine thousand teaching Buddhism, seven thousand running hospitals, orphanages, and so on). Finally, a small number of elders would run sixty centers of religious cultivation (*hsiu-lin*), at which a thousand monks would meditate and recite buddha's name.[4] This accounted for only thirty-six thousand of China's half a million monks. What would have happened to the rest is unclear. Perhaps T'ai-hsü expected that many of them would disrobe to avoid manual labor and military service, both of which he is said to have favored for monks. With the sangha reduced to scholars and functionaries, there would not have been funerary specialists to perform rites for the dead, but this objection carried no weight with T'ai-hsü, for such rites were something of which, by now, he tended to disapprove. Indeed, he seems sometimes to have had grave doubts about monkhood itself.[5]

7   T'ai-hsü wearing the new vestment that he designed as part
of his campaign to bring the clergy up to date. It combines
a secular cut with a miniature of the 25-strip pattern worn
by monks when lecturing.

One of his earlier schemes was to build a national Buddhist
center in the capital, which would consist of a monastery, a university, a library, and a museum. Into the museum would be
moved all Buddhist images so that the other buildings would be
free of them. Idolatry was only to be tolerated as "an accommodation to the weakness of the masses." Presumably this weakness
was to be given more play in the monasteries and preaching halls

that he planned to retain at the provincial and local level. He must have realized that the scheme would find little support in Chinese Buddhist circles, since he says that he would build this national Buddhist center if he "could raise the money from abroad."[6]

Among T'ai-hsü's main objectives in reorganizing the sangha was to win it a higher status. "Monks are always religious recluses," he said, "taking no interest in the affairs of the community or the country and they are in turn slighted by the government and the ruling classes."[7] In the summer of 1918 he took the first of a series of steps to rectify this. After discussions with Chang Ping-ling and Wang I-t'ing, he set up the Bodhi Society (Chüeh-she) in Shanghai. It was intended to serve as a springboard for publication and ultimately for the reform of the sangha.[8] Before the year was out, it began to publish "The Reorganization of the Sangha System," which had lain in manuscript since 1915, as well as the first number of a quarterly magazine, *Chüeh-she ts'ung-shu*. At the end of 1919 T'ai-hsü decided to move the headquarters from Shanghai to Hangchow, where a follower of his had recently bought a small temple, the Ching-fan Yüan, on the West Lake. At the same time he changed the quarterly into a monthly, the inaugural number of which came out in the first lunar month of 1920 under a new name: *Hai-ch'ao yin*—"The Voice of the Sea Tide" (that is, the Buddha's voice). It was to be the most durable of all the Buddhist periodicals launched during the Republican period, and as of 1967 was still being published.

In 1922 T'ai-hsü took another step forward when he opened a seminary in Wuchang, whose graduates could serve as the agents of reform. It exercised an increasing influence on the many other schools for Buddhist monks that were set up then or later (see Chapter Six).

In 1923 he started the first of a series of "world Buddhist organizations" that helped to make him the Chinese monk best known abroad. None of the series was durable and their immediate influence was slight. But they served to interest Chinese Buddhists in the ecumenical ideal, and, somewhat indirectly, they led to the principal ecumenical body that exists today.

WORLD ORGANIZATIONS

T'ai-hsü's international debut was not made, as in the case of his ecclesiastical reforms, with any master plan. Indeed, he seems to have started by accident. In 1922 one of his lay followers, Yen Shao-fu, had visited Lu Shan near Kuling in Kiangsi province. Lu Shan was the mountain where, fifteen centuries earlier, Hui-yüan had launched the cult of Amitabha and created a model of strict monastic life. Now its monasteries were largely in ruins. Throughout Kiangsi, Buddhism was at a low ebb, while Kuling was a popular summer resort for foreigners, including many missionaries.

Yen Shao-fu decided to so something about reviving this ancient Buddhist center. He acquired some land near the remains of the Ta-lin Ssu and put up a small wooden building that could serve as a lecture hall. The following year (1923) he returned with T'ai-hsü so that the latter could use the hall to give a summer lecture series. Accompanied by other disciples, they reached Lu Shan on July 10. At some point during the next few days Yen Shao-fu, apparently on his own initiative, hung up a sign in English and Chinese that read: "World Buddhist Federation—Shih-chieh Fo-chiao Lien-ho-hui." Soon after this, T'ai-hsü had a visitor, Professor Inada Ensai of Otani University, who had gone to see him in Wuhan and, finding him away, had followed him to Lu Shan. Professor Inada noticed the sign and this led them to discuss the possibility of collaboration between Chinese and Japanese Buddhists in spreading the dharma in Europe and America. Inada stayed on to deliver one lecture after the series began on July 23.[9]

From then until August 11, one or two lectures a day were given by visitors (like K. L. Reichelt) or disciples (like Ch'ao-i), but mostly by T'ai-hsü himself, who spoke on such topics as "Buddhism and Science" and "Buddhism and Philosophy." The audience swelled to about a hundred, as various foreigners summering nearby dropped in. One such was Edo Sentaro, the Japanese consul in Kiukiang. Attracted by the sign, he came every day. This encouraged T'ai-hsü to visit him in Kiukiang after the lectures were over. He pointed out to him that, aside from Inada and himself, no other Japanese had taken part. Could Japan use its Boxer Indemnity funds to send some delegates the next year? Edo promised to submit the proposal to Tokyo, and this led T'ai-hsü to apply to his own government for permission to hold in 1924 "the First [Conference of the] World Buddhist Federation."

Both governments approved, and the conference—the first of its kind in China—was held at Lu Shan on July 13–15, 1924. There were ten Chinese delegates, mostly monks close to T'ai-hsü. Representing Japan were Saeki Teien, abbot of the Horyuji Temple and head of the Hosso sect; Kimura Taiken, professor of Indian philosophy at the University of Tokyo; and Mizuno Baigyo, who in 1904 had helped Chinese monks to resist confiscation and was well qualified to act as interpreter.[10] As in the previous year, vacationing foreigners also attended.

Discussion at the conference centered on the future exchange of Buddhist teachers and students between China and Japan; on relations with countries like Burma and Thailand, where Buddhism was of the Theravada school; and, more generally, on the unification of Buddhists everywhere, first in China, then in Asia, and finally throughout the world. To this end a proclamation of intent was drawn up; a constitution was adopted;[11] a headquarters site was chosen in Wuhan; dues were fixed; and members and officers were elected. Most significant of all, perhaps, it was decided that the following year a conference would be held in Tokyo.

This decision was implemented. In November 1925 Japan played host to the East Asian Buddhist Conference, which will be described in Chapter Nine. Hence there was no meeting at Lu Shan. T'ai-hsü went there that year, but merely to set up a summer course in Buddhist studies and English, the purpose of which was to prepare four monks to go abroad and spread the dharma in Europe and America. In May 1926 he returned to Lu Shan for the last time, staying just long enough to have one meal and collect his books.[12] The World Buddhist Federation had become a thing of the past.

It was active, therefore, only two summers. It was scarcely an "annual" affair, as Wing-tsit Chan calls it,[13] nor was it really the beginning of a "world Buddhist movement," as claimed by T'ai-hsü's biographer. Among those who took part, the latter tells us, were "several persons, English, German, Finnish and French, who acknowledged themselves to be Buddhists, among whom was Ai Hsiang-te."[14] Ai Hsiang-te is none other than the Norwegian Lutheran missionary, K. L. Reichelt, who in his own account of the conference in 1923 states that he gave an evangelical address on the first chapter of John.[15] Perhaps he chose the text too well (in Chinese it has a Buddhist flavor). Mention is elsewhere made of Russian, Burmese, and American delegates,[16] but it seems likely that they had no more authority to represent the Buddhists of their respective countries than Reichelt had to represent the Buddhists of Norway (or was it he who was referred to as "the delegate from Finland"?). The only accredited foreign representatives appear to have been the Japanese.

Elected to the council of the World Buddhist Federation in 1924 was Reginald Johnston, who had once published a book about Chinese Buddhism,[17] but was hardly a Buddhist himself. In fact, he had refused to attend the conference in 1923, as had Liang Ch'i-ch'ao, who was also listed as a council member—an honor of which he was perhaps unaware at the time. It seems almost certain that three other council members (Ti-hsien, Yin-kuang, and Ou-yang Ching-wu) had not authorized the use of their names, since they were not on good terms with T'ai-hsü.

In brief, the World Buddhist Federation fell somewhat short of representing either Buddhism or the world. It was essentially a meeting between the Japanese and T'ai-hsü. Yet it was a significant step ahead in his career, for it showed that he had learned how to create organizations on paper and how to think on a global scale. It also gives us an insight into his motivation, which in the course of the conference he explained to Reichelt as follows: "Many of them [the Christians] only come in contact with ignorant and immoral Buddhist monks strolling about in the streets. They think all Buddhists are of this type and that we are all given over to dark superstitions and do not really cultivate religion. We have started this conference movement to show you that it is not true." Reichelt comments that "the voice and burning eyes of T'ai-hsü were witness to a very real inner pain and grief. The same was the case with the other Buddhists attending the conference. *They all spoke about it.*"[18]

Motivated partly by this "pain and grief," T'ai-hsü went on to create a whole series of "world" organizations. Already in 1923, when the first lectures at Lu Shan were underway, he decided to rename the Buddhist New Youth Society in Peking. On July 29 it became the World Buddhist New Youth Society, although it was still the same organization with little more than high hopes and tea cups.[19] In 1924 a World Buddhist Women's Association was "just being organized."[20] Nothing more is heard of it.

On April 6, 1925, pursuant to the constitution of the World Buddhist Federation adopted the previous summer, T'ai-hsü established a China chapter, called the Chinese Buddhist Federation (Chung-hua Fo-chiao Lien-ho-hui) with headquarters at the Kuang-chi Ssu in Peking. Its immediate purpose was to legitimize the dispatch of delegates to the East Asian Buddhist Conference in Tokyo that autumn as representatives of all the Buddhists in China.[21] Elaborate by-laws were drawn up providing for branches in every province and district. Four branches were reportedly established (Hunan, Honan, Chekiang, and Szechwan). But after the East Asian conference was over, the Chinese Buddhist Federation evaporated.[22] About this time T'ai-hsü decided that the World Buddhist New Youth Society in Peking should organize a World Propaganda Team (Shih-chieh Hsüan-ch'uan Tui) to spread the dharma first in China, then in Europe and America. Telegrams were sent out to all the large monasteries, signed by T'ai-hsü and others, calling for support of the scheme. Nothing came of it,[23] probably because he had antagonized the senior monks who headed the large monasteries. Nor does anything appear to have come of the All-Asia Buddhist Education Center (Ch'üan-ya Fo-hua Chiao-yü She), which he set up in 1927.[24]

When T'ai-hsü had attended the East Asian Buddhist Conference in 1925, the man behind it, Mizuno Baigyo, wrote an article saying that he had known T'ai-hsü only a little over ten years, but "Japanese Buddhists had found in him a new colleague and a good partner in spreading oriental culture through the world . . . I hope that Buddhists of both countries will take him as their central figure (*chung-hsin*)."[25] T'ai-hsü's international aspirations received a further stimulus at the conference when the German ambassador, von Solf, invited him to Germany. Things foreign had great prestige in China at this time, and it occurred to T'ai-hsü that the best way to get his ideas accepted at home would be first to get them accepted abroad.

In 1928, soon after a meeting with Chiang Kai-shek in June, he was able to get official backing for a world tour. He and two lay followers left Shanghai on August 11 and spent nearly nine months in France, England, Germany, the United States, and Japan. He cut a wide swath, not only because he was the first Buddhist monk to be seen in the streets of Western cities, but also because he was treated at Chinese legations like a visiting dignitary and was provided with enough money to make sizable donations for the support of the European Buddhist groups he visited and even for the creation of new groups. In Paris, for example, he gave 5,000 francs toward the establishment of a World Buddhist Institute, which was to unify Buddhism and science as the basis for missionary work throughout the world. He helped to set up its Paris chapter, which was to serve as "European headquarters," and he created other chapters from organizations already existing in Nanking, Singapore, London, and Berlin. He proposed a budget of £200,000, to be raised mostly in China. All this so impressed his new-found followers that one of them, A. C. March, said: "T'ai-hsü is a very practical man. He is no dreamer . . . Now that China has definitely entered the work of establishing Buddhism throughout the world as a universal religion, we may expect great results to follow."[26]

But they did not follow. The Paris chapter, which became Les Amis du Bouddhisme, soon turned away from T'ai-hsü, and the others (like the Buddhist Lodge in London) relapsed into independent existence. More serious, perhaps, was the fact that he had failed to win the respect of leading intellectuals, particularly in France. Although his biographer speaks of the favorable reviews that greeted his lectures there,[27] a Chinese informant who was living in Paris at the time furnishes a different story.

According to him, T'ai-hsü's arrival had been publicized by Louis Laloy of the Institut des Hautes Etudes Chinoises, and

Sylvain Lévi, professor at the Collège de France, who invited
him to lecture at the Musée Guimet. Despite pleas from the Chinese community in Paris (which felt that its prestige was at
stake), T'ai-hsü decided to lecture extemporaneously. He refused
to provide an outline for the interpreter, and the only interpreter
he could get on this basis was a Chinese student who knew little
or nothing about Buddhism. Worst of all, he would not accept
the idea that a Paris audience might be more critical and better
informed than an audience in China. When he faced the hall
filled to capacity at the Musée Guimet, he gave a rambling, in-
coherent, amateurish talk about the similarities of Buddhism,
science, and Marxism. It was anything but a success. Laloy said
later to my informant: "Nous nous sommes trompés," and Lévi
asked the Chinese minister in Paris if he could not arrange to
have a better representative of Chinese Buddhism come to
France. At T'ai-hsü's next lecture the hall was almost empty.

Although this account is not consistent with the picture of a
triumphal tour given by T'ai-hsü's followers, it is confirmed in
the pages of the journal of the very group that had invited T'ai-
hsü to lecture:

> We are grateful to the Chinese monk who has started the move-
> ment: at the same time we have noticed with some concern that there
> is perhaps a certain misunderstanding between him and his French
> listeners . . . He is bent on showing [Europeans] that he is familiar
> with all the philosophies and sciences of the West . . . that there is
> no incompatibility between Buddhism and science. It is at least forty
> years since the conflict between science and religion ceased to in-
> terest anyone in Europe, but it is possible that his arguments will
> prove very striking to Asians who have been Westernized, that is,
> Americanized. In short, it would seem to us that His Eminence T'ai-
> hsü has not taken into account the mentality of the countries to
> which he wants to bring the light of the law . . . French orientalists
> who have given such a fine welcome to His Eminence T'ai-hsü ob-
> viously have not the least intention of being converted to Buddhism.[28]

Even his principal follower in Paris, Grace Lounsberry, looked
back on his fumbling with displeasure. The next year he received
a letter from her that stated: "If we are to have the pleasure of
welcoming you again, it is most necessary to bring a Chinese
versed in Buddhism who speaks French and English correctly—

8 T'ai-hsü in London, 1929.

so much that we wished to ask or hear from you was lost through interpreters not learned in Buddhism . . . Our policy is to publish only the texts or works written by thoroughly instructed Buddhists, as so much inaccurate thinking has been spread abroad."[29]

In England and the United States (where he lectured at Yale, Chicago, the Hartford Seminary Foundation, and the Berkeley School of Religion), his audiences appear to have been less critical of what he had to say and more appreciative of his engaging manner, impressive title (His Eminence the Venerable Abbot T'ai-hsü), and spectacular appearance (he lectured to them in the red robe and regalia of a dharma master).[30] He told them that he was touring the West "in order to educate the public there with regard to the Buddhist revival in China."[31]

Encouraged by the contacts he had made, T'ai-hsü returned to China in May 1929 and at once set to work on the Chinese sector of the grand plan he had inaugurated in Paris. Attached to his seminary in Wuchang was a library of perhaps a hundred thousand volumes. He renamed it "the Library of the World Buddhist Institute."[32] Later he decided that his other seminaries should also become sections of the institute, each specializing in one branch of study. For example, the seminary in Amoy would specialize in Japanese; the seminary in Peking would specialize in English; and the Chungking seminary would specialize in Tibetan. The headquarters of the World Buddhist Institute (and the only part of it not in existence by this time) would be in the Fo-kuo Ssu in Nanking, which its abbot was persuaded to offer to T'ai-hsü in 1931. In the end the offer could not be accepted because of a lack of funds. Support was forthcoming neither from the laity nor from the Chinese Buddhist Association (Shanghai, 1929), with which T'ai-hsü was engaged in a bitter feud. The lack of funds soon forced some of his seminaries to close down. The others continued to operate just as they had before, although they were sometimes referred to by T'ai-hsü as sections of the World Buddhist Institute, which was, as one of his disciples put it, "imaginary."[33]

T'ai-hsü's global ambitions received new stimulus in 1935 when he met the Venerable Narada, from the Vajirarama in Ceylon, who was visiting China at the time. The two of them agreed that Chinese monks should go to the Vajirarama and study Theravada Buddhism. Five went in 1936, received the Theravada ordination on arrival, and began studying Pali, English, and Theravada doctrine. But they soon scattered and disrobed, so that in the end little came of this effort to carry out the plan that T'ai-hsü's teacher, Yang Wen-hui, had first considered forty years earlier.

In 1939, after further abortive efforts to organize internationally,[34] T'ai-hsü embarked on a new tour, this time as head of the Chinese Buddhist Goodwill Mission. The mission was subsidized by the Nationalist government, since part of its task was to win support for China's war of resistance against Japan. It left Chungking in November 1939 and returned in May 1940, after visiting Burma, Ceylon, India, and Malaya. One of its hosts in Ceylon recalled that thousands came to hear T'ai-hsü during his speaking tour of the island. He expounded the doctrine, described Buddhism in China, and called for cooperation between Chinese and Sinhalese Buddhists (but did not, according to this informant, call for support against the Japanese). By not eating meat he impressed people as an ascetic; and by not eating after noon he showed his respect for the Theravada rules, all of which he tried to observe. Reverend Fa-fang interpreted for him from Chinese to English and Dr. G. P. Malalasekera from English to Sinhalese.

As a result of the tour, Fa-fang was invited to accept a lectureship in Mahayana Buddhism at the University of Ceylon. He was an experienced teacher, having been on the faculty of one or another of T'ai-hsü's seminaries for almost two decades. But his English was not good enough for him to teach effectively abroad. Perhaps with the idea of training younger men, he brought over two more Chinese monks in 1945. After a few years of study, both of them disrobed and returned to China. Fa-fang himself died in Ceylon in 1951. T'ai-hsü's efforts abroad had apparently come to very little.

Yet he had accomplished more than was immediately apparent. During the tour in 1940, he had spoken privately to Dr. Malalasekera of the need for a world Buddhist organization. They agreed that it would have to wait until after the world war, which hampered communication and the raising of funds. Then in 1947 T'ai-hsü died, and that appeared to be the end of it. But in 1950 the World Fellowship of Buddhists—the first authentic world Buddhist organization—was founded by Dr. Malalasekera, who said that he set it up "because T'ai-hsü inspired me to do so." Thus the ecumenical impulse that had originated with Dharmapala in 1893 and had been transmitted from Yang Wen-hui to T'ai-hsü to Dr. Malalasekera, returned to reach its fulfillment in Ceylon a half century after it began there.

DOMESTIC ORGANIZATIONS

Although some of T'ai-hsü's efforts in education and journalism were productive and durable, he experienced almost as much frustration in trying to organize the Buddhists of China as in trying to organize the Buddhists of the world. We have already taken note of the Bodhi Society, the Buddhist New Youth Society, the Chinese Buddhist Federation (Peking, 1925), and the Chinese Buddhist Education Association, all of which faded out in the early and middle 1920's.

In June 1928 T'ai-hsü resolved to try again. On June 23 he went to see Chiang Kai-shek, who also came from Chekiang, and urged the desirability of forming a Buddhist group that would unite monks and laymen. Chiang sent him on down to various government officials, to whom he spelled out in greater detail his plans for a national Buddhist association, that is, an association for the Buddhist religion (fo-chiao hui). The officials told him that this was not a good time to promote religion (the anti-religious movement of the early 1920's had recently revived) and suggested that he set up an association for Buddhist studies (fo-hsüeh hui). The word "studies" (hsüeh) implied that Buddhism was to be investigated as a philosophy rather than practiced as a religion.

Chafing under these restrictions, T'ai-hsü set up the preparatory committee of the Chinese Buddhist Study Association (Chung-kuo Fo-hsüeh Hui) in Nanking on July 28, 1928. It was intended to serve as the model for a new organization that would embrace all the Buddhists of China.[35] That is, like the Bodhi Society ten years earlier, it was to be a wedge of study in the door of reform. After it was formally inaugurated, however—on November 29, 1929—it turned out to be nothing more than a sort of "Sunday Evening Club," whose ten to twenty members met once a week at the Wan-shou Ssu in Nanking and listened to a lecture on the sutras given by T'ai-hsü when he was available, or by others when he was not. Sometimes up to several dozen nonmembers would also come to listen. During the Sino-Japanese War the group moved to Chungking, where it held Sunday lectures at the Ch'ang-an Ssu.

The Chinese Buddhist Study Association was small and ineffectual, but holding the presidency of it provided T'ai-hsü with a title that he could use to advantage. Hereafter he set up no further domestic organizations. His goal became instead to win control of the Chinese Buddhist Association (Shanghai, 1929)—as he finally did in 1945.

T'AI-HSÜ AND SCIENCE

One of the pillars on which T'ai-hsü rested his organizing efforts was the compatibility of Buddhism and science. Early in his career he had realized that science was the wave of the future. How could he, as a Buddhist, find a way to ride it? He had never had a scientific education: indeed he had received little formal education of any kind (nor should it be forgotten that he had become a monk because he wanted to acquire supernatural powers). But he soon decided that science could and should serve Buddhism as an ally, if not as a handmaiden. Thus astronomy, he said, confirmed the statement in Buddhist scripture that "space is endless and the number of worlds is infinite, for all are in mutual counterpoise like a network of innumerable beads"; and that "the world is maintained on a 'windwheel' (axis) which is suspended in a vast and empty space." Biology confirmed the statement in Buddhist scripture that "in a single drop of water Buddha can behold eighty-four thousand microbes," a phenomenon that T'ai-hsü had first become aware of many years before when he peered through Yang Wen-hui's microscope in Nanking. As to evolution, it was Buddhist scripture which first revealed that "all life emerges from a certain concentration of matter in the form of a nucleus" and that "life rises from a nucleus body of microbes."

But science, he believed, was the inferior branch of knowledge: "Scientific methods can only corroborate the Buddhist doctrine; they can never advance beyond it." "Buddhism . . . holds that science does not go far enough into the mysteries of nature and that if she went further, the Buddhist doctrine would be even more evident. The truths contained in Buddhist doctrine concerning the real nature of the universe would greatly help science and tend to bring about a union between science and Buddhism." "Astronomy, physics, mathematics, chemistry, natural history, etc., can all be explained by Buddhism, which has much to reveal to scientists, and this union of Science and Buddhism is what we most desire."[36]

In T'ai-hsü's view the common metaphysical basis for Buddhism and science was Dharmalaksana philosophy, according to which everything in the world was ideation only. T'ai-hsü taught this in his seminaries and wrote voluminously about it in books and articles that attracted wide attention. He has been credited by his admirers with achieving an important reinterpretation, which in effect reconciled Dharmalaksana with Avatamsaka and T'ien-t'ai idealism. He himself claimed that it was "elucidated with modern ideas, made use of modern science, and agreed with Einstein's Theory of Relativity."[37]

There was nothing new in this attempt to find common ground for Buddhism and science. It had been made before and would be made again—sometimes with ludicrous results.[38] But the hope that T'ai-hsü frequently expressed for a *union* between Buddhism and science makes one wonder if he did not hope for an ideological or even an organizational union, just as he hoped for a union between Chinese Buddhism and Buddhism elsewhere. Since he also believed that Buddhism was identical with Sun Yat-sen's political ideology of the Three People's Principles ("Buddhism is the ultimate goal of the Three People's Principles and the Three People's Principles are Buddhism put into practice"),[39] it would appear that he looked forward to presiding over ever grander syntheses.

T'AI-HSÜ'S METHODS

Whatever his goals may have been, T'ai-hsü's methods were those of the promoter. He understood the importance of getting lay sponsors who had money and status. One of his sponsors has told me that when T'ai-hsü asked him to become the head of a large Buddhist club, he had been his lay disciple for only a year and did not understand Buddhism very well. But he held a high government post. "Therefore," as he puts it, "T'ai-hsü decided that I would make the best president, since what Buddhist organizations needed then were influential backers. I accepted because I revered him. Once the members realized he favored me for the post, they voted me in unanimously."

T'ai-hsü spent much of his time maintaining contact with such followers by travel and correspondence, usually to good effect. In 1922, for example, he sent some student monks to Szechwan. Through his lay followers there, he arranged for them to be officially welcomed by the governor. Their arrival made headlines, and their public lectures were well attended. They used the approach that T'ai-hsü had taught them. They would begin by admitting that Buddhism "had become incrusted with many superstitions," that monks were lazy and ignorant, and so on. Having thus disarmed their audiences, they would go on to advocate the reform of the sangha, the revision of Buddhist doctrine "along the lines of modern philosophy," and the use of Buddhism "to elevate people and to improve social conditions." In other words, they implied that Buddhism was in tune with the new ideas that were then sweeping China. Their mission was a great success. Many business and professional men, who had not been interested in religion before, became supporters of the mission and began the practice of daily meditation. A Young Men's Buddhist Association was organized.[40] We might not be wrong in thinking that some of the converts were glad to see a Chinese religious group displaying as much vigor and modernity as the Christians.

There seems to be no doubt that T'ai-hsü was aware of the importance of giving the Christians effective competition, even if it meant borrowing their methods to do so. For example, at his

street chapel in Hankow when the doors were opened wide in
the evening, passers-by could see an image of Amitabha, brilliantly lit by electric bulbs. Music from an organ invited them
in. Once the hall had filled, a sermon was given on Pure Land
doctrines, followed by short testimonies from T'ai-hsü's followers.
On the roof of the building there was a reliquary, to which members of the audience were taken afterwards. The sarira relic was
not only brilliantly lit but surrounded by mirrors, so that almost
anyone was capable of seeing its marvelous radiance.[41] T'ai-hsü
centered the preaching on Pure Land doctrines "because this
was all that ignorant people could understand"—although at his
seminary nearby he encouraged students to master the abstruse
doctrines of Dharmalaksana philosophy. K. L. Reichelt, on whose
description the foregoing is based, concludes: "In this way Buddhists could compete better with Christians, who had made so
much progress in China especially through evangelism in street
chapels. T'ai-hsü, who actually had little use for the ways of faith
and worship, found it expedient to use this method as a preparation with the crowds."[42]

To intellectuals T'ai-hsü talked about Buddhism and philosophy, Buddhism and science, Buddhism and economics, Buddhism
and social reform. People who attended his lectures at Chung-
hua University in Wuchang and West China Union University in
Chengtu recall that the students were intrigued by the novelty
of listening to a Buddhist monk, particularly on a Christian
campus. "He held the students spellbound," one missionary told
me. Since his Chekiang accent was too thick to be generally
understood, his staff used to hand out mimeographed summaries
ahead of time (efficient staff work was one of his fortes).

Sometimes T'ai-hsü would miscalculate and nearly overturn in
the new waves he was trying to ride. At his Wuchang seminary
he encouraged student monks to read the left-wing periodicals
that he had placed in the reading room. In 1922 some of them
began to form patriotic political cells and were soon showing less
enthusiasm for study than for the political meetings that they
slipped out at night to attend. One evening a search of their
rooms turned up "revolutionary documents" and "obscene pictures" (indeed, according to this account, they had been in the

habit of moving on to brothels after the political meetings were over). Nine students were expelled. In the spring of 1923 the seminary was surrounded and searched by the authorities. Some students were arrested as subversives, and it is said that only T'ai-hsü's influence saved them from execution. Later fifteen students were expelled from his seminary in Amoy for creating "serious disturbances."[43] No wonder that conservative members of the sangha would not allow their disciples to study under T'ai-hsü and become "new monks" (hsin-seng). One of the reasons they began to establish seminaries of their own was to give their disciples somewhere else to go.[44]

It was partly because T'ai-hsü was a prophet without honor in his own land that he made such a strenuous effort to acquire prestige abroad. On his world tour of 1928-29, for example, he spoke of his efforts to cooperate with Dharmapala twenty years earlier and, more recently, of the anti-Buddhist movement in China, which he boasted of holding in check by having organized a conference shortly before he came to Europe.[45] Actually it had been Yang Wen-hui with whom Dharmapala was in correspondence, and the conference T'ai-hsü had just organized was simply the preparatory meeting of the Buddhist Study Association, which had no effect whatever on the anti-Buddhist movement. He also told his European audience that after the Chinese revolution "the progress of Buddhism in China was stopped until I revived the movement a few years ago."[46] This was an exaggeration almost as preposterous as some of the titles conferred upon him by the more impressionable foreigners—for example, "the Supreme Abbot T'ai-hsü, the Buddhist Pope of China."[47]

Because the Chinese Buddhist Study Association and the Chinese Buddhist Association had such similar names—names often translated into English identically—and because they were founded in the same year,[48] outsiders often took T'ai-hsü to be the head of the latter instead of the former, that is, they thought he was in charge of the principal Buddhist organization in China. This was a misunderstanding that he did little to discourage. In 1942, for example, he used his connections with the Foreign Ministry to get himself listed in the *Chinese Year*

Book as head of "the Chinese Buddhist Association," which had
made "outstanding contributions [in] awakening the masses to
the country's cause." Few readers realized that this was a splinter
group and not the national organization.[49] In 1950 Fa-fang told
the inaugural conference of the World Fellowship of Buddhists
that T'ai-hsü had headed the national organization from 1928
until his death in 1947. For most of this period, as we have seen,
he had actually been at loggerheads with it.[50]

But it would be wrong to picture T'ai-hsü as nothing but an
unscrupulous self-promoter. In his own eyes his promotions were
justified by the cause they served. For example, when I asked
one of his disciples why he kept naming his organizations "world-
this" and "world-that," I was told that this nomenclature had
not been intended to stake any claim to represent the world's
Buddhists, but merely to express the hope that they would
unite.[51] Foreigners who met T'ai-hsü abroad did not find him
aggressive or pretentious. It was quite the reverse. One of his
English hosts on his world tour recalled that he was "sweet . . .
very quiet, and had a lovely smile." According to a woman he
met in France, he was "a wonderful person, with a tremendous
presence. One really felt his saintliness." In Ceylon a prominent
layman remembered that "he was so saintlike and looked so
holy." Sanctity, gentleness, and dynamism ("he was bursting
with energy") were the qualities about him that most impressed
people abroad. Despite the language barrier (he spoke no foreign
language), they found him an appealing personality.

Foreigners who met T'ai-hsü in China, however—especially
if they had other Buddhist contacts there—seemed less likely
to form a favorable opinion. John Blofeld, for example, admired
his energy as an organizer, but objected to his penchant for
invoking science, competing with Christian missionaries, and
putting modernization ahead of religious practice. "He was a
man of immense learning and some wisdom, but no one, least of
all himself, thought of him as a sage or spiritually enlightened."[52]
A European Buddhist who often saw T'ai-hsü in Shanghai spoke
more harshly: "He was a man with a gift of making himself
important."

This very gift was what most appealed to his Chinese followers. They were proud of his ecumenical pioneering, his proposals for institutional reform, his schools and periodicals, his forays into science, and his ultimate success in winning organizational control of Chinese Buddhism; but above all they were proud of his status. "He was a great man," as one of them said to me. "He was recognized by the intellectuals. He was known to Buddhists all over the world." In a sense he was offering the Buddhist component of the national revival for which there was such a longing.

Although his followers included extremely able monks and influential lay devotees, they did not amount to more than a minute fraction of the Buddhist community. Most other Buddhists felt ambivalently about him. They were pleased that one of their own had managed to become so famous, and they acknowledged the value of some of his ideas, but he did not correspond to their concept of what a monk ought to be. He seemed to them to talk about Buddhism more than he practiced it. The monks they most respected—Hsü-yün, Yin-kuang, Ti-hsien, Hung-i, Lai-kuo, T'an-hsü—were persons for whom practice was of the essence, who remained aloof from the world rather than seeking for status in it, who wanted to restore Buddhism to what it had been rather than to make it into something new. They feared that, if it were made into something as new as T'ai-hsü seemed to be proposing, it would no longer be Buddhism.[53]

Chapter IV

THE LAY BUDDHIST
MOVEMENT

THE last two chapters have dealt with the struggle between T'ai-hsü and the conservatives for leadership of the monastic community. This community, with its three quarters of a million monks and nuns, was set apart from the rest of the population by clerical dress, shaven heads, and an ascetic way of life. Its two hundred thousand monasteries and temples were built in a distinctive style and often had rich holdings of farmland.[1] In other words, it was an establishment, both readily identifiable and rich enough to invite control or exploitation.

The Buddhist laity was another matter. Almost all Chinese were partly or occasionally Buddhist, just as they were partly Taoist or Confucian. Even the few who were most exclusively Buddhist—those who had taken all three steps in the lay initiation—looked and lived like their fellow citizens. More important, perhaps, was the fact that lay Buddhist groups did not own large amounts of property, usually nothing more than a clubhouse that was indistinguishable from the buildings around it. Therefore the lay community was inconspicuous, difficult to identify, and offered little that outsiders—or insiders—could control or exploit. It attracted no external predators and was the scene of no internal struggle. There was no need for national leadership.

For these reasons, local Buddhist societies,[2] composed largely of lay people who had joined in order to take part in meritorious activities, differed markedly from the national Buddhist associations or branches thereof, operated by monks to defend the monastic establishment. The monks did not look to their associations as places to earn merit, which they were earning already by their monastic life: what they wanted was a lobby. The laymen felt no need for a lobby: what they wanted was a *tao-ch'ang* —a place where they could practice the religion. At monasteries they were usually allowed to be little more than spectators. They wanted to become participants: to recite buddha's name and chant the liturgy; to study and propagate the doctrine; and to carry out good works that exemplified the compassionate bodhisattva ideal.

This was not the first time that lay people had banded together for such purposes. Since the Six Dynasties (220-589 C.E.), there had been societies for reciting buddha's name, for study, and for publication.[3] But it would appear that by the mid-Ch'ing few of them drew their members from the educated classes, partly because the law discouraged them.[4] This did not mean that there was no interest in Buddhism among the educated. In the early and mid-Ch'ing there had been such well-known devotees as P'eng Ch'i-feng and his son P'eng Shao-sheng; Wang Wen-chih and Lo Yu-kao.[5]

During the late Ch'ing the number of devotees appears to have entered a period of rapid growth. To some extent this must have been because it was the time of troubles that started with the Taiping Rebellion in the mid-nineteenth century and ended with the civil war in the mid-twentieth. Just as Buddhism had taken root among the literati during an earlier time of troubles (100-600 C.E.), now and for similar reasons it enjoyed a resurgence of popularity among those whose Confucian commitment was weakening as the official ideology proved bankrupt, and who saw in Buddhism a refuge from economic, social, and intellectual disorientation. Liang Ch'i-ch'ao wrote that "among the late Ch'ing 'Scholars of the New Learning' there was almost none who did not have some connection with Buddhism."[6] Its popularity grew not only among the literati but also among the rising bourgeoisie. The development of Western treaty ports in central China was creating a new class of entrepreneurs who had surplus income and whose links with Confucianism were weaker than those of the merchants of earlier times.

Disorientation increased during the Republican period, and by 1920 the shift toward Buddhism was beginning to be noticed by Western observers, who spoke of the significance of the "number of accessions from the learned class. Many officials, disheartened by the present confused political situation, have sought refuge in the monasteries. Some of them are now abbots of monasteries and are using their influence to build them up. All over China there are Confucian scholars who are giving themselves to the study of Buddhism and to meditation. Some of the Chinese students who have studied in Buddhist universities in Japan are propagating Buddhism by lecture."[7]

We hear this from many observers,[8] and well-known examples can be cited. Hua-wen, the abbot who rebuilt the Fa-yü Ssu in the 1890's, had already held several high government posts before he became a monk.[9] Ch'ü Ying-kuang, a former governor of Shantung and Chekiang, became disgusted with the partisan strife and after 1925 devoted the rest of his life to Tantrism and Buddhist relief work.[10] In October 1933 Marshal Sun Ch'uan-fang, one of the principal warlords defeated by Chiang Kai-shek, decided that "the great nation of China has reached such a critical period that I want to forget it all by becoming a Buddhist"; and he prepared to take the robe.[11] Ts'en Hsüeh-lü, a military man in Kwangtung, "got sick of killing people" and became a follower of Hsü-yün in 1937.[12]

It was against this background that lay Buddhist groups proliferated during the Republican period. No one knows how many there were in all.[13] They tended to come and go like bubbles in a ferment, so that little trace is left of them. Yet the ferment cannot be doubted. It has been my own experience, when collecting material for this book, that almost every new source mentions the names of groups I have never heard of before, often in places I would have never expected to find them—Chahar, for example, or Kansu, or Sian. Usually there has been nothing more than their names. There has been no way of knowing to what extent they were active or for how long. But even their nominal existence would indicate that the spores of the lay Buddhist movement had blown far and wide.

There were, on the other hand, certain main centers of lay activity, particularly the larger cities where there were the wealth and the leisure for it—Shanghai, Wuhan, Peking, Hangchow, Ningpo, Foochow. Here one found Buddhist groups that were solid and successful.

TYPES OF LAY SOCIETIES

Many of the smaller groups tended to specialize. For example, merit clubs (*kung-te lin*) operated vegetarian restaurants in Shanghai, Hankow, Foochow, and elsewhere.[14] To avoid eating meat was in itself highly meritorious, since it reduced violations of the Buddhist first commandment—not to kill. But this was *missionary* vegetarianism. At the cashier's counter there was often a contributions box for the release of living creatures (to save them from the slaughter house), and almost always there were sutras and tracts for sale, many of which advocated sparing life. As the customer paid his bill, his eye could not miss the display of literature, usually quite inexpensive. Even if he already had a copy, why not get another and gain the merit of presenting it to someone? Buddhist vegetarian food is delicious. I would not go so far as to say that vegetarian "chicken," made largely from beancurd, is indistinguishable from the real thing, but it is certainly tasty and the Buddhist treatment of mushrooms is (to my palate, at least) the best in the world. Thus the vegetarian restaurants offered their patrons the rare opportunity to combine self-indulgence with mortification of the flesh. It is little wonder that they multiplied in metropolitan areas during the Republican period. Indeed their multiplication, if it could be traced from old city directories and guidebooks, would be one yardstick for the spread of the Buddhist revival.

A second type of specialized activity was carried on by the study group, whose members met periodically to discuss sacred texts or to listen to lectures on them by visiting monks. Sometimes they specialized in the texts of one school, as, for instance, the San-shih Hsüeh-hui in Peking, which studied and published Dharmalaksana treatises.[15] Comparable groups existed in Shaosing, Ningpo, Tsinan, Hangchow, Chen-chiang, Nanking, Canton, and Yingkow.

The third and probably the most popular specialty was reciting buddha's name. This was carried on by pure karma societies (*ching-yeh she*), lotus societies (*lien-she*), and recitation clubs (*nien-fo lin*). Their members got together periodically to chant the name of the buddha Amitabha in much the same way as monks at a monastery. They would chant his name while circumambulating, then chant it seated, then sit in silent concentration on the idea of Amitabha. This was one cycle of work, lasting up to an hour and a half. At the end of each cycle they would assign the merit generated thereby to the benefit of themselves and others, so that all might be reborn in the Western Paradise.[16] Sometimes a monk would be invited in to lead them, particularly for a recitation week in winter. Then for seven days they would recite four to eight cycles a day, that is, up to twelve hours, with time off only for lunch and supper (and some preferred to fast after twelve o'clock noon).

The larger lay Buddhist groups did not confine themselves to this or any other special activity. They worked on many lines. For example, the Buddhist Pure Karma Society[17] in Shanghai, founded in 1925, ran an orphanage and an out-patient clinic with free Chinese medicine for the poor. It collected money to clothe and feed not only the city's poor, but victims of flood and famine in other parts of central China. It offered to its intellectual members a place where they could meet and discuss Buddhist philosophy; to its pious members a hall where they could carry on religious practice (such as the recitation of buddha's name on Sunday); and to everyone, including the interested public, an opportunity to attend lecture series on Buddhist texts. It published a journal, the *Ching-yeh yüeh-k'an* (Pure Karma monthly). It operated its own transmitter (XMHB, "The Buddha's Voice"), which put on nightly broadcasts and was, so far as I know, the first Buddhist broadcasting station in the world. At its spacious headquarters in four acres of the Enlightenment Garden on Hart Road, there was a shrine-hall where the seven to ten resident monks performed morning and afternoon devotions, which lay members could attend. There were also rooms for Buddhist visitors: one bhikkhu from Ceylon told me that he had stayed there in 1934 and 1936 and had spoken about Theravada Buddhism over the radio. Finally, the society housed both the national headquarters of the Chinese Buddhist Association (Shanghai, 1929) and the headquarters of its Shanghai branch.

Money to support these varied activities came from the members (numbering about a thousand), among whom were many rich businessmen. The man who had donated the premises, for example, was Chien Chao-nan, head of the Nan-yang Brothers Tobacco Company, two of whose wives subsequently became nuns. Some members also belonged to one or more of the other lay societies in Shanghai, such as the World Buddhist Devotees Club[18] and the Shanghai Merit Club (which operated a vegetarian restaurant).

Although all these organizations were solid and successful, I have been unable to find an informant who served as an officer of any of them. I have, however, had many hours of conversation with the man who was for fifteen years the president of the Buddhist Right Faith Society in Hankow (Han-k'ou Fo-chiao Cheng-hsin Hui).

THE RIGHT FAITH SOCIETY

In 1939 this was called "perhaps the most active Buddhist laymen's association in China."[19] Fifteen years earlier it had already made a favorable impression on J. B. Pratt, who visited its "large excellent building" with an auditorium, temple, lecture hall, offices, and a primary school for boys. Pratt was told that it had three thousand members in Hankow alone and that "preaching services were held in its lecture hall every evening."[20]

The founder and first president of the Buddhist Right Faith Society was Wang Sen-p'u, a successful businessman who was a director of the Chamber of Commerce. He founded it in 1920, and it was formally inaugurated the next year.[21] Either then or soon afterwards he donated his house to serve as its headquarters, and for the rest of his life he gave much of his time to this and other Buddhist activities. Wang was very fat and so kind-hearted that he used to be called "Amitabha." When he walked up to the steps of the Society (in spite of his corpulence he preferred walking to being driven), the beggars would spot him from afar and cluster around crying, "Mr. President! Mr. President! Amitabha! Amitabha!" He would empty all the money he had in his pockets before going in the door.

Both Wang and his successor (my informant, who succeeded him as president about 1931) had taken the Refuges with T'ai-hsü and were therefore officially his disciples. T'ai-hsü had a special relationship with the society, in which he held the title of Guiding Master (tao-shih). Whenever monks were needed to lecture on the sutras, lead the ritual on festival days, or handle the hand-chime and wooden fish during the recitation of buddha's name, they would be sent over for the purpose from T'ai-hsü's seminary, which lay across the river in Wuchang. In return, the society underwrote the seminary's annual deficit, which was not a large sum, since its total budget was usually less than $6,000 a year. When my informant succeeded Wang Sen-p'u as president, he also succeeded him as patron (yüan-hu) of the seminary. There were, as we might say, interlocking boards of directors.

The dues of ten dollars a year were remitted for poor members, but paid regularly by the prosperous businessmen, civil servants, and professional people who made up more than half the membership. But the total income from dues was only enough to cover overhead and the salaries of the permanent staff.

Money for all the good works supported by the Right Faith Society was raised on the fifteenth day of the eighth lunar month. Wuhan's bankers and businessmen would be invited to a party, and they came knowing what lay in store for them. As they chatted, the president would go around with a contributions book and ask each of the guests, "Now what can I put you down for?" Everyone was ready to give at least a few hundred dollars; some gave one or two thousand. By the time the party was over, there might be pledges in hand for a hundred thousand. After inflation began, pledges in rice were preferred.

A hundred thousand Chinese dollars (equivalent at that time to less than half as much in United States currency) was not a sum that could make any perceptible impression on the mass misery of China, whether its spending had been concentrated or dispersed. The Right Faith Society chose to disperse it:

1. It operated a clinic that gave free medical attention and treatment to the poor. Four Western-trained and four traditional Chinese doctors donated their services in rotation, so that one of each category was on duty every day. (Poor patients in China often distrusted Western medicine.) Prescriptions were filled at no charge.

2. It operated a free primary school for about a hundred children of poor families in the neighborhood. At first parents were skeptical and applicants were few. Later, when they saw that it was well run, they applied in large numbers. The school was housed in a building down the street from the society's headquarters.

3. It donated coffins to families who could not afford them.

4. It donated three to five thousand dollars at the end of every year to the Ching-chieh T'ang (Hall for Honoring the Abstinent), in which several hundred indigent widows who had not remarried were housed, fed, and clothed. Along with its donation, the society sent a monk or a layman to preach the dharma to them or to lecture on the sutras. The Ching-chieh T'ang was operated by the Hankow Charitable Association (Tz'u-shan Hui), which was not a Buddhist group.

5. Also at the end of each year it distributed food to needy families. This was not intended to maintain them over a long period, but simply to give them the equivalent of a "good Christmas dinner." Each family received milled rice at the rate of two sheng per adult and one sheng per child, which was enough for two or three days' consumption at New Year's.

6. Fires were common in Hankow. The society would set up soup kitchens to serve congee to the victims.

7. Floods were also common. The society would dispatch small boats to rescue the marooned and supply food to many who needed it, as, for example, during the great flood of 1931. Even animals were rescued. In 1926 the floodwaters carried thousands of small turtles under the railing on top of the

Yangtze embankment and left them stranded there, whereupon the populace began to collect them for food. The provincial governor was persuaded to dispatch soldiers and police to guard them. Then the Buddhists themselves sent in workers with long bamboo brooms to sweep them back into the river—a notable instance of the meritorious release of living creatures.

Probably personal relationships played a role in some of the society's charitable efforts, but it tried to be businesslike and impartial. For example, poor families had to apply at its headquarters to get the New Year's allotment of rice. Field workers would then go to their homes to see whether they were really in need and, if so, to issue them coupons that could be exchanged for rice during the last two weeks of the year. An audited statement of the society's income and expenses was published annually so that donors could know how their money had been used.

Charity accounted for the largest outlay of funds, but it was not the work to which the members gave most time. There was good attendance at the lectures on the sacred texts, sometimes lasting for a week, sometimes for months. The dharma was also propagated in a monthly magazine, the *Cheng-hsin yüeh-k'an.* Members had the use of a fine Buddhist library that had been acquired along with Mr. Wang's house. Hundreds of them would come to recite the prescribed liturgy on the birthdays of Sakyamuni and Kuan-yin or to take part in "recitation weeks," the merit arising from which they would usually transfer to the benefit of their ancestors. Although it is true that some of the members were illiterate old women whose interest in Buddhism was chiefly devotional, they followed rather than set the tone. The management was firmly in the hands of well-educated male devotees, elected by ballot. Membership was not, however, exclusive: any respectable person could join who was sponsored by two existing members. The total was three thousand persons.[22]

The most important thing about the Right Faith Society, perhaps, was the paramount role of lay people. Monks and nuns could neither join nor serve on the staff. But the ten to twenty lay staff members lived almost as if they were monks themselves. They had rooms at the headquarters, in which their wives were not allowed to pass the night (they could go home if they wished to have sexual intercourse). They took their meals there, always vegetarian, and abstained from alcohol. They accepted low salaries of twenty-to-thirty dollars a month. Most striking of all, these functionaries performed the full liturgy of morning and evening devotions in the great shrine-hall upstairs. They played the roles of precentor, succentor, and duty monk, although they did not formally hold these titles. They struck the liturgical instruments with as much expertise as if their heads had been shaven and as if they had been wearing monks' robes.[23]

The Right Faith Society was not affiliated with the Chinese Buddhist Association, which had its own branches in Wuchang and Hankow. As in other metropolitan areas, monks and laity were organized separately, since they had different purposes. In the smaller cities, however, there were often too few of them for separation to be practical. For example, in Ying-ch'eng, which lay about eighty-five kilometers southwest of Hankow, there was only one Buddhist group, the Ying-ch'eng Buddhist Society. In the 1930's it had a few dozen members, clerical and lay, including the district magistrate. Its head was the president of the district Chamber of Commerce. Because the principal temple of the town, the Shou-ning Ssu, owned very little land and there was not enough demand for Buddhist services in the countryside to enable its five or six resident monks to keep body and soul together, the Ying-ch'eng Buddhist Society paid their entire annual deficit, amounting to $200–300.[24] In return, the monks cared for members' ancestral tablets in the hall of rebirth.[25] Originally the society had not been affiliated with the Chinese Buddhist Association, but after the Second World War it became one of its branches. The Right Faith Society, in Hankow, did not. This illustrates a trend toward reversing the traditional relationship between sangha and laity.

THE GROWING ROLE OF THE LAITY

During the T'ang and Sung dynasties lay groups had usually been founded and led by monks. During the Republican period the initiative for most of them came from laymen; and monks, if they took part, were reduced to the role of instructors in

liturgy and professional lecturers. On the other hand, the Chinese
Buddhist Association was of, by, and for the sangha—at any
rate until 1945. As we have seen, its *raison d'être* was to protect
the monastic establishment. Although it did have lay members,
some of whom were elected to its executive council, they played
a subordinate role. After 1945, however, the association was
brought more under lay control. Its new charter gave laymen
in and out of government a larger say in its affairs, and more of
them were elected to its executive council. Yet many large,
purely lay groups like the Right Faith Society did not become
branches of the association. They retained their autonomy, unlike
the smaller local groups that included the sangha along with
the laity. This reflected an overall trend for the sangha to become
increasingly subject to the laity, while the laity was becoming
increasingly independent of the sangha.

Another trend in the changing lay-sangha relationship was
toward a weakening of the distinction between the two sides.
It became somewhat more common during the Republican period
for lay devotees to take part in the performance of mortuary
rites, which had normally been reserved to monks.[26] It also grew
more common for them to go to a monastery and join the monks
in meditation or in reciting buddha's name. This seldom took
place at conservative monasteries like Chin Shan, but at the
Nan-hua Ssu under Hsü-yün laymen were allowed to sit in the
meditation hall for the evening period, and at the Ling-yen Ssu
under Yin-kuang they could pass the whole day in the hall for
reciting buddha's name. In either case their participation was
in the nature of a trial or adventure, lasting for a few days or
weeks. From one person, however, I have heard of a monastery
where laymen practiced meditation side by side with the monks
throughout the year.

This was the Mi-le Yüan, near the Hsi-chih gate in Peking.[27]
During the Republican period, like so many of the other five
hundred Buddhist temples in the capital, it had become vacant.
The last of its original monks died or moved away. It was then
taken over by two outsiders who, although they had no extraordinary gifts, were pious and pure enough to win a small following among the laity. About 1935 they were joined by a very

different sort of monk, named Chen-k'ung. Refusing to accept
the abbotship, he became the rector, that is, the officer in charge
of religious instruction.[28] His talent attracted more lay supporters,
including some rich industrialists. Soon their donations became
large and regular enough so that the resident monks, whose
number rose to fifteen or twenty, were not obliged to earn their
livelihood performing rites for the dead, as were most of the
monks in Peking, but could work at meditation instead.

Among the lay supporters there were also some intellectuals.
Half a dozen of them now moved into the monastery and began
to work with the monks. Sitting in silence behind them, they
took their meals in the refectory. They sat with them in the
meditation hall too, from early morning to late at night, that is,
for the whole daily program of meditation. This program was
approximately the same as at Chin Shan or the Kao-min Ssu,
where laymen were seldom allowed even to enter the meditation
hall.[29] Chen-k'ung had a connection with the Kao-min Ssu, since
he was a pupil of one of its rectors.[30]

It is true that certain differences remained. The lay participants
did not attend morning and afternoon devotions; the monks did.
The lay participants wore ordinary Chinese gowns rather than
the monastic ch'ang-kua. They slept in comfortable guest rooms
rather than on the common platform of the meditation hall. They
could come and go as they pleased, whereas the monks could
only enroll at the beginning of a semester and then had to take
part in every period of meditation until it ended.

Furthermore, none of the lay participants could perform the
duty of giving signals on the board and bell or of patrolling the
hall during periods of seated meditation in order to strike
anyone who dozed an awakening blow.[31] It would have been
inappropriate for a monk to be struck by a layman, whereas the
laymen were most certainly struck by the monks, not only for
dozing when seated but also for letting their thoughts wander
during circumambulation. It was Chen-k'ung himself who struck
the hardest, though outside the hall he was mild and courteous.
During circumambulation, as soon as he saw that anyone's mind
was not on his work (and Chen-k'ung could tell at once), he
would strike him over the shoulders and cry, "What is it?" He

struck monks and laymen with equal vigor. When it came to the routine of meditation itself, there was no distinction between the two. They walked together, sat together, ate *fang-ts'an* together in the evening period, and had an equal right to ask for private instruction.[32]

What made this even more interesting was the character of the laymen involved. Almost all of them were intellectuals who had made a study of Buddhist texts and doctrine before they ever set foot in the Mi-le Yüan. Most were university graduates. My informant, for example, had just taken a university degree in physics. (He was teaching at Oxford at the time of our interview.) He did not regard the year and a half he had spent in the meditation hall as religious practice, but as "something like an experiment in a laboratory." The same was true, he said, for the other laymen there. "None of them was the typical pious devotee who had blind faith only . . . In the beginning they were not obedient followers, but were very inquisitive and sharp in challenging. They became Chen-k'ung's followers only after they were defeated by his unsurpassed wisdom, since he could point out their fallacies immediately."

What sort of monk was it who could win over Chinese intellectuals, most of whom were either scornful of Buddhism or accepted only the most theoretical part of it? He was a monk who disdained theory and intellectualism. Said my informant:

He was almost illiterate. He had no use for scholarship and was not very polite to members of the intelligentsia. He used to urge his followers to do, not to read. In his view, reading even the sayings of Ch'an masters and the accounts of how they became enlightened was a waste of time. At the Mi-le Yüan there was no summer session of lectures on sacred texts [as there was at most of the better monasteries]. I had heard lectures by T'ai-hsü, T'an-hsü, and Tz'u-chou [all eminent monks], and before I met Chen-k'ung I had had the idea of visiting the famous monasteries in the south, like Chin Shan and so on. But after I met him and tested him for a long time, I gave up all my previous intentions, because I had already found some one at the level of the T'ang masters, like Te-shan and Lin-chi, in flesh and blood in the twentieth century, although he was not at all famous. The tradition of Chin Shan and the fame of other masters, like Hsü-yün, could not attract me any more. The phrase "lion's roar" [the voice of a buddha] is used very frequently in Buddhist scriptures, but I have heard the actual "lion's roar" myself.

Regardless of how we judge this appraisal of Chen-k'ung as a Ch'an master, and despite the lack of confirmation from other sources, there seems no need to doubt that systematic joint cultivation was carried on by monks and laymen at the Mi-le Yüan. It should be noted, however, that the superior status of monks was preserved. They sat closer to the abbot in the refectory, and closer to the front in the meditation hall. Laymen, as we have seen, could be beaten by monks, but not vice-versa. Only monks held official positions, while laymen were treated as guests (which may be one reason why, according to my informant, their more comfortable quarters and greater freedom were not resented by the monks who sat beside them). So although we may say that at the Mi-le Yüan the distinction between sangha and laity had weakened in respect to the substance of religious work, it was preserved in respect to most formalities.

We read of one group, however, in which even the formal distinctions had begun to weaken: the Hankow Buddhist Women Devotees Club (Han-k'ou Fo-hua Nü Chü-shih-lin). Both lay women and nuns belonged. Those who lived in the club were required to stay three years, or if they left earlier they had to pay for the full three years of food. This and other regulations were said to have been strictly enforced for all the "pure sisters" (ching-lü), as the members were called. Any member, whether belonging to the sangha or the laity, could hold offices elsewhere reserved to the sangha: guest prefect, proctor, precentor, succentor, and secretary. The head (lin-chang) was a man.[33]

None of my informants had ever heard of such a lay-monastic hybrid. All said that, though a layman could perform the function of a precentor, he could not formally use that title. This was the case at the Right Faith Society where the lay staff members acted as precentor, succentor, and so forth, but were not so called; and where, if a devotee was lecturing on a sacred text, he would not be referred to as dharma master (fa-shih, the title used by lecturing monks), but as "Devotee So-and-So."

It therefore appears that it was far less common for laymen to appropriate the titles of monks than to appropriate their functions. But both kinds of appropriation were underway; and as laymen did more and more that had previously been done by the monks, they inevitably came to need monks less and less.

One might have expected the monks to be alarmed by this trend, but instead many of them appear to have encouraged it, perhaps because they believed that over the short term there was more safety than danger in raising the number of lay Buddhist enthusiasts, some of whom could be counted on for protection against the enemies of the monastic establishment. Whether this would have proved true in the long run is another question.

If the strength of the lay Buddhist movement was the enthusiasm generated by the transformation of lay people from spectators into participants, its weakness was the indifference of the youth.[34] Buddhist youth associations were started in Peking, Shanghai, Wuhan, Chungking, Chengtu, and elsewhere, but all of them appear to have been ephemeral.[35] Few young Chinese accepted T'ai-hsü's claim that Buddhism was more scientific than science and more socially concerned than socialism. In general, only after people had reached mature years did some personal disappointment or the fear of death turn them toward Buddhism.

For very few people, young or old, did Buddhism become a symbol of national identity. This had happened in Ceylon and Burma, where colonial authorities had shown a Christian bias, and it was later to happen in Vietnam. But in China there were too few committed Buddhists; religious commitment was a private matter, traditionally unrelated to politics; and the need for modernization was more acutely felt than in Theravada countries. Therefore Buddhism failed to capture either the loyalty or the imagination of the more nationalistic Chinese.

Chapter V

BUILDING AND PUBLISHING

Some cultures delight in maintenance, others in reconstruction. The Japanese and the English, for example, preserve their antiquities with loving daily care. The grounds are kept as neat as a clock, and the broken roof tile is replaced within the year. In China, on the other hand, litter tends to accumulate, particularly in the back parts of a building. The broken tile may wait until those around it have to be replaced or the rafter has rotted or the roof has fallen in. Then repair becomes reconstruction—a Major Project, for which it is possible to feel some enthusiasm. In the meantime the tiles that fall may be left lying in the courtyard, the appearance of which is not improved (in the case of monasteries) by the robes and gowns that the monks often hang out to dry there. The English visitor shakes his head, just as he does when he sees the Hong Kong millionaire being driven about in a new Rolls Royce by a chauffeur with rolled-up shirt sleeves. A monastery with litter and laundry in the courtyard, he thinks, can only be in a state of moral and physical decay.

This is not to say that there was no day-to-day maintenance of buildings or that better monasteries did not have better maintenance, but only that there was a lower ratio of mainte-

9   Monks' gowns drying in front of the library of the Hsi-ch'an Ssu, Fukien.

nance to reconstruction than in countries like England and Japan. Even in the most flourishing Chinese monasteries, where the rules were strictly kept, some buildings were allowed to fall into such a state that they had to be wholly reconstructed. This continued to be so during the Republican period.[1]

RESTORATION

Reconstruction (*ch'ung-hsiu*) should be distinguished from restoration (*chung-hsing*). The latter was required when not one or two but most or all the buildings of a monastery were in disrepair, when the number of residents had dwindled to a handful, probably with little talent or discipline, and when the only remedy was the accession of an eminent abbot who could completely reform and rebuild. He would bring with him a few able young monks who had had administrative experience at a good monastery. With their help he would soon have a "tight ship." Dust would be swept away and rubble cleared. Waste and pilferage would be stopped, and rents efficiently collected. The daily rites would be fully reinstated and the monastic rules strictly enforced. Then would come the task of physical reconstruction. Every eminent monk had lay followers among the rich and powerful who were glad of a chance to "get in on" the merit and prestige that would arise from restoring a famous old monastery. The rich would donate money to put up buildings and to purchase farmland; the powerful would sometimes make it possible to recover farmland that had been lost in the period of decay. After a few years of hectic effort, the monastery would be as large and splendid and its monks as pure and diligent as they had been one century or five centuries before. The abbot who had brought this about would be revered, after his death, as "the

10   A new shrine-hall under construction in 1929 at the Wan-fu Ssu, Fukien, to replace one destroyed by a flood the previous year.

ancestral master responsible for the restoration" (*chung-hsing tsu-shih*).

But nothing lasts, particularly where there is no central authority to maintain standards. Sometimes after a few decades, sometimes after a few centuries, there would be a disastrous fire, or the monastery would be pillaged in a rebellion or would fall into the hands of an incompetent or unscrupulous abbot who failed to enforce the pure rules or violated them himself. In any case the élan of the restoration would fade. This would cause the best monks to go elsewhere, depriving the monastery of their administrative talents. Maintenance and repairs would be neglected, and income-producing property would be lost by either carelessness or encroachment. Against encroachment the monastery would now have little protection, since it would have forfeited the respect of the laity by its failure to enforce the rules. As income declined, more monks would leave. As the monastery emptied (losing, so to speak, the mandate of heaven), popular support would tend to drop off faster, so that still more monks would leave.[2] The process would accelerate geometrically, until in the end the monastery reached the same state of decay as before it had been restored. Then, if it were old and famous enough, it would be restored again. This was the monastic cycle, similar to the dynastic cycle in Chinese history—even to the use of the same term (*chung-hsing*) for restoration. Some monasteries had gone through nearly a dozen cycles of restoration and decay.[3]

During the Republican period, as at other times, many were at the nadir of the cycle. At least fourteen were restored by a single eminent monk, the Venerable Hsü-yün (see p. 34): on Chi-tsu Shan in Yünnan, the Hsi-chu Ssu (Po-yü An), Chu-sheng Ssu (Ying-hsiang Ssu), Hu-kuo Ssu, and Hsing-yün Ssu; in Hsia-yang, Yünnan, the Lo-ch'üan Ssu; in Kunming, the Yün-ch'i Ssu (Hua-t'ing Ssu), Sung-yin Ssu, Sheng-yin Ssu (a subtemple of Yün-ch'i); in Foochow, Fukien, the Yung-ch'üan Ssu (Ku Shan); in Kükiang, Kwangtung, the Nan-hua Ssu, Ta-chien Ssu, Yüeh-hua Ssu, and Yün-men Ssu; and in Kiangsi, the Yün-chü Ssu.

Details on four of these restorations will suffice to illustrate the pattern. In 1904, when Hsü-yün first arrived at Chi-tsu Shan in northern Yünnan, he found that all the temples there had become hereditary, that is, they were no longer operated as if they belonged to the sangha as a whole but were treated as hereditary private property by individual monks. For this reason the pilgrims who came to Chi-tsu Shan were not given the food and shelter that was their due. Hsü-yün wanted to build a place for them, but the heirs of the mountain would not allow it.[4] Eventually he enlisted the help of lay devotees in Ta-li, some of whom were high officials. They arranged for him to get a ruined temple, the Po-yü An, which with their donations he gradually repaired, enlarged, and opened to all pilgrims. He drew up and enforced a code of rules, instituted meditation, lectured on the sutras, and held an ordination to which some seven hundred persons came to take their vows. "Thereupon all the monasteries on the mountain began gradually to reform. They put on their robes, ate vegetarian fare, held devotions in the shrine-hall, and allowed pilgrim monks to stay."[5]

Hsü-yün's second major restoration was launched in 1920. Here is his own account:

The Hua-t'ing Ssu in the Western Hills of Kunming [the capital of Yünnan] was an illustrious, ancient monastery set in the most lovely scenery. Its monks had been unable to keep it up, and it was falling to pieces. Recently, moreover, they had formed a wish to sell it to some Europeans, who were going to make it into a club. The local authorities had given permission for this. I thought it was most unfortunate and said as much to T'ang [T'ang Chi-yao, the governor of Yünnan and Hsü-yün's disciple]. I asked him to preserve this famous site. T'ang took my words to heart and talked it over with Wang Chiu-ling and Chang Cho-hsien. Together they reached a decision. They held a vegetarian feast, to which they respectfully invited me, and handed me a red card asking that I become the abbot of the Hua-t'ing Ssu and restore it. After they had asked three times, I accepted the card.[6]

Hsü-yün rebuilt the monastery in handsome fashion, although he was unable to increase the landed endowment proportionately (so that a shortage of food developed as the number of resident monks approached a hundred). He changed the name from Hua-t'ing Ssu to Yün-ch'i Ssu, in order to honor the memory of the great Ming dynasty monk, Chu-hung, who combined the practices of Ch'an and Pure Land at the original Yün-ch'i Ssu in

Hangchow. It was at the Hua-t'ing Ssu that the English Buddhist, John Blofeld, spent nine months in the 1930's. He testifies to the "magnificent scale" on which its buildings had been restored.[7]

By the time of Blofeld's visit, Hsü-yün had long since left Yünnan and taken over two important monasteries in southern China. The first, Ku Shan, was the largest in Fukien, where Buddhism was still relatively vigorous. Ku Shan's buildings had been reconstructed and the landholdings enlarged in the middle of the nineteenth century, and they were still in excellent condition. There were four hundred monks in residence.[8] But, as at Chi-tsu Shan, many features of the private, hereditary temple had crept in. In particular, monastic offices were for sale. Anyone could purchase the title of rector and then live free of charge in an apartment at the monastery for the rest of his life, training his private disciples exactly as if it were his hereditary place of tonsure.[9]

In 1928 Hsü-yün had made a lecture tour of southeastern China, ending up in Shanghai. Early the next year Ta-pen, the abbot of Ku Shan, died at the age of eighty-two. Hsü-yün was summoned and asked to take over by no less a person than Yang Shu-chuang, minister of the navy and governor of Fukien, and Fang Sheng-t'ao, a former governor.[10] Because of Hsü-yün's loyalty to Ku Shan, as the place in which he had originally been shaved and ordained, he "could not but accept." He soon canceled the ranks that had been purchased and got rid of the monks who had purchased them. No longer were novices permitted to be trained there. Instead, a seminary was started for ordained monks. Discipline was tightened and the atmosphere improved. Ku Shan became again a proper public monastery.[11] This was not the kind of physical restoration that Hsü-yün had brought about in Yünnan and was soon to bring about in Kwangtung. Rather, it was institutional reform.

In 1933 General Li Han-hun, the head of the North Kwangtung Pacification Office, became distressed at the condition of the Nan-hua Ssu, the most illustrious monastery in Kwangtung province. Here in the T'ang dynasty had lived the Sixth Patriarch, and here after death his mummified body had been preserved for thirteen hundred years. The Nan-hua Ssu had last been restored by Han-shan in the early seventeenth century, but since then had fallen into dilapidation and decay.[12]

General Li had some minor repairs made in 1933–34 and sent his secretary to a prominent Hong Kong businessman for help in raising $15,000 toward a more extensive reconstruction. The businessman replied that $15,000 would be too little, but that no amount of money would be enough unless they found the right person to take over the abbotship. He suggested Hsü-yün, from whom he had received the Refuges three years earlier at Ku Shan. When they sent him a telegram, Hsü-yün accepted with alacrity. He had recently had two dreams in which the Sixth Patriarch appeared to him and said: "The time has come; you must return home." When he arrived at the Nan-hua Ssu in the autumn of 1934, he found it in a dreadful state. There were not even chairs to sit on. The half dozen monks still in residence had been raising chickens—slaughtering and eating them in violation of the most fundamental Buddhist rule. As soon as they heard he was about to arrive, they had got rid of the whole flock; and the incumbent abbot, informed of the plan for a restoration, agreed to yield his post.

With money from Canton and Hong Kong, the main halls began to be repaired or rebuilt. Regular meditation was instituted. Monks and lay people came to be ordained every spring. The number of monks in permanent residence soon went over a hundred. Increasing income was derived from donations, the performance of rites, and the land the monastery was now acquiring—almost one hundred acres of fruit and forest land provided by the local authorities at the direction of Li Han-hun and about ten acres of paddy that he helped Nan-hua recover from squatters. By 1941 the reconstruction was 80–90 percent complete.[13]

Nan-hua became the focus of Buddhist activities in Kwangtung, where for two decades antireligious forces had been rampant. Hsü-yün, who had resigned as abbot of Ku Shan in 1935, also restored the neighboring Yün-men Ssu, which was the seat of the Yün-men school of Ch'an Buddhism, and another famous monastery of the province. Only in 1953 did he leave Kwangtung for the Yün-chü Ssu in Kiangsi—his last restoration. Although Hsü-yün seems to have restored more monasteries than anyone

11 The relic pagoda at Ch'i-hsia Shan before and after the monastery was rebuilt around it.

else during the Republican period, other monks were similarly
active. Elsewhere I have told the story of the Ch'i-hsia Ssu near
Nanking. Completely destroyed during the Taiping Rebellion,
it was reconstructed on an impressive scale by Tsung-yang with
the help of high officials and prominent businessmen.[14] The same
thing happened at the Ling-yen Ssu near Soochow, the Tou-
shuai Ssu (Shih-tzu Ling) near Nanking, and the Ch'ung-sheng
Ssu near Foochow.[15] Other monasteries demolished by the Taipings had already been restored in the late Ch'ing.[16]

A high incidence of restoration was equivocal. Where it followed a great disaster (like the Taiping Rebellion), it showed
that Buddhists still had the administrative vigor and popular
support to rebuild what had been destroyed through no fault of
their own. Where it followed a period of slow internal decay, it
showed that, whereas some Buddhists were vigorous enough to
rebuild, other Buddhists had become slack and weak enough to
make rebuilding necessary.

NEW MONASTERIES

An unequivocal sign of vigor was the founding of entirely new
monasteries. During the T'ang, the golden age of Chinese Buddhism, it is likely that more were founded than in any other
period of Chinese history, partly because so many T'ang rulers
were patrons of Buddhism. In the Ch'ing dynasty state patronage
was intermittent, and under the Republic it ceased altogether.
Private patronage suffered from the economic dislocation of the
times. It would not have been surprising, therefore, if no new
monasteries at all had been constructed after 1911, except where
the growth of population and wealth created both the need and
the means, notably in Shanghai.[17] Yet new monasteries were, in
fact, started elsewhere. At least four were the creation of the
Venerable T'an-hsü (no connection with T'ai-hsü): the Leng-
yen Ssu, Yingkow, Liaoning (founded in 1921); the Po-jo Ssu,
Changchun, Kirin (1922); the Chi-le Ssu, Harbin, Heilungkiang
(1922); and the Chan-shan Ssu, Tsingtao, Shantung (1931).

These were all large public monasteries—places where abbots
were publicly elected, unordained novices could not be trained,
and pilgrim monks could stay as long as they wished. The Leng-

yen Ssu had about seventy residents, the Chan-shan Ssu about a hundred. In both cases the majority were students enrolled in their seminaries. T'an-hsü and his fellow disciples also founded two smaller monasteries and restored three others, large and small, in north China.[18]

Some Western authorities have maintained that Chinese Buddhist temples were founded to improve geomantic influences (*feng-shui*) and thereby to avert natural disasters.[19] This was not the motivation of T'an-hsü. He was simply following the resolve of his illustrious master, Ti-hsien, to revive Buddhism in north China and in particular to revive the T'ien-t'ai sect. The lay people who gave the necessary money did so to gain merit. They were attracted by the excitement of creating something large and new for their religion and their community. The very size was exciting ("let's build a really *big* temple," some of them would say). Once they felt a commitment to the project, they saw it through, despite the high cost. The Leng-yen Ssu, for example, cost between two and three hundred thousand dollars— a very large sum in the China of those days.

New construction was probably a fair indicator of the amount of lay commitment to Buddhism. But it was more than that. Once when I was talking to the abbot of Chin Shan about the plans to establish a certain temple, I ventured the opinion that it would require a lot of money. He disagreed. "Temples," he said, "are of a different nature from schools and things like that. With or without money, it is possible to get them started so long as you have the right men. The thing depends on the character of the monks involved." He applied this not only to the construction of new monasteries but to the restoration of old ones. If he was correct, then we have just seen evidence that at least a few of the "right men"—able monks—continued to exist in China down to the end of the Republican era.

Because of the twofold relationship between monastic construction and the prosperity of Buddhism, it would be useful to prepare a graph showing the incidence of building and repair in different provinces over recent centuries. Unfortunately the necessary information has yet to be gathered. Certain figures have been compiled from district gazetteers by C. K. Yang, R. H. Myers, and Wolfram Eberhard, but gazetteers seldom provide the details needed to differentiate the complete restoration of a major monastery with hundreds of monks from the redecorating of a small temple with a handful of monks or none at all. Ten instances of the former would indicate a high level of Buddhist prosperity, whereas ten instances of the latter might mean little more than a slight increase in the demand for funeral services because of rising population. In the compilations available so far, no distinction is made between the two categories.[20] As to monastic histories, which are likelier to provide the data necessary for such a distinction, few of them have been brought up to date.

It is true that Western observers in China during the late Ch'ing dynasty depicted many monasteries as decaying, whereas Western observers in the Republican period frequently mentioned the Buddhist building activity they had seen underway.[21] But this is not good enough evidence that the level of construction had actually risen. Quite aside from the fact that these observations were scattered and unsystematic, they may reveal more of a change of bias than a change of conditions. Despite a rise in influential converts (see p. 74), there is little reason to assume that there was more building activity or greater monastic prosperity under the Republic than a century earlier. We shall return to this point in the final chapter.

PUBLISHING

For Chinese Buddhists, printed matter was more than a medium for instruction in religious truth. When a Buddhist bought himself the reprint of a sutra, he may have wanted to study eternal verities, but he almost certainly felt that he was acquiring merit —good karma—by paying for the book (since the money helped a press or a bookshop that was spreading the dharma), and that by reading it he would be taking part in the Buddhist practice which was most respectable in the eyes of a Confucian society. Many religious practices could be dismissed as superstitious or heretical by unfriendly literati, but the study of an ancient text —even a Buddhist text—was considered to befit the scholar and the gentleman.

Hence as a growing number of laymen became interested in Buddhism over the century before 1950 (and as their need for respectability increased vis-à-vis Christianity, science, and so on), the flow of printed matter, which had been a modest stream after the Taiping Rebellion, became a veritable flood. There were other factors besides this growing lay commitment. Inquisitorial censorship had ended with the revolution of 1911. Western technology accelerated printing and circulation, while Western ideas provoked intellectual controversies in which Buddhism became involved. Further stimulus came from the discovery of the manuscripts and art of Tunhuang, from the revival of Buddhist schools like the Avatamsaka and Dharmalaksana, from the private and official interest in Tibetan Buddhism, and from the need to understand the history of China's relations with India and Japan.

The achievement that has most impressed some observers was the reprinting of three editions of the complete Tripitaka, as well as parts or sequels thereof.[22] This is certainly evidence of Buddhist wealth and piety, but it does not necessarily indicate readership. The Tripitaka, with its millions of words, was like Dr. Eliot's five-foot shelf—decorative and inspiring. It was usually the individual sutras, printed and purchased separately, that were well-thumbed. According to one source, 537 Buddhist titles appeared between 1920 and 1935.[23] Another source states that as of 1935 there were sixty-eight separate institutions publishing and selling Buddhist books in China.[24] In 1950 the Central Scriptural Press in Peking had on hand thirty *million* copies of five hundred titles.[25] Yet it was only one of three Buddhist publishing houses in that city—and in Shanghai there were seven.[26] Aside from these new ventures, which started after 1911, sutras were still being printed at monasteries like the T'ien-ning Ssu in Changchow and at the Chin-ling Scriptural Press in Nanking.

The main categories of books published, apart from the sutras themselves, were: (1) reprints of lectures on the sutras by well-known monks; (2) translations of the sutras into the colloquial language; (3) interpretations of doctrine and exhortations to practice (often printed by lay devotees at their own expense); (4) summaries of Buddhism and excerpts from the Tripitaka (compiled by evangelistic groups); and (5) scholarly studies of Buddhist history. There were regrettably few biographies of contemporary monks or new editions of monastic histories.[27]

If the sale of books was an index of personal commitment and scholarly interest in Buddhism, periodical sales were an index of the activity of the new clubs and associations to which many of the committed lay people belonged. The first Buddhist periodical to appear was *Fo-hsüeh ts'ung-pao* (Buddhist miscellany), issued monthly in Shanghai from October 1912 through June 1914. It was followed by the *Fo-chiao yüeh-pao* (Buddhist monthly; 1913), *Fo-kuang* (The Light of the Buddha; 1915), and *Chüeh-shu* (Enlightenment; 1918), the quarterly that became *Hai-ch'ao yin.* Although its headquarters often moved from place to place, it remained in the hands of T'ai-hsü while he was alive and of his disciples after he died in 1947. No other Chinese Buddhist journal appears to have had such a long history, and probably none came to be so influential in calling for the institutional reform of Buddhism.

The banner of reform was carried by other journals as well. They denounced corrupt and superstitious practices, and, although they were opposed to Christianity, they printed articles advocating the reorganization of Buddhism along Christian lines with church membership and married priests. Many of these reformist periodicals were edited by disciples of T'ai-hsü or by monks under his influence. For example, the editor of *Hsien-tai seng-chia* (Modern sangha) was Ta-hsing, a graduate of T'ai-hsü's seminary in Wuchang, and its editorial offices were at his seminary in Amoy. In its pages one can find the most indignant allegations of the malevolence, corruption, and stupidity of T'ai-hsü's conservative opponents.

Magazines of a different kind were published by groups like the Pure Karma Association (Shanghai), the Buddhist Devotees Club (Changsha), and the Right Faith Society (Hankow). We know that some of these groups were conservative, and most of them appear to have been interested primarily in religious practice and study rather than in institutional reform. However, since few copies are available, generalization is risky.

In all, about seventy Buddhist periodicals appeared during the Republican period. Fifty-seven of them are listed in Appendix 1. This may sound like an impressive number, but the majority had few readers and a short life. They testify to a widespread ferment which, under different external conditions, might have solidified

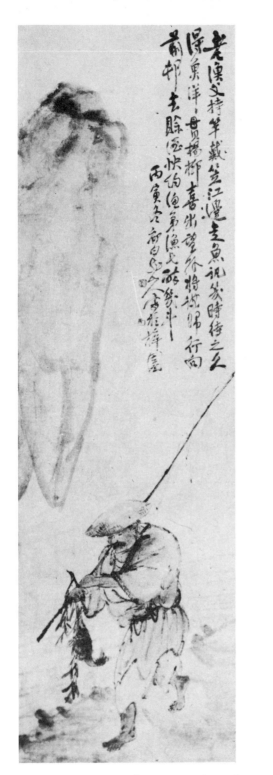

12 Two paintings by Wang I-t'ing, the prominent devotee. On the left a fisherman; on the right Kuan-yin.

into something durable and significant. In actuality, little was produced in the way of distinguished writing, creative thinking, or original research. A few Buddhist scholars like T'ang Yung-t'ung and Chou Shu-chia enjoyed a wide reputation, but Buddhism had no Hu Shih.

When it came to the creative arts, there was even less in which Buddhists could take pride. It is true that Eight Fingers was admired as a poet; that Tsung-yang, Hung-i, and Wang I-t'ing were skilled painters in traditional modes; and that some of the craftsmen who supplied temple images had a feeling for line and the expression of religious ideals. But there was no artist monk of the caliber of Mu-ch'i. Many monks could scarcely tell good art from bad. A visitor to a large Chengtu monastery in 1924 noted that in front of the Buddha image in the great shrine-hall stood a lithograph "advertising a well-known baby's food and showing the Prince of Wales in oriental robes, kneeling among the varied Asiatic worshippers."[28] This typifies a deficiency in taste that was only too common in the sangha. In this respect Buddhist China was comparable to Christian America of the same period. Piety was authentic, but it does not seem to have borne artistic fruits. We have no way of knowing whether there would eventually have been an *aggiornamento* of religious art and architecture (like that in Europe and more recently in America), but no signs of it were obvious by the time the Communists took China.

Chapter VI

BUDDHIST
EDUCATION

T HE monastic schools that began to be set up in 1904 were something new, but education for monks was not. Under a system that had existed for centuries, many monks had learned a few basic texts while they were novices living in small temples.[1] After ordination some of them had gone on to study the monastic rules (the Vinaya) at a Vinaya school, and more of them had studied the doctrine as apprentices of a professional lecturer. Such were the main elements in the traditional system of education.

TRADITIONAL EDUCATION

The Vinaya school was not a common institution. Indeed, I have been able to get a firsthand account of only one—at Pao-hua Shan, the leading ordination center of central China.[2] After its spring ordination ended on the birthday of Sakyamuni (the 8th of the fourth lunar month), most ordinees returned to their home temples. A certain number, however, who wanted to perfect their performance of ritual and observance of the rules, would enroll in the Vinaya hall (*hsüeh-chieh t'ang*), which ran for three months; then some of them would enter the board halls (*pan-*

t'ang), where they might remain for two or three years. This whole curriculum formed what I call a "Vinaya school," although no such collective term is used (so far as I know) in Chinese.[3]

The vinaya hall could hardly be called a school. It was simply a dormitory, whose residents followed the same program as the main body of monks at Pao-hua Shan from the 15th of the fourth to the 15th of the seventh lunar month, that is, for the period of the summer retreat.[4] It was extremely arduous. There were five periods of devotions each day instead of the usual two; three periods of circumambulating in the main courtyard; two periods of meditation; and a lecture of one and a half hours on some sacred text. In spite of the hot summer weather, the solemnity of the work made it necessary for the monks to wear their outer robes most of the time, so that they sweated profusely and, even with a daily bath in midafternoon, "we really stank," as one informant told me.

This was the program with which those enrolled in the vinaya hall were kept busy from 3:00 A.M. to 9:00 P.M. Apart from the lecture, they had no opportunity for theoretical learning. They learned by doing, and what they did most of the day was to chant the sutras during devotions. They had not yet qualified to *study* chanting. That came only after they entered the board halls in the middle of the seventh month.

There were two board halls: a bell-board hall and a west-board hall.[5] Both were laid out like a meditation hall, with a platform at each end for sleeping, but instead of the center of the room being empty, so that there was space to circumambulate, it was occupied by tables and benches.[6] Students enrolled first in the bell-board hall, and when they had learned the system of signals on the bell and board,[7] they were promoted to the west-board hall. There were no marks or examinations. Promotion was based on seniority. Each student received a serial number according to the date of his ordination and his position on the roster of ordinees. If he was caught breaking a rule, one of the common penalties was to lower his number, which meant that his term in the bell-board hall was prolonged. Most students managed to get through it in about a year.

Apart from learning signals on the bell and board, the work

of the two halls was the same: study of liturgy and ritual. This included, for example, the pronunciation of the Chinese characters used to transliterate Sanskrit names and incantations and the magical gestures employed to "release the burning mouths" (one of the commonest rites for the salvation of the dead).[8] Every element of the largest of the mortuary rites (the *shui-lu fa-hui*) had to be mastered in full. Another subject was the ritual of ordination: the entire formulary both for those ordained and for those ordaining had to be learned. The semiannual ordinations at Pao-hua Shan provided an opportunity for practice, since the student monks of the board halls served as instructors of the ordinands.[9] Furthermore, since mortuary rites were concomitant with ordination, these could be practiced too.

The board hall was an odd sort of school because there were no teachers. The seniors taught the juniors. The only monastery officer was an assistant instructor (the lowest of the four instructorships[10]), whose duty was limited to keeping order and meting out punishment to those who broke the rules. He did not give "Explanations" of how to meditate (as he would have if he had been an instructor in a regular meditation hall). When during certain periods each day the students sat in the posture of meditation, the sort of "work" (*kung-fu*) they did was up to them. They studied ritual in small groups: one of the more advanced students taught three or four of the less advanced. No learned monk came in to supervise; nor did anyone inspect the notebooks into which the juniors copied the notes of the seniors (copying was the activity to which they devoted the most time).[11] If something was copied wrong, it went uncorrected, and this happened fairly often because, as one informant explained, "some students were rather sloppy in copying." He himself still had four thick volumes of what he had written down forty years earlier in a meticulous hand. They appeared to contain about 1500 pages, and he valued them so highly that he would scarcely let me look at them before he hurried them back to safekeeping. He had spent four years in the Vinaya school at Pao-hua Shan.

Many young monks, whether or not they had been through a Vinaya school, studied Buddhist doctrine under the ancient system of apprenticeship. They would seek out a dharma master (*fa-shih*) to whom they would attach themselves as pupils. When he traveled about the country to lecture on the sutras, especially during the summer retreat at large monasteries, they would accompany him. Dressed in a red robe and seated on a dais, he would expound a given passage from 2:00 to 4:00 P.M. At 5:00 P.M. the audience would reassemble to hear one of his pupils expound the same passage again (a different pupil each day, in rotation). Later in the evening, members of the audience would meet with the pupils for individual consultation on difficult points.[12] After spending several years as the understudy of a dharma master who specialized on this sutra or that (and most did specialize), a monk could become a dharma master himself and pass on what he had learned to his own pupils.

This system of apprenticeship continued well into the Republican period. It had the merits and shortcomings of all such systems. It produced a very small number of monks who knew the traditional interpretation of a few texts very well indeed, but it did not encourage originality or adaptation to changing times. On the other hand, quite a large number of monks from different monasteries attended lectures as members of the audience and even the least attentive must have learned a smattering of Buddhist doctrine, so that the educational effect, though it may have been superficial, was broad—broader, at any rate, than the effect of the Vinaya school, where the work was largely intramural.[13]

For the ordinary monk who had not attended a Vinaya school and had learned only a smattering from lectures, lack of education was no handicap to his career. Whether he was a contemplative in the meditation hall or an administrative officer or a pilgrim or hermit, he did not need to know the finer points of the Vinaya or the doctrine particularly well. Nor did he need to know them if he decided to earn his livelihood performing rites for the dead. Lay people expected him, through his pure life, to accumulate merit, which he transferred through ritual to their benefit. If he had a deep understanding of doctrine or was punctilious in following the Vinaya rules, he was perhaps considered a more potent accumulator of merit, but lay people did not insist on this. So long as he could chant the sutras and ate no meat, it was probably enough.

If it was enough for the ordinary monk, however, it was not

for the lecturer, who had to be thoroughly trained in textual exegesis. After 1900 the loss of imperial protection, as we have seen, led to the need for more lecturers—particularly lecturers who could present Buddhism to the laity in terms that spoke to a modern, secular world. This meant that the traditional system of monastic education had to be reformed and expanded and that new kinds of monastic schools had to be created.

SEMINARIES: KUAN-TSUNG

I call these new schools "seminaries," although in Chinese different terms were used and the differences were significant. When their immediate purpose was to forestall confiscation, they went by the same name and had almost the same curriculum as the schools that the would-be confiscators wanted to establish. That is, they were called *hsüeh-t'ang*. Where the threat of confiscation was slight and the founding monks were conservative, both the name and curriculum of the *hsüeh-t'ang* were avoided in favor of something more traditional, such as *hsüeh-chieh t'ang* (Vinaya hall).

In 1922 a new term came into use when T'ai-hsü set up the Wuchang Institute for Buddhist Studies (Wu-ch'ang Fo-hsüeh-yüan).[14] Many of the innovations he made there proved popular, and by 1945 almost all the seminaries in China had become "institutes for Buddhist studies" in name, if not in substance. To varying degrees they adopted what T'ai-hsü had adopted from lay schools and abroad.

Seminaries, no less than other Buddhist organizations in the Republican period, came and went like bubbles in a ferment. Without making any special search, I have collected the names of seventy-one of them (see Appendix 2). As of 1936 forty-five were reported to be in operation.[15] Most were forced to close by the economic distress that followed the Japanese attack in the summer of 1937, but new ones continued to be founded and old ones revived right up to the Communist victory in 1949. Rather than attempting to generalize about so many ephemeral institutions, I shall describe some of the few that proved durable and served as exemplars for the rest.

One such was the seminary started in 1913 by Ti-hsien, the

eminent T'ien-t'ai monk, at the Kuan-tsung Ssu in Ningpo. By 1918 it was offering a three-year course devoted entirely to Buddhist texts, with the lectures given by Ti-hsien himself.[16] At that time it was known simply as a research center (*yen-chiu she*). In 1929 an elderly layman was invited in to teach traditional literature (*kuo-wen*). Soon afterward, elementary courses in other non-Buddhist subjects were added, and by the early 1930's the seminary had been given the name Hung-fa Hsüeh-yüan (Academy for Spreading the Dharma) and consisted of four sections.

The elementary section was called the Vinaya hall. Its program was more modern than at Pao-hua Shan. Young monks (usually under eighteen) not only learned rules and etiquette, but also received the rudiments of a primary education, reading the Confucian classics, Chinese history, geography, and arithmetic. Knowledge of Confucian classics was important if monks wanted to be able to explain Buddhist texts or ideas in terms that would find favor with an educated audience. Indeed, according to one monk who had enjoyed great success as a lecturer on Buddhism, a thorough Confucian training was his most important asset.

The next section was called the preparatory course (*yü-k'o*). Here the study of Confucian literature continued and the study of basic Buddhist texts began, particularly the *Lotus Sutra.* Other sutras often studied were the *Surangama, Heart, Diamond, Vimalakirti, Lankavatara, Bhaisajyaguru,* and *Avatamsaka,* the *Sutra of Perfect Enlightenment* (Taisho 842), and the *Sutra in Forty-Two Stanzas.*

The third section was called the research center (the name used for the whole in 1918). There students devoted themselves exclusively to Buddhism, paying special attention to treatises and commentaries and becoming acquainted with different interpretations.[17] In the fourth and highest section, known as the dharma propagation center (*hung-fa she*), they learned how to give public lectures on the texts they had mastered.

The Vinaya hall had its own classroom, whereas the other three sections worked together. Everyone enrolled in them would be present when, daily at 2:00 P.M., the abbot would ascend the dais in his red preaching robe, seat himself in lotus position, and formally expound a passage from the text then being studied, just as he would if he were a dharma master lecturing during the summer retreat. When he finished at 4:00, the students went to afternoon devotions, next to supper, and then reconvened for the evening session, during which those enrolled in the preparatory course had to listen to those in the propagation center practice lecturing—that is, practice reciting what they had heard from the abbot earlier in the day. (Attendance was optional for the research center.) The next morning the abbot, as chief lecturer (*chu-chiang*), or one of his assistants (*fu-chiang*) would come to audit the recitation—still of what the abbot had said the day before. Students chosen by lot would speak for five to fifteen minutes apiece. The morning session lasted from 8:00 to 11:00 A.M. and was followed by a rest, lunch, recitation of buddha's name, and an hour of T'ien-t'ai meditation (*chih-kuan*) from 1:00 to 2:00 P.M.

One might have expected beginners to study an easy text and senior students a more difficult one, but since the three upper sections were a "one-room schoolhouse," what everyone studied was the same. An alumnus said: "At first we did not understand very well, but as we heard things over and over again, the meaning became clearer." When a student in one of the lower sections had made some progress, he would be orally examined, and if it was found that he could explain a test passage satisfactorily, he would be promoted to the next section. Although in theory the four sections comprised a twelve-year course, it was not necessary to spend three years in each. All the alumni I interviewed had skipped a year or more.

There was no blackboard and no taking of notes; no written examinations, no marks, and no diploma. On graduation, students received only the red robe of the dharma master as a token that they were now qualified to teach. Thus there was little here that differed from the traditional system of lecture apprenticeship. Except in the first section (the Vinaya hall), there was no accommodation to either the content or the methods of modern education. One of the alumni compared it to the old Chinese private school.

The discipline was inordinately strict. No students were

allowed to leave the premises, and even their mail was censored. One of them told me that once when he bought some beancurd from a vendor, the abbot saw it and beat him with a rattan whip. Students also found it difficult to keep up academically. They used to practice their passages for the day during morning devotions. They were supposed to be chanting the liturgy, of course, but with the voices of three or four hundred other monks to cover them, no one noticed that they were doing their homework. Some students could not take the rigors of the program and died of tuberculosis.

On the other hand, there were certain advantages. As at other seminaries, education was free. Students were housed, fed, clothed, and given a monthly allowance of one Chinese dollar during the entire term of their enrollment. They were able to devote themselves wholly to study, with no need to earn money taking part in rites for the dead, and they could look forward to emerging well qualified to make their names in spreading the dharma. But the atmosphere was too old-fashioned for many of the younger monks. One of the alumni recalled that he had had enough of it after only two years: "I was not even learning the formulas used in writing letters." Since departure was only permitted on promotion from a section, he left surreptitiously and made his way to T'ai-hsü's South Fukien Seminary where he found what he wanted—modern teaching methods and a more philosophical approach to Buddhism.

T'AI-HSÜ'S SEMINARIES

The origins of the South Fukien Seminary can ultimately be traced back to 1921, when Tan Kah-kee, a prominent citizen of Amoy, decided to endow a new university there. He petitioned the Fukien provincial government for a site, asking that they confiscate a large tract of land that belonged to the Nan P'u-t'o Ssu, the leading local monastery. The petition was eventually granted, and Nan P'u-t'o lost some of its best rice-fields. In 1925, fearing further encroachment, the abbot decided to start a school.[18] To head it, he invited Ch'ang-hsing, who

had already made a name for himself teaching at seminaries in
Kiangsu and Anhwei. When the abbot retired in April 1927, he
was succeeded by T'ai-hsü who, the monks believed, would be
able to protect them against "the dangers threatening Buddhist
monasteries."[19] T'ai-hsü also took over as head of the school,
where he introduced the methods and approach that he had
already perfected in Wuchang. He changed the name from
Ching-hsien Hsüeh-fo She to Min-nan Fo-hsüeh-yüan. He instituted written entrance examinations, diplomas, and a regular
marking system in which 60 percent was the passing grade.[20]
Lectures were given by an instructor (*chiao-shih*) as they would
have been in a Western classroom, not by a lecturer seated on a
dais in a red robe, as at the Kuan-tsung Ssu. The instructor
walked around and used a blackboard, while the students sat
taking notes. Although sometimes the instructor would ask them
questions about their reading, they were expected to answer briefly
in their own words, not to repeat mechanically what they had
heard the day before. Most young monks found that they learned
much faster this way. The use of the blackboard was particularly
important: the Chinese language has so many homophones and
Buddhism has so many technical terms that verbal instruction
was at best inefficient and often incomprehensible. They also
found it exciting to be for the first time active participants in
classwork rather than reverent auditors. The work was still
arduous. According to a former student at the seminary, there
were five hours a day spent in classes on Buddhist texts, three
hours a week on the history of Buddhism, and eighteen hours
a week on secular subjects, with one hour of homework to be
done each morning and evening. The secular subjects were traditional literature (six hours a week), Japanese (five hours),
history and geography (five hours), and psychology (two hours).
There was no course in mathematics.

As first reorganized by T'ai-hsü, the South Fukien Seminary
had a six-year curriculum: three years of the regular course
(*p'u-t'ung k'e*) that has just been described; and three years of
specialization (*chuan-hsiu k'e*). In the mid-1930's the latter was
discontinued for lack of students. At the same time, a lower

school was added, offering three years of elementary traditional literature, history, geography, and basic Buddhist texts—a curriculum like that of the Vinaya hall of the Kuan-tsung Ssu. But it was not known by any such old-fashioned name as "Vinaya hall." Instead it was called the "Seminary for Fostering the Orthodox" (Yang-cheng Fo-hsüeh-yüan). In the late 1930's it had an enrollment of about fifty, while in the regular course there were about thirty. Both levels ceased operating in 1939, to be revived briefly after the war.

At both levels the students in each class were taught separately, as they would have been in a modern secular school. It was not a "one-room schoolhouse" like Kuan-tsung's. Furthermore, although students had to attend morning and afternoon devotions and formal meals in the refectory, they did not take part in any program of meditation or reciting buddha's name. The goal was to stimulate, not to still, their minds. The day off was Sunday rather than the traditional eighth, fifteenth, twenty-third, and thirtieth of the lunar month. They could play ping-pong—a levity unheard of at the Kuan-tsung Ssu.

Another major difference lay in the type of instructors, many of whom were laymen. At the Kuan-tsung Ssu, laymen were hired only when no monk could be found to teach a subject and, in general, subjects were avoided which no monk could be found to teach. At the South Fukien Seminary, on the other hand, one of T'ai-hsü's lay disciples gave courses on Buddhist logic. History, geography, and psychology were taught by another lay disciple, Professor Ch'en T'ing-mo of the University of Amoy, who used the same syllabus as that of an upper middle school. Japanese was taught by a Japanese layman. All this may have been partly because T'ai-hsü himself had been taught by a layman, and partly because of his misgivings about the state of the sangha.

Most of what has been said above applies to all the five seminaries controlled by T'ai-hsü. Each had about the same proportion of lay faculty and, at any given time, much the same curriculum and teaching methods. Each, however, specialized in a different language. In Amoy it was Japanese; in Chungking, Tibetan; in

Wuchang and Peking, English; in Sian, Pali. Thus each seminary was meant to serve as one department of the World Buddhist Institute mentioned earlier.[21]

None were located in rich monasteries, probably because T'ai-hsü was unpopular among the conservative monks who controlled them. He therefore depended largely on lay donations. His Wuchang Seminary, for example, was set up in secular buildings sold to at half price by a lay devotee. Its operating expenses, as we have seen, were covered by a subsidy from the Right Faith Society.

The curriculum T'ai-hsü was using in the 1930's differed from what he started out with at the Wuchang Seminary in 1922. The latter had been borrowed from a Japanese Buddhist university, and it included a wide assortment of the best known sutras.[22] By about 1935 these were no longer studied. They had been replaced by treatises and commentaries, particularly those dealing with Dharmalaksana idealism, hetuvidya logic and Abhidharma analysis—all newly popular at that time. This represented a shift of emphasis from Buddhism as a religion to Buddhism as a philosophy. One monk who was enrolled at the South Fukien Seminary in the late 1930's, when asked if he had studied the *Surangama Sutra*—a favorite with most Chinese Buddhists—dismissed the question with perceptible contempt. I gathered that such texts were considered by T'ai-hsü to be beneath the notice of advanced students. I have already alluded to another individual who studied for two years at the conservative Kuan-tsung Ssu and then transferred in disgust to the South Fukien Seminary. During one of our interviews the conversation turned to a fellow student of his at Kuan-tsung who, far from leaving in disgust, had pursued his studies there for nine years. "Him?" said this informant. "He is uneducated."

The Kuan-tsung Ssu appears never to have adopted the modern educational methods advocated by T'ai-hsü, perhaps because of his old feud with its founder, Ti-hsien, whom one of his followers had called "a traitor to Buddhism." It remained resolutely conservative. But other seminaries, no less conservative to begin with, did modernize step by step. This was more often in terms of teaching methods than curriculum. That is, many introduced blackboards, marks, and diplomas, but few dropped the study of basic sutras in favor of the study of treatises and commentaries.[23] Nor should their innovations be attributed entirely to the example set by T'ai-hsü. Secular curricula and modern teaching methods had been adopted by Buddhist *hsüeh-t'ang* as early as 1905, and they had spread to other Buddhist schools before T'ai-hsü started the Wuchang Seminary in 1922.[24] It was in his approach that T'ai-hsü broke new ground. He imbued students with his desire to raise the prestige of Buddhism and showed them a way to go about it, that is, by connecting religion with the secular movements of the day.

THE T'IEN-NING SEMINARY

The huge T'ien-ning Ssu in Changchow housed the seminary that may be said to have gone furthest in modernization—partly because it was the most old-fashioned to begin with. It was also the only one to be located in any of the four leading Chinese monasteries. At the other three (Chin Shan, Kao-min, and T'ien-t'ung) priority went to the work of the meditation hall and, in any case, their pre-eminence made them relatively immune to confiscation. The T'ien-ning Ssu, on the other hand, had felt a threat to its property as early as 1901, when certain people in Changchow had tried to set up a modern school and asked the monastery to assign some of its revenues. The senior monks felt that if they contributed toward one school, they would soon be asked to contribute toward others. So they decided to start one themselves. Accordingly they set up a free school for lay children (*i-hsüeh*) with a three-year course.[25]

In 1920 an extraordinary ordination of fifteen hundred monks was held at the T'ien-ning Ssu to commemorate the casualties of 1860, when Changchow had been sacked by the Taiping rebels and thousands had died. (Sixty years is the Chinese equivalent of a centennial.) When the abbot discovered that many of the ordinees had received little or no education, he decided to do something about it. Accordingly he moved the lay school to a small temple about half a mile away, where it became a "com-

plete primary school" with sixty pupils in six grades. The premises
that had formerly housed it at the monastery were enlarged and
converted into a seminary for the poorly educated ordinees. The
abbot refused to call this a *hsüeh-t'ang* because the term implied
a neglect of religious practice. Instead he called it the "T'ien-ning
Vinaya Hall" (T'ien-ning Hsüeh-chieh T'ang).[26] It included three
or four classrooms, an infirmary, and an uposatha hall. In the
latter every night after supper the students did an hour of pros-
trations before the buddha image and twice a month, on the
so-called uposatha days, they recited the 250 monastic vows. In
general, the curriculum was similar to that of the board halls
at Pao-hua Shan: it was composed of rules and etiquette, ritual
and chanting, and regular meditation. The focus was on religious
practice, not on study of the doctrine, and the teachers, of course,
were all monks. Thus it was very old-fashioned indeed.

When one of my informants became abbot in 1931, he decided
that the Vinaya hall did not answer the needs of the times. He
therefore changed its name to *fo-hsüeh yüan* (because this was
the name now being adopted by other monastic schools) and
invited an experienced teacher, Te-i, to become dean.[27] The curriculum was divided into six separate half-year courses, and
modern methods of instruction were introduced. Although Te-i
specialized in lecturing on Dharmalaksana commentaries, he
taught the principal sutras besides. His reforms were a major step
toward modernization.

In 1938 Te-i retired. His place was taken by Min-chih, a
dharma discipline of the T'ien-ning Ssu, who had just graduated
from T'ai-hsü's seminary in Wuchang. Full of the new ideas he
had imbibed there, he added secular subjects to the curriculum
so that it paralleled the curriculum at government-operated middle schools. Lay instructors were brought in: English, for example, was taught by an engineer from a locomotive factory. Study
of the treatises of the Dharmalaksana, T'ien-t'ai, and Avatamsaka
schools displaced study of the basic sutras. An extra three years
were added for those who wished to do research. This represented a higher stage of modernization and completed the shift
in emphasis from religious practice to philosophical expertise.
Throughout these twenty years of change, the T'ien-ning Semi-

nary was one of the largest in China, with about two hundred students usually enrolled.

THE LEVEL OF EDUCATION

There is no doubt that the seventy-odd seminaries established in the first half of the twentieth century raised the educational level of the sangha. The question is, how much? A rough guess suggests that they may have turned out a total of about 7500 graduates (see Appendix 2). This would have not amounted to even 2 percent of the monks in China. Furthermore, not all had received a good education. Some seminaries were "sloppy" (*ma-hu*), as one alumnus put it. The teachers knew little more than the students, and the range of subjects was limited. Among the scores of alumni I have interviewed, less than half appeared to know written Chinese as well as the average graduate of a lay middle school. Moreover, whereas tens of thousands of Chinese laymen speak excellent English, I do not know of a Chinese monk anywhere in the world who speaks more than a few halting words. Even those who have lived overseas for decades usually speak no foreign language at all and depend entirely on lay devotees to act as their interpreters in spreading the dharma.

It cannot be denied that the educational opportunities of monks were inferior. Not only did seminaries have lower standards, but their curricula separated them from the regular Chinese educational system, so that they could not get government approval as counterparts to middle schools. Government universities, which would recognize, for example, the diploma given by a Christian middle school, would not recognize the diploma of its Buddhist rival. Therefore Buddhist monks at Chinese universities were rare. One graduate of the T'ien-ning Seminary, who applied to National Central University after 1945, was admitted, I heard, solely because of the influence of the lay devotee who financed him. Four graduates of T'ai-hsü's Sino-Tibetan Buddhist Institute are said to have attended a university in Chengtu during the war. At first they were restricted to auditing, because their English was inadequate. In the second semester they became regular students. I could not find out whether they had graduated. In fact, I know of only one person who, when already a monk, received a degree. He had been put through Tsinghua University during the 1930's by his rich hereditary temple in Kiangsu.

Despite its shortcomings, the monastic educational movement should not be belittled. If we consider how old-fashioned the system was before 1900 and the extra burdens imposed by the necessity of learning Buddhist texts as well as secular subjects, and if we remember that the monks were not being helped by mission boards or Boxer indemnity funds, we can better appreciate the amount of educational progress they made during the Republican period.

THE METAPHYSICAL INSTITUTE

Standing almost with its back turned to monastic education was the Metaphysical Institute in Nanking. Not a seminary, but unique of its kind, it exemplified the anti-clerical views of its creator, Ou-yang Ching-wu. After the failure of his audacious attempt to take over all the monasteries in China (p. 34), Ou-yang had retired to his farm in Kiangsi, where he spent the next two years in study. In 1914 he returned to the Chin-ling Scriptural Press and took up the collation work that had been left in his charge by Yang Wen-hui. That same year he started a "research department" which was, in effect, a school where he taught private pupils. Then came the death of Ch'en Hsi-an, who had been the principal assistant at the press for thirty years and had been left in over-all command. At about the same time, Ch'en I-fu, the next in command, resigned. That left the field clear for Ou-yang. He had not been particularly close to Yang Wen-hui, under whom (before his death in 1911) he had only worked for about two years, but now it was he who took over Yang's domain.[28]

In the autumn of 1919 he made the research department into a separate institution in a separate building and called it the "Chinese Metaphysical Institute" (Chih-na Nei-hsüeh Yüan).[29] The building is said to have belonged to Mei Kuang-yüan, the

younger brother of Mei Kuang-hsi, one of Ou-yang's principal
supporters. The initial operating expenses were covered partly
by Chang T'ai-yen, whom he had come to know when he was
studying Tantrism in Japan (1907–08), and partly by Tsung-yang,
who was just then embarking on the restoration of Ch'i-hsia
Shan.[30] Students had to pay merely for their room and board. In
1921 the institute began to offer a university course (*ta-hsüeh
chuan-k'o*), which was renamed "Dharmalaksana University"
(Fa-hsiang Ta-hsüeh) in the autumn of 1925. Only middle-school
graduates could enroll, and nearly half of them came from
Kiangsu and Kiangsi, the latter being Ou-yang's home province.[31] By this time, the institute had sections for publishing, research, and general business. Its journal, *Nei-hsüeh*, which
commenced publication in 1924, served as one of the main
channels for Ou-yang's contributions to Idealist philosophy—contributions that played a major role in a minor current of modern
Chinese intellectual history.[32]

The Northern Expedition, which reached Nanking in March
1927, was as ominous for the Metaphysical Institute as it was
for many other Buddhist organizations. Troops were quartered
on the premises. Although they decamped after Ou-yang appealed for help to friends in official circles, regular classes could
not be resumed on the same basis as before. This was because
part of his income had been coming from supporters of the
Peiyang warlords, whom the Northern Expedition had ousted.[33]
The institute continued to operate in Nanking on a reduced
scale until the next disaster—the Japanese attack of 1937. Then
it moved to Szechwan.[34]

The most important thing to be said about the institute is that
it was of, by, and for the laity. Of the forty students enrolled
at its "university" in 1925, only six were monks and, of the
fifteen members of the staff, only one was a monk and he was
a librarian, not a teacher. The curriculum centered on Dharmalaksana texts and doctrines and was gradually broadened to
include such subjects as Confucian classics, seal characters,
rhymes, and drama. Originally Ou-yang had, like Yang Wen-hui,
followed the doctrines of both the Dharmalaksana and
Madhyamika schools. About 1922, however, he accepted the

thesis of some Japanese scholars that the *Awakening of Faith in the Mahayana* was a forgery.[35] This set him at odds with most Chinese Buddhists. A layman who went to the institute in 1931 found it almost impossible to talk to him about Buddhist doctrine, and so what he studied under him that year was Confucian philosophy. He urged Ou-yang to work out a combination of Buddhism and Confucianism in order to make China stronger in resisting Japan. Ou-yang agreed to follow this suggestion.

By this time, because of the effect of the Northern Expedition, the operation was much smaller. The only teachers were Ou-yang and his perennial assistant, Lü Ch'eng, and there were no more than twenty students.[36] They did not attend classes, but worked on their own under Ou-yang's guidance. Only in the summer were formal classes held.

Since both Ou-yang and T'ai-hsü had a low opinion of the sangha and were enthusiastic about Dharmalaksana philosophy, one might think that they would have made good allies. But Ou-yang's interpretation of Dharmalaksana was different from T'ai-hsü's, and he found it difficult to get along with monks of any kind, reform-minded or otherwise. For his part T'ai-hsü had taken strong exception in 1920 to a sentence in the new by-laws of the Metaphysical Institute: "We are on principle opposed to fostering the selfishness that is implicit in becoming a monk."[37] This, needless to say, gave even greater offense to conservatives like Ti-hsien and Yin-kuang. When one of my informants asked for Yin-kuang's approval to study at the Metaphysical Institute, that eminent Pure Land master replied: "Ou-yang Ching-wu is a great king of devils and you may *not* study under him."

The hostility of monks did not trouble Ou-yang. He ignored them rather than arguing with them. As one of his former disciples put it: "Well-known abbots never came to the institute and Ou-yang never went to their monasteries. He considered that monks were ignorant and stupid. They did not understand Dharmalaksana doctrines. They were not qualified to discuss Buddhism with him. How could there have been any argument?"

It is said that initially monks were not even allowed to enroll at the institute. Later Ou-yang admitted a few, but they were neither treated with deference nor permitted to lead other students in religious cultivation. Religious cultivation, in fact, was banned. Though residents at the institute observed certain ascetic principles (vegetarian food and no sexual relations with their wives on the premises), they were not supposed to meditate or recite buddha's name or perform morning and evening devotions or have Buddhist services performed when relatives died. Ou-yang was opposed to all ritual and, in particular, to the "worship of idols." Buddhism originally had not had such things, and he wanted it to return to that primeval purity. He stood for "destroying superstition."

He was also jealous of his prerogatives. The story is told that in the early 1920's Liang Ch'i-ch'ao, who had studied for half a year at the Metaphysical Institute, was asked to be guest of honor at a dinner party. Ou-yang was also invited. As soon as he saw that the seat of honor was allocated to Liang, his pupil, whereas he, the master, had a secondary seat, he made for the door. Liang understood, had the seating rearranged, and persuaded him to return.

Ou-yang never took part in the work of other Buddhist groups and seldom lectured outside the institute. This was at least partly because of his thick Kiangsi accent: he usually found it difficult to make himself understood. His isolation, combined with his prickly personality and his contempt for most of what most Buddhists believed in, prevented him from exercising much direct influence on them. Undoubtedly the books and the journal that he published attracted the notice of scholars, and his school became a major attraction for touring foreigners who had an interest in Buddhism, but his actual following was confined to a handful of philosophical Buddhists. This does not diminish his significance. Like T'ai-hsü he exemplified the new trend—the shift from sutras to treatises, from devotions to research, from the religious to the secular—a shift that called into question the ultimate future of the sangha. Monks who were trained to place academic activities above all others became further and further removed from their original role; and to many of them there would eventually seem less and less relevance in the monastic vows.

Chapter VII

SOCIAL ACTION BY THE SANGHA

THERE were several respects, curiously enough, in which it was out of keeping with the Buddhist tradition for monks to engage in social-welfare work as we ordinarily think of it. First of all, it reversed their accepted relationship with the laity. The laity was expected to provide for the sangha, emphatically not vice versa. The sangha earned merit by religious cultivation; the laity earned merit by supplying the wealth that made this possible. In the second place, the most urgent task of the sangha vis-à-vis those suffering from want or disease was to teach them how to avoid rebirth. What good could come of relieving their distress? Since it had been caused by misdeeds in previous lives, relief would only postpone the inevitable expiation.[1] Nor were monks exempt from the nearly universal feeling in China that the beggar or the invalid should be taken care of by his family. Under the family system, charity began and usually ended at home. Such attitudes were to some extent offset by contrary feelings: by the bodhisattva ideal of helping all creatures, by the desire to earn merit, and by ordinary human sympathy. Therefore, although organized charity on the part of the sangha may have been uncommon, we do hear of instances of individual or occasional welfare work. In 1904, for

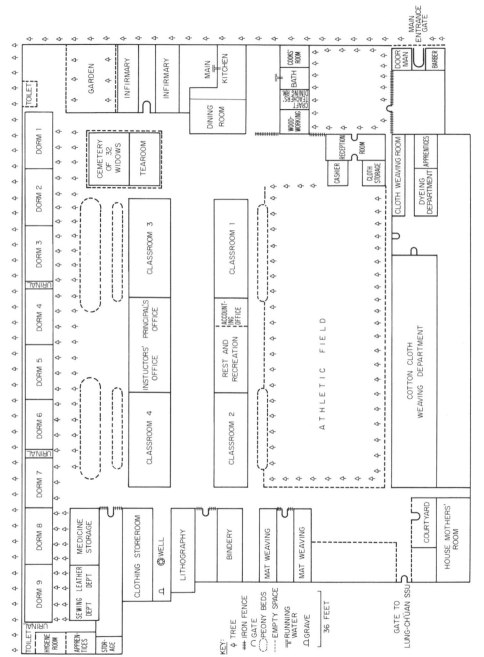

13 Diagram of the Lung-ch'üan Ssu orphanage.

example, when Hsü-yün was traveling through a mountainous part of northern Yünnan, he met an eighty-three-year-old monk working on road repairs. He told Hsü-yün that he had entered the sangha when he was young; at twenty-four he had found peace of mind in the meditation hall at Chin Shan; and later he had gone on a pilgrimage to Tibet. When returning from Tibet through northern Yünnan, he had found this stretch of mountain road so rough that he "took pity on the men and horses that had to travel it." Hence for many decades he had been working on it alone, living in a hut by the roadside, and going out every day with a pick and shovel. When he talked to Hsü-yün, he had finished about nine tenths of what he had set out to do.

Monks used to do other kinds of good deeds as the occasion arose. They buried dead bodies along the road, released animals in distress, and picked up scrap paper for burning (in the Chinese view any paper with writing on it should come to an honorable end). Monasteries sometimes offered shelter to victims of flood or fire and to the poor distributed food, clothing, or coffins paid for by rich lay donors.[2] But it was not until this century that institutionalized charity—social action along modern lines—came to be undertaken by the sangha.

THE LUNG-CH'ÜAN ORPHANAGE

According to Mizuno Baigyo, the first instance was the orphanage of the Lung-ch'üan Ssu in Peking.[3] This was also one of the few such enterprises on which we have plentiful information. Between September 1918 and December 1919 it was visited by field workers engaged in a sociological survey of Peking being conducted by the Princeton University Center in China. Their report states:

The orphanage is run by the temple priests. It is caring for some 250 boys who are full orphans or have only a mother living and whose relations are unable to care for them. It admits only boys who are under twelve years of age and their behavior must be guaranteed by some shop or friend of the family. Once admitted the boys can stay apparently as long as they want to, as some thirty-seven of the inmates are over nineteen years of age. These, however, are simply given a home and must earn their living either by working in the orphanage or finding work outside.

All the boys are given school work, industrial training, and a daily lecture of an hour on religious subjects. Twelve boys are in the Higher Primary, five are in Middle School, and one is even attending the University.[4] Printing, tailoring, carpentering, dyeing, shoe-making, weaving, and mat-making are the industries taught.

The boys live in dormitories, eighteen in a three *chien* room, twelve by thirty feet. They all sleep on one long *k'ang* or built-in bed that runs the full length of the room. They are given three meals a day rather than the two customary in most of the government institutions.

The budget of the institution amounts to practically $10,000 a year. It is met principally by individual contributions made to the temple, but some official funds are supplied. The Municipal Council contributes $1 a month, the local Board of Education $5 a month, while the police furnish $60 worth of rice each month. The Five Saints Nunnery gives $20 a month.[5]

As far as could be seen, the institution is well managed, the boys are well cared for and are given school and industrial training. They certainly are turning out a very creditable type of work.[6]

Five years later, when J. B. Pratt was in China, he visited this and other orphanages. "The children of these institutions," he wrote, "are well cared for, carefully educated in the usual elementary subjects with modern methods, and in addition each is taught a trade. Daily worship in the Buddhist shrine is required and the fundamentals of the Buddhist religion—especially the Five Precepts—are inculcated."[7] In accordance with the First Precept, the children ate no meat.

I had several interviews with the monk who had served as manager of the Peking orphanage in 1925. He said that he had been asked to take charge of it because Tao-hsing, then abbot of the Lung-ch'üan Ssu, was a Hupei man like himself. He corroborated what I had learned from documentary sources and offered an important item of additional information: although the head of the orphanage (*yüan-chang*) and the manager (*kuan-li*) were monks, the instructors in the primary school and vocational classes were all laymen. Unlike their Christian counterparts, the monks did not directly participate in the daily care and education of the children in their charge. This did not mean that they felt no personal involvement. They had been the first to conceive of the orphanage and had worked hard to bring it into being. Its significance, in fact, can only be appreciated in the light of their motivation, on which we have their own testimony.

Tao-hsing states that he had been awakened, as from a deep sleep, by the events of 1900, the year of the Boxer Rebellion and the Dowager Empress' flight from Peking. Suddenly he had realized how urgently China needed new schools. A few years later he accepted the care of a couple of orphans. This gave his master, who was then abbot, the idea that the monastery should start an orphanage, not only to advance the cause of education but "to accord with the Buddhist principle of compassion." Tao-hsing had already had the same idea, but felt that it was beyond their resources. The next year, however, the orphans were noticed by a friendly official from the Ministry of Education. When he heard what the monks wanted to do, he slapped the table in approval and said, "To take pity on orphans was the way in which the ancient kings showed their kindness: today it is an important task."

Support was soon forthcoming from members of the Peking General Chamber of Commerce who were lay disciples of the abbot.[8] They provided the money to put up a set of buildings that were opened on August 14, 1908. There was room for over a hundred orphans, but this soon proved insufficient and the following year they gave $10,000 for a much larger set of buildings, which included classrooms, workshops, and living quarters for 162. One of the two Buddhist devotees who helped to manage the orphanage in its early years was Wang Tzu-chen. He wrote that he himself had lost his father and mother as a child and had endured "indescribable poverty and hardships," so that he had a very personal reason for participating in work of this kind.[9]

These are almost the only statements we have about the reason why Chinese Buddhists started a specific charitable enterprise. Note the mixture of motives that is revealed. Parallel to the Buddhist principle of compassion was the Confucian principle of "following the way of the ancient kings." Underlying both was a

concern for education in the interest of nation building. Con-
spicuously absent was any mention of the motive we hear so
much about in the case of monastic schools: the protection of
property. However, though the latter may not have been intended, it was the eventual result. About 1913, according to the
former manager, President Yüan Shih-k'ai decided to confiscate
the whole of Lung-ch'üan Ssu. When news of this reached the
abbot, he invited Yüan to come and see his orphans doing setting-
up exercises on a plot of vacant monastery land. The viceroy was
delighted with this calisthenic spectacular and said that the
confiscation would not take place after all.

I have found no statistics on the total number of such institutions started by the Chinese sangha, but there must have been
many. Another large one was jointly operated by Chin Shan and
Chiao Shan at the Ho-lin Ssu in Chen-chiang. It cared for about
one hundred children from 1919 until 1937, when the Japanese
invasion cut deeply into monastic income. Like the Lung-ch'üan
Ssu, Chin Shan and Chiao Shan had only one of their own monks
on the staff: the resident manager. All the teachers and other
personnel were laymen. The responsibility assumed by the monasteries was simply to pay their salaries and provide rice for them
and the orphans.

In 1918 Yüan-ying started the Ningpo Buddhist Orphanage
with 110 "students."[10] We hear of another at the K'ai-fu Ssu in
Changsha and of yet another at the Nan P'u-t'o Ssu in Amoy.[11]

OTHER WELFARE ACTIVITIES

No comparable effort was made in the field of medicine. Clinics
existed, but none appear to have been large-scale. According to
several informants, it was not uncommon for monasteries to retain
a Chinese practitioner who dispensed herbal remedies once or
twice a week. The operation of hospitals, however, was usually
beyond their means.[12]

More work was done in the field of education. We have already
seen how the T'ien-ning Ssu started a free school in order to
forestall the attachment of some of its revenue.[13] At about the
same time, the Liu-yün Ssu in Shanghai set up a lay primary

school with four hundred students. Tuition was nominal or remitted altogether. Although it was located just behind the monastery, the monks did not take any part in its operation, not even to give courses on Buddhism. The teachers were all laymen working on salary.[14]

Other lay schools were operated in conjunction with seminaries or by several monasteries jointly.[15] About 1919, for example, six large monasteries on Mount Nan-yüeh set up a boarding school there that attracted pupils from all over the province of Hunan. According to my informant, who headed both the school and the largest of the supporting monasteries (the Chu-sheng Ssu) just before the Mainland fell to the Communists, its dormitories (built especially for the purpose) housed about one thousand boys. He said that they made the best academic record in Hunan and that a hundred percent of them passed their middle-school entrance examinations. (A remarkable record indeed! Perhaps he was referring to a certain year only.) The curriculum was the standard one prescribed by the Ministry of Education, and the teachers were all laymen, except for a monk who gave a course in Buddhist doctrine; nor did any of the graduates, according to this informant, ever become monks.

The Sino-Japanese War brought new demands for social action by the sangha. For centuries its members had been exempt from military service, but this privilege came to an end when conscription was introduced in 1933. At first the monks were little affected, but with the Japanese attack there came a real danger that they would be sent to the front, where they would have to kill human beings and eat animal foods from field kitchens, thus breaking their most fundamental vow. The Chinese Buddhist Association (Shanghai, 1929) petitioned the central government to allow them to serve in an ambulance corps instead.[16] This request was granted, and a "sangha rescue team" (*seng-chia chiu-hu tui*) was formed in July 1937, made up of about 120 monks. After brief training, it took part in the August battle of Shanghai, transporting wounded soldiers and refugees from disaster areas to various receiving stations around the city. According to a Buddhist source, "observers said that the monks were the bravest among those going back and forth during the

14   After the Japanese attack in 1937 the Yü-fo Ssu, Shanghai, provided shelter
for refugees. Nurses are hastening down the steps in front of the monks.

battles." One monk was killed. After the fall of Shanghai, the
team followed the army to Nanking, where it continued its
work. Yüan-ying, then head of the Chinese Buddhist Association,
went to Southeast Asia to raise money for it from overseas
Chinese. In Singapore he collected enough to organize a second
sangha rescue team in Hankow, while in Kuala Lumpur and
Penang he raised enough to organize a third team in Ningpo.
After these cities fell, some of the Hankow team followed the
army to Hunan, Szechuan, and Shensi.[17]

The war also gave monks the opportunity to play their more
traditional role in offering asylum to people in distress. Hsü-yün
sheltered refugees at the Yün-men Ssu in northern Kwangtung
(as he had previously done during civil wars in Yünnan).[18] In
the four months following the rape of Nanking at the end of
1937, Ch'i-hsia Shan is said to have housed and fed thirty thousand persons.[19] Those who could not be accommodated indoors

were housed in tents. The monastery used up its own stores of grain and then borrowed grain from others. The Japanese occupation authorities objected to this on the grounds that disorders might arise from such a large concentration of people. Many of the monks themselves objected because they were afraid that when the grain stores were used up, they would starve. But the abbot and his dharma brothers were not to be dissuaded. Besides ordinary refugees they sheltered several Nationalist army officers, whom the Japanese would have shot, by dressing them up as monks.[20] This was not unusual. A former member of the Nationalist underground in central China has told me that he and his colleagues were often given refuge in temples and that, as a consequence, temples were burned and monks were executed.

In the early 1920's T'ai-hsü read in a newspaper that Christian evangelists had obtained permission to visit Chinese prisons and preach the gospel. Prisoners had been converted and later discharged as new men. "Why should not Buddhists do the same?" thought T'ai-hsü, and so the monks studying under him at the Wuchang seminary began a program of prison visiting.[21] The idea spread to Peking and later to Shanghai, where a city magistrate arranged for lectures to be given to convicts in the hope that they would become Buddhists and reform. In the 1930's this work was carried on by both the Pure Karma Society and the Chinese Buddhist Association.[22]

THE SANGHA'S APPROACH TO SOCIAL WELFARE

Prison work may have seemed like an innovation, but for centuries the sangha had been reforming criminals by accepting them as monks—a method of reform which, as even a missionary acknowledged, was often quite successful.[23] The sangha had always helped orphans in a similar way, by recruiting them. It had always relieved the sick by reciting penances to cancel the bad karma that was causing disease. It had always provided education by preaching the dharma.

Unfortunately, these compassionate measures came to be regarded as old-fashioned after 1912. Worse than that, they had not prepared the sangha to undertake the new, institutionalized forms of social welfare that were now expected of it: orphanages, clinics, and modern schools. Here is why, when such institutions were set up, they were seldom staffed by monks. Monks simply had had no experience with that sort of thing: they were not doctors, and, as teachers, few could satisfy the qualifications required by the government.[24] But this was not the only reason for their failure to participate. Often, I think, it was because of a certain lack of enthusiasm. Many welfare enterprises were started because the monks felt obliged to, not because they found the idea intrinsically attractive. They were happy to put up the money and let it go at that. Why did they feel obliged to? Some observers emphasize the threat of confiscation; others the need to compete with Christian missionaries. Mizuno, for example, states flatly that schools and orphanages were set up because of the example provided by the Christian missionaries.[25] On the other hand, the informant who headed the school of Nan-yüeh told me that prior to the threat of confiscation monks had seen Christian welfare efforts going on for decades but had done nothing to imitate them. It was therefore, he said (almost indignantly), this threat and not the Christian example that caused them to start orphanages and schools, including the one at Nan-yüeh. Legally they had yet another reason: according to regulations issued in 1929 and amplified in 1935, monasteries had to devote a certain part of their income to charitable enterprises.[26] But generally speaking, they ignored this requirement, which was no better enforced than other laws governing Buddhism, as we shall see in the next chapter.

The paucity of Buddhist social-welfare efforts might lead a Western observer to erroneous conclusions about the place of monasteries in the community. He might suppose they were generally regarded as parasitic institutions that consumed but did not contribute. This was indeed what the Confucian enemies of Buddhism had long argued, but with no perceptible effect on popular attitudes. Quite aside from their religious functions, so important to the elderly and bereaved, monasteries played a major role as centers of community life, especially for amusement and recreation.

If, for example, the residents of cities like Hangchow and Soochow had a holiday, how did they spend it? Many of them would go out to the temples in the neighboring hills. The walk was invigorating, the scenery beautiful. There were pagodas to climb, caves to explore, ancient rock carvings, and the art and architecture of the monasteries themselves. Even the illiterate, as they strolled about, could tell their children some of the legends connected with what they were seeing. The educated could read the ubiquitous inscriptions, which gave them a chance to display their erudition and pleased their historical sense. Many of the visitors, particularly the women, would repair to an altar to pray, offer incense, and consult the bamboo divination slips. The Delphic phrasing of the slips was always good for animated discussion. About noon, under the shade of the trees in the monastery courtyards, they would open their picnic baskets or eat a leisurely vegetarian meal arranged by the monks. Then followed an afternoon of chatting, games, and the noisy fun without which a holiday was not a holiday. Often several temples would be visited, each with its sights and shrines. When they reached home, everyone would feel it had been a day well spent. They were refreshed not only by the respite from toil, but by the contact with nature, with history, and with the spiritual world.

A BUDDHIST FESTIVAL

Photographed by Henri Cartier-Bresson

At the end of March 1949, when north China had already fallen to the Communists and their occupation of south China was only a matter of two months more, Henri Cartier-Bresson visited Hangchow. As he wrote, there was "a great longing all over the country for peace." Every year at this time in Hangchow there was a day of pilgrimage to offer thanks for divine favors as well as prayers for the future. In 1949 Buddhist leaders decided that peace should be the object of special prayers. Perhaps larger numbers of people than usual streamed over the causeways across the West Lake (one of China's beauty spots) and into the hills beyond, dotted with dozens of monasteries. M. Cartier-Bresson went too and took the photographs on the following pages. This was one of the last unfettered manifestations of Buddhism in China.

Pilgrims head toward the hills beyond the West Lake.

A religious procession passes the lake on the way to the Ling-yin Ss
where participants will give thanks for having their prayers answere
Green and white banners read "Clear the way" (for someone importa
to follow), and smaller placards bear the name of Kuan-yin, the godde
of compassion.

hese three boys—or their parents—have probably recovered from an
ness after vowing that they would repay a divine cure by performing
penance. Each of them has pinned to the skin of his chest a talismanic
aque, from which an incense burner is supposed to be suspended; but
e cord is attached where it passes over the rack, which bears the
eight. Similarly another incense burner is supposed to be suspended
om the flesh of the right arm, but the towel prevents onlookers from
eing whether it really is. Nonetheless, to carry the heavy, carved
ooden rack is an ordeal in itself, and another towel is needed to keep
eat out of the eyes. The penitent who follows the boys wears a cage
vered with cutouts of the Buddha.

More people on the road, one rich enough to afford to ride, others on foot. Note the bag—the badge of the devout pilgrim—worn by the woman on the left. The characters read "Visiting the mountains to offer incense" and "Recite buddha's name with the whole heart."

beggar lolls with palm outstretched, the stump of one leg encouraging donations.

A party of rich pilgrims reaches the side gate of the Ling-yin Ssu, the largest and most famous monastery in Hangchow, dating from the Six Dynasties. The sign over the gate states that a Mr. T'an donated money for the path.

A monk of the Ling-yin Ssu stands before the great shrine-hall. Probably he is a guest prefect, in charge of caring for visitors. An earlier shrine-hall was destroyed by the Taiping rebels and reconstruction was completed in 1911 at a cost of $200,000, the largest timbers being of Oregon pine.

Inside, all sorts of people are offering incense; the soldiers' prayers for peace must be especially fervent.

Near the altar some schoolboys rest on the monks' kneeling pads. The seated image is the Buddha; standing on his right is his disciple, Ananda. Notice the votary candles and pennons. Perhaps the boys have been discussing the back pair of candles, which read: "The universe is contained in a grain of maize; at the rock of the next life is the soul of the last." This refers to a well-known story about a T'ang dynasty monk who, just before his death in north China, told a friend to meet him twelve years later in Hangchow. The friend kept the appointment and found him reborn as a shepherd at the nearby temple of Shang-t'ien Chu.

Having made their offerings or simply admired the interior, the visitors descend the steps of the great shrine-hall. M. Cartier-Bresson noted the contrast between the "young girls from Shanghai in slacks and sharp square shoulders, who have read all the movie magazines" and the "peasant women so full of dignity in their blue dresses."

In the tea garden, wives chat while husbands watch the passers-by. The woman on the right has a pilgrim's bag inscribed "Amitabha"; and the woman wearing the rosary seems to be handling a sprig of willow, often stuck into the hair or dress at this time of year. There was a saying: "If you don't stick in a willow sprig at Ch'ing-ming, no one will remember you after you die."

Some pilgrims bring a picnic; others order a vegetarian meal from the monastery kitchen; others buy snacks from vendors like this girl, who is selling water chestnuts.

After a little refreshment it is pleasant to saunter about enjoying the sights and taking part in gentle amusements—such as a snapshot on the shoulder of the Laughing Buddha (right background).

The Laughing Buddha (Pu-tai) was a Sung dynasty incarnation of Maitreya, the buddha of the future. In that life he was an eccentric monk who loved children; he would have been delighted to find them standing all over him.

Illiterate peasant women are not the only serious pilgrims. Here two men, looking well-educated and possibly father and son, make the round of sacred carvings and caves, carrying their incense in pilgrims' bags.

Strollers often catch a view of the West Lake. The causeway across it was built by the eleventh-century poet, Su Tung-p'o, when he was governor. Planted on it alternately are willow and peach trees, the green to set off the blossoms.

Some visitors have a personal problem on which they wish to consult a fortuneteller like this one, whose booth stands on the way to the monasteries and who seems to be a man of education and varied talents. Divination could be a respected profession in China. The figurines are Chi-kung and Kuan-yin; and the framed picture portrays Chiang K'ai-shek, General MacArthur, and perhaps Li Tsung-jen. In front of the picture are rolls of *ch'ai-tzu*—ideograms to be analyzed for clues to the future.

Other pilgrims have spiritual matters to attend to. They ask the monks to perform a service for the benefit of some deceased member of the family. During the service, written prayers are burned and thus conveyed to the other world. Here a monk is inditing such a prayer, while one of his brethren looks on.

The heart of the festival: prayers for peace are recited by the monks in the great shrine-hall. As is customary in China, laymen feel no need to attend. The sign on the pillar reads: "Make a donation toward the building of the Thousand Buddhas' Pavillion." Images of the twenty-four devas can be seen in the background.

The most devout pilgrims go on to the higher and more distant monasteries. This gate marks the start of the path to the Fa-hsi Ssu (better known as Shang T'ien-chu), named on the sign. A mendicant monk sits in the foreground beating his "wooden fish" and sounding his hand chime to keep time while he chants. Approaching from beyond the gate is a blind lute player. The leaves are just beginning to bud in the early spring.

Worshipers smile with satisfaction at the offerings they have just made within. Notice the absence of people in Western dress at this upper monastery, which was rebuilt about 1929.

The end of a long day finds different expressions on the faces of pilgrims as they walk past the gate where their journey began.

Chapter VIII

SANGHA AND STATE

BUDDHIST monks in China were often called *fang-wai*, meaning "outside the secular world." They were said to "owe the king no homage and their kinsmen no obeisance." Monks ordained before 1900 have assured me that if they had been invited to visit the court, they would not have had to kowtow to the emperor as other citizens did.[1] Whether this was so or not (and I have found no eyewitness account of such a visit in the late Ch'ing dynasty), it is undoubtedly true that monks were exempted by law from taxation, conscription, and the corvée, and that this exemption was honored by the local authorities. They were also exempt from police investigation.[2] Prosecution for a crime was usually abandoned when a criminal—even if guilty of a capital crime—entered the order.[3] By law the ordination of criminals was forbidden, but this and most other laws that applied to the internal affairs of the sangha had fallen into disuse, so that the monastery was even more outside the world in practice than it was on paper. It enjoyed government protection without having to put up with government control.

Such a privileged position for the sangha during the late Ch'ing dynasty may seem hard to credit when we remember the mandarinate's traditional hostility toward Buddhism, which it had long regarded as an ideological challenge to Confucian orthodoxy, a drain on the national income, a breeding ground for sedition, and a stimulus to popular superstition. But most officials, however hostile, were reluctant to dispense with the sangha's assistance in protecting the community from natural disasters; or to risk the displeasure of the emperor, who hoped that the merit accumulated on his behalf by the sangha would assure him of health and longevity. Furthermore, even among the most Confucian of the literati, there was a certain respect for Buddhism's ancient contributions to Chinese culture. The relative strength of these contradictory feelings varied, as did the positiveness of the emperor's personal patronage, so that the official treatment of Buddhism oscillated between hostility and support and remained deeply ambivalent. There is scarcely a recent dynastic reign in which measures were not taken to inhibit the activities of the sangha. Yet there is also scarcely a reign in which we do not discover favors being lavished on Buddhist monks and monasteries. The K'ang-hsi Emperor, many of whose edicts were anti-Buddhist, helped to restore the monasteries of the sacred island of P'u-t'o Shan, explaining that his motive in doing so was the hope that the compassionate Kuan-yin would send down blessings on the people and "lead them

15 A Buddhist sutra, the *Yao-shih ching*, copied by the K'ang-hsi Emperor in his own hand and bestowed on the Hsi-ch'an Ssu, Fukien, as a mark of favor.

to the salvation which she offers to all sentient beings."[4] He himself stayed at various famous monasteries, on which he conferred imperial holographs and sometimes new names.[5] The Yung-cheng Emperor did likewise. After Pao-hua Shan burned in 1734, he ordered it rebuilt at a cost of twelve thousand ounces of silver.[6] He was interested in Ch'an and had a meditation hall set up in the palace. The Ch'ien-lung Emperor, who said that it was "desirable to decrease gradually the number of monks and temples and ultimately to do away with them altogether," stayed at the Ch'i-hsia Ssu near Nanking on five different occasions—a mark of high imperial favor.[7] Ch'ing patronage of Buddhism continued to the end of the dynasty. In 1906, for example, an imperial edict conferred a new name and certain regalia on a monastery in Yünnan, and local officials were ordered to protect and respect the abbot.[8]

The unending contradiction between the desires to suppress and to support is well exemplified in the field of law. The provisions of the Ch'ing Code, if they had been put into effect, would have decimated the Buddhist establishment. They stipulated, for example, that a monk had to be over forty years old before he could accept a disciple, and then he could accept only one. Nor could this single disciple come from a family with less than three sons. The penalty for violation was fifty blows of the long stick and a month in the cangue. If officials who knew of a violation failed to report it, they too would be punished.[9] Nonetheless, during the last few years of the Ch'ing dynasty monks of all ages were freely accepting several disciples apiece, many of them from families with less than three sons.

The code provided an even stiffer penalty (one hundred strokes of the long stick, followed by banishment to a border region), if a monk erected a temple—or even enlarged one—without getting permission from the emperor himself.[10] Yet in the last years of the Ch'ing dynasty, temples were being freely erected and enlarged all over China without permission from anyone.

Perhaps the best known restriction covered the issuance of ordination certificates. If monks were ordained without being given a certificate that the government had supplied, they were to be punished with eighty blows and returned to lay life.[11] Yet in the last years of the Ch'ing, ordination certificates were privately printed and issued without government control of any kind.

These statements about actual practice as opposed to the prescriptions of the law are based largely on interviews with three monks who were ordained in 1894, 1898, and 1902 and who traveled through many parts of the country in the years immediately following. They snorted derisively at the idea that the sangha was restricted by the regulations cited above or by any of the other articles in the code, such as the ban on public begging and preaching, the requirement that monasteries report to the district magistrate any visiting monk who did not have an ordination certificate, the insistence that monks observe mourning regulations and practice ancestor worship, and so on. "There were never any such laws as these!" said these three informants as they were separately interviewed. When I produced photostatic copies of the relevant sections of the code, they were startled but still maintained that they themselves and all the monks they knew had regularly carried on the prohibited practices. The laws, they concluded, must have been "empty."

If this was the case, perhaps one reason was that the officials who might have enforced the laws were less anti-Buddhist than is generally believed and were guided not so much by law as by custom. That is, they were reluctant to interfere where custom was working smoothly. So long as the sangha did nothing to impair public order, it was left to manage its own affairs. But if a monk became even slightly involved in something heretical or subversive, then the district magistrate could consult the code and strike him down with at least twenty dire regulations that he had been breaking (like most other monks) throughout his career. This fits in with the Confucian attitude toward law[12] and is supported by the nature of criminal cases in which Buddhist monks became involved.[13]

Another reason why the control of the sangha was weak was the weakness of the organs set up to control it. From earlier dynasties the Ch'ing had inherited a hierarchy of sangha officials (seng-kuan), each official being responsible for the activities of

the monks and nuns in his area, for whom he played an intermediary role with the authorities. In the capital there was an
office headed by a *seng-lu ssu;* in every prefecture there was a
seng-kang ssu; in every department there was a *seng-cheng ssu;*
and in every district there was a *seng-hui ssu.* Except for those in
the capital, they held the ninth or lowest official rank. They were
appointed by and reported to the local government, although
their appointments had to be approved by the Board of Rites in
Peking.

According to the Ch'ing monks interviewed, although this
ecclesiastical hierarchy continued to exist until the end of the
dynasty, it was largely powerless and inactive. Those appointed
to it were not necessarily eminent abbots: they were simply
monks who resided near the yamen from which the area was
governed. "Theirs was just an empty title," as one informant put
it.

Western visitors to China were sometimes told of monks who
held jurisdiction over all local monasteries and who had the right
to punish breaches of the monastic rules by sentencing offenders
to beating, confinement, or return to lay life.[14] It would be
natural to suppose that they enjoyed the same authority as the
ecclesiastical officials of an established church in the West. But
closer inquiry often brought out a different picture. After fourteen years in Foochow, Justus Doolittle wrote that the monks
there were "professedly under the control of an officer living in
the southeastern quarter of the city who, according to the report,
was formerly a priest himself and who received his title of office
directly from Peking for the special purpose of governing them.
It is, however, found to be the fact that he has little or no real
authority over them, except in unimportant matters, they being
more immediately under the superintendence and jurisdiction of
the abbots of their respective monasteries."[15]

This is not to say that nowhere in China during the late Ch'ing
dynasty was control of the clergy actively enforced. There may
have been zealous magistrates, particularly near the capital, who
went by the book. Throughout the country, if a monk committed
a secular crime or outraged public decency, he was either punished by the authorities or turned over for punishment to the

appropriate sangha official. Furthermore, a few sangha officials were eminent monks whose views would have carried weight with their brethren even if they had not been holding that office. But on the whole it would appear likely that the laws directed at the sangha were seldom applied, and that the persons immediately responsible for their application were seldom active, so that the Buddhist monastic establishment was just what it was said to be—outside the secular world.

REPUBLICAN LAWS AND THEIR ENFORCEMENT

Only after understanding the privileged position of the sangha under the Ch'ing dynasty is it possible to appreciate the changes that followed the revolution of 1911. Imperial patronage and protection came to an end. The Ch'ing Code gradually lapsed; its more restrictive provisions on the clergy were never effectively revived. But, as we have seen, these restrictions had been largely nominal, and the sangha gained less by their disappearance than it lost by the passing of its imperial protectors.

The first step toward re-establishing government protection and control was taken in June 1913, when the Ministry of the Interior promulgated the Provisional Measure for the Control of Monasteries. This made an abbot legally responsible for the care of monastic property and prohibited him from alienating it by sale, mortgage, or donation. It also prohibited outsiders from forcibly occupying it.[16] The sangha could scarcely take exception on either count. Reputable monks had always been opposed to the sale of the fixed assets of public monasteries except in an emergency and with the approval of all the leading officers. Not only land and buildings (title to which were in the monastery's name) but furnishings, books, and works of art were considered to be owned in common by the entire sangha. It was as important to protect them from unscrupulous abbots as from greedy local officials.

The government's next step, however, was far less welcome. In 1915 the Ministry of the Interior formulated a measure that restored several of the restrictive provisions of the Ch'ing Code and in some other respects went even further in interfering with monks and monasteries. One of the articles, for example, governed what monks could say when they spoke in public. They were limited to doctrinal exegesis, moral exhortation, and "stimulating patriotic thoughts." The local authorities had to be notified five days beforehand of the time and place of a speech and to be given a curriculum vitae of the speaker (article 15). Under article 17 all monks were to receive ordination certificates issued by the Ministry of the Interior (just as they used to receive them from the Board of Rites). If they had already been ordained, they were to receive registration certificates. In either case their names were to be reported to the Ministry and go on file. Any monk without an official certificate was to be refused permission to stay at monasteries as a guest (*kua-tan*) or to take part in the rites for the dead that were the main source of personal income for the clergy. More serious perhaps was article 23, under which an abbot who violated the monastic rules was subject to censure and dismissal by the civil authorities. The latter were thereby given a lever that they could use to pry away monastic land and buildings. Another such lever was provided by their right (under article 10) to approve a monastery's alienation of its property for use in the public welfare.[17] It is little wonder that many Buddhists opposed the measure on the grounds that it "gave local officials great powers to restrict monks and to encroach on religious property."[18]

Buddhist opposition was strenuous, but unsuccessful. Indeed it provoked Yüan Shih-kai's suppression of the Chinese General Buddhist Association, and the measure was passed by Parliament and promulgated as Presidential Edict No. 66 on October 29, 1915. It might have put an end to the freedom that the sangha was now enjoying *de lege* as well as *de facto*, but, with Yüan Shih-kai's early death, its provisions were only intermittently and locally enforced. It turned out to be important mainly as a forerunner of later attempts to interfere with internal monastic affairs.

Nation-wide enforcement of any law was out of the question until China began to be unified under the Nationalists in 1926–1928. On December 7, 1929, the new government promulgated Regulations for the Supervision of Monasteries and Temples,[19] which are still the law of Nationalist China. They dealt mainly with the use and protection of monastic property. Articles 5 and 6 repeated earlier provisions that the ownership of real estate and sacred objects was vested in the monastery as an institution, not in its abbot as an individual; and required that all such property be registered with the local authorities. Its transfer had to be approved not only by these authorities but by the local Buddhist association. This gave the associations a semiofficial role for the first time. Since they were controlled by the sangha, it meant theoretically that monks now had a defense against official efforts to take over their property.

Other provisions of the new law were more restrictive. Every abbot had to be a citizen of the Republic of China (article 6). He was only permitted to use the income from monastic property for spreading Buddhist doctrine, for the support of religious practice, and for "other proper expenses" (article 7). Monasteries were required to undertake activities—commensurate with their financial ability—in the fields of charity and public welfare (article 10).[20] If an abbot was not a Chinese citizen or if he alienated monastic property without government approval or misused the income derived from it or failed to undertake activities in the fields of charity and public welfare, then he could be dismissed from office by the local government authorities (article 11). The authorities were not, however, empowered to dismiss him for violating monastic discipline, as they had been in 1915. Disciplinary violations were now considered an internal matter, outside their jurisdiction.[21] Nor could they normally interfere in the choice of an abbot's successor. This was also considered an internal matter, to be handled in accordance with the customs and rules of each monastery, whether these provided for appointment by the retiring abbot or for a public election.[22] Only under three conditions—if a monastery had been abandoned or its abbot had disappeared, if there was no one of his lineage to take over, and if there was no local Buddhist association to choose a successor—could the local authorities select an abbot, and even then they were supposed to consult the leading monks of the area.[23] Abbots could make or break a monastery; their selection was the fulcrum of the administrative process. The fact that it was normally to be left in the hands of the monks themselves was more significant than the minor and contingent forms of interference that the new law provided. More significant still was the omission of the principal restrictive provisions of the Ch'ing Code. There was no attempt to control tonsure, ordination, building temples, receiving pilgrims, soliciting donations, public preaching, mourning observances, or worship by women.[24]

Furthermore, under articles 3 and 12, two kinds of establishments were entirely exempted from the force of the regulations: monasteries located in outlying areas (Mongolia, Tibet, Sinkiang, and Tsinghai), where separatism would have been exacerbated by any attempt at control; and temples in China proper that had been established by private individuals, that is, built with funds from their own pockets and not through public solicitation.[25] Such temples and their property could, for instance, be freely alienated by the monks in charge of them. This left mainly the larger institutions subject to the regulations of 1929—and even here there was the question of enforcement. In practice few monasteries registered their property (as required by article 5); even fewer engaged in charity and public welfare (article 10); and yet I have not heard of an abbot who was dismissed for failing to do so (article 11). Probably more significant was the violation of article 9, which required that all monasteries and temples submit semiannual statements of income and expenses to the local authorities. Such statements were not submitted by rich monasteries close to the seat of national government (for example, Chin Shan and the T'ien-ning Ssu), and so it seems likely that poorer institutions did not submit them either.[26] As one abbot said to me: "The 1929 regulations were as good as empty. They existed in name, but from the first to last they were never enforced."

The organ of government primarily responsible for their enforcement was the Ministry of the Interior, which issued most of the executive orders that concerned the sangha. It shared this responsibility with the Ministry of Social Affairs after the latter was created during the war. The two ministries, as we have seen, jointly set up the Committee for the Reorganization of Chinese Buddhism in 1945 (p. 46). Standing outside and above them was the Kuomintang Party, whose approval was required on all important measures from 1928 to 1946, when China was still in the "period of tutelage." At the local level, jurisdiction over monasteries was exercised by provincial bureaus of civil and social affairs, by finance organs in tax matters, and by public-security organs in other matters (such as the registration of property).

Acting as an intermediary between the monasteries and these official organs was the Chinese Buddhist Association, which notified its members of government actions and forwarded to the government its members' views and complaints. It also enjoyed certain specific powers under the regulations of 1929. It had the right to ratify transfers of monastic property and priority in selecting an abbot for an abandoned or disputed monastery. According to a later law, it could recommend to the local authorities that an abbot be removed from office for violation of the monastic rules, and could mete out the penalties for him or any other violator.[27] Unfortunately these powers, like the complaints it forwarded, were largely ineffective. On June 20, 1936, its national headquarters protested that "local government authorities sometimes erroneously regard Buddhist associations as cultural groups, only allowing them to study their religion but not to concern themselves with monastic property that has been taken over or to regulate religious activities." On August 1, 1936, the Ministry of Interior sent a directive to provincial and municipal organs reminding them that "Buddhist associations of all levels everywhere in the country are religious groups. Under the Regulations for the Supervision of Monasteries and Temples and the charter of the Chinese Buddhist Association, they have certain obligations and rights with respect to the supervision and preservation of monastic property and the enforcement of religious rules."[28] This directive might seem to have augured well for the Buddhist cause. As it turned out, it was a boon of little value, purchased at a high price. Local officials continued to ignore the rights of the association and its branches, while the Ministry of the Interior soon called on it to amend its charter so as to place itself more fully under the control of party and government organs at every level. Article 5 of the amended charter (adopted in November 1936) put this very clearly: "The Association shall be under the direction of the People's Training Department of the Executive Committee of the Central Kuomintang and under the control of the Ministry of Interior. The branch associations for provinces, special municipalities, and famous mountains shall be under the direction and control of the national association and of local government organs and Kuomintang headquarters." The same applied to districts and municipalities.

At all levels the party and government were now to receive reports on the association's activities, rules, and membership. Every monk and nun was required to join, and, if any one of them was excused, this had to be reported to the Ministry of the Interior. As a double check, article 6 called for registration of the sangha—and of its property. There was even a bow to political indoctrination. Part of the association's program was now to be "research work on the Three People's Principles," and members could be expelled for opposing them.[29]

In the United States it would be found shocking if, let us say, the National Council of Churches were placed under the control of the FBI and Christian pastors were required to accept the Democratic Party platform. But this is because Americans are used to freedom of religion. What Chinese citizens were guaranteed by the draft Constitution of 1936 was not freedom of religion, but freedom of religious *belief;* and, like other freedoms, it could be "restricted in accordance with the law."[30] Furthermore, the Chinese were accustomed to governments that looked on religion as potentially subversive. Even liberals, who might have protested the official control of political groups, were happy to see it applied to religious groups. The Buddhists themselves were happy to be controlled because it meant that they also had a chance to be protected.

THE LAW VERSUS THE ENEMIES OF BUDDHISM

On balance, surprising as it may seem, Republican laws provided more for the Buddhists' protection than for their control: in particular, for protection against those who wished to "borrow" or confiscate monastic property. This was the effect not only of the omnibus regulations of 1913 and 1929, but also of various *ad hoc* measures. In 1917 and again in 1930, for example, decrees were issued giving the abbot of a monastery the right to start a civil suit against government administrators who attempted to take over its property for educational purposes.[31] A similar decree of 1932 casts interesting light on the distinction between common property (*kung-ch'an*) and public or government property (*kuan-ch'an*): "Any monastery or temple that has a head monk in residence and has been constructed or repaired with donations raised by the head monk, whether or not it ought to be abolished (*wu-lun ying-fou fei-chih*), is nevertheless common property and not government property, and may not be made use of or demolished by any group."[32] A special target of protective legislation was the lay devotee who, after donating monastic property, tried to repossess it; or in other cases tried to interfere with the monastery's internal administration and even expel the abbot. All this was forbidden by law.[33]

The high-water mark in government recognition of Buddhist property rights came in 1931 after a group of deputies in the National Assembly, led by a Tibetan, Lo-sang Ch'u-ch'en, introduced two proposals. The first called for restoration to the sangha of all the properties that had been confiscated to date. The second provided that a memorandum be sent to all government organs, reminding them that infringement of monastic property rights by any government units or individuals, including the police and the army, was punishable by law. On August 1, 1931, President Chiang Kai-shek responded with an executive order (*hsün-ling*) to the effect that the first proposal would be impracticable, but approving the second.[34] Such was Chiang's authority that the movement then underway to confiscate monastic property collapsed (see p. 44).

The reason for this series of protective measures was, as we have seen, that confiscation and borrowing of temples had been common since 1912. Most often they had been used as barracks. Illustrious monasteries like the P'i-lu Ssu in Nanking, the Chao-ch'ing Ssu in Hangchow, the K'ai-fu Ssu in Changsha, the Hei Ssu in Peking, and the Tz'u-en Ssu in Sian had been taken over by the military. Sometimes the circumstances were such as to arouse indignation even among non-Buddhists, as can be seen in the following passage from an article by Bishop Tsu.

We recall the fate of the Lung-hua Ssu, an ancient and famous monastery in the western suburb of the city of Shanghai. In pre-Republican days it enjoyed wide popularity, not only on account of its architecture but also of its beautiful surroundings. In the spring time its courtyards were thronged with pilgrims and children who came to worship and to enjoy the many colored peach blossoms . . . Then came the Revolution of 1911 and with it the battalions of new soldiers in khaki uniforms. Some were dispatched to Shanghai for its protection. But there were no barracks and the government had no money to build them. Someone with a business mind, but little capacity for spiritual values, suggested that the commodious equipment of the Lung-hua Ssu was available and the army could have it for less than a song, for the monks were powerless to resist. And so one morning soldiers came, turned out the monks, and established themselves there. That was eight years ago and the khaki-uniformed soldiers are still there. The droning voices of the bonzes in their chanting, the temple bells, and the footsteps of the pilgrims in spring time have all disappeared and in their place one hears the mingled notes of bugle and drum and the measured thud of soldiers' boots resound-

16 Two soldiers stand guard at the entrance of the Lung-hua Ssu, Shanghai, 1922.

ing in the yards as they practiced the goose-step to the rhythm of the "left-right" of the leader. A sight which one can hardly forget on entering the main hall is to see, in place of the beautiful tapestries, candle sticks, kneeling stools, and burning lamps—the paraphernalia of worship and adoration—the entire floorspace crowded with stacks of rifles with shining bayonets, soldiers-kits, and camp-beds—the paraphernalia of war and destruction. But in the center there remains the majestic image of Buddha, seated on a raised platform, with the serene and unperturbed face, looking down upon the strange sight with infinite pity for poor humanity thus gone astray.[35]

The Lung-hua Ssu apparently remained in the hands of one army or another until the end of the Sino-Japanese War. Then, after a brief reprieve, the Communists marched in. As of 1962, according to one visitor, it was being used as barracks and parade ground for the public security forces.

Military occupation did not necessarily exclude the continued residence of monks. Sometimes a few of them stayed on in a small corner of their former domain. In other cases the army was satisfied with taking over empty rooms only. Then the monks might be able to carry on much as usual. The Kuang-hsiao Ssu in T'ai-chou, one of the largest monasteries in northern Kiangsu, had to quarter soldiers—dozens or hundreds of them—intermittently from 1935 to 1949. Yet its fifty-odd monks managed to maintain the round of daily devotions and at times to operate a seminary and an occupational training center. Chin Shan kept its famous meditation hall going when hundreds of Japanese prisoners, guarded by a detachment of Nationalist troops, were housed there in 1945. The largest monasteries had so many buildings that religious exercises could be largely isolated from such uninvited guests, particularly if the latter behaved well. Some did; others treated the monks with contempt and vandalized the buildings they were occupying. It depended not only on the attitude of the commanding officer, but on the reputation of the monastery. At Chin Shan, for example, the troops are said to have been orderly.

No compensation was given for vandalism or for ordinary wear and tear, and few monasteries in the late Republican period had the resources to make good the damage that was done. On the other hand, when the authorities were occupying most of a tem-

17 The great shrine-hall of the Kuang-hsiao Ssu, Canton, in 1909.

18 The great shrine-hall of the Kuang-hsiao Ssu in 1928; the sign over the new gate reads "Kwangtung Judicial School."

ple for a long period, they had an incentive to keep it structurally sound—to replace the rotten joist and leaking roof tile. Maintenance tended to be better, perhaps, when the occupiers were civil authorities. Photographs taken of the Kuang-hsiao Ssu, Canton, in 1909 and 1928 show this ancient temple looking sprucer after it became a school, though the improved maintenance was at the expense of all religious function: in 1928 the Buddha hall itself was plastered with Kuomintang slogans like, "The Revolution has not yet been completed. Comrades strive on!"[36]

No statistics are available, so far as I know, that reveal the incidence of confiscation and show how it rose and fell in different areas at different times.[37] It depended in part on the prosperity of Buddhism. Many informants have confirmed what Reichelt wrote in the 1920's: "If any [monastery] buildings stand empty or activities slacken, both buildings and worldly possessions are very quickly confiscated for public purposes."[38] Whereas the authorities hesitated to encroach on a monastery that was strictly operated and full of monks, they needed only the slightest pretext for occupying one that was on the decline and had many empty rooms. Since there were more such monasteries in outlying provinces than in central China, the incidence of confiscation was generally higher there.

Political developments also had their effect. From the beginning of the Republic, confiscation had probably been most widespread in Canton. This was partly because Buddhism there was on the decline, partly because Sun Yat-sen was in need of money to build an army, and partly because many of his associates were antireligious in outlook. "Shortly following the Revolution of 1911 the city of Rams [Canton], the seat of revolutionary thought, was the first to set an example in eradicating superstitious practices by taking idols from the temples and dumping them in the river."[39] In the ensuing years most of the large monasteries and small temples of the city were confiscated, sold, or demolished.[40] Heavy taxes were imposed on the fees charged by monks for mortuary rites and even on the tinfoil used in making the paper images that were burned for the benefit of the deceased. These antireligious levies became so pervasive that in 1924 an Italian flag was seen flying on a paper automobile to save it from confiscation in hell.[41] The government was indifferent to religious sensibilities. For example, in order to free land for agriculture, a mass exhumation of graves was ordered in the countryside around Canton. Despite the popular reluctance to disturb ancestral bones, this was ruthlessly carried out. Just as under the Communists in 1958, coffin boards could soon be seen serving many uses—even to bridge irrigation ditches.[42]

Such was the religious policy of the government that set out in 1926 to take over the rest of China. In many areas, when the troops of the Northern Expedition arrived they devastated monasteries, smashed images, and turned temples into schools and police stations.[43] Antireligious decrees were issued, and the suppression of "superstitious activities" became one of the tasks of the new bureaus of public safety.[44] Soon, however, came the split within the Kuomintang. The Communists were expelled from party and government posts. Conservatives and elder statesmen were taken into the government and gradually their influence made itself felt. By 1929 the tide had begun to turn in favor of religious tolerance rather than "suppressing superstition"; and of the protection rather than the destruction of Buddhist monasteries.

This does not mean that destruction ceased. For one thing, many areas remained outside Nationalist control. The Moslem general Pai Chung-hsi is reported to have driven out the monks and destroyed almost all the monasteries in Kwangsi.[45] Feng Yü-hsiang did much the same in some northern provinces.[46] A resident of Honan in 1931–32 recalls that Feng's troops went about Buddhist temples breaking the heads off stone and bronze images and using wooden ones for fire wood (a policy suggested to him by his Christian advisers). Even where the Nationalists were in control, a new wave of destruction was brought about by the Japanese war. Images were seized and melted down to make bullets. Temples were caught in the line of fire. In 1937, for example, two large Shanghai monasteries were bombed out, while a little distance up the river, Chiao Shan (Silver Island) was shelled and partly destroyed when the Nationalist army used it as a strongpoint in blocking the Japanese advance along the Yangtze. According to one informant, the Ch'an-yüan Ssu on Hsi

19 The Mi-yin Ssu in Ning-hsiang, Hunan, after it was destroyed in 1918 by
disbanded troops on the rampage.

20 Like a crucifix in a bombed cathedral, Maitreya survives the Japanese air
raids on Chungking.

T'ien-mu Shan was totally destroyed by bombs after it had been "borrowed" to house the Cheking provincial government.

Borrowing had continued all along in areas under Nationalist control, despite President Chiang's executive order of August 1, 1931, which had to be repeated in 1936.[47] Now the needs of the war caused more temples than ever to be occupied, particularly by troops, and victory did not bring an end to new encroachments. The situation continued to be so chaotic that on May 28, 1946, another order was issued, this time jointly by the National Military Council and the Executive Yüan, prohibiting all government and military units from illegally occupying or damaging monastic property. Many monasteries posted copies of this decree at their main entrance and, as one monk said, "sometimes it had a certain effect."[48]

From first to last, "a certain effect" was all that could be claimed for the law's protection of monastic property rights. It was usually most effective when it had the support of local officials.[49] For example, if notices like those just mentioned were signed by the mayor or the garrison commander, they were more likely to be respected than if they bore the signature of a ministry in Nanking. There was, indeed, an ongoing struggle between the central and the local authorities. From the start of the Republican period, the former could afford to champion Buddhist rights in the abstract and often had ulterior reasons for doing so, whereas the local officials were faced with the concrete problems of setting up schools, agricultural associations, prisons, and police headquarters, all of which required floorspace. This led to a clash of interests.

In 1924, for example, a district Buddhist association in Anhwei province complained to the Administrative Court in Peking that many hundreds of temples there had been occupied or confiscated. The Anhwei authorities had justified this under Presidential Edict No. 66, to which they gave the following interpretation: all the property of a temple could be taken over if no monk resided there; most of it could be taken over if its monks were not conversant with Buddhist scripture (leaving them just enough so that they could start life anew as laymen); and "quite a lot" could be occupied even if the residents were learned monks. The

Administrative Court ruled that this interpretation was erroneous and ordered the Anhwei authorities to return all the monastic property in question to the original owners. It is not clear whether the court's order was carried out.[50]

The central government seems to have interceded most firmly when local officials acted less from need than from bias. In 1927, for example, at the height of the antireligious movement the Farmers' Association in Feng-hua, Chekiang, "borrowed" a nunnery there, took the sacred images outside, and smashed them to bits. Later the nunnery was returned to its owners. When the head nun tried to raise money to recast fifty-one of the images, the local Kuomintang committee member sent a letter to the district magistrate asking that she be ordered to cease and desist, on the grounds that she was practicing idolatry and promoting superstition. The case was referred by the Chekiang Civil Affairs Department to the Ministry of the Interior, thence to the Executive Yüan, and finally to the Kuomintang Secretariat. In 1931 the latter instructed both government and party organs that the nun should be allowed to put up her images and that religious rites should not be interfered with.[51] In 1932 the Ministry of the Interior ordered provincial and municipal authorities to penalize bookshops selling literature that ridiculed or profaned any religion.[52] On at least three occasions—in 1930, 1935, and 1946—the central government ordered local authorities to desist from levying taxes on Buddhist rites for the dead, such as the tax mentioned earlier in Canton.[53]

The purpose of this tax was not merely to draw on monastic income, but to discourage the very practice of religion. An antireligious movement had been launched in 1922–23, partly as a reaction to Christian militance and partly under the stimulus of the humanist ideas of Bertrand Russell and John Dewey and the Marxist ideas of returned students. It abated for a time and then revived in 1927–28. On November 12, 1928, the Society to Abolish Superstition was set up in Peking; it promptly petitioned the government to return China's monks and nuns to lay life and to prohibit them from performing rites for the dead. The petition, of course, was rejected. Three years later, similar societies were set up in Chekiang, determined not only to laicize the sangha

21 The World Student Christian Federation meets at Tsinghua College in Peking, April 1922. This meeting triggered the antireligious movement that came to be directed against Buddhism as well as Christianity.

and abolish mortuary rites but to do away with talismans, *yin-yang*, prayers, and even gatherings to chant the sutras.[54] These ideas found support at the provincial level of government. In Kwangsi, for example, the sale and burning of incense, candles, and paper offerings were prohibited as of January 1, 1929.[55] In Yünnan it was said to have become illegal in 1935 to make obeisance to an image of the Buddha.[56] Even the central government was not immune. The New Life Movement, which Chiang Kai-shek launched in 1934, inveighed against the burning of incense.[57]

Yet no prohibition of religious practice (so far as I can learn) was ever incorporated into national law. For one thing, it would have caused too much resentment to make an exception for Christian practice (as extraterritoriality or foreign pressure would have required). For another thing, Buddhism had too many friends in high places who were ready to use their influence to protect the monks and monasteries they admired. They, rather than the laws or the machinery of the Buddhist Association, were the shield and buckler of the sangha when danger threatened.

FRIENDS IN HIGH PLACES

If local officials encroached on monastic property, the abbot was supposed to complain through the nearest branch of the Buddhist Association, which would attempt to dissuade them. If nothing came of this, the complaint would be referred to the provincial branch and finally, perhaps, to the national headquarters, which would take the matter up with the Ministry of the Interior in Nanking. But the officials of the ministry usually had neither the inclination nor the power to impose their will on local officials in matters of this kind. Therefore, whenever Buddhists were in a position to do so, they would bypass official channels and make direct use of personal connections. When, for example, the Wuchang Buddhist Institute was occupied by a military detachment in 1929, a prominent local devotee happened to know the commanding officer. He persuaded him to move the detachment elsewhere. A similar problem, after all appeals to the law had failed, was resolved through the good offices of a devotee who was private secretary to Chiang Kai-shek. President Chiang personally ordered the military to vacate.

There were several cases in which monasteries received highly placed help in recovering lost land and income. One such involved the struggle between the Ch'i-hsia Ssu and Huang Chih-fu. The Ch'i-hsia Ssu was a famous monastery outside Nanking. Huang was the principal of the Ch'i-hsia Township Normal School, which was being built on the slopes of Lung Shan adjoining the hill on which the monastery stood. Both hills belonged to the monastery, and both were claimed by Huang. When his workmen began fencing off these claims with wire netting, the monks tried to interfere and were driven off with fists. When they returned in force to give blow for blow, Huang had them arrested. Some of them spent a year or two in prison. In 1929 the monastery started legal proceedings, but got no satisfaction. Nor did it receive any help from the district officials to whom it appealed. Finally after Chi-jan, a prior of the Ch'i-hsia Ssu, was arrested for the third time, one of his brother priors wrote to Lin Sen, the President of China, who had taken office in 1931. Lin often stayed at the monastery and was friendly with its senior

officers. When he heard how they were being treated, he indignantly intervened, had all the monks in prison released, and
issued orders for the normal school to desist from further encroachment. Middlemen slowly negotiated a compromise agreement, signed in April 1937, whereby the Ch'i-hsia Ssu agreed to
lease 140 *mou* of its land to the school for the nominal sum of
$50 a year.[58] At another time the monastery received the help of
Lin Hsiang, head of the Supreme Court, in recovering the use of
420 *mou* of farmland that had been lost after the Taiping Rebellion.[59]

Chin Shan, just down the Yangtze from the Ch'i-hsia Ssu, had
such good connections that in 1929 the government sent in troops
to collect its grain rents from obstinate tenants.[60] That same year
near Foochow a company of the Fukien army was stationed at
the Ch'ung-sheng Ssu to prevent mischief by neighboring peasants, who were angry because the monastery had recovered
ownership of land they had been treating as their own. It had
almost certainly been recovered with the help of officials who
were friends of Ta-pen, its illustrious abbot.[61]

Troops were also dispatched to monasteries that expressed a
need for security during ordinations. For example, Europeans
who went to be ordained at the Ch'i-hsia Ssu in 1933 found it
guarded by a detachment of cavalry under the command of a
German instructor, von Bodin. One day President Lin Sen himself drove up to see how the ordinees were getting along and to
emphasize the protection being extended by the central government.[62] Thus, while some monasteries were being rudely occupied by the army, others were being protected by it. Of course
it is likely that instances of the former were more common. The
Ch'i-hsia Ssu, perhaps since it was so close to the capital, seems
to have enjoyed particular favor and influence.

The same applies to certain monks. The Venerable Hsü-yün,
for example, is portrayed as having so much influence that he
could arrange a truce between government and insurgents in
Yünnan, prevent a punitive expedition against Tibet, and secure
the dismissal of a hostile official. This last episode is said to have
taken place in 1913, when the chief of civil affairs for Yünnan,
Lo Jung-hsüan, was creating difficulties for the newly founded

Yünnan-Tibetan Buddhist Association. The leaders of the association asked Hsü-yün to go to Peking and intervene on their behalf. The premier at that time was Hsiung Hsi-lin, a Buddhist devotee, who "did a good deal to help"—so much, in fact, that the difficult Mr. Lo was transferred to Peking. His successor, Jen K'o-ch'eng, made every effort to assist Buddhist activities.[63]

In 1921 Hsü-yün is said to have persuaded T'ang Chi-yao to relinquish the governorship of Yünnan in order to avoid bloodshed with Ku Pin-ch'en; and in 1926 he secured an agreement that the troops there would cease molesting the peasants.[64] Probably Hsü-yün's role in these events has been exaggerated, but there seems little doubt that he was widely respected in the highest official circles.

The number of Buddhists in these circles is not generally realized, partly because many of them considered that their religious life was a private matter, not to be advertised in a world that might consider it backward or superstitious. Among high-ranking Buddhist officials who held office at one time or another during the Republican period (some quite briefly), there were at least two chiefs of state, four prime ministers, nine officers of ministerial rank, and seventeen provincial governors and warlords.[65]

Unfortunately for the sangha, it would appear that as the years went by, the number of such patrons in office declined. Many of them were elderly as well as old-fashioned, and they simply died off. Their places were often taken by Christians and modernizers who were indifferent to Buddhism or actively hostile toward it. They naturally appointed like-minded colleagues, so that whole departments "went over." Looking through a file of Buddhist magazines, I once found scrawled across the top of one issue: "The Foreign Ministry despises Buddhism." As to the local officials, fewer and fewer of them—Buddhists aside—had any feeling that monasteries, through their accumulation of merit, provided insurance against locusts and drought.[66] The old basis for official patronage no longer had much validity.

Yet the friends of Buddhism in their seesaw contest with its enemies were never routed. There was never a general persecution. In fact, aside from the widespread encroachment on their property, monks appear to have fared as well as the rest of the

population, if not better. Although their farmland and urban
real estate were subject to taxation, monastery premises in both
city and countryside were tax-exempt, as were donations received
for meals and lodging. This was provided by law and, according
to my informants, the exemption was honored.[67] Monks also enjoyed a privilege denied the ordinary citizen in being permitted
to serve on first-aid teams rather than on the front line. Yet they
enjoyed the ordinary citizen's civil rights: they could vote and
stand for election, and they were not subject to arrest for anything remotely connected with their vocation. The only monks
who were arrested or imprisoned during the Republican period
for other than common crimes appear to have been those who
collaborated with the Japanese.

The Nationalist government had no program to assist the
sangha. It never paid for the repair of monasteries or provided
subsidies to elderly monks (as the Communists were to do after
1950). But it also had no program to utilize or indoctrinate the
sangha, which was left to fend for itself.[68] The Ch'ing dynasty
had been effective in protecting it, ineffective in regulating it.
The Republic was ineffective in both. This provided stimulus
(the threat of confiscation) without restraint—an invigorating
combination.

MONKS IN POLITICS

Arthur Wright attributes the "failure of the Buddhist revival"
partly to its apolitical character.[69] Whatever the truth is about
the revival, it appears perfectly correct that after the 1911 revolution the sangha stayed out of politics. There were no longer
revolutionary monks like Tsung-yang and Ch'i-yün, if only because the groups preparing for the *next* revolution were militantly
antireligious. Monks did not belong to political parties, did not
hold public office, and generally speaking did not even take advantage of the right to vote. They felt that such activities would
violate the spirit if not the letter of the monastic rule. They recalled the example set by Hui-yüan, the founder of the Pure
Land school: "His shadow never left the mountain, his footprints
never entered the secular world. When he bade farewell to

guests, he went only as far as the Tiger Creek."[70] At some monasteries a list of twenty-four regulations was displayed twice a month. One of them stated, "Whoever delights in talking politics and whose heart is bent on secular matters will not be allowed to live in the monastery."[71] Political passions were considered extremely disadvantageous to religious practice and therefore to the accumulation of merit. Hence they could lead to the loss of financial support from lay devotees.

Probably the closest thing to a "political monk" during the Republican era was T'ai-hsü. Although he never held public office, some informants have reported hearing that he was a member of the Kuomintang. Others (in a position to know, although perhaps not to speak frankly) have categorically denied this. In any case, he did openly advocate participation by monks in secular activities, partly in order to fulfill their duty as citizens, partly to win greater prestige for Buddhism.[72]

T'ai-hsü's political sympathies originally lay with the Left—the socialists and anarchists—and this still appears to have been his attitude in the early 1920's. Soon, however, perhaps because he had his fingers burned by encouraging radicalism among his students, or perhaps because he felt that prestige for Buddhism could best be won by supporting the central government, or perhaps simply because he was getting older, T'ai-hsü became politically more conservative. In 1924 he wrote an article entitled "A Warning about the Communist Party," in which he said that the latter ought to be called "the party of killing and destruction, not the party of common property" (which is what its name means in Chinese). The only way to eliminate private property, he said, was to eliminate the ego on which it was based, and this could be only accomplished by Buddhism.[73] Although T'ai-hsü may not have belonged to the Kuomintang himself, he certainly cultivated good relations with some of its important members. A photograph taken in the late 1920's shows him standing contentedly beside Chiang Kai-shek. As we have seen, he received Nationalist government subsidies for two foreign tours and for the operation of his seminary near Chungking.

Other Chinese monks, although they seem to have avoided any connection with partisan politics, did not stand aloof from the defense of their country. Politics were bad, but patriotism was good. We have already noted how Yüan-ying, the president of the Chinese Buddhist Association, tried to organize resistance against Japan and how, once the Sino-Japanese War broke out, resistance and relief work was carried on at various monasteries (pp. 127-129). It is not always clear whether such work exemplified patriotism or compassion. In 1939, for example, many of the monks of the Nan-hua Ssu began to give up their evening meal so that the grain they saved could be donated to China Relief; and they held daily rites for the benefit of the souls of those killed in the war. In 1941 their abbot, Hsü-yün, took the $200,000 he had received in pious donations over the preceding two years and gave it to the Kwangtung provincial government, again for China Relief.[74] Even those monks who risked their lives sheltering members of the underground may have been motivated as much by the bodhisattva ideal as by a desire to defend the nation.

The defense of the nation included (in the eyes of most monks) its defense against Communism. They did not consider this a partisan political struggle. As one informant said, "We could oppose the Communists without political partisanship simply on the grounds that they were devils who were harming all mankind." In Communist guerilla areas—for example, in northern Kiangsu after it was occupied by the New Fourth Army in 1940–41—many of the leading monks had been treated as landlords, dispossessed, and sometimes executed. The Buddhist establishment had no illusions about what a Communist victory would mean.

For their part, the Communists appear not to have been interested in trying to win over or infiltrate the sangha. I have heard of only one Communist Party member who became a monk, and he did so not in order to infiltrate but to escape arrest after Chiang Kai-shek's suppression of left-wing groups in Shanghai in 1927. Under the religious name of Hung-miao, he lived an exemplary monastic life for many years. In 1946 he received the dharma of the famous Ling-yin Ssu in Hangchow (one of whose officers is the source of this story). Soon afterwards he became its abbot. Although he did not openly advocate Communism, he allowed party workers during the late 1940's to distribute their propaganda through the shops outside the monastery. When Communists took Hangchow, they organized struggle meetings against the other officers of the Ling-yin Ssu, but never against him.

A few young monks were interested in Marxism and, as the Republican period wore on, they may have come to hope for a Communist victory. But I have heard of none who became an activist or a party member. Among refugees from the Mainland today, Buddhist monks are the most uncompromising of the anti-Communists.

Another question sometimes raised is involvement in secret societies. It is difficult to prove that something has never happened, especially something that would have been kept secret if it had, so I can only say that repeated inquiry has revealed no evidence to suggest that secret societies had any appreciable Buddhist membership or organizational links with monasteries or lay clubs. Certainly the Buddhist distaste for heterodoxy and desire for merit worked against it. In the case of lay devotees, if one of their clubs participated even indirectly in the ulterior, worldly aims of a secret society, the merit its members gained through religious practice would have been vitiated.[75] In the case of monks, there was every reason for them to remain outside the secular world. Otherwise they risked losing not only personal purity (and hence lay support), but also whatever was left of their old, privileged status. As we have seen, there had long been a kind of tacit understanding that if they did not meddle in secular matters, the secular authorities would not meddle in theirs. During the Republican period, with the threat of confiscation hanging over them, they would have been foolish indeed to weaken their claims under that compact.

Chapter IX

FOREIGN CONTACTS

THE Ch'ing government frowned on its people having contact with foreigners almost as much as did the Communist government after 1949. During the Republican period, however, there was a forty-year interlude during which foreigners could travel freely in China and Chinese found it relatively easy to go abroad. This was also the period when foreign ideas and ways of doing things enjoyed the highest esteem, when the impact of the West was at its zenith. The Buddhist monastic establishment could not remain unaffected, although, being "outside the secular world," it was affected somewhat less than other segments of Chinese society. Sometimes the foreign impact on Buddhism was circuitous—such as the Western military victories, which led to the call for modern secular schools, which led to the confiscation of monasteries, which led to the establishment of Buddhist associations and seminaries and to social action by the sangha. Yet in other ways foreign impact was direct. Chinese Buddhists, for a variety of reasons and purposes, interacted with persons who belonged to the non-Chinese world.

CONTACTS WITH JAPAN

From the sixth through the seventeenth century, imports of Chinese Buddhism had been entering Japan. In the late nineteenth century the process was reversed. Japanese Buddhism began to be exported to China, partly because of the Japanese parishes that were springing up in the treaty ports and partly because of the possibilities for the use of Buddhism as an instrument of foreign policy.

These possibilities were discussed as early as 1871, only three years after the Meiji Restoration. At that time some of the Meiji leaders favored a military expedition against Korea, in order to give employment to the samurai as well as to revive ancient military virtues. This was opposed by other Meiji leaders—men like Iwakura Tomomi, who believed that Japan had to be modernized before it could hope to win a war. On the eve of Iwakura's departure for two years of study and negotiation with the Western powers, he received a memorandum from Eto Shinpei, one of the most ardent members of the war party. Balked on Korea, Eto had a new scheme: the conquest of China. "China is the battleground of Asia," he wrote. "Those who do not take possession of her are endangered; if, however, you do take possession of her, you control the situation in Asia." Accordingly Eto proposed that military and naval preparations should be made, intelligence collected, and strategy decided upon; then on the ground of some discourtesy to Japan, China should be struck down with a single blow.

What interests us here are the methods he proposed for the collection of intelligence. "Two percent of the Chinese are Confucians or Christians. The rest are Buddhists like our own people. Therefore we should now despatch priests to live in China and spread the dharma or practice the religion, so that they may be utilized for strategic military work such as making the Chinese people more peaceable and collecting intelligence." This was point four in Eto's sixteen-point memorandum. In Japanese it sounds a little vague, but points nine and ten were precise: "Priests should be selected from the various sects and despatched to China as spies (kanja) . . . In order to make geographical investigations of China, several [lay] people should be very secretly selected and dispatched, possibly intermingled with the above-mentioned priests or possibly on some other basis."[1]

Eto was himself a Buddhist, having lived for a time in a temple, but we do not know whether he communicated his ideas to the leaders of the Japanese sangha. Therefore we cannot say whether his ideas played any role in the decision, reached soon afterwards, that missionary work in China should be undertaken by the Higashi-Honganji chapter of Jodo Shinshu, the larger of the two Pure Land sects. Somewhat nobler motives are attributed to Otani Kosho, its twenty-first hereditary patriarch. First, he considered that China's power as a nation had been weakened by the corruption and decadence of Chinese Buddhism and so, by purifying the latter, he hoped to strengthen China and repay her for all the cultural gifts that Japan had received. His second motive, which is more credible, was to help Japanese Buddhism prove its usefulness to the nation in the face of the anti-Buddhist movement then underway.

Therefore in July 1873 he sent one of his priests to reconnoitre. This priest, Ogurisu Kocho, went first to Shanghai, then quickly proceeded to Tientsin and Peking, where he settled down in the Lung-ch'üan Ssu to study Chinese under one of its monks. Like his compatriots of a half century later, he took a special interest in Lamaism, frequenting the Yung-ho Kung and making a pilgrimage to Wu-t'ai Shan. His findings suggested the possibilities not only for missionary work in China, but also for an alliance of the Buddhists of Japan, China, and India in order to bring about an ecumenical revival of their religion. When he returned to Japan in August 1874, his report strengthened Otani's determination to take some positive action.[2] Before long, the Higashi-Honganji drew up a new creed, which emphasized that glorious death in military service would be rewarded by rebirth in the Western Paradise; and spoke of brotherhood with the Chinese against unfilial barbarians.[3] Then in May 1876 Otani, accompanied by Ogurisu Kocho, went to Tokyo to talk to Terashima Munenori in the Foreign Ministry about the problem of China missionary work. We are not told the substance of their conversation, but in August of that year a branch temple opened its doors in Shanghai, staffed by six priests, including Ogurisu. It was "the first Japanese religious organization in China."[4]

Almost immediately, more personnel were sent to staff it, first

six priests and three laymen, then an additional twelve. Although
some of them conducted services for the Japanese residents of
Shanghai, most of them devoted themselves to the study of
Chinese, which only Ogurisu could speak well enough to use
when preaching. By 1877 a special school had been set up in
Peking, where the best accent could be acquired.

These energetic efforts did not lead to the growth of Chinese
congregations. Indeed by 1885 missionary work had been virtually
abandoned, since "it was impossible to get together more than
one or two people to preach to."[5] This was attributed partly to
Chinese contempt for Japan as a country that was imitating the
West, and partly to the inability of Japanese missionaries either
to protect converts or to carry on social-welfare work as effectively as their Christian competitors. Another reason they advanced was that "in China the decadence of the sangha was so
pronounced that Buddhism had lost the confidence of the people.
Japanese members of the sangha tended to be looked at in the
same light."[6] Actually, it seems probable that Japanese priests
were looked at in a far worse light, since they married and ate
meat. The whole concept of the decadence of the Chinese
sangha—a concept that served first to justify the Japanese missions and then to explain their lack of success—is open to
question (more will be said about this in Chapter Eleven).

It was not until 1895 that conditions improved. The defeat
of China at the hands of its despised little neighbor stirred interest in learning how that neighbor had progressed so quickly.
Furthermore, the trade agreement signed in July 1896 gave the
Japanese certain extraterritorial rights in the treaty ports—rights
that enabled them to offer the same protection as their Christian
competitors, but with the added advantage that converts did
not have to abandon ancestor worship. The Higashi-Honganji was
quick to profit by this. It opened not only temples but schools.
The schools advertised for students with pointed slogans, such
as: "Nations rise and fall on talented men, and talented men are
produced by education." The courses they offered were in the
Japanese language and in standard modern subjects. At least
four such schools were opened in 1898-99.[7] It is doubtful that

their only purpose was to help China grow strong by producing men of talent. Rather it was to make sure that some of its men of talent were oriented toward Japan.

Even more realistic were the efforts underway in Fukien province, where the Japanese were trying to create a sphere of influence across the straits from their newly acquired colony of Formosa. The aim was not merely to build up parishes, but to use the missions in the same way as the European powers. Thus in the summer of 1900, when the powers were busy up north with the Boxer Rebellion, it seemed like a good time to occupy Amoy. The Japanese High Command decided to do so at the end of August. All that was needed was a *casus belli*. Two years earlier the Higashi-Honganji had rented a private house in the city and fitted it up as a temple. On August 23rd the priests moved out all their valuables and, shortly after midnight on the 24th, the abbot rushed to the Japanese consulate with the news that his temple had been burned by a mob. It was certainly in flames, but the only Chinese observed in the vicinity had been trying to extinguish them. A small force of Japanese marines immediately landed to protect Japanese property. Full-scale bombardment and occupation was planned for August 31st. Unfortunately the Japanese cabinet delayed its final approval just long enough for British warships to arrive, loaded with troops. The plan had to be canceled, and Japan's first "missions case" ended up as something less than a success.[8]

A more subtle approach was already on the way. In 1899 the East Asian Cultural Alliance had been established to create an anti-Western, anti-Christian united front among the peoples of the East. Visits were being exchanged with Buddhists in Thailand, China, and India. In 1904 Dr. Inoue Enryu, after returning from a trip to India, proposed that the Japanese should establish a great Confucian-Buddhist university that would serve the whole Buddhist world and maintain branches in Korea, China, and Mongolia.

Other possibilities for maneuver were created when Chinese officials began to confiscate monastic property. As we have seen, the Japanese priest Mizuno Baigyo advised his Chinese brethren to start schools in order to "get the jump" on the confiscators;

and to apply for protection to the headquarters of the Higashi-Honganji in Japan. The latter was pleased to accept the affiliation of some thirty-five monasteries in Chekiang province toward the end of 1904 and sent its representatives to protect them.[9] A test case soon occurred when a Hangchow monastery was threatened with having part of its premises turned into a technical school. On January 10, 1905, with a blaze of firecrackers, a large wooden plaque was installed over the front gate, reading: "Public place of worship of the Imperial Japanese Shinshu sect—Honganji chapter." This caused consternation among literati and officials throughout the province. The governor appealed, without success, to the Japanese consul. The Japanese priests stood pat on their passports. Peking wrung its hands, but said that they would have to be respected. The best that the local officials could do was to get the plaque removed: foreign protection remained in force.

This is said to have been the signal for general resistance by the monasteries of neighboring provinces against the confiscation of their property. In Fukien and Kwangtung they began to place themselves under the Japanese wing. Such was their faith in the immunity this conferred that in Canton on February 26, 1905, a lay school established on monastery land was completely destroyed by a group of infuriated Buddhists. The newspaper *Shen-pao* briefly castigated the Chinese monks for their insolence in accepting Japanese protection against their own laws and protested vigorously against Japanese interference—but then fell silent, apparently because it was not immune to Japanese influence itself. These developments frightened the Chinese government, which proceeded to cancel the authorization for local officials to confiscate monastic property. Affiliation with the Honganji died down.

In any case it had been limited to the area of the treaty ports, where Japan had acquired missionary rights in 1896. She had tried to claim the same rights elsewhere, invoking the "most-favored nation" clause, but without success. This was still true in 1915, when the fifth section of her Twenty-One Demands (including parity with Western missionaries) was rejected by Yüan Shih-K'ai. During the whole first twenty-five years of the

Republican period, her missionary work in China was admittedly "hindered by conditions"[10]—a phrase that must allude to anti-Japanese feeling, which was growing particularly strong with respect to Buddhism. Eto's plan to use priests for espionage had been published in 1900 and was soon implemented. "Following the Russo-Japanese war," states a Japanese source, "as the power of the militarists grew, some Japanese missionaries received special 'defense funds' from a certain government agency for carrying on military intelligence work . . . This made the Chinese feel that the missionaries were not only suspect, but a positive threat." In these circumstances very few new temples were established.[11] Instead there was a return to the idea of ecumenical cooperation.

In 1923-24, as we have seen, the Japanese Foreign Ministry took an interest in the Buddhist meetings held at Lu Shan under the auspices of T'ai-hsü. In 1924 it arranged for Japanese delegates to be present and to offer their country as the site for a similar meeting the next year. Accordingly, the East Asian Buddhist Conference was held in Tokyo on November 1-3, 1925.

This was perhaps the first international Buddhist conference of modern times.[12] Small delegations of three members each came from Taiwan and Korea. Twenty came from China.[13] Most of them were close to T'ai-hsü or shared at least some of his views about the modernization of Buddhism.[14] Seventeen were laymen—two each represented the Buddhist New Youth Society, the San-shih Hsüeh-hui, the World Buddhist Devotees' Club, and the Metaphysical Institute. There was not one representative of the famous monasteries of central China.

T'ai-hsü, literally and figuratively, took the center of the stage.[15] He pointed out that, whereas the Chinese excelled at religious cultivation, the Japanese excelled in organizing, propaganda, and community service. A Sino-Japanese liaison committee was set up to put these complementary talents to work, with Wang I-t'ing as the Chinese representative, and resolutions were passed for action in the fields of education and social welfare. Also included in the conference was a symposium on Buddhist doctrine, at which T'ai-hsü gave papers on the theory of *alayavijnana* and on the secularization of Japanese Buddhism.

Plans were made to hold the next East Asian Buddhist conference in Peking—plans that never materialized.

After the meeting, the Chinese delegates were given an eighteen-day tour and were treated with flattering deference. Everywhere they were entertained by local government officials. In Kyoto they were welcomed by a crowd of ten thousand. Their host both at the conference sessions and on the tour was none other than Mizuno Baigyo. "It was chiefly through his good offices that the great conference in Tokyo was brought into being."[16] Among those present were representatives of the Ministry of Foreign Affairs. The latter had supplied the largest financial subsidy for the conference, which obviously fitted in with the perennial effort to expand Japanese influence in the Middle Kingdom.[17]

This fact was not lost on some of the Chinese delegates. They were only too well aware that, as one of them put it, "Japan's mouth had long been watering for China" and that the conference they were attending was essentially a piece of propaganda. At one point Mizuno spoke of China and Japan as being elder and younger brothers and said that Japan's friendship for China was based on her gratitude for the Chinese culture she had adopted. Retorted Hu Jui-lin, an outspoken old devotee who had been governor of Fukien under the Ch'ing, "Don't start talking about gratitude or you'll frighten us . . . The last time there was talk about Japan's gratitude to China, it was followed by the Twenty-One Demands."[18]

Still, most of the Chinese delegates must have felt that by coming to Tokyo they had more to gain for their religion than to lose for their country. They saw the hope not only of a central role in the world Buddhist movement, but also of higher status for Buddhism at home, where a Japanese connection would impress their adversaries. Thus three years later when the Japanese Buddhologist, Tokiwa Daijo, was touring the monasteries of southeast China, he met Yüan-ying, who was soon to set up the Chinese Buddhist Association (Shanghai, 1929) in an effort to protect monastic property. Yüan-ying said that Tokiwa's visit had given him courage and that, from then on, one of the arguments he would use to win over public opinion for the protection of Buddhism was the existence of chairs of Buddhist studies at Japan's imperial universities. Japan was a country that had successfully modernized; yet she paid attention to Buddhism.[19]

This did not mean that the Japanese form of Buddhism was uncritically regarded in China. When T'ai-hsü was addressing the East Asian Buddhist conference, he said quite frankly that Japanese monks were too sectarian and nationalistic; too much tainted by modernism and, compared to monks in China, less devout in their religious life and unable to undergo austerities. Strange words from T'ai-hsü, but so strongly did he feel about it that, when he returned from the conference, he decided that the Chinese sangha could not model itself upon its counterpart in Japan, since monks there married and ate meat.[20] For their part, the Japanese thought that Chinese Buddhists were ignorant of modern critical methods and content to take a traditional approach to Buddhist texts.[21]

Nonetheless, for the next ten years Buddhist exchanges happily continued between the two countries. Japanese scholars toured China to collect material on Buddhist history and art, while

22   Tokiwa Daijo on one of his many tours, at the
     K'ai-yüan Ssu, Chaochow.

Chinese went to Japan to study.[22] Ostensibly to promote such exchanges, several Sino-Japanese organizations were formed.[23] It would not be too cynical to suppose that some, at least, of their backers in Japan hoped to use them as instruments for political penetration, whereas most if not all of their Chinese backers hoped to use them to mobilize Buddhist opinion in Japan against that country's aggressive policy.

The brutal invasion of central China in 1937 put an end to such hopes and to the era they symbolized. No longer could either side expect to use the other for ulterior purposes, as in the preceding decades. What now began was a dreary era of military occupation, in which Buddhism, like other facets of Chinese life, had to be controlled, adapted, and integrated into the Japanese imperial scheme. Ultimately it had to be displaced by Japanese Buddhism. Therefore, as a Japanese source puts it, "where Nippon's army went, its religion went too."[24]

Since 1870 only about a dozen permanent temples had been established, nearly all in Shanghai, but now between 1937 and 1942 some thirty-five were opened, not only in Shanghai, but in Nanking (six temples), Hankow (four), Hangchow (three), Soochow (two), Wuhu (two), Wusih (two), Chen-chiang, Kiukiang, Yangchow, Changchow, and many smaller cities.[25] Most of the parishioners were Japanese—in three cases entirely so[26]—but at four temples out of five there were at least a few Chinese parishioners, and at one out of six the Chinese were in a majority. The conversion of China had begun (or so the Japanese may have thought).

Not all Chinese monks and devotees could follow their government to Szechwan. Those who remained had to cope with the realities of foreign occupation. They had no choice but to accept the increasing number of Japanese priests who came to work in China, living in Chinese monasteries or in Japanese research institutes, and in return they went to Japan themselves. In 1939, for example, over twenty Chinese monks were selected by competitive examination. As one of them told me, he was twenty-two at the time and had been serving as a sacristan (*i-po*) at Chin Shan. He wanted to go partly because he was curious about the state of Japanese Buddhism. Also he believed that if he learned the language, he would be better equipped to cope with the occupation forces on his return. "If I knew Japanese, they would not be able to bully me. I would be able to reason with them." After qualifying in the examinations, he spent his first year on language study in Tokyo, his second at Otani University, and his third at the Mampukuji outside Kyoto, which is the most Chinese of Japanese Zen monasteries. He was very politely treated. When I asked (a little tactlessly) whether the Japanese government did not have a policy of trying to use Buddhism to subdue China, he replied with some sharpness: "*I* was not utilized by them. That was not the way they behaved toward me." He said, however, that other monks who had gone to Japan were looked on as collaborators when they returned, and some had to change their names. I have heard elsewhere that after the victory in 1945 several high-ranking monks were imprisoned as collaborators in Shanghai and one was executed in Canton.[27]

During the long years of the occupation, the principal vehicle for Japan's Buddhist policy was the Central China League of Religious Federations. This had been created by the Japanese Military Intelligence Bureau in October 1938.[28] It was "under the direction and supervision of the military authorities." Throughout a series of bureaucratic changes over the ensuing years,[29] its official purposes remained the same: to coordinate and control Japanese religious groups in central China and to promote their cooperation with Chinese counterparts. To the latter end the league established at least a dozen Japanese-Chinese Buddhist associations (described below). Those existing in November 1940 formed the Japanese-Chinese Buddhist Federation. In April 1941 an East Asian Buddhist conference was held in Nanking; and in May 1943 the Greater East Asian Buddhist Federation was founded in Shanghai, with Count Otani as president and Chu Min-i (the puppet Foreign Minister) as vice-president. Branches were then set up to supplement or supersede existing organizations. It is difficult to say how far these elaborate efforts got beyond the stage of paper work.

Japanese-Chinese Buddhist associations were to be found in

Nanking, Shanghai, Hangchow, Wusih, Soochow, Chen-chiang, Changshu, Pengpu, Nantung, Wuhu, Hofei, and Kiukiang. They were staffed by three categories of personnel: Chinese monks, Japanese priests, and local Chinese officials. If the head was in one category, his deputies would be in the other two. Among the membership, the sangha (mostly Chinese) generally outnumbered the laity. The work of these associations is variously described as relief, arranging lectures, and providing guidance for seminaries and devotees' clubs.[30] The real work, of course, was mobilizing China's Buddhists to carry out Japanese policy (thus offering a preview of the Communist treatment of Buddhism after 1949).

Although members included the Panchen Lama and the Chang-chia Living Buddha, only a few well-known Chinese monks appear to have been involved. Among them was Shuang-t'ing, the abbot of Chin Shan, who headed the Japanese-Chinese Buddhist Association in Chen-chiang.[31] According to one of his disciples, the Japanese authorities told him quite frankly that, if he refused this post, there would be "very serious consequences." Shuang-t'ing felt that his first duty was to protect Chin Shan—doubly vulnerable since Nationalist officers had been hidden in a cave there during the Japanese attack. Therefore he accepted. One reason for his decision was that the parent body, the League of Religious Federations, was committed to "do its best when Chinese monasteries and temples applied for protection." According to several informants, it generally succeeded. Well-known Buddhist institutions cooperating with the Japanese encountered few difficulties: not many monasteries were harmed.[32] Sometimes the occupation forces behaved badly (for example, one soldier killed a monk at Chin Shan "because of a language difficulty"), but most of those who visited the immense shrines seem to have treated them with respect or reverence.

The activities of Japanese Buddhists in China from 1871 to 1945 puts them in a darker light than I think they deserve. They were caught between conflicting loyalties. Some, no doubt, enthusiastically cooperated in their government's long effort to subjugate China, but others must have been troubled by com-

23   Japanese soldiers nap in a small temple during the advance in Honan, 1938.

punctions that even the alleged decadence of Chinese Buddhism could not dispel. There were many, I believe, who did their best to help their Chinese brethren within the confines of a national policy of military aggression.

CONTACTS WITH TIBET

Just as Buddhism was used by Japan to serve political ends in China, so it was used by China to serve political ends in Tibet. Indeed this Chinese use of Buddhism had a much longer history, going back to the early Ch'ing dynasty when the K'ang-hsi Emperor had sent an army to expel the Dzungars from Lhasa and install the seventh Dalai Lama. That initiated Ch'ing influence not only over the Tibetans but also over the Mongols, who belonged to the same theocratic system. K'ang-hsi and his successors became the patrons (*danapati*) of Tibetan and Mongolian Buddhism, which suited their Manchu mentality no less than it satisfied their political needs.

After the collapse of the Ch'ing dynasty, the Tibetans began to consider themselves an independent nation. Successive Republican governments tried to persuade them that they were not— that they were one of the five races of China and that Tibet was Chinese territory. In the effort to revive imperial policy, Buddhism was among the better cards in a poor hand: that is, the Chinese could still argue that Tibet was bound to China by a common religion. This was not altogether factitious. For example, one of the rites for the dead most commonly performed by Chinese monks—the *fang yen-k'ou*—was of Tibetan origin. Mountains like Omei and Wu-t'ai Shan had long been equally sacred to Chinese and Tibetan pilgrims and had provided the venue for Sino-Tibetan syncretism.[33] Most important of all, the Tibetan school of Buddhism had once flourished in the home provinces and could be made to flourish there again.

The Buddhism of Tibet was of the Tantric variety, noted for its use of magical gestures, diagrams, and incantations. During the T'ang dynasty it spread to China too, and from China it spread to Japan. This resulted in three distinct Tantric traditions —Tibetan, Chinese, and Japanese—which have had a complicated history. The Chinese form was suppressed by the end of the Ming but, when the Ch'ing dynasty became patrons of the Tibetan form, they established its temples in Peking and several other Chinese cities. These were entirely staffed by lamas who lived as they would have at home, spilling yak-butter tea on their magnificent brocades and occasionally performing the masked demon dances that became a favorite subject for Western photographers. After 1911 such lama temples fell on evil days, so that little of any form of Tantrism, native or foreign, remained alive in China proper. It was in this situation that some Chinese Buddhist devotees decided to import Tantrism for the second time from Tibet and for the first time from Japan. To them, as to some Europeans of that era, Tibet was a land of precious secrets, which they resolved to learn. It is difficult to ascertain the relationship between this personal interest and government policy, to say which came first and how each stimulated the other.

Government policy first entered the picture in the autumn of 1912, when President Yüan Shih-k'ai gave an audience to the Chang-chia Hutukhtu. Chang-chia was the last of a line of living buddhas who, since the seventeenth century, had served as trusted intermediaries between the Chinese government and the Dalai Lama. From the middle of the eighteenth century they had lived in Peking, where they ranked first among the metropolitan lamas and were lodged in the largest Peking lamasery, the Yung-ho Kung. The last of the line, born about 1889, also lived part of the time at Wu-t'ai Shan, over which he had been given jurisdiction by the Ch'ing government.[34] Considering this historical background, one can understand why Yüan Shih-k'ai wanted to consult him on Buddhist and borderland affairs.

Chang-chia took advantage of the opportunity. He urged Yüan to give equal protection to Buddhism of every sect and suggested that the problem of Mongolia and Tibet could be solved through religion. Later he was given a warm welcome by the Chinese sangha, whose members appreciated the leverage he had provided toward securing government protection of their monasteries.[35] That is, the government could not successfully use Buddhism as a tool for cementing relations with Tibet if it allowed Buddhism to be persecuted on China's own territory. This may explain why it was a Tibetan deputy who introduced the protective legislation of 1931 (see p. 143).

There seems to have been little further official action regarding Tibetan Buddhism during the first decade of the Republican period. It was the Japanese rather than the Tibetan form of Tantrism that attracted Chinese interest. Wang Hung-yüan, Kuei Po-hua, Ou-yang Ching-wu, Ta-yung, and others went to Japan to study under Shingon masters. In 1923, however, an important development occurred. For many years the Dalai Lama had suspected the Panchen Lama of cooperating with the British or the Chinese in order to undermine his supremacy, which he now decided to assert by levying taxes in the area under the Panchen's direct control. Summoned to Lhasa, the Panchen fled to India and in 1924 reached China. It would appear that his arrival—together with that of another important lama, who was also at odds with the Dalai—activated Chinese interest in the use of Buddhism for the recovery of Tibet. This other lama was No-na (1865-1936), a living buddha whom the Dalai had kept in prison for five years. In 1923 he escaped and in February 1924, as soon as he reached Peking, he was given a decoration by the Chinese government. He and the Panchen began touring China, lecturing on Tantric Buddhism, and winning many followers, among them high officials. Their followers were not merely taking part in a charade to support government policy; they were genuinely interested in the novelty, if not the profundity, of Tantric doctrine and in the acquisition of paranormal powers.[36] No-na was credited with all six *shen-t'ung* (seeing and hearing at a distance, reading thoughts, changing shape, knowing the past and future, and resolving all difficulties). When he lectured, it is said that tiny white relics would spray from his body and land on the audience. His disciples formed the No-na Students' Society (No-na T'ung-hsüeh Hui) to provide him with living and traveling expenses and to pay for the publication of his lectures.

Soon more Tibetan lamas began to tour China and to win disciples in the same way. The government was courteous to all of them; and to some it gave official posts and religious titles.[37] The Panchen was particularly favored. Not only did he become a member of the Mongolian-Tibetan Affairs Commission (as did

No-na and others), but he was chosen a state councilor in 1934 (a most prestigious office) and for some years received a subsidy to maintain his office in Nanking.[38] Whereas the government honored No-na with a fairly modest title ("Wise, Enlightened Teacher, Protector of the Nation"), the title it gave the Panchen implied that he ranked supreme in the Tibetan hierarchy—a claim that caused less worry in Lhasa than the possibility that the Chinese might escort him home with an army of occupation. Such a plan was actually underway when he died in 1937, after thirteen reluctant years as a Chinese pawn.

It is doubtful whether any of the lamas who toured China in the 1920's and the 1930's wanted to betray their native land. A few, like the Panchen, were at odds with Lhasa, but most were simply taking advantage of an opportunity to add to their prestige. That is, when they returned to Tibet after touring the cities of China, administering initiations to prominent Chinese, and receiving honorific titles from the Chinese government, they enjoyed a higher status in their own locality—not unlike returned students. On their tours they were also able to raise money for their home temples. Finally, they could bring the true dharma to displace what they considered to be the impurities of Chinese Buddhism. In Western books it is usually the Tibetan form of Buddhism that is called impure, but the lamas believed that this stricture more properly applied to the Chinese form since it was not, like theirs, of purely Indian origin. They pointed to many indigenous Chinese accretions, as, for example, the paper money, houses, and boats that were burned at funerals; the Chinese musical instruments used to accompany chanting; the clothing worn by monks (all of which was Chinese except for the *kashaya* robe); vegetarianism (not authorized, in the Tibetan view, by the Buddha); and Ch'an methods of meditation, which had been rejected in Tibet in the T'ang dynasty.[39] Many lamas thought that whereas complete enlightenment could easily and quickly be won by their own methods, Ch'an had never helped anyone to reach any enlightenment at all. This was partly because it did not place enough emphasis on formal study. In Tibet, Buddhist texts were studied hard, analyzed with hetuvidya logic, and then expounded in a stylized debate between students using shouts

and gesticulation to pour scorn on one another's interpretation—
all of which was considered beneficial to spiritual progress and
was entirely lacking in China. (This picture of the Tibetan attitude toward Chinese Buddhism comes mainly from a Chinese
convert who, as we shall see below, spent thirteen years in Tibet.)

The success enjoyed by the lamas on their tours—their prominent disciples and official honors—inevitably aroused the resentment of Chinese monks. Most Chinese monks were skeptical of
the efficacy of Tantric practices, which seemed to be a mixture
of Brahmanism and magical hocus-pocus. But a few of them took
a different attitude; indeed, they set out to master Tibetan Tantrism themselves. We do not know the degree to which this was
promoted by government policy. We know only that in 1924, the
same year that the Panchen and the No-na arrived in China,
Chinese monks began preparing to go to Tibet to study.

The first group prepared at a school set up by T'ai-hsü in Peking (to be discussed in the next chapter). The majority of its
graduates got no farther than the Tibetan borderlands, but three
reached Lhasa—Neng-hai, Ch'ao-i, and Fa-tsun. Fa-tsun returned
in 1934 to become the principal of the Sino-Tibetan Institute outside Chungking. This was the second Tibetan school that
T'ai-hsü established. Nearer Lhasa than its predecessor, it too
prepared monks for study in Tibetan monasteries, and was perhaps the only Chinese Buddhist institution to enjoy a government
subsidy during the Republican period.

The government took an increasingly active role as its plans
for the Panchen Lama matured. In December 1936 the Mongolian and Tibetan Affairs Commission inaugurated a program for
the regular exchange of Chinese and Tibetan monks. Two Chinese were to be selected annually by the Chinese Buddhist Association and sent to Lhasa for five years of study; two Tibetans
were to be chosen by "local government of Tibet" for study in
China. Early in 1937 the Nationalists invited Shirob Jaltso, an
eminent scholar, to lecture at five Chinese universities. "This was
the first time a Tibetan instructor had been provided for Chinese
university students."[40] Shirob, like the Panchen and No-na, was
at odds with Lhasa. Soon he too received a series of official
posts.[41]

Lhasa, of course, understood the thrust of Chinese policies. It did not permit organizational links between Buddhists in China and Buddhists in Tibet; nor did it give its blessing to many of the Tibetan lamas who went to China on lecture tours. (Most of the lecturers came from Sikang, over which it had no political jurisdiction.) On the other hand, it did not view their activities with unrelieved dismay.[42] There was the hope that if Tantric Buddhism became popular in China and if enough Chinese officials and businessmen became disciples of Tibetan masters, it would create an influential body of opinion opposed to any invasion of Tibet (just as Chinese Buddhists hoped that collaboration with their coreligionists in Japan would serve to retard the Japanese military). This may explain why Chinese monks were permitted to come to Lhasa to study and to remain for many years.

The effort by each side to use religion for its own political purposes can be seen in the career of one of my informants. Born of a poor family in Nanking, he had become interested in Buddhism as a young man. He got to know Lü Ch'eng at the Metaphysical Institute, who urged him to go to Tibet so that he could learn the language and someday return to translate Tibetan books. In 1933, already a monk, he enrolled at T'ai-hsü's school outside Chungking and became a disciple of a lama on the faculty. After three years in linguistic and religious study, he attracted the attention of the Mongolian and Tibetan Affairs Commission. In 1936 the commission assigned him to the Central Political Institute, which had been set up by the Kuomintang to train cadres. In 1937 he left for Lhasa, where he lived for eight years at the Drebung monastery—the largest monastery in Tibet, if not in the world—and received his *geshe* or doctoral degree. Evidently he won the confidence of the Lhasa authorities, for he spent the remainder of his thirteen years there running a Chinese school they had set up for Tibetan children and at the same time working at the Lhasa office of the Mongolian and Tibetan Affairs Commission, so that he continued to play the dual role of monk and political agent. This is not to imply that there was anything sinister in what he was doing. It was simply that the Chinese government had enabled him to pursue his interest in Buddhism for their own purposes, which he naturally expected to serve.

The presence in China of more and more Tibetan lamas and of Chinese monks returned from Lhasa stimulated the interest in Tantrism among the laity. Interest was also stimulated by patriotic hopes and fears. Some devotees believed that Tantric rites could unite the people psychologically and perhaps even protect them supernaturally. They recalled that when the Mongols tried to invade Japan in 1281, the Japanese had recited a mantra from the *Jen-wang hu-kuo ching*.[43] Thereupon a great typhoon had destroyed the Mongol fleet. In the same way China's enemies might be defeated in the twentieth century. During the spring of 1925 T'ai-hsü lectured regularly on the *Jen-wang hu-kuo ching* in Peking's Central Park. Sometimes a thousand persons came to listen, and many of them took the primary initiation, receiving a religious name with the character *jen*[44] to link them with the patriotic sutra they had just heard. About this time a Bodhi Society was started in Peking and in 1934 another Bodhi Society was set up in Shanghai, to promote the translation and study of Tantric texts. In Shanghai the Panchen was president and the members included some high-ranking former officials.[45] Such societies (which existed in many other cities besides) were regular stops on the lecture tours of Tibetan lamas and Lhasa-trained Chinese monks. Tantrism was in the midst of a small but spreading revival when the Communists took China in 1950.

CONTACTS WITH THERAVADA BUDDHISTS

The Japanese and Tibetans were Mahayana Buddhists with whom it would be natural for Buddhists in China, also Mahayanists, to have a close relationship. The same did not apply to the Theravadins of Southeast Asia—in Burma, Ceylon, Thailand, and Indochina. Not only did they have a different kind of Buddhism (which many of them regarded as "pure" in contrast to the "corrupt" Mahayana), but there was a much greater language barrier than between China and Japan, which used the same ideograms. Until Dharmapala's abortive visit to Shanghai in 1893, there had been no significant contact between Chinese and Theravada Buddhists for many hundreds of years. We have already noted how Dharmapala's ideal of a world Buddhist movement took root in China, first under Yang Wen-hui and later under T'ai-hsü. If the ideal was to be realized, there had to be not merely contact but communication. Few Chinese Buddhists knew English, which was already the ecumenical language in Southeast Asia, and almost no Theravada Buddhists knew Chinese.

Efforts to break down these barriers centered in cosmopolitan Shanghai. Sometime in the late 1920's Kuan Chiung, the distinguished founder of the Pure Karma Society, discovered a young Cantonese in a Shanghai law firm who was both proficient in English and interested in Buddhism. His name was Wong Mow-lam (or, in Mandarin, Huang Mao-lin). Kuan made it possible for him to resign from his job and, in 1928, to begin translating Chinese Buddhist texts into English. In 1930, as a further step toward expanding ecumenical communication, Wong was made editor of a new magazine, *The Chinese Buddhist*, published in English. Copies were sent to Southeast Asia and Europe; and soon letters from foreign Buddhist organizations were being published in its pages, soliciting Chinese correspondents and cooperation. This gave the Chinese real hope of winning a better image for Chinese Buddhism in the world at large and counteracting "the wrong impression that Buddhism is only fitted for the superstitious orientals," as Wong Mow-lam had put it in his first issue.[46]

Before long it was decided that Wong should go abroad to study Theravada and explain Mahayana or, as we might say today, to start a dialogue. With the sponsorship of the Pure Karma Society, he set out for Ceylon on February 3, 1931. He spent three years there learning Pali and Sanskrit. If he had returned to China, he might have played an important role as an interpreter between the two divisions of Buddhism. Unfortunately he drowned while out swimming one day, and *Chinese Buddhist*, which had already suspended publication, was never revived.[47]

In 1934 the Ceylonese bhikkhus Soma and Kheminda came to China to return Wong's visit. When they reached Shanghai they found no facilities for study and went on to Japan. Nonetheless, during their brief stay they spoke on the Buddhist radio station, XMHB, and met many Chinese devotees. They were followed the next year by Narada, another bhikkhu from the same temple (the Vajirarama in Colombo). Narada visited Shanghai, Hangchow, Soochow, and Hankow, and had a meeting with T'ai-hsü. In 1946, Soma and Kheminda again went to China, this time accompanied by Pannasiha, to teach Pali at T'ai-hsü's seminary in Sian. When their boat docked, they found that the civil war had broken out in Shensi and that Sian was inaccessible. After spending three months in Shanghai they returned home.

Whereas Asian Buddhist visitors to China came mostly from Ceylon, Chinese Buddhists went not only to Ceylon but to Thailand, Burma, India, and Indochina. Usually they went as pilgrims or for reordination[48] or to minister to the overseas Chinese, but sometimes their purpose was to study the Pali language and Theravada doctrine.

In December 1935 four Chinese monks left to undertake such study in Thailand, where they were welcomed by the Supreme Patriarch and lodged in a royal temple.[49] Before long at least one of them disrobed. Shortly thereafter five other monks were sent to Ceylon, where they received a Theravada ordination on May 6, 1936, and began what was to have been a three-year program of Theravada studies (as mentioned in Chapter Three). One by one they disrobed and scattered.[50] In 1940 Fa-fang arrived. He had been teaching in T'ai-hsü's seminaries since the early 1920's, and soon became lecturer in Mahayana Buddhism at the University of Ceylon. In 1945 he brought over two younger Chinese monks. They too disrobed.[51]

One reason for this notably unsuccessful record may have been that the sense of monastic vocation was undermined by exposure to foreign life and ideas. Another reason was the attitude of the hosts. From the Theravada point of view the Mahayana ordination was invalid. In fact some Theravadins considered that Mahayana Buddhism was such a dangerous heresy that its destruction would be a blessing for the world.[52] They saw no question of dialogue but only of correcting error. In this atmosphere Sinhalese laymen are said to have discriminated against the Chinese and refused to accord them the same deference they

gave to the Sinhalese monks, as, for instance, always taking a
lower seat and presenting them with *dana*. Hence the Chinese
monks became disillusioned and left. This information comes
from a Mahayana informant, whose account may be slanted.[53] In
any case, it seems likely that the Sinhalese were entirely unaware
of the sensibilities they were offending.

In China itself the attitude toward Theravada Buddhism was
ambivalent. On the one hand, the Chinese regarded it as too
narrow. Naturally they could not approve of its rejection of
Mahayana doctrine and its air of superiority. On the other hand,
a small but growing number of Chinese Buddhist intellectuals,
both monks and laymen, were coming to accept the thesis that
Theravada was indeed closer to Buddhism in its original form
than was Mahayana. Quite aside from the changes the latter had
undergone in India, there were the Confucian and Taoist accretions of which they became aware as they studied the history of
Chinese Buddhism in the newly established seminaries. Furthermore, as expounded by the Buddhist intellectuals of Ceylon and
Burma, Theravada seemed less vulnerable to the charge of
"superstition" and more compatible with the pronouncements of
science. The elite of the Theravada sangha seemed to be less involved in purely ritualistic activity and to devote a higher proportion of their time to preaching and meditation. For all these
reasons, and also because of the desire to join forces with the
Theravadins in spreading Buddhism in the West, Buddhist exchanges between China and Southeast Asia grew in number during the 1930's. In 1935-36 not only were students sent abroad,
but the Chinese donated four sets of the Tripitaka (two for
India) and acquired a plot of land to build a Chinese Buddhist
temple at Nalanda (the great Indian Buddhist university of the
seventh century). A "propaganda group" was organized to correspond and exchange news with Buddhists in the West. At a few
Chinese monasteries some monks began to observe certain rules
that had been observed in early Indian Buddhism and perpetuated in the Theravada countries. For example, in the new Pure
Land center at Ling-yen Shan, meals after noon were taken in a
"room for medicinal eating" rather than in the refectory, and
many of the monks who lived there ate only in the morning. It

became slightly less uncommon than it had been to observe the summer retreat (*vassa*), to recite the Pratimoksa twice a month, and to insist that a monk be twenty years old before he took the bhikshu vows.

Some of the Chinese monks who had gone abroad for reordination in Theravada countries made it a point, when they returned, to wear a saffron robe rather than the Chinese black, gray, or brown. Since it still had a Chinese cut, it symbolized, as one of them told me, their desire to reunite the two divisions of Buddhism. In a small practical way this exemplified the Chinese instinct to reconcile differences in a higher synthesis rather than to take an exclusive position on one side or another.

CONTACTS WITH CHRISTIANS

This instinct to synthesize can also be seen when it comes to Christianity. Many Chinese Buddhists regarded Christ as a bodhisattva (a buddha-to-be) whose life and teachings exemplified Buddhist principles.[54] Several syncretistic sects came into being between 1850 and 1950 that purported to combine Buddhism with Christianity, Taoism, and other beliefs. Partly because of such universalism, when Christian missionaries began to appear at Buddhist temples in the mid-nineteenth century, they had been treated with the utmost courtesy and kindness. For example, in 1850 an eminent abbot near Hangchow recommended an adjoining piece of land for the building of a Christian church. He made the recommendation despite his own experience of missionaries who, as he gently suggested, ought to "show greater tolerance for the customs of other religions."[55]

Tolerance was certainly not their outstanding trait; nor was it outstanding among the Christian tourists and businessmen—at any rate they called themselves Christian—who found it increasingly fashionable to regard things Chinese as inferior and absurd—particularly the "bonzes." Since they also found that the loveliest spots in China had been utilized by the "bonzes" to build monasteries, which were often the only places to stay on travels or holidays, the result was friction.

The chances for friction were less if all or part of a declining

monastery had been rented outright, as was common in the
Western Hills outside Peking, at the foot of Omei Shan in Szechwan, and sometimes on the southeast coast. The few monks involved either vacated the premises entirely or moved to a rear
building where, grateful for tenants, they were ready to put up
with whatever they had to. The situation was different when
Christian visitors stayed as guests at a prosperous monastery with
a full complement of monks. In 1924, for example, a doughty
Philadelphian, Harry A. Franck, visited Mt. Omei. Despite the
prohibition on the import of meat, of which he was fully aware,
he brought along several cans of it, as well as two live chickens
for slaughter on the very top of the sacred mountain. No sooner
had he arrived than he began to bargain over the price of accommodations, thus degrading the monastery to the status of a hotel.
(He should, of course, have waited until he was about to leave
and then made an unsolicited gift.) Since he felt that he was
being overcharged for the charcoal on which to cook his chickens, he took pleasure in making the abbot "lose face by coming
himself late in the evening and pretending to verify the weighing."

24   Westerners picnicking at the T'an-che Ssu in the Western Hills, Peking.

The next day Franck professed surprise at the "half-hostile attitude towards foreigners . . . [of] the fat, lazy monks." Elsewhere he calls them "cynical-looking young loafers." Yet he complains that (in spite of their laziness and cynicism) they had spent a good part of the night at their devotions, which he describes as such "a whooping and shrieking and general caterwauling as should have banished the most belligerent horde of devils as effectually as it did the sound sleep from which it frequently tore me."[56]

One could cite dozens of similar passages from the reminiscences of Western travelers and old China hands.[57] It may seem remarkable that after a century of such contact, the monks continued to be hospitable and courteous to foreigners who treated them with even a modicum of respect. But barbarian boorishness was easy to excuse, since it only confirmed the Chinese sense of superiority. Nor was this sense threatened by Christian polemics, against which the monks usually managed to make a fairly good showing. When Timothy Richard interviewed a leading Peking monk, he was asked, "Who sent you to China? Your sovereign?" Richard answered: "No, I would not have come to China if I had not felt that God had sent me." The monk said: "How do you know what the will of God is?" Richard's reply is not recorded, but in recounting the conversation he urged that Buddhism should not be judged by the ignorance of the ordinary monk.[58]

What did trouble the Buddhists was their inability to compete with the Christians materially. They did not have the unlimited funds that seemed to be available to missions, so that even if they wanted to, they could not build schools or orphanages on the same scale. Nor did they have the extraterritorial privileges that made it possible for missionaries to offer converts protection from Chinese law. Particularly resented was the fact that the 1929 Regulations for the Supervision of Monasteries and Temples applied to Buddhist and Taoist institutions, but not to Christian ones, which were of course exempt by "extrality." Furthermore, even before the end of the Ch'ing dynasty, monasteries had occasionally been turned over to Christian missionaries, who only had to dot the *wang* in order to make a Hall of Guardian Kings (T'ien-wang Tien) into a Hall of God (T'ien-chu Tien).[59]

For all these reasons, the Buddhist attitude toward Christianity gradually hardened. Anti-Christian feeling, which had first developed in response to Jesuit inroads during the Ming dynasty,[60] began again to displace the usual attitude that all religions were different aspects of a universal truth. It became common (presumably more so than it had been before 1860) for monks to warn their lay disciples against reading Christian books. The lay initiation often included an abjuration of heterodoxy.[61] I have been told by one eminent abbot that those Christians who are militantly anti-Buddhist and call the dharma "nothing but lies" will be reborn in hell and punished by Yen-lo Wang. Even persons sympathetic to Buddhism have not escaped censure. K. L. Reichelt, the Lutheran missionary, found much to admire, particularly in Pure Land devotion, and he incorporated Buddhist elements—including an incense burner!—in the altar arrangements of his Christian Mission to the Buddhists, first in Nanking and later in Hong Kong. The architect for the mission buildings in Hong Kong was no less a person than Johannes Prip-Møller, who designed them in the pattern of the Buddhist monasteries that he had spent four years studying. There was a refectory, library, and a wandering-monks hall, where pilgrims could stay in the usual manner. Gradually they were introduced to Christian doctrine and to such diversions as swimming, games, and language instruction. Many of them became converts, some even Christian pastors. The ingenuity of all this has seemed Machiavellian to some Chinese Buddhists. One abbot bitterly called it "that place that specializes in destroying Buddhism."[62]

CHRISTIAN CONVERTS TO BUDDHISM

The humiliations that Chinese Buddhists had suffered vis-à-vis Christianity, when added to the humiliations they felt as Chinese vis-à-vis the West, made it very sweet for them to find that a few Western Christians had been converted to Buddhism. They gave a handsome welcome to B. L. Broughton, the vice-president of the Maha Bodhi Society of London, who spent six weeks touring Chinese Buddhist institutions in 1933 and was the first Englishman to receive the bodhisattva ordination.[63] They also welcomed

Dwight Goddard from Santa Barbara, who came soon afterwards to get help with translations; M. W. Anthony, the first American to receive the bodhisattva ordination (on May 26, 1936); John Blofeld, who stayed at many monasteries in the late 1930's; and Miss Ananda Jennings, who went to study meditation at the Nan-hua Ssu in 1949. Probably the most famous Christian convert was Trebitch-Lincoln, born Ignatz Trebitsch in 1879. The son of a rich Jewish grain dealer near Budapest, he received an orthodox Hebrew education, but thereafter the variety of his *curriculum vitae* has few parallels in modern times.

From 1897 to 1904, having joined the Lutheran Church, he worked as a Christian missionary to the Jews of Hamburg; then to the Jews of Montreal as a Presbyterian, later as an Anglican; and finally he became curate of an English country village. This last proved stifling to his talents, which, after a couple of fallow years in London, blossomed again from 1906 to 1909, when he served as the director of a socio-economic survey of Belgium. The success of the survey led somewhat circuitously to a seat in the House of Commons, but this too proved stifling. He began to speculate in Rumanian oilfields, lost heavily, and, to cover his losses, signed his patron's name to a large cheque.

In 1915, posing as a German spy, he escaped to the United States, where he supplied military intelligence to the Federal authorities in Washington while intermittently eluding the New York police. He was finally extradited on the forgery charge to spend three years in an English prison. After his release in 1919 he joined the plotters of the Kapp Putsch in Berlin. When that failed he sold information about other protofascist plots to several European governments, ending up again behind bars. By 1922 he was ready to shake the dust of Europe from his feet. He headed for China.

In China he served as adviser to a succession of warlords (Yang Sheng, Wu P'ei-fu, Ch'i Hsien-yüan). It was one of the happiest times of his life, affording full scope for intrigue and political imagination. Before long, of course, he found himself overextended and began to travel—first to Europe, then to the United States, then back to China, where he resolved to enter a Buddhist monastery. For this purpose he went to Colombo,

Ceylon, in 1925. Soon he was living in the Vidyalankara monastery school and had mastered the doctrine well enough to be giving lectures himself at the Young Men's Buddhist Association. He displayed the same intensity as in his earlier religious phase —until in 1926 there came the news that his son was about to be executed for a sensational murder in England. He went back to save him, failed, and spent the next two years as a Buddhist missionary in San Francisco. Then he dropped completely out of sight.

In May 1931 he reappeared, to be ordained under the name of "Chao-k'ung" at Pao-hua Shan, the most illustrious ordination center in China.[64] This was apparently the first time that a European had become a Chinese Buddhist monk. Chao-k'ung did not want it to be the last, and so he went off to scour Europe for disciples. On July 25, 1933, he arrived in Shanghai with twelve of them—English, French, Italian, German, and Austrian, the women outnumbering the men by two to one. After he had given them a few months' training at his small temple in the French Concession, they were ordained at Ch'i-hsia Shan in a ceremony that lasted over forty days. Aided by an interpreter, they went through most of the same exercises as the hundred and forty Chinese who were ordained at the same time; this was not the "easy" ordination that was given to foreigners in Taiwan during the 1960's. A most eminent monk, Ch'ing-ch'üan, the retired abbot of Chin Shan, came to preside. Members of the diplomatic corps attended, as did "tens of thousands" of lay visitors, and stories were run by many newspapers in Nanking and Shanghai.

Despite this success, Chao-k'ung never seemed able to shake off misfortune. He had to live on borrowed money. He was suspected of being a Russian, German, and British spy—suspicions he did nothing to dispel by the wild-eyed books and articles he authored on international affairs. Two of his disciples committed suicide, one died, and others he expelled in his fits of rage. Although three of them eventually returned to Europe and worked intermittently as Buddhist missionaries, they did not bring back more Europeans to be ordained, as many Chinese monks had hoped. Nonetheless, the latter still speak of Chao-k'ung with affection and pride. Despite his checkered career (of which they

25 Chao-k'ung at his own ordination in 1931.

26   Chao-k'ung and his disciples before they were ordained in 1933: eight nuns in the front row; four monks in the back row; Chao-k'ung in the center with two Chinese nuns and two lay devotees.

are largely ignorant), it was he who at the end of a century of Christian privilege had enabled them to turn the tables on the missionaries.

CONTACTS WITH CHINESE OVERSEAS

Overseas Chinese tended to be more conservative and religiously inclined than their cousins at home. They did not face the task of modernizing China. The antireligious movements that swept the Mainland during the 1920's found few echoes in Singapore and Penang. Also, the roots of most of the overseas Chinese lay not in the official classes, which had a commitment to Confucianism, but among the poor and uneducated. Except for food, clothing, and shelter, they spent more of their income on religion than on anything else.[65] This was not only because of their religious

inclinations, but also because of their cultural pride, which was
all the stronger for residence in an alien environment. As some
overseas Chinese families prospered, generation by generation,
they became lavish patrons of Buddhism, both where they lived
and when they returned home. Monks from China therefore
made fund-raising tours of the overseas communities. Monasteries
in certain parts of China received much of their income from
overseas pilgrims.

Monks traveled not only to raise funds, but to spread the
dharma and to visit the holy places of Buddhism. One of the
most inveterate travelers of the past century was Hsü-yün. In
1889 he visited the holy places of Tibet, India, Ceylon, and
Burma. In 1905 he went to spread the dharma in Burma, Malaya,
and Taiwan. In Malaya alone ten thousand persons became his
disciples after hearing him preach. Here and elsewhere, almost
all of his audience was Chinese since he spoke no foreign language—this was not the beginning of a dialogue with the Theravadins. On a tour in 1907, however, he won a foreign disciple—

27   The ordination at Ch'i-hsia Shan in December 1933.

no less a person than the King of Siam. Interested to hear that Hsü-yün had been in a trance for nine days, the King came to see him, invited him to the royal palace, took the Refuges with him, and gave him a large tract of land, which Hsü-yün allocated to the use of the Chi-le Ssu in Penang.[66]

Sometimes he did not get so royal a welcome. In 1916 he was on his way back from Rangoon, where he had gone to get a Buddha image (another common motive for trips abroad).[67] When he reached Singapore, he was taken off the boat on the suspicion of being a revolutionary. Along with five other monks he was hustled to the police station, questioned, bound, beaten with fists, put out in the hot sun and not allowed to move. "If we moved, we were beaten. They gave us nothing to eat or drink and would not allow us to go to the latrine. This went on from six in the morning to eight at night." Finally some of his disciples heard about his plight and got him released on bail. The reason for his detention was said to have been a desire on the part of the Singapore police to please their "good friend," Yüan Shih-k'ai.[68]

Hsü-yün was not the only monk who went on pilgrimages and lecture tours overseas. In 1902-1906 Yüeh-hsia is said to have visited Japan, Southeast Asia, India, and even Europe.[69] Tao-chieh visited India, Burma, Malaya, and Ceylon. Overseas travel became commoner as ships and trains made it more convenient, as Chinese abroad became increasingly able to finance it, and as certain institutional relationships developed. The most important of these relationships involved the overseas sub-temple. Sub-temples were wholly owned branches of a large monastery. Most were in mainland China, but Ku Shan near Foochow had a sub-temple in Penang called the Chi-le Ssu. Its origins went back to 1885, when a delegation of Ku Shan monks was sent to Penang to raise money. One of them, Miao-lien, won a large following among the laity there. This enabled him to construct between 1891 and 1904 an immense, rather garish set of buildings that still covers a whole hillside outside the city. It is, in fact, the largest Chinese temple in Malaya. Under local law it was an independent institution, but in Chinese Buddhist eyes it was a branch of Ku Shan: the parent institution had the right to appoint its abbots and to audit its accounts. There was frequent intercourse between the two, since not only did officers go out to take up their appointments, but novices and devotees from Penang went back to Ku Shan to be ordained.[70] The Chi-li Ssu provided Ku Shan with a base for raising funds overseas and benefited financially itself. For example, Yüan-ying stayed there in 1939 when he was raising funds for the sangha rescue teams, but such was his eminence that the temple enjoyed a sharp increase in the donations for its own improvement and repair.[71]

One of the reasons for the success of the Chi-le Ssu was that most of the residents of Penang were of Fukienese extraction.[72] They could understand the dialect of the monks sent out by Ku Shan and were proud of the fact that it was the largest monastery in their native province. Penang, one might say, was in Ku Shan's sphere of influence. Another such sphere was Taiwan, also settled by immigrants from Fukien. Although there was no sub-temple there, Ku Shan lay just across the straits from Tamsui, so that travel back and forth was quick and convenient. The elite of the Taiwanese sangha went to Ku Shan to be ordained and to receive a few years of training.[73] Their names are given in its ordination yearbooks, along with the names of many Taiwanese lay ordinees. According to one informant, the Japanese authorities encouraged this religious traffic with the mainland and facilitated entry and exit procedures. Perhaps they saw a new way of using Buddhism for their own ends.

I have not heard of other monasteries in China that had such widespreading or deep-rooted connections overseas. Ku Shan may have been unique. But it was extremely common for monks and lay pilgrims to go back and forth between overseas Chinese communities and the "famous mountains" at home. Even at Wu-t'ai Shan near the Inner Mongolian border, one could find pilgrims from Singapore. In 1936, when Tai Chi-t'ao was on his way home from Europe, he stopped in Manila to lay the cornerstone of a new Buddhist temple sponsored by a group of overseas Chinese who, since 1930, had been serving as the Philippines distributor for a Buddhist publishing house in Soochow.[74] Here as elsewhere in Southeast Asia, Buddhism was a link with the motherland.

Chapter X

SECTS AND
DISSENSION

EXTERNAL attack may unify or divide. It is more likely to divide when different elements in the community under attack see different avenues to survival. Such was the case with Chinese Buddhism during the first half of the twentieth century. It was split into cliques and parties, not based on sectarian traditions but on conflicting views of vital issues, such as the relative importance of study and practice.

Sects continued to exist. Some gained in popularity while others declined. But they were not like sects in Christianity. A Chinese monk could belong to this or that sect in any one of several senses, of which the most basic was genealogical. That is, he necessarily belonged to the sect of his master and his master's master, just as a monastery necessarily belonged to the sect of the monk who had founded it. This kind of adherence was largely nominal, with no bearing on doctrine and practice. Most Chinese monks considered that the doctrines of all sects were true and their practices efficacious, but that for each individual, at any given stage of his spiritual development, certain doctrines and practices were more useful and congenial than others. Thus a monk might belong by lineage to one of the Ch'an (Zen) sects, but study T'ien-t'ai doctrines and practice Pure Land recitation.

This was extremely common, and it became even more so during the Republican period.[1] The reason was simple: there was no way to renounce one's lineage. Since most Ch'ing dynasty monks had belonged to the Lin-chi sect of Ch'an, their disciples after 1912 had no choice but to belong to it also. Many of them, however, having been tonsured in the Lin-chi sect and ordained under the Vinaya sect, went on to the newly established seminaries, where the texts they studied might be T'ien-t'ai, Avatamsaka, or Dharmalaksana. All of them recited buddha's name, since this was part of the standard daily liturgy at Chinese monasteries, and some of them were affected by the resurgence of Pure Land that centered on the Ling-yen Ssu near Soochow. Here, under the leadership of Yin-kuang, the reciting of buddha's name was raised to the same level of articulation and intensity as the Ch'an practice of the meditation hall; and it was carried by Yin-kuang's followers to other parts of the country.[2] So great was his influence that after his death he was generally recognized as the thirteenth Pure Land patriarch.

T'ien-t'ai, Avatamsaka, and Dharmalaksana are often grouped together under the general name of doctrinal schools (*chiao-men*). They received more attention not only as their texts entered the curriculum at seminaries, but also because they were championed by eminent monks: Ti-hsien, for example, championed T'ien-t'ai. "It was only by his efforts that the T'ien-t'ai school again became prosperous . . . More than one hundred thousand persons followed him as his disciples."[3] One of his disciples, T'an-hsü, established five large new monasteries in north China (see pp. 96-97). This was another factor in the resurgence of Pure Land, since those who studied T'ien-t'ai doctrines generally advocated Pure Land practice.

The revival of the Dharmalaksana sect[4] was led mainly by lay intellectuals, starting with Yang Wen-hui, and may be at least partly attributed to the interest aroused by the recovery of lost texts from Japan. This interest was heightened by similarities with European Idealist philosophy, which was just then being introduced. Probably more original writing was devoted to Dharmalaksana than to any other school during the Republican period. Ou-yang Ching-wu developed his own brand and made it the focus of study at his Metaphysical Institute. Han Te-ch'ing did likewise at the San-shih Study Society in Peking, while Hsiung Shih-li tried to amalgamate Dharmalaksana with Neo-Confucianism. Its advocates also included Wang Yu-chi, who founded the World Buddhist Devotees' Club in Shanghai; and T'ai-hsü, who was its leading exponent within the sangha.

The doctrines of the Avatamsaka sect were expounded by at least three eminent monks: Yüeh-hsia, Ying-tz'u, and Tz'u-chou, who lectured far and wide on its basic sutra. Yüeh-hsia even established a short-lived Avatamsaka University in Shanghai.[5] With respect to religious practice, there was a tendency for students of Avatamsaka to employ the Ch'an system of meditation.[6]

The rise in popularity of these sects did not mean that others went into eclipse during the Republican period. The Vinaya sect continued to flourish at certain monasteries that specialized in ordination, the most important being Pao-hua Shan near Nanking. There were also monks (Hung-i and Tz'u-chou, for example) who carried on theoretical studies of the Vinaya. As to Ch'an, it was still being vigorously practiced at monasteries like Chin Shan and the Kao-min Ssu, which were looked upon as models of monastic life and served as training grounds for the clerical elite. The most revered of all modern Chinese monks, Hsü-yün, was an advocate of Ch'an who treated the meditation hall as the focal point of the many large monasteries that he revived (see Chapter Five). He also made it a point to receive and transmit the dharma of all five Ch'an sects, including Fa-yen, Yün-men, and Kuei-yang, whose lineages he thereby preserved from extinction.[7] Other famous Ch'an masters were active too—Yeh-k'ai, Ch'u-ch'üan, Jung-t'ung, and Lai-kuo. However, it does seem to be true that, while Ch'an remained strong in certain monasteries, elsewhere the time and energy that the previous generation would have devoted to collective meditation now went into textual studies.

THE ESOTERIC SCHOOL

Mention has yet to be made here of the Esoteric or Tantric school. In Chapter Nine we saw how it was reintroduced from

Tibet and Japan. Here we shall examine the institutional consequences of this, first as seen in the Buddhist College for the Study of Tibetan, which T'ai-hsü opened in Peking on October 11, 1924.[8] It was housed in the Tz'u-yin Ssu near the Fou-ch'eng gate, one of the many declining monasteries in the capital, whose monks were glad to find tenants for empty buildings. Only five monks remained and, except for their own living quarters, they rented the entire compound to the college: three shrine-halls, a refectory large enough to seat the fifty students, kitchens, latrines, office, and apartments. In order that each student might have his own room, two new rows of apartments were constructed.

Of the fifty students, about two thirds were monks and the rest laymen. They lived in the same row of apartments and sat indiscriminately in the great shrine-hall (whereas elsewhere in China monks took precedence)—the laymen even wearing street clothes (rather than the clerical gown that was normal in this situation).

The purpose of the school was to prepare students to go to Tibet for further study. At the center of the curriculum, therefore, was the study of the Tibetan language, taught by a Chinese layman. The principal was a monk, Ta-yung, who gave a course in Esoteric Buddhism, which he had studied in Japan. T'ai-hsü, when he happened to be in residence, lectured on Hinayana and Mahayana treatises, particularly the *Ch'eng wei-shih lun*. Sometimes the Panchen Lama came over to teach Tibetan gathas.

The only Tibetan who was regularly attached to the school was a high-ranking lama from Sikang, Dorje Tsripa Gegen. He was noted for having a temple in Mongolia and a sister who was married to a British consul. His main responsibility was to preside over three sessions a day of religious exercises, conducted in the principal shrine-hall. Here, where Chinese monks had once stood to chant the liturgy, the students sat on cushions, as silent as in a meditation hall, each concentrating on the mantra or sutra that was most suitable to his character and stage of development. This kind of work involved certain risks. If a student's concentration wavered, one of the spirits attracted by the religious activity might take possession of his body; or if he concentrated on the wrong thing (literally "entered heterodoxy"), he might begin to shake all over. In either contingency the lama in charge knew how to bring him out of it, by throwing a handful of dry rice hard against his face. The lama could also *induce* possession. On one occasion, by reciting a powerful mantra, he summoned the spirit of an apsaras—a kind of Buddhist angel— into the body of one of the students. The latter knew only Chinese and Tibetan but at once began speaking in Mongolian, apparently the language of the apsaras in question. At all times, because of uncertainty as to how the spirits were going to be-have, the students would give notice of their arrival by snapping their fingers when they entered the shrine-hall.

It may seem strange that T'ai-hsü, who hoped to forge a union of Buddhism and science, should have created an institu-tion like this. It is true that he never took part in the Tantric exercises himself, but we may wonder why he wanted his stu-dents to do so when it could have made him vulnerable to the charge of encouraging superstitious practices. The reason was this: before uniting Buddhism with science, he wanted to unite the component parts of Buddhism itself. He felt that it would be incomplete without its Tantric component, which he therefore decided to revive. He planned to modify it and then to combine it with existing schools so as to produce a new, unified Buddhism, both esoteric and exoteric, in which adepts who knew the secrets of Tibetan lamas would live the pure life of Chinese monks. That is why, for example, although lamas are permitted to eat meat, the food served at his Tibetan College was strictly vege-tarian. Another reason for his interest in Tantrism was his eager-ness to prove that the Buddhist religion was not a mere relic of the past, but could serve the cause of national reconstruction. He was in touch with the Panchen Lama soon after the latter reached China and is said to have suggested his nomination to take the place of the Jebtsundamba Hutukhtu, the Mongolian Grand Lama and chief of state, who had died in 1924 (the year the Panchen arrived). Chinese irredentism towards Tibet and Mongolia offered T'ai-hsü his first big chance to make himself useful to the government.

His Tibetan school in Peking lasted two years, during which it was supported by several rich devotees,[9] so that tuition, room, and board were entirely free for those enrolled. After the first class had graduated, it closed down. About ten of the fifty graduates headed for Tibet. As we have seen, three of them reached Lhasa, but most got no further than Sikang, the border area between eastern Tibet and Szechwan. This was true of Ta-yung himself, the principal. He died in Sikang in 1929.

The successor school was set up by T'ai-hsü near Chungking in 1931 (the Sino-Tibetan Buddhist Institute). It was even more secularized,[10] operated for a much longer period (until 1949), and a higher proportion of its graduates seem to have reached Lhasa. It might therefore have had a greater long-term influence on the practice of Buddhism in China proper. The same may be said of the efforts of Neng-hai, an ascetic and much respected monk who had been a Nationalist general before he took the robe. After studying in Lhasa, he became the abbot of Chin-tz'u Ssu in Chengtu, which had previously been a typical Chinese monastery. Neng-hai turned part of it into an institute to translate and publish Tibetan scriptures, but, more important than that, he introduced Tibetan liturgy and meditation methods. At least some of the two hundred and fifty monks enrolled were bound to carry these methods elsewhere and thus contribute to a partial Tantrification of Buddhism in China. That is, when the Communists won in 1950, not only was Tantrism being revived as a separate school, but it was one component of a new amalgam that men like T'ai-hsü and Neng-hai hoped to make the Chinese Buddhism of the future.

THE ANTISECTARIAN TREND

While the popularity of different sects rose and fell during the Republican period, there was also a new trend against thinking in terms of sect at all. Monks and monasteries announced that they belonged to no sect or to every sect. In large measure this was simply an extension of the doctrinal inclusiveness referred to at the beginning of the chapter. Yet it also represented a protest against monopolistic private control of public monasteries, in many of which the abbotship was restricted to members of a particular religious lineage—resulting in a kind of family ownership that made for continuity but offended outsiders and violated, to some extent, the Buddhist tradition.[11]

Hence, for example, the illustrious T'ien-t'ung Ssu, which was Ch'an by lineage, became nonsectarian early in the Republican period. The abbot no longer had to receive the dharma of the Lin-chi sect to which it had belonged. This did not mean a total rejection of ancestry: the tablets of deceased Lin-chi abbots continued to be worshiped, and the Lin-chi board still hung in the meditation hall. But the monastery now belonged, as one investigator was told, to all sects.[12] Other institutions decided that they were nonsectarian on the basis of the varied work they carried on, even though the abbotship was restricted to this or that lineage. The last abbot of the T'ien-ning Ssu, for example, which was still Lin-chi in succession, told me that it "did not belong to any one sect, since it had a meditation hall [Ch'an], a hall to recite buddha's name [Pure Land], and a seminary for the study of doctrine [T'ien-tai, etc.]."[13] He himself had studied under T'ai-hsü, who was strongly opposed to the sectarian approach, partly because of his ideas about the unification of Buddhism and partly because lineal succession excluded his disciples from taking over important monasteries.

Sect thus became less than ever a basis for division and dissension during the Republican period. Buddhists were divided over the issues they thought critical for the future of Buddhism: study versus practice, philosophy versus religion, religion versus superstition, clergy versus laity. But they were divided in the first place by regional and personal loyalties.

REGIONAL LOYALTIES

Regionalism has long been an endemic feature of Chinese society. Differences of dialect and custom have made it easier to work with people from one's own area. Thus most of the large monasteries of Kiangsu came to be controlled by monks from a few districts in the northern part of the province.[14] Kiangsu monasteries had much in common with those of Chekiang: exemplary meditation halls, strict enforcement of the rules, and sizable landed income. Therefore, despite differences of dialect, the senior monks of these two provinces worked closely together, and they were in demand wherever Buddhism was less prosperous. That is, a guest prefect from Chin Shan might be invited to become abbot of a monastery in Szechwan, even in preference to a Szechwanese. When a Szechwanese, on the other hand, stayed in the wandering-monks hall at Chin Shan, he found the life unusually harsh and, if he enrolled in the meditation hall, he found it nearly unbearable. Yet he could see that this and other Kiangsu monasteries were endowed with great wealth and enjoyed close connections with patrons and high officials, who were royally treated when they came to stay. The senior monks may have lived a hard and simple life while in office, but once they qualified for retirement they were given comfortable private apartments, where they could spend the rest of their days without a care. It was perfectly possible for outsiders to work their way up in this system, but the fact was that most of those who had done so were natives.

All this aroused the resentment of monks who were not from Kiangsu and Chekiang. I remember talking to an abbot from Hunan, who had been at pains to impress upon me the high caliber of the meditation halls in his home province. "In Hunan," he said, "people seldom struggled for the abbotship, but there were fierce struggles in the monasteries of Kiangsu and Chekiang. Money was at stake. The Kiangsu people did not care about religious cultivation. Their specialties were money and fame. Chin Shan has been no good for decades." I have often heard such expressions of resentment against the "great abbots of Kiangsu and Chekiang" voiced by monks from other parts of the country.

It is interesting that among the twenty-four tonsure disciples and grandson-disciples of T'ai-hsü, there was not a single Kiangsu monk and only one from Chekiang, T'ai-hsü's native province. The reader may recall that it was the elders of the large monasteries of Kiangsu and Chekiang who prevented him from getting control of the Chinese Buddhist Association in 1931. Nor did they ever provide quarters for any of his schools or publications. It was not enough to be a native by birth: one had to be one by outlook, and T'ai-hsü's outlook was that the monastic system in these two provinces was ripe for reform.

If regional loyalty was a major divisive factor, personal loyalty was a minor one. Certain eminent monks had a large number of followers, who tended to look upon themselves as an elite; other monks, whose following was smaller, resented it. This may explain why some informants belittled Hsü-hün, claiming that his age was exaggerated and that his reputation was based less on his sanctity than on the miracles attributed to him.

DIVISIVE ISSUES

Study versus practice. The most basic and pervasive of the issues dividing the Buddhist community was the proper relationship between study and practice. Should a Buddhist devote himself to textual research and intellectual understanding of the doctrine, or should he spend his time in devotions, meditation, and reciting buddha's name? The extreme views were that he should do exclusively one or the other. For example, I was told by a youthful enthusiast for Ch'an: "Chinese Buddhism does not emphasize theory but practice, that is, the practice of the Vinaya rules and religious exercises. Scholarship and theory are obstacles. Scholars are so full of knowledge that they cannot be good at religious exercises." This was precisely the view of Chen-k'ung, the rector of the Mi-le Yüan in Peking who used to tell his disciples that reading sutras was a waste of time and that they should not read about what to do, but do it (see p. 84).

Far at the opposite extreme stood Ou-yang Ching-wu, with his contempt for everything but abstruse metaphysical and textual research; and almost as extreme was T'ai-hsü. In T'ai-hsü's plans to reform the sangha, he provided for a token quantity of religious cultivation, but at most of his own seminaries there was little or none. He himself rarely took part in meditation, reciting buddha's name, or even in daily devotions. What he emphasized was scholarship. On the lecture platform and in print, scholarship was the only element of Buddhism that would impress intellectuals, especially the young Chinese and foreign intellectuals on whom he felt the future of Buddhism depended. Furthermore, since they were the prime target, traditional scholarship was not enough. It had to be combined with a knowledge of Buddhism abroad, foreign languages, and science.

Between the two extremes lay many gradations of emphasis, some heavy on practice, others on study, others on balance. The abbot of Chin Shan, for example, told me: "In studying the dharma, you must first learn the scriptures and get to understand the main ideas. Afterwards you must devote yourself to religious cultivation. That way you cannot go amiss. If, on the other hand, you learn the scriptures but do not cultivate your own mind, it is like talking about a feast of the most nourishing delicacies and never getting a scrap to eat."

Some monks saw the need for balance on a rather different basis. In their eyes the important thing was to save all sentient beings. The Chinese sangha, they felt, had withdrawn too completely in pursuit of its own salvation and had been doing too little to spread the dharma among the laity. Yet the dharma could best be spread by persons who not only studied but exemplified it, and this meant that religious practice could not be ignored. That is why Yüeh-hsia's Avatamsaka University included a meditation hall and why Ying-tz'u and his disciples took part in seven weeks of intensive meditation every year at a Ch'an monastery. It is interesting that both Yüeh-hsia and Ying-tz'u refused to serve as abbots.[15] They were in favor of the practice carried on in the meditation hall, but spurned the administrative work that supported it. Ying-tz'u went so far as to forbid his followers to take any monastic office at all. To serve as abbot or prior, he told them, meant preoccupation with money. The same time could be better spent studying the sutras and lecturing on them to the laity. This alone was to follow the true bodhisattva path and "to pay back the kindness of the Buddha."

Philosophy versus religion. Closely connected with the issue of study versus practice was the question of the nature of Buddhism: was it a philosophy or a religion? In the eyes of many Chinese, philosophy was respectable while religion was not. The study of philosophy, particularly if it involved recondite ideas and textual criticism, was the prerogative of the scholar class, which throughout most of Chinese history had enjoyed the highest status in the community. The practice of religion, on the other hand, was conspicuous among the poor and uneducated; and during the Republican period, under the influence of Western intellectuals, it also became old-fashioned. That was one reason why in 1928 T'ai-hsü named his group in Nanking the Chinese Buddhist *Study* Association, and why after the Communist victory the principal new Buddhist monthly was named "Modern Buddhist Studies." The distinction between Buddhism as an object of study (*fo-hsüeh*) and Buddhism as a religion (*fo-chiao*) seldom comes through in English translation ("Modern Buddhist Studies," for example, simply calls itself *Modern Buddhism*), but it is important in Chinese. More than once Chinese friends have told me of a father or grandfather who took up Buddhist studies in his old age, emphasizing that his interest was purely philosophical, not devotional; this made him very different from the "simple-minded populace" that went to monasteries to burn incense and also very different from the monks who lived in monasteries, reciting sutras and practicing meditation. If he took an interest in any monastery, it was because of its historical or cultural significance or because of its usefulness to the community as a resort or retreat.

One of the leading advocates of the philosophical approach was, of course, Ou-yang Ching-wu. He regarded religion as superstitious. When the Japanese invited him to the East Asian Buddhist Conference in 1925, they were careful to address him as "Mr.," not as "Devotee" (*chü-shih*), the title commonly accorded Buddhist laymen, which he would have considered an insult. Liang Ch'i-ch'ao, had a similar attitude, as reflected in the following paragraph:

The Chinese have always been badly tainted with the poison of superstition; as Buddhism (*fo-hsüeh*) became prevalent, all sorts of belief in evil spirits and unorthodox doctrines as well as methods for public deception and popular delusion were revived in its wake . . . Students of Buddhism little realized that Buddhistic teachings (*fo-fa*) frowned upon this; indeed they acted in such a way as to further the trend, and even men who had been pillars of the New Learning twenty years ago talked about it avidly. If this [trend] continues un-

changed, then Buddhism will become a great obstacle in our intellectual world, and even those of us who have always treated Buddhistic
teachings with respect will henceforth be tongue-tied and afraid to
discuss it any more.[16]

What Liang Ch'i-ch'ao saw in Buddhism was a philosophy
that would serve as the basis for a Chinese renaissance—or
rather for a Chinese reformation. "The dawn of modern European
history came from two great waves: one, the revival of Greek
thought, which was the Renaissance; and the other, the resurgence of primitive Christianity, which was the Reformation.
Our country's new turning point hereafter should also develop
in two directions: one, the emotional which [involves] a new
literature and a new art, and the other, the rational, which
[involves] a new Buddhism."[17] It is not clear whether this course
of events was being predicted as inevitable or advocated as
something that could be brought about by vigorous effort. But
reading between the lines, one can sense, I think, that Liang
saw in Buddhism a weapon of defense against the cultural
imperialism of the West.

I shall never forget the way a disciple of Ou-yang's explained
to me the basic position of the Dharmalaksana school. First, he
said, there is Being (*sat, yu*) and non-Being (*asat, wu*). Then
there was realization of the unity of Being and non-Being. This
was the realization of Ch'an, which looked at anything from
three points of view (as Being, as non-Being, and as both Being
and non-Being). Then there was the concept that Being and
non-Being were alternatives, and finally the concept of "neither
Being nor non-Being." These had been grasped in the Dharmalaksana, so that it approached an object at the five levels and saw
it as five phenomena. As he concluded this explanation, he began
to laugh triumphantly. Here was the supreme formulation. I
asked if it had comforted Ou-yang Ching-wu in his many
tribulations and was told that it had.[18] In a culture where the
ultimate reality is textual and where the word may be more real
than the object, one can see the appeal of such doctrines to
those whose self-respect is imperiled.

Some intellectuals during the Republican period thought that
Confucianism had failed to save China from Western dominance

and that Taoism was too closely associated with the popular and the heterodox. Therefore they decided that they were Buddhists. This solution, however, only created the new problem of how they were to make Buddhism into something socially and intellectually acceptable, and what their relationship was to be with the others who considered themselves Buddhists, in particular Buddhist monks.

Clergy versus laity. Ou-yang, as we have seen, looked with contempt on Buddhist monks. He rarely visited their monasteries or welcomed them at his institute. This was partly because he considered them unversed in philosophy and preoccupied with practice, and partly because he was affected by the long-standing Confucian hostility toward monasticism. The Confucians justified their hostility on three grounds. In the first place, monasticism was of foreign origin, having come from India. Second, it was unfilial, since monks neither served their parents nor perpetuated their families. Third, it was antisocial, since they were parasites who consumed without producing and were not subject to taxes, conscription, or the corvée. But there were also anticlerical tendencies developing within Buddhism itself. Some lay devotees after years of studying the dharma came to realize that they knew more about it than the average monk; or, if they were active in social-welfare work, they saw that the average monk was doing far less than they to exemplify the Buddhist principle of compassion. Even with respect to religious cultivation, devotees who carried it on at home or in a Buddhist club came to feel that they were as good at liturgy and meditation as the monks who had trained them and that their home or club was in some respects more what a monastery should be than the monastery itself. All of this made them reluctant to accept the assertion that only as monks could they get beyond the third stage of the bodhisattva path.[19] Nor were they impressed by this or that monk just because he had sat in the meditation hall at Chin Shan. He had, of course, given up family life, but to some lay Buddhists this very fact may have been a subconscious challenge. He had "gone the whole way," whereas they remained householders. When they asked themselves, "Why is he any better a Buddhist than we are?" there may have been a certain satisfaction in being able to reply that he probably was not and to add, "Whatever he can do, we can do better."

This decrease in respect sowed bitterness in the hearts of members of the sangha, most of whom believed that their ascetic life, through its accumulation and transfer of merit, contributed to society in an important way. They were naturally disappointed when they discovered that this contribution was no longer valued so highly. A sincere monk, who had given up sex, wine, meat, and other creature comforts, who had worked many hours a day at chanting and meditation, and who had perhaps burned off some of his fingers as an offering to the Buddha, was not, of course, doing all this to win public applause—but nonetheless it must have been galling to find that some devotees simply wanted to know why he was not running a kindergarten.

The split between the sangha and the laity should not be overdrawn. The devotee who looked down on *most* monks might feel deep respect for *some* monks, and probably a majority of devotees continued to look on *all* monks as useful in the accumulation of merit and essential for the performance of ritual. For their part, monks were usually glad to see devotees taking a more active part in religious cultivation, since it increased their commitment to Buddhism and, on balance, the likelihood of their support of the sangha.

This worked to limit the hostility and sense of competition resulting from the trend for more laymen to engage in clerical activities while more monks became secularly active. Indeed this very trend, if projected into the future, would have eliminated the distinction between the clerical and the secular and therefore the possibility of competition and hostility. Already there were laymen who lived like monks and monks who lived like laymen. Examples of the former are provided by a staff of the Right Faith Society, by the intellectuals attending meditation at the Mi-le Yüan, by the devotees enrolled at T'ai-hsü's Tibetan institutes in Peking and Chungking, by the Buddhist club members who performed rites for the dead in Yünnan, and by those institutions where lay people regularly held monastic offices. As to monks, in some country districts they could be found living at home with wives and children and putting on their robes only to perform official duties.[20] Even within the orthodox sangha there was a radical splinter group that wanted to change the rules so that monks could marry.[21] In terms of the Vinaya rules, a married sangha would have been no sangha at all.

Religion versus superstition. The Chinese term for superstition, literally translated, means "erroneous belief." Naturally every one condemned it. The problem was that different people, even within the Buddhist community, had different ideas as to which beliefs were erroneous. The majority of monks and devotees, who believed in the efficacy of Buddhist rites,[22] were looked down on as superstitious by a progressive minority who did not, while those progressives who still took part in religious cultivation were looked down on as superstitious by metaphysicians like Ou-yang Ching-wu. The origins of this kind of snobbery can be traced back to Hsün-tzu (298-238 B.C.), the Confucian philosopher who asserted that the gentleman—the Superior Man—considered ancestor worship to be purely symbolic, whereas when the common people practiced it, they thought they were actually serving the ghosts of the dead (*Hsün-tzu* 19:21). Eventually religious attitudes became a criterion for class distinction: any educated person who betrayed a literal belief in ghosts or in the efficacy of rites for the dead was in danger of being lumped with the "ignorant masses."

Let me quote from two interviews to illustrate how this danger has affected Buddhists in recent decades. The first interview was with the abbot of Chin Shan, whom I was questioning about the volunteer plenary masses that used to be held by the monks at his monastery. Once a year during a long and elaborate ceremony, each of them put up soul tablets for his master and parents so that they might receive part of the merit being generated and thereby be aided toward a better rebirth.[23] It seemed to me that the number of monks participating would be a fairly good index of belief in the efficacy of rites for the dead. This was the point of my first question.

"Were there many monks at Chin Shan," I asked, "who preferred *not* to put up tablets and who took no part in the plenary mass?"

"Why?" the abbot replied. "It did not cost them anything."

"But perhaps some of them were opposed to putting up tablets."

"There was no reason for opposing it."

"For example, you know that here in Taiwan Reverend So-and-So does not approve. He does not favor soul tablets. He says that they are not a good thing. Some monks of T'ai-hsü's school . . ."

The abbot interrupted me: "They did not come to Chin Shan. If you came to Chin Shan, you had to follow Chin Shan's rules."

"So when there was a volunteer plenary mass, everyone definitely had to . . ."

"Definitely put up two tablets."

"If he did not put up the two tablets," I asked, "would the proctor reprimand him?"

"That couldn't have happened. There was nothing like that."

"You were at Chin Shan thirty years. During those thirty years was there any change in this respect?"

"There was no change."

"Every one still wanted to put up two tablets?"

"Of course they did."

"There was no modern . . ."

"If they were modern, they did not come to Chin Shan," he said, laughing. "We were old stick-in-the-muds (*wo-men shih lao fu-pai*)!"

The second interview was with a disciple of T'ai-hsü. He began by saying that rites for the dead were an expression of filial piety and acknowledged that sometimes they might be effective in releasing souls from hell. (I never have found a monk who was willing to condemn these rites completely—perhaps because of the fear of losing lay patronage or arousing the anger of fellow monks.) But, he said, rites for the dead were not a part of the orthodox Buddhist tradition. They had been created in response to popular demand. "The Chinese sangha has never opposed them, but we who expound the sutras and spread the dharma often criticize them. They were not a feature of Buddhism in ancient times, yet because people think they were, they look down on Buddhism as superstition. When you write about this, you must make it clear that these things are old Chinese customs, but do not belong to Buddhist thought."

At the end of our interview I asked him to convey my best wishes to a monk who was a neighbor of his. "I am not acquainted with him," he replied.

"But he lives at such-and-such a temple quite near you," I said.
"O yes, I know."

"Do you work on different lines?" I asked.

My informant smiled contemptuously and made the gesture of striking a wooden fish, saying: "He is tok-tok-tok . . ."—that is, he was the sort of monk who performed rites for the dead.

This illustrates what was referred to earlier—a kind of pecking order, keyed to superstition, within the Buddhist community. There was also such a pecking order in Chinese society as a whole. I have found that the Buddhists considered the Taoists superstitious; the Confucians considered the Buddhists superstitious; the Christians considered them all superstitious and were considered superstitious themselves by the Confucians and the Communists.

Conrad Brandt once remarked: "Superstition is somebody else's religion." This is true in a special way among Chinese, many of whom fear the charge of superstition in the same way that French intellectuals fear the charge of naiveté. In a Republican handbook on the city of Canton, devoted mostly to proud descriptions of its progressive administration, public utilities, and the sewage system, there is a table headed "Religious Beliefs of the Citizens of Canton." It lists 14,000 Buddhists, 6,500 Christians, 2,500 Mohammedans, 1,500 Confucians, 1,000 Taoists, and 1,099,000 atheists—a figure of which Moscow itself could be proud.[24]

The fear of being snubbed as superstitious has resulted in all sorts of anomalies. A Buddhist layman once told me that his father used to copy the *Diamond Sutra* or the *Heart Sutra* with a vermillion brush on yellow paper and then burn the characters on the anniversary of the birth and death of his mother. "It was not superstitious," said this informant. "It was not like the ignorant people who burned paper cars and houses during a plenary mass. I myself grew up under the influence of the May Fourth Movement and I am very much against superstition. When my father burned sutras, it was an act of filial piety."

Similarly a most eminent lay Buddhist, whom I had just heard disparaging "superstitious monks," proceeded to tell my fortune from the lines on my face. Then he said he could "make all the buddhas and bodhisattvas descend," that is, come down to his household shrine. He had me sit across from it, lighted two candles, and put them on the altar. The halo of the candles was supposed to grow larger and larger before my eyes until the Buddha paintings that hung on the wall came to life. Unfortunately this did not happen, and I said so. "Yes," he commented, "the size of the halo is proportionate to the reach of the mind of the observer." This particular devotee had made a deep study of Buddhist texts and was accomplished in religious exercises. He was also a cosmopolitan, equally at home in French, English, and Chinese. Another Buddhist layman, no less cosmopolitan, once told me that Chinese astrology was superstitious and had no scientific basis, but that *European* astrology was really dependable.

The most impressive witness to the fear of being called superstitious was someone whose identity I shall take pains to conceal, since he has both my gratitude and respect, and I find it hard to write about this question without appearing to mock, though nothing is further from my intent. This informant, who had been educated and lived in the West, was descended from a devout Buddhist intellectual who had played a major role in launching the Buddhist revival. His embarrassment over his forbear's piety was constantly at odds with his filial pride and his honesty. He kept emphasizing that the forbear had been very much opposed to superstition. He had been a scholar, interested in Buddhism only as a philosophy. He loved science and did not chant the sutras. He did not visit monasteries to offer incense or eat vegetarian food. No, his biography erred in saying that he used to sit in meditation and recite buddha's name. Although he had been active in the reprinting of Buddhist sutras, he did not believe in missionary efforts to spread the dharma. The purpose of reprinting was solely to facilitate scholarly research.

But as our talks went on, facts began to emerge that did not entirely fit this picture. My informant mentioned that his forbear ate vegetarian food on Kuan-yin's birthday. It was true that he had taught his children to recite the *Diamond Sutra* sitting in lotus position. And there was a year when he made every one in the family recite buddha's name for an hour a day to cancel the bad karma of a brother who had gotten into difficulty. Perhaps his biography did not, after all, err in stating that he often sat in meditation. Yes, he had hoped to reach the Western Paradise after he died, although he did not expect to be reborn at the highest level since he had not regularly abstained from meat and sex. When his mother died, he called in monks to perform Buddhist services for the usual seven weeks. After one of his daughters became a Buddhist nun, he did not allow the others to follow suit, but they did burn nine scars on their forearms. All this was true, but the important thing was that he had been a scholar, a *chün-tzu,* who had nothing to do with "vulgar superstition."

This ambivalent attitude toward religious activity was not a new phenomenon. Hackmann wrote, in the late Ch'ing dynasty: "It is often maintained that the faithful adherence to Buddhism, as regards the laity, is confined to the lower classes. It may well be that the cultured Chinese, the official, contemptuously smiles and scoffs at the superstitions of Buddhism. But this apparent contempt is not always genuine. Even high-placed officials, of mature age, not infrequently submit to Buddhism when the thought of death and the uncertainty of their future fate begins to weigh heavily upon them. They generally arrange matters so as to court observation as little as possible. A private chapel near their house or their place of business is the scene of their devotions, and the help they afford to monks and monasteries is rendered with all privacy."[25]

Soothill puts it more caustically. After describing the honors he saw paid by local officials to a new set of the Tripitaka, he adds: "Thus does the disdainful Confucian officer bow at the shrine of Buddha, just as readily as he does at any and every other shrine. He will recite a Buddhist chant 'as a sure cure for a stomach ache' and call in the Buddhist priests to release his father's soul from Hades, all the while in his heart despising the man and sneering at his methods."[26] Similar remarks have been made by many other outside observers.[27]

It is certainly true that for the Chinese intelligentsia religious practice has usually been a private pursuit, associated with withdrawal from society or at least from the public eye. Its incidence is therefore peculiarly difficult to estimate. In the early 1920's, for example, one of the leaders of the Young China Society was Ch'en Ch'i-t'ien. Later he played an active role in modernizing education and after the war served as minister of industry and commerce. He is one of the last people who might be suspected of an interest in Buddhism, inasmuch as the Young China Society in 1920 had voted to exclude from membership any person who had religious faith, and in 1922 Ch'en himself had been asked to chair a conference of the Federation of Anti-Religionists. Yet the fact is that he had repeatedly withdrawn from active life to immerse himself in Buddhist studies and once, for several months, had practiced meditation half an hour twice a day, sitting on his bed. To what extent this was religiously motivated is unclear. He says merely that it helped him to calm his mind and concentrate better while reading. But the religious significance of such activities was emphasized in some of the texts he read (for example, the *Awakening of Faith*).[28]

During the Republican period there were many others whose interest in Buddhism was discreet and whose motivation was obscure. Some of them were probably religiously committed; others must have felt no more committed to Buddhism than Westerners feel committed to Hinduism when they practice yoga as calisthenics. It is perhaps hardest of all to interpret behavior regarding rites for the dead. Many a bereaved son who was ostensibly antisuperstitious wanted to feel that he had done everything he could for his parents after they died. Hence he would have Buddhist monks perform their rites. Afterwards he might explain his act as "custom" or a "gesture of respect" and voice greater indignation than ever against "ignorant monks" and "popular superstition." Or, if he was more sophisticated and less on the defensive, he might attribute his behavior to half belief.

Half belief, as found in China, was a kind of doublethink, an ability to entertain mutually exclusive ideas as each was useful and appropriate, so that ideas matched the complexity of life and human needs. The origins of this point of view can be traced back to Taoist relativism and to the injunction of Confucius: "Sacrifice to the spirits as if they were there." The Chinese have

28 The bereaved eat a vegetarian meal while rites for the dead are underway.

always had a genius for makebelieve. Rather than rejecting the imagined in favor of the real, they have in the past been able to appreciate both, and thereby to accept and reject superstition simultaneously.

Thus in May 1963 a ghost named Old Huang was found to be haunting Murray Barracks in Hong Kong, which then housed the Resettlement Department. With the approval of the Colonial Government he was exorcized in an impressive ceremony, with nearly a hundred Buddhist monks taking part. Afterwards there was a lively exchange of letters in the English-language press, attacking and defending the government action. One of the communications from a Chinese reader ran as follows:

Sir, I do not believe in ghosts, but there were occasions when I was scared stiff myself. Ghosts may be unreal but the fear of ghosts is as real as a deep cut on a bleeding arm. Try sitting yourself in the dark some chilly night and imagine all the ghost stories you have heard, you would soon find yourself in a shaky condition and would perhaps scream aloud as if some ghost had actually tapped you on the shoulder from behind.

It is useless to argue with those who believe in ghosts and in houses being haunted because it is impossible to prove to them the truth of something that does not exist physically. Nor would it be practicable to ask so many people to visit the psychiatrists or lock them away in mental asylums.

Here is where a religious ritual comes in handy when other means fail. To the nonbelievers, the smell of incense, the beating of the gongs and whatnot and the monotonous chanting of the monks or priests may seem humorous, but to the believers, the continuous ritual concentration of reverence to both men and spirits does seem to be able to create a feeling of reassurance in the psychology of the ghost victims and thereby changes or pacifies the disturbed atmosphere of the haunted houses.

It is therefore not superstitious but wise to respect a religious ritual, though not necessarily believing in it, as long as it is capable of serving a good purpose of mystic cure.

In the past, at any rate, a related ambivalence has been found in the attitude toward orthodoxy. On the one hand, many Chinese intellectuals have appeared to be conformists, almost mesmerized by the word *cheng*, which means not only "orthodox" but "correct" and "symmetrical." Probably a majority of Chinese have felt that it was important to be considered *cheng* in terms

of whatever system of belief they adhered to. In Taiwan one can
see Chiang Kai-shek's personal name, Chung-cheng, "right on
the mark of orthodoxy," outlined by trees planted over several
acres of mountainside. When I was there last, the character
chung had become obscured by undergrowth. Only *cheng* stood
out, sharp and clear, visible from miles away. Across the Formosa
Straits, what the seventeen million members of the Communist
Party have feared most of all was the charge of "altering the
orthodox" (*hsiu-cheng*), the standard term for revisionism.

Yet most Chinese—including many intellectuals—have had
another side to their nature. They have been able to take off
their orthodoxy like street clothes and stand revealed in a tolerance so broad that Westerners might be taken by surprise.
There has been no concern for consistency, no need to reconcile
the contradictions of different ideologies, but simply an instinctive feeling that everyone in his own way was right and that
every system of thought, however heterodox, had its own orthodoxy and could be fitted into a higher synthesis. In the case of
Buddhism this meant not only that there was less reason for
sectarian controversy, but also that the same individual could
approach religion in different ways and at different levels, for
each of which he kept a separate mental compartment. Therefore the simultaneous rejection and acceptance of superstition
created no problem.

This sophisticated tradition would seem to be coming to an
end. Many of the Chinese who have studied abroad or become
converts to Christianity or Marxism are doctrinaire, exclusivist,
and orthodox in the Western fashion. They reject anything that
Westerners might call superstitious, regardless of its practical
and therapeutic benefits.

Conservatism versus reform. The great majority of Buddhist
monks and laymen during the Republican period were conservative, both religiously and politically. For them the golden age of
Buddhism lay in the past, so that improvement meant restoration, not reform. That is not to say that they refused to innovate.
Their attitude might be compared to that of the "self-strengthen-
ers" of a half century earlier. Buddhist practice was the essence:

modern schools and social action were the expedient means, to be employed only as might be necessary to protect or strengthen the essence.

There were, however, a small number of monks who liked reform for its own sake. To them the vision of sweeping away the past was deeply satisfying. Many were followers of T'ai-hsü. In theory they had renounced the secular world: in fact they were caught up in some of its swiftest currents and hence were furious with impatience at the conservatives who refused so much as to wet their toes. One can respect the sincerity of these Young Turks and sympathize with their desire to get Buddhism "into the swim," but one cannot help wondering if there was not an irreconcilable contradiction between their aims and their vows.

Not all the reformers were in T'ai-hsü's camp. His ideas were merely the best publicized. I recall one monk who had been presented to a temple at the age of ten because of his father's disillusionment with life. When we met, he was fifty-three. He had spent many years studying at Buddhist seminaries and had not left the Mainland until 1957, so that he had gone through "struggle" and "ideological remolding." Yet I got the impression that many of his ideas antedated his exposure to Marxism.

Early in our first interview, he expressed the view that wandering monks preferred to stay in small hereditary temples rather than in large public monasteries, which, he said, did not have so lofty a religious tradition. This was the opposite of what I had heard from everyone else. The adage runs: "When I sleep, may it be in a public monastery. It is impossible to practice the religion at a small temple." Asked to explain his criticism of public monasteries, he replied:

"They had been taken over by the people of orthodox lineage, who were able to get their grip on monastic property. The luxury they enjoyed as abbots was appalling. They had great airs, and in their dealings with outsiders they were snobs. [He himself was an outsider from Shantung.] The regulations at places like T'ien-ning and Kao-min [in Kiangsu] were too strict, and they were in accord neither with the Buddhist spirit nor with primaeval Buddhism. Collective meditation was too mechanical as well as too arduous. During meditation weeks at the Kao-min Ssu, monks not only became mentally deranged, but some died. Collective meditation was a delight for the 'old hands,' but misery for beginners. *The Code of Rules of the Kao-min Ssu*[29] is a perfect example of the feudal thinking and the monop-olization of power by the abbots. [He himself had never held any monastic office at all.]

"As to T'ai-hsü, his ideas on reform were good—for his day. Con-ditions have changed and are constantly changing, so that the reforms needed at any given moment differ from those needed earlier. Bud-dhist seminaries were too old-fashioned. They did not speak to the times, nor deal with the point of view of the youth. Japanese Buddhist education did, and that is why it is the Japanese who are spreading Buddhism today in the United States and elsewhere. Whatever in Buddhism is not in accord with science must be discarded."

"But if you did that, what would be left?" I asked.

"The basic truth of Buddhism," he replied.

"What is that?"

"Ch'an," he said.

Other reformers were more eccentric. One such, who came from Canton, considered that the reason for the decay of Bud-dhism in China was that it was actually Brahmanism in disguise. In his view, the only remedy was to purge it of Brahmanistic elements. His friend T'ai-hsü had wanted to establish a new system for the sangha, but he himself had preferred to reform the doctrine. Hence he had set up a series of "new Buddhist in-stitutes." He continued:

Chinese Buddhism has been too heterogenous. Take the big temples. You had your rules, I had my rules. This was bad. As to expounding the scriptures, you had your way, I had my way. Each person's inter-pretation was different. This was worst of all. The scriptures belong to Buddhism; they are not yours or mine. So things have got into confusion. For centuries Chinese Buddhism has had no future. There have been no people of talent. You know T'ai-ts'ang [the abbot of Chin Shan]? He is a rice worm. The various Buddhist associations have been useless—empty names. Seminaries have just been in it for the money. They teach "Chinese Buddhism," but the real Buddhism they don't know how to teach. They all talk about "eminent monks." That does no good whatever. That's all Ch'an talk—Hsü-yün's school. None of it can be relied on. I am not in favor of meditation. It is not a good thing. It is part of Brahmanism and essentially useless. As for enlightenment, it cannot be depended on. It is a very bad thing be-cause it enables those who have it to mock those who do not. It is not Buddhism, but heterodoxy (*wai-tao*). Sakyamuni did not speak of becoming enlightened. He only said that he had attained the Way. He did not say what the Way actually was. He did explain the Wonderful Law (*miao-fa*) and this explanation has real value. The *Surangama Sutra* is fake. The *Avatamsaka Sutra* is also fake. Some parts of the *Lotus Sutra* are fake, since the translator did a poor job . . . No, I do not know Sanskrit, but I can tell which parts are fake simply by reading the translation and I have edited them out of the new edition that I have prepared.

There are always those who delight in saying that everyone else is out of step but them (like this eccentric Cantonese), just as there are those who feel bitterly about a system in which they have not prospered (like the monk from Shantung) and others who want to change the system in order to win status and prestige (like T'ai-hsü). Obviously these are not mutually exclusive motivations, and all of them affected, to some extent, the various coteries of Buddhist reformers.

What the conservative majority wanted, on the other hand, was to preserve and restore, not to reform: to rebuild monasteries that had fallen into decay, to follow the models still embodied at Chin Shan and the Kao-min Ssu, and to adhere strictly to ancient rules. Almost all conservatives—from Hsü-yün to Ying-tz'u—took the same position on the issues discussed in this chapter. They put at least as high a value on practice as on study. For them, Buddhism was at least as much a religion as it was a philosophy. They did not consider that religious rites were superstitious. In their eyes innovations in Buddhism had to be justified on the grounds that its essence was thereby preserved. A seminary, for example, might properly be started in order to forestall the confiscation of monastic property; or it might be set up to train more monks to resume their ancient role of lecturers on the sutras. But its purpose could not be to produce a new kind of monk who was so secularly oriented that he verged on the anticlerical.

It was precisely here that the conservatives differed most vehemently with T'ai-hsü. Already in 1910 his first book had called for the transformation of Chinese Buddhism into a lay movement. Buddhism had been held back in China, he said, because it had been in the hands of the sangha.[30] That was the position that he was to hold for the rest of his life: basic disapproval of the monastic system to which he belonged. Two years later he participated in the "invasion of Chin Shan"—and attempted to change the system by force. Thereafter, both to excuse his participation and to justify his grandiose plans for reform, he exaggerated its defects. He almost outdid the Confucians and the missionaries in their scorn of superstitious and ignorant monks. Although this got him into the strategic position where he could not be scorned as superstitious himself, it also increased the friction with the conservatives. They felt that he was a kind of class traitor, who was "fouling his own nest" and violating the ties that bound him to his own masters, teachers, and brethren. His rejection of their values, his flair for self-promotion, and the airy way in which he disposed of them in his proposals to reorganize the sangha—all this they found wholly exasperating. It is little wonder that they would not allow their disciples to study under him and that they blocked all his bids for leadership until, during the Second World War, he managed to outmaneuver them. That is, when he finally won control of the Chinese Buddhist Association in 1945, it was not because he had won them over. It was because he had made himself the Buddhist whom non-Buddhists had heard most about, who had proven most useful to the government, and whose ideas seemed most in tune with the times.

In 1929, an American woman visited the T'ien-t'ung Ssu, where several of T'ai-hsü's teachers had served as abbot, and found that the senior monks there did not approve of T'ai-hsü. "They say he does not practice his religion. They think there is none to compare with my friend Yin-kuang, [who] has a much greater influence than T'ai-hsü [and] is more widely read by the general public." Soon afterward she visited Yin-kuang himself and asked the great Pure Land monk if "he felt no stir when he read of T'ai-hsü's attacks on him. It did seem to me that he at last warmed to his subject and that his deepset eyes were lit with some sort of fire . . . [To him] T'ai-hsü with his rushing here and there knows nothing of what Buddhism means."[31]

This is typical of the widespread feeling against T'ai-hsü and the tension that built up as conservatives struggled with reformers over issues affecting the survival of Buddhism—a tension that continues to this day. I remember interviewing a lay devotee from Szechwan, who spent his time teaching Ch'an meditation to a number of disciples and writing articles about Ch'an monasticism. He told me that he had no traffic whatever with monks from Ch'an monasteries. Monks were ignorant, he said, and knew very little either about monasticism or about Ch'an. I had heard elsewhere that he had been a monk himself in his youth, but to me he flatly denied the fact. Probably most revealing of all was the letter he had sent me before we met:

I am a person who prefers to be independent and withdrawn from the world. Indeed I look down upon all those who have so little discrimination as to get involved in worldly affairs. Hence very few people abroad know about me. But many of my pupils are well-known scholars and professors. In fact, they are all older than I am.

Why do I mention all this? Because one of my pupils inspected your letter (he is a lecturer at the University of Taiwan) and thought that you were probably the person who came to Taiwan last year to get information about the monastic system. At the time they all laughed about the fact that the people you went to see [Buddhist monks] were not the right ones to answer your questions. For our part, we make it a practice to avoid talking with the ordinary type of person who has only superificial knowledge, but pretends to know a great deal. If you do not approach us in the proper way, we will politely refuse to see you. As I heard the story, one reason they laughed was that already a student from Harvard had come to ask to study under me, from whom it became clear to me that it would be another two or three hundred years before you people understood the true spirit of Chinese culture. Because I advocate treating all men as equals, just as the Buddha did, and placing education above distinctions of class or race, just as Confucius did, therefore I have decided to send you four of my books.

Chapter XI

CHRISTIAN STEREOTYPES AND BUDDHIST REALITIES

At the conclusion of the preceding volume I suggested that the Western picture of Buddhism in modern China had been painted in darker colors than it deserved. I promised that in the present work I would explain how and why this had happened. Many of the factors have now been touched on; what remains is to show how they coincided— that is, how it was a historically logical coincidence for diverse groups to cooperate in the denigration of Chinese Buddhism.

First among these groups were the Confucians, who controlled the writing of history until 1912. They had traditionally censured Chinese Buddhism because they regarded it as heterodox and wasteful, and because they were competing with the Buddhists for imperial favor. Second, there were the Chinese novelists who began, about the same time as Chaucer and for similar reasons, to use the corrupt monk as a stock character: he was more interesting than the saintly ascetic. Third and more recently, there

have been splinter groups within the Chinese Buddhist community itself. T'ai-hsü and others like him had to justify their
effort to reform the sangha by exaggerating its defects. Fourth,
there have been Japanese Buddhists and Buddhologists, the former required by imperial policy to view Chinese Buddhism as
corrupt and the latter feeling an instinctive preference for the
ancient over the modern: one sign of modern decadence (in their
eyes) has been the intermingling of sects kept separate in Japan.
Fifth, there are the Chinese Communists who, as they write and
rewrite history, must justify their insistence that Buddhism rid
itself of the "dirty things" in its "feudal" past and serve socialist
construction.

Most of all, however, our picture of Chinese Buddhism—particularly of its condition in the nineteenth century—has been
darkened by Christian missionaries. During that period it was
they who did the most investigating on the spot, since they had
to take the measure of their opposition and to collect evidence of
the need for their work. By portraying the worst of what they
saw in the sangha, they could underline the importance of saving
its followers and stimulate those who were dropping pennies in
the China Missions box at home. There were also larger historical
reasons for their bias. From the sixteenth century onward Jesuit
missionaries had found that they could only work in China at
the pleasure of Confucian officials and only convert China by
converting the officials first. Hence they chose to see Confucianism as a rationalistic philosophy compatible with Christianity—
indeed as the ideological foundation on which a Christian China
could be built. They readily accepted the orthodox Confucian
pronouncements that Buddhism was a superstitious heresy confined to the ignorant masses—all the more readily because so
many Buddhist practices were also found in Catholicism (such
as celibacy, self-mortification, incense, rosaries, tonsure), with
the result that Catholic missionaries were in danger of being
confused with their pagan antagonists unless they disassociated
themselves by vigorous condemnation. These same "Romish
practices" were equally repugnant (for different reasons) to the
Protestant missionaries who began to arrive in the nineteenth
century. They were glad to accept the Confucian-Jesuit stereo-

type of Chinese Buddhism and to give it wider circulation than ever before.

Of the six persons writing extensively in English on Chinese Buddhism between 1840 and 1912, five were missionaries and the sixth dedicated his most important work on the subject "to all missionaries of every Christian creed laboring in China."[1] Aside from these six, there were dozens of others like them who incorporated their impressions of Buddhism in books on China in general. They had scarcely a good word to say until the 1920's— not at any rate, about Buddhist practice. Some of them found points to admire in Buddhist doctrine, but there were almost none who did not condemn the monks and monasteries that were supposed to exemplify it.[2] Most of them, indeed, took an attitude of churlish arrogance that in our ecumenical age makes odd reading. In 1845, for example, the Reverend George Smith (later Bishop of Hong Kong) spent a few days at the T'ien-t'ung Ssu, one of the model monasteries of China. Here is the entry he wrote in his journal for September 16:

I was disturbed at an early hour by a priest groaning in the anteroom and uttering doleful sounds, as he prostrated his body before the hideous idol, after relighting the perfume sticks. I remonstrated with the poor creature, who, with a vacant stare, asked me whether there were no Buddhist priests in my own country, and what idols we worshipped. I gave him a tract, which he was unable to read, and which I therefore received again. In the afternoon I passed through some lesser temples, in which a few priests were performing their customary mummeries. I was at length attracted to the principal temple [of the T'ien-t'ung Ssu], in which about thirty priests were engaged in celebrating the evening service . . . Some of the priests, while repeating the sounds, secretly held out their hands toward me, making signs for some of the books which I carried under my arm. At length they all bowed down for some minutes before the idol, with their muffled faces on the ground. The sight of such an instance of delusion overcame all hesitation on my part; and proceeding at once into the temple, I passed between the rows of priests and placed a tract before each of them, as they lay on the pavement beating their heads. The tract contained a remonstrance against the sin of idolatry . . .

In the evening I proceeded to an out-temple, distant a few hundred yards, where two priests were stationed. They appeared to take pleasure in exhibiting the ugly little idols which were enshrined within the principal hall. As I remonstrated with them, in the presence of many other persons, on the folly of asking me to worship such senseless blocks, I proceeded to point to the idols with my umbrella; whereupon the principal idol soon gave way to the force with which, in my carelessness, I poked its various parts. The whole assemblage burst into a loud laugh, on which I was emboldened to show how little the other idols could help themselves. As I gave them a slight thrust they trembled, tottered, and tumbled from their thrones. The people again laughed heartily, as the priests tried for some time in vain to make one of the idols maintain its sitting posture, the fall having disordered its component parts. Thinking that this liberty might put their good humour to too severe a test, I became more serious in my manner, and spoke of the wrath of God on those who thus dishonour his name. The only intelligible reply which I received was, that it was the Chinese custom to worship idols. In an adjoining room were a number of pikes lying in different directions. With these the priests armed themselves in case of robbery or depredation.[3]

Although the pikes were not wielded against Bishop Smith, he received a poor impression of the state of Chinese Buddhism:

The greater portion of these monks are either brought to the temple in childhood by their needy relatives or have been driven to find asylum within its walls by their poverty or crime in later years. The priests themselves acknowledged to me that this was often the case . . . Here these wretched specimens of humanity live together in idleness. No community of interest, no ties of social life, no objects of generous ambition, beyond the satisfying of those wants which bind them to the cloister, help to diversify the monotonous current of their daily life . . . The greater part of these wretched men saunter around with an idiotic smile and vacant look and appear little removed in intellect above animal creation . . . They abstain from animal food and repeat their daily routine of O-me-to Fuh till the requisite amount of purity and merit has been gained and the more devout are enabled to revel in the imaginary paradise of absorption . . . and become a part of Budh himself. How glorious in contrast to such meager hopes are the substantial realities which the Gospel reveals! 1 John iii.1-3.[4]

The next half century saw a vast expansion of the missionary effort in China, but little change in the attitude—or even in the surnames—of its leaders. In 1906 the Reverend Arthur H. Smith, "forty years a missionary in China," wrote the following: "Buddhism . . . has long since degenerated into a mere form. Its priests, like those of Taoism, are for the most part idle, ignorant, vicious parasites on the body politic. The religion, like many of its temples, is in a state of hopeless collapse."[5]

Neither of the Smiths had made a special investigation of the subject and, if their judgment is at fault, it may be attributed to ignorance. But Buddhism fared little better at the hands of missionaries who had devoted years to its study. The Reverend E. J. Eitel told a lecture audience in Hong Kong in 1870:

As to the [Buddhist] priests, they are certainly not very numerous in China; they are mostly recruited from the lowest classes, and one finds among them frequently the most wretched specimens of humanity, more devoted to opium smoking than any other class in China. They have no intellectual tastes, they have centuries ago ceased to cultivate the study of Sanskrit, they know next to nothing about the history of their own religion, living together mostly in idleness and occasionally going out to earn some money by reading litanies for the dead or acting as exorcists and sorcerers or physicians. No community of interest, no ties of social life, no object of generous ambition, beyond the satisfying of those wants which bind them to the cloister, diversify the monotonous current of their daily life.[6]

Does this last sentence have a familiar ring? It well may, for Eitel borrowed it, without the benefit of quotation marks, from Bishop Smith (three paragraphs above). We can see a tradition developing before our eyes.

Another German, the Reverend Heinrich Hackmann, who began as a Lutheran pastor in Shanghai, spent much of his life investigating Buddhist practice, not only in China but throughout Asia. Like an increasing number of missionary writers, he dwelt on the moral depravity of the Chinese sangha. "The moral level of the monks is a very low one ... Their religious duties are purely mechanical, carried out within their own restricted circle, and their life, instead of being an example of self-conquest, becomes a life of utter idleness ... All their intercourse with laymen is in connection with business ... Immorality of various kinds is but too common . . . Whoever is familiar with the outward signs of opium smoking can recognize smokers among the monks frequently enough, especially in the larger town monasteries."[7]

Even De Groot, not a missionary but a scholar, tells us that at many Buddhist institutions only the spacious temple halls exist, but the clergy who crowded them to make their hymns resound, have all but a few disappeared. Nuns are a rarity, and no longer dwell in cloisters, but in houses among the laity. With the greater part of the convents, religious wisdom has vanished. Theological studies belong to history; philosophical works have well nigh disappeared, and to collect a complete Tripitaka in China has become an impossibility. Propagation of the doctrines of salvation through preaching, which the Mahayana principles laid upon the sons of Buddha as one of the highest duties, has long since ceased. In short, from whatever point of view one considers the matter—conventual life is at best a shadow of what it was in past centuries.[8]

BUDDHIST REALITIES

Are these charges supported by the available evidence? Was Chinese Buddhism at the end of the Ch'ing really in so dark a state of decline and decay? Leaving aside such subjective complaints as the monks' "vacant look" and "revolting food," let us review the principal charges systematically.

(1) *The sangha was dwindling.* A census of 1667 showed 110,000 monks in China. A survey of 1930 showed 500,000.[9] Even allowing for considerable understatement in the earlier figure, there appears to have been an increase in the size of the sangha over two and a half centuries. Because no figures are available for the late Ch'ing dynasty, we cannot be sure how much of this increase occurred between 1850 and 1911, the years that concern us here. But it seems probable that some of the increase occurred during this period, if only on the basis of evidence supplied by the missionaries themselves. According to their observations, for example, the number of resident monks at the T'ien-t'ung Ssu near Ningpo increased from about 100 in 1845 to more than 250 in 1920. A similar increase seems to have taken place at Ku Shan near Foochow. The monastic population of the sacred island of P'u-t'o Shan apparently rose from 600 in 1845 to 2,000 in 1923. Intermediate figures indicate that in each case the increase came gradually.[10] This and other evidence seems to support the hypothesis that in central China, at any rate, the monastic population was on the rise during the late Ch'ing.

(2) *Buddhist scriptures were out of print and monks did not*

study them. Ten years before De Groot wrote that "to obtain a complete Tripitaka in China has become an impossibility," Timothy Richard was complaining that he had searched north China in vain for "standard Buddhist works" and that in the whole empire not one bookshop in a hundred had them for sale.[11] This was somewhat disingenuous. Already for three decades large-scale scriptural printing had been under way in Kiangsu—as Richard was well aware, for he had visited one of the scriptural presses in 1884. Indeed, he had long since purchased a complete set of the Tripitaka for £32.[12]

In 1895 he visited Hangchow, apparently for the first time, and was "surprised to find a Buddhist Tract Society shop in the city." Soon afterwards he went to T'ien-t'ai Shan where he found "a fine Buddhist library in good condition."[13] At about this time another observer noted the pomp and ceremony with which a new monastery near Wenchow received "from the north a valuable copy of the Buddhist classics."[14] The fact that "all the local mandarins ... went out in full dress to pay honor to it" suggests that it was the Lung-tsang edition of the Tripitaka, printed at the Po-lin Ssu in Peking. On at least four other occasions between 1890 and 1911, sets of the Lung-tsang Tripitaka were acquired by Chinese monasteries.[15] Yang Wen-hui was not altogether accurate in calling it a "dead letter" (see p. 3). Furthermore, such monasteries as the T'ien-ning Ssu in Changchow and Ku Shan in Fukien had their own presses with thousands of printing blocks in active use. Even Bishop Smith, when he visited the T'ien-t'ung Ssu in 1845, received a set of "sacred books."[16]

But were the sutras read? If, as many a missionary writer maintains, the sangha was illiterate, then they obviously could not have been. The available evidence suggests, however, that a majority of monks *were* literate and, in fact, better able to cope with the difficulties of Buddhist texts than laymen of the same educational level, since they were familiar with the technical vocabulary.

But do we not hear from some of the monks themselves that the Tripitaka usually stayed on the shelf except for the sixth day in the sixth month, when it was taken out for an airing? Wei-huan wrote in 1939 that "the Tripitaka in monasteries was looked on with awe, but never studied. It was kept in libraries and sunned once a year. Sometimes, but not very often, the monk in charge of the library might take a fancy to 'look' through the whole Tripitaka from the beginning to the very end, spending three years, without trying to understand the scriptures very thoroughly.[17]

In the first place, the monk who wrote these lines was a follower of T'ai-hsü. He had a vested interest in pointing up the need for reform and particularly the advantages of T'ai-hsü's new system of monastic education, of which he was himself a product. In the second place, the point that he appears to be making is a red herring. The Tripitaka was a vast corpus of six to eight thousand chapters. To read the whole of it was a misplaced effort for anyone but the professional scholar. We might as well call someone a poor Christian because he had not read the Apostolic Fathers. What mattered was whether or not monks read—and understood—the handful of basic texts.

Even where it is clear that the monks were engaged in reading them, Western observers have managed to discount the fact. When that formidable Englishwoman, Mrs. C. F. Gordon Cumming, visited a large Ningpo monastery in 1879, she noted that "in the library some students were droning drearily over the religious classics, which are said to be as dull as they look.[18] Poor Buddhists! Their only hope of winning the respect of such visitors lay in their next incarnation, when they might (if they had merited it) be reborn as beef-eating country parsons.

The way in which the largest number of monks studied Buddhist texts before 1912 was to attend the lectures often held at the larger monasteries, particularly in summer.[19] Once again we find that the testimony of missionaries must be read with caution. In 1890 Timothy Richard wrote that, since his arrival in China nineteen years before, he had never "heard a single public sermon from a Buddhist priest in China, nor heard of anyone else who had heard one."[20] De Groot concurred: "In the present corrupt era the clergy is too ignorant to preach sermons and the great mass [of the monks] is too stupid to understand them."[21] But in 1895, only five years after Richard had made the pronouncement just quoted, he was surprised to find that at T'ien-t'ai

Shan "there was a custom of preaching daily from the fourth to the eighth month."[22] About 1920, the Reverend Lewis Hodous wrote retrospectively: "A few years ago Buddhist sermons, however serious, were only listened to by monks and by a few pious devotees."[23] This is somewhat different from saying (as did Hodous' predecessors) that they were not listened to at all.

Chinese sources, of course, often refer to lectures on sacred texts given by eminent monks during the late Ch'ing dynasty (see p. 235ff). At least two of my own informants lectured widely in China between 1895 and 1911. They did not, however, make any special effort to apprise the missionaries of what they were doing.

(3) *Monks were of lower-class origin and had entered the sangha simply to escape poverty.* The first point in this complaint reveals more about the missionaries than about the sangha. Many of those latter-day followers of a carpenter's son liked to associate with the "best people," who, being Confucian officials, stood ready to confirm the darkest view of Buddhism, like their predecessors in the time of Matteo Ricci. Thus Herbert Giles quotes the eminent Ch'ing Confucian, Lan Ting-yüan, to the effect that nine tenths of monks and nuns "had been given to the priests when quite little either because the parents could not afford to keep them or in return for some act of kindness . . . These cloister folk do a great deal of mischief amongst the populace wasting the substance of some and robbing others of their good name."[24]

The truth about the background and motivation of monks (in recent times, at least) is far more complicated. Few of them entered the clergy as young children—closer to one tenth than nine tenths. Most entered in their teens and twenties for a variety of personal reasons: because of disappointment in love or business, because of illness or the death of relatives, or because they liked the monastic atmosphere or wished to devote themselves single-mindedly to the study and practice of Buddhism. Nor did most monks come from impoverished families. According to the little evidence available, they came from all levels of society, but particularly from the lower middle class—poor by our standards but not by theirs.[25]

(4) *Monks merely went through the motions of their religious exercises.* When he visited the temples of P'u-t'o Shan, the Reverend Charles Gutzlaff, who combined the distribution of tracts with the role of interpreter for British opium smugglers, was outraged by the lack of decorum. "None of the officiating persons showed any interest in the ceremony, for some were looking around laughing and joking, while others muttered their prayers. The few people who were present, not to attend the worship, but to gaze on us, did not seem, in the least degree, to feel the solemnity of the service." Robert Fortune, the English botanist who had also stayed at P'u-t'o Shan, quotes this passage and remarks: "What Mr. Gutzlaff says is doubtless true, but after residing for months in their temples, at different times and in different parts of the country, I have no hesitation in saying that such conduct is very far from being general . . . I have generally been struck with the solemnity with which their devotional exercises were conducted. I have often walked into Chinese temples when the priests were engaged in prayer and although there would have been some apology for them had their attention been diverted, they went on in the most solemn manner until the conclusion of the service as if no foreigner were present."[26]

It is understandable that different persons at different times might receive different impressions,[27] but what arouses suspicion is to find a single observer apparently adjusting his account to suit his audience. In 1902 Hackmann visited the T'ien-t'ung Ssu. He was allowed to enter its meditation hall and watch the monks at work there, a privilege until then accorded, so far as I am aware, to no other European at a model monastery in China. Here is what he wrote:

Entry was forbidden to unauthorized persons, as a notice in front of it announced, but the *tu-chien* [provost] allowed me to enter and so I walked quietly through the door. Within there was a solemn dimness and complete silence. All around the walls, as in the dormitory, were benches with cushions, upon which people sat here and there, perhaps twenty in all. No one paid any attention to me. They sat there, their gaze apparently turned inwards, with their legs crossed and hands laid together in the well-known posture of the Buddha sunk in meditation. There was not a sound to be heard. It was a strange sight. I stood there, watching for several minutes. They sat motionless, almost like statues. Then came the distant sound of a gong. At once, one of them got up and struck with a stick upon the bell hanging over him. Its notes shrilled again and again in the stillness that had reigned till now. Suddenly they all jumped up, put their dress in order, and walked still silent out the door. Most of them were young people and I would guess that this was a training for persons who had not long since entered the monastery. I had come in just at the end. When I wanted to witness another sitting in the afternoon, I was not permitted to do so.[28]

Three years after this was published in a missionary house organ, Hackmann described Buddhist meditation in a book for the general public: "Those who meditate betake themselves to the hall of meditation and in a certain prescribed attitude exercise their minds on the problem of abstraction. But almost everywhere, where meditation is still practised, it has changed into a lifeless and formal thing. This is especially evident where these meditations are worked out in company, as is customary in some monasteries, which boast of old tradition with regard to this rite. They differentiate between sedentary and ambulatory meditation. They are merely external exercises, carried out in a prescribed order."[29]

In his first account, written just after he had been to the T'ien-t'ung Ssu, Hackmann was obviously impressed by the seriousness of what he had seen. By the time he wrote the second account, he had decided that meditation was "lifeless and formal." Was this because he had been to more meditation halls and verified with some delicate instrument that what went on there was simply "external exercise"? Perhaps he had, although T'ien-t'ung's is the only hall he seems to have visited. There is at least one other possibility: that it would ill suit a Christian pastor to be favorably impressed by what he saw of Buddhist meditation.

It is obvious that many monks some of the time, and some monks most of the time, merely went through the motions of their religious exercises. This is true in every religion—indeed in every human activity. How many of Hackmann's parishioners in Shanghai, I wonder, were able to keep their minds on the prayers they heard him read each Sunday morning—and did the good

Doctor always manage to do so himself? There is some truth in this charge against the monks, but it is only a partial truth and of little significance. The motivation of animals is gauged in the laboratory by the magnitude of the shocks they are ready to incur in order to reach food. Similarly, perhaps, the degree of religious commitment felt by those monks who chose to live at large public monasteries can be gauged by the discomfort this entailed—discomfort so great and so well hidden from the laity (particularly in the meditation hall) that it cannot have been a mere commercial show. Many of them must, I think, have had genuine and fairly strong religious goals.

(5) *Buddhist monks were immoral and violated the monastic rules.* It is true that the nonhierarchical structure of the Chinese sangha left many of its members free to violate the rules, and some of them made themselves conspicuous by doing so. Usually they lived at small hereditary temples that were often in a state of disrepair; it is precisely from such temples that reports of immorality come.[30] The missionaries have little or nothing to say about the large public monasteries that have just been mentioned. Indeed they seem to have been unaware of the all-important distinction between public and hereditary institutions. Only rarely do we get even a hint of it, as when MacGowan remarks in some puzzlement that the monks of the Kuo-ch'ing Ssu were "strictly moral, being under a discipline too stringent for everyday monks, who find life there intolerable, although comfortable and free quarters are supplied."[31]

While missionaries did not (so far as I am aware) fabricate their reports of immorality in the sangha, they portrayed it as common to monasteries and temples without distinction of type—indeed, as so nearly universal that even if it could not be seen, it could be assumed. Hackmann writes: "Where the monks are under the rule of a strict abbot, who cares for the reputation of his monastery, these things are kept in the dark."[32] Giles had something similar to say about the consumption of meat and wine: "Whatever may be the forbidden dainties in which the brothers indulge beyond the limits of the cloister or in their own private apartments, it is quite certain that here before the eyes of the

public the commandments of the Buddha are in no way infringed."[33] This implies that the observance of the rules in public
was evidence of their violation in private. No comment seems
necessary.

(6) *Monks were generally despised.* Matteo Ricci was not the
first to report this. The missionaries who immediately preceded
him—Gaspar da Cruz and Martin de Rada—had already noted
how much less respect the clergy enjoyed in China than in Europe.[34] This has been one of the most persistent generalizations
about the Chinese sangha.

It is a fact that in some regions the clergy was not respected
to the degree it was in others,[35] and that in all regions one could
hear contempt expressed in public by literati who might show
respect in private. Since most monks came from rural areas and
many of them spoke with a strong rural accent, there was also a
tendency for city people to look down on them. Finally, they
were set apart from the rest of society by their dress, diet, and
mode of life. They were "odd" and so, like witches, they were a
natural object of transferred hostility.

All this may be true, but it is peripheral. What chiefly determined the prestige enjoyed by the individual monk was the type
of monk he was. There were several types, all clearly recogniz-
able and categorized as such by the Chinese. The missionaries'
charge that the monks were generally despised arose from the
failure to appreciate this fact. As in the case of monasteries, they
did not discriminate.

The most conspicuous type was the "wild monk" or "wine and
meat monk," who was noted for his indifference to the dietary
rules—and sometimes for brawling and thievery. He may have
been an entertaining fellow, but hardly an object of respect.
Another type often seen in the streets was the mendicant who
went from door to door soliciting money. The Chinese tended to
regard beggars as idle parasites, rejected by their families, and
made no exception for Buddhist monks. (It seems likely that
Ricci was mistaken for such a mendicant when he began to
spread the Gospel by going from door to door dressed in Buddhist
robes, which he soon exchanged for the Confucian scholar's
gown.)

Far more numerous were the "call monks," who earned their livelihood performing rites for the dead. Amounting to perhaps 80 percent of the sangha, they lived in hereditary temples, from which they went out "on call" to the houses of the bereaved. Hence they too were often seen in the streets. They seldom took part in meditation and ascetic practices; nor did they usually study or lecture on sacred texts.[36] There is no doubt that educated Buddhist devotees tended to look down on them as ignorant and commercial. But such devotees made up less than two percent of the population. The majority of the people did not insist on the higher forms of religious practice, about which they knew very little. Vegetarianism and celibacy were the most they expected of the clergy. So when there was a death in the family, they were satisfied to have call monks perform the customary rites.[37]

None of these types were mutually exclusive. Call monks sometimes begged and mendicants were sometimes "wild." But distinct from them all was another type: the monks engaged in religious cultivation (*hsiu-hsing seng*). Living much of the time in large public monasteries and seldom seen in the street, they devoted themselves to meditation, study, lecturing, and ascetic practices. They had the respect of educated Buddhists and were recognized even by non-Buddhists as a clerical elite.[38] Indeed they were an inconspicuous part of the Confucian establishment, often sought after by those emperors, scholars, and officials who happened to take an interest in Buddhism. If one chose to think of them as the prime representatives of the sangha, then it was anything but despised; whereas if one chose (like some missionaries) to think of it as represented by mendicants or "wild" monks, then it was anything but respected.

(7) *Monks did not go out to spread the doctrine among the laity.* It is true that prior to the Buddhist revival they did not *go out* to do so. When they expounded the sutras, it was inside the monastery and their audience consisted largely of monks. At any rate, there is seldom any mention of lay people in documentary sources, where the conventional phrasing is "Reverend X expounded the Y sutra at the Z monastery; there were N hundreds of people in the audience (*t'ing-chung*)."[39] We cannot tell how

many were monks and nuns and how many were male and female
devotees. In at least two instances, however, lectures were arranged by lay people: in 1905 Hsü-yün expounded the *Surangama
Sutra* in Kuala Lumpur and the *Bhaisajyaguru Sutra* in Malacca.
It is probably safe to assume that, when lay people made the arrangements, they also attended. Furthermore, right after many
of his lecture series, Hsü-yün administered the Refuges to hundreds or thousands of lay people, some of whom may have been
converted because they had heard him speak. In 1904 three
thousand people took the Refuges with him after his lectures in
Kunming. In 1905 over ten thousand did so after his lectures in
Malaya.[40]

I have already mentioned two informants who lectured widely
in China between 1895 and 1912. When asked about lay attendance, they insisted that it was no different in those years from
what it had been in the T'ang dynasty or from what it became in
the Republican period: there were most certainly lay people in
the audience. "When the lecture took place at a lay Buddhist
club," said one informant, "the laity predominated. At a monastery there were usually—but not always—more monks. In north
China, male devotees outnumbered females. In central and south
China, the reverse was true. In Kwangtung province, evening
lectures were common; elsewhere they were given in the morning. Usually the audience would thin out after the first few
sessions in a series. The social lions and lionizers, the wives and
children of devotees, would lose interest. Middle-aged devotees
stayed longer. Many of the elderly sat through every session to
the end of the series, even when it lasted a year. In any case it
is nonsense—arrant nonsense!—to say that before 1912 lectures
were attended only by monks."

Such participant testimony must command our respect, but
it is not altogether accurate, as one can see from the first sentence.
Before 1912 there were no lay Buddhist clubs; the principal
venue for lay attendance did not exist. The truth lies somewhere
between what we hear from these conservative informants, vigorously defending the condition of Buddhism in the good old days,
and what we hear from the followers of T'ai-hsü, eager to take
credit for starting the mission to the laity. In other words, before

1912 lectures were a regular feature of monastic life,[41] and lay people were welcome to attend, but no special effort was made to attract them. Nor did monks often go forth from the monastery to seek them out, partly because of the laws against so doing[42] and partly because the idea of aggressively spreading the dharma was foreign, if not distasteful, to most of the sangha.

Evidence of this intramural passivity is the fact that so many outside observers were impressed by the evangelism of the Republican period. To complete the quotation from Hodous, writing about 1920: "A few years ago Buddhist sermons, however serious, were only listened to by monks and by a few pious devotees. Today such addresses are advertised and are usually well-attended by the intellectuals. Often women are found listening . . . Not only monks, but laymen trained in Japan are delivering lectures on the Buddhist sutras. The favorites are the *Awakening of Faith* and the *Saddharma-pundarika Sutra*."[43]

Between 1912 and 1950, after the revival began, eminent monks like Ti-hsien, Yin-kuang, Ying-tz'u, Yüeh-hsia, Yüan-ying, Hsü-yün, T'an-hsü, T'ai-hsü, Hung-i, Yüeh-hsi—perhaps twenty in all—lectured in Shanghai, Nanking, Wuhan, Peking, Tientsin, Hangchow, Canton, Hong Kong and Chungking, and in smaller places like Yingkow, Harbin, Amoy, Swatow, Changsha, Kunming, Kweiyang, and Sian. The growing popularity of such lectures was partly due to the spread of mass media. Buddhists not only felt the need but they had the means to attract new converts. We know of course that these means did not exist in the nineteenth century.

(8) *Monks did no social-welfare work.* In terms of modern forms of social welfare, this charge appears to be entirely justified. I have yet to learn of a single school, orphanage, or clinic operated by the sangha before 1900. Its humanitarian role was realized in other ways, as we have seen.

This completes our review of the allegations against Chinese Buddhism as it existed before the revival began. On items 7 and 8, it is guilty as charged. Regarding 4, 5, and 6, a partial truth has been presented as a whole truth. The first three charges are, according to the evidence available, false.

Buddhists are entitled to make countercharges. First, their missionary critics generalized from insufficient data and assumed that what they had not seen did not exist. Just as De Groot in Amoy knew nothing about the scriptural presses in Kiangsu, so Timothy Richard, when he was still in north China, knew nothing about the lectures at T'ien-t'ai Shan. Hence they assumed that printing and lecturing were a thing of the past. If they had been more persistent in their inquiries, they would have found out sooner not only about lecturing and printing, but about the model monasteries like Chin Shan and the Kao-min Ssu, which, if they visited, they never mention.[44]

In the second place, although the missionaries' lack of persistence in searching out the good things in Chinese Buddhism is understandable, it is not so easy to excuse their determination to see nothing but evil. Such was their bias that even when there was something to be admired, they could turn it into something to be deplored. Nevius, for example, wrote that "it is worthy of notice, as an indication of the character of the people and the art with which Satan suits the forms of idolatry to the minds of his deluded victims, that there is nothing horrid or indecent in the appearance of any of the idols of China."[45] Similar passages have already been cited from the pens of Hackmann and Giles.

Because of their bias, missionaries did not distinguish the good from the bad or, if they did, the bad was all they reported. They should not be singled out, however, for selective reporting and distortion. These were common failings among foreigners in China, for reasons that we shall presently examine.

THE GROWTH IN UNDERSTANDING

Early in the Republican period, the picture of Chinese Buddhism began to be modified. It was modified, at least, in the eyes of Westerners who happened to read certain new books and articles which, for the first time, sought to approach the subject without religious bias. The earliest important example was the detailed study of the art and architecture of the sacred island of

P'u-t'o Shan, where the German architect, Ernst Boerschmann, had spent the month of January 1908.

[The monastic library] is a beautiful, impressive place . . . Here sit the more learned of the monks in contemplative peace, removed even from the minor disquiet of the monastery, at the highest point on its central axis, and immerse themselves in the mysteries of Buddhist doctrine. From the heavy cupboards they took out the precious books and explained much to me most readily. They are just as proud of their books as one of us would be. To be sure they said sadly that there was no point in explaining their doctrines to me, since I did not believe in them . . .

Everything makes an impression of orderly administration . . . The longer I am in the monastery, the more I am struck by its operation and by the conduct of the monks. Only rarely does one of them give the appearance of stupidity. In the afternoon I had a long conversation with two of the monks, who were extremely free, open, and self-confident, and who behaved impeccably. They were very well posted on the political problems of the railways. They asked whether we Germans had been first in getting the concession for the Peking-Hankow line, which I had to answer in the negative; and whether the big library in Berlin really had as many Chinese books as they had heard, which I could affirm.[46]

After observing a party of pilgrims—"hard-faced people who were really touching in their genuine devoutness" and whose religious needs were served by the monks "in a way that was a pleasure to see"—Boerschmann then makes the following remarkable statement: "The temple interests me more and more because here one can see active religious practice. Life and human needs are really involved. This religion is certainly not dead; the furthest one can go is to say that it is spiritually impoverished by formalism . . . Until we Europeans have mastered the subject, we should not allow ourselves to make a superficial adverse judgement about this religion, which, in spite of philological investigation, is still today a closed book for everyone."[47] Boerschmann wrote this on the basis of observations not merely at P'u-t'o Shan, but at sacred mountains and monasteries in fourteen provinces over a two-year period. Unfortunately, his book (written in German) had very few English and American readers when it was originally published, and today it is virtually unobtainable.

The English-speaking world got its first chance to read a defense of Chinese Buddhism in a volume by Reginald Johnston, published in 1913. Johnston not only defended it, but he attacked its attackers, the Christian missionaries, for their "fanatical intolerance" and "gross discourtesy."[48] The very vigor with which he stated his views impeded their acceptance.

It was perhaps inevitable that the first successful apologist should have been one of the missionaries themselves: the Reverend K. L. Reichelt. As early as 1920, when he proposed the establishment of the Christian Mission to the Buddhists, he had kind words to say. He explained that he had been in China for seventeen years, stayed in many monasteries, known many monks, participated in their daily worship and in their "solemn and quiet meditation in the 'changtang' [ch'an-t'ang]." He acknowledged that there were "so many black spots in their monasterial life, so many bad characters and pitiful backsliders. But this is only one side of their life; though it is unfortunately the side always most strongly emphasized. I have found in addition so much sincere piety, whole-hearted and holy devotion and beauty of character among monks that my soul has been filled with wonder."[49]

A few years later Reichelt argued even more pointedly. Admitting that "the inferior type of monk" was the one most often met with in China, he went on: "The many pious and high-principled monks live withdrawn in their cells and are unknown to the world. We, however, who have had a glimpse behind the scenes, know that there are such and that they are not inconsiderable in number. They too must be taken into account when the Buddhist society is judged."[50]

Reichelt's reappraisal was supported by his friends Lewis Hodous and Johannes Prip-Møller, as well as by several other writers.[51] But they could not remove from the shelves of the world's libraries the dozens of books and articles that their predecessors had written, nor the hundreds of books and articles for which these had served as sources. A stereotype of Chinese Buddhism had been printed. It proved convenient and indelible.

Even today, when reading recent scholarly work on the subject, one can sense in the background the ghost of Bishop Smith, waggling his umbrella.

In a book published in 1964—the best general history of Chinese Buddhism that has appeared so far—Professor Kenneth Ch'en of Princeton University concludes on the note that in recent years "moral and spiritual decadence was universal."[52] For "the most complete account of Buddhism in modern China," he recommends his readers to the work of Professor Wing-tsit Chan.[53] Writing in 1950, the latter reported: "The clergy is notoriously ignorant and corrupt. Temples are either in a poor state of preservation or saturated with an atmosphere of commercialism. Masterpieces of descriptions of this sad picture are to be found in the works of J.J.M. De Groot."[54] To some it may seem strange that Professor Chan, after a year's field work in China, should refer his readers to De Groot for descriptions of monasteries and provide none himself. But what seems even stranger is the gratuitous sarcasm and condescension with which he approaches his subject.[55] The effect of the stereotype is virtually unimpaired.

One reason for this is that Reichelt, the leading champion of Chinese Buddhism's good repute, was doubly handicapped. His indifference to sinological minutiae made him suspect in the eyes of scholars.[56] The warmth of his understanding aroused the resentment of missionaries, who became, in fact, deeply suspicious of his efforts to draw closer to the Buddhists. After his death many of the decorations embodying Buddhist motifs were removed from his mission at Tao-fung Shan.

Another reason for the persistence of the stereotype has been the effect of certain distorting factors, which have played a role in more than one Western misconception about China.

DISTORTING FACTORS

Almost everyone who went to China from 1840 on fell victim to a reaction. In the eighteenth century, European intellectuals had considered the Ch'ing empire to be the model civilization. In the nineteenth century, as traders and travelers encountered

Chinese realities, they found almost nothing of the model they had heard about. The pendulum swung from uncritical adulation to cynical contempt. Until about 1950 most old China hands felt that "John Chinaman" could never get *anything* quite right.

There were many minor but effective factors that exacerbated this feeling. One was the Westerners' failure to develop sensory check-valves. Stinks and hubbubs that the Chinese scarcely noticed, because they had learned to screen them out, became for Westerners the most striking element in a situation.[57] Similarly they were struck by dirt, which they associated with moral deficiency. I recall talking to a European Buddhist who had traveled widely in China, sometimes staying at monasteries where the bedbugs were so plentiful that she preferred to sit up all night. "No monastery," she said, "was well-run. Nothing in China was well-run. Everything was dirty, filthy, noisy, full of fleas, and disorganized."

"But were some monasteries relatively better run than others?" I asked.

"Oh yes, some looked clean and swept—but," she added bitterly, "there were still bedbugs. I did not get a good impression of the state of Chinese Buddhism."

Another minor factor has been physiognomic provincialism. Western descriptions of Chinese monks are peppered with sentences like the following: "Most of them had a stupid and unintellectual appearance . . . All had a kind of swarthy paleness of countenance, which was not agreeable to look upon."[58] The reader may recall the impression made on Bishop Smith by the monks of the T'ien-t'ung Ssu: "The greater part of these men saunter around with an idiotic smile and vacant look and appear little removed in intellect above animal creation." When a missionary's wife visited the same monastery eighty years later, she felt that most of its monks "looked like ex-brigands."[59] If the reader wishes to see for himself, he can scrutinize the faces of hundreds of monks in the pages of Prip-Møller, where he will find some that are certainly unprepossessing. To save him trouble I have included three photographs here. Figure 30 shows a party arriving on P'u-t'o Shan: note the cross-eyed monk on the far right. Yet the monk in Figure 31, who is also ocularly ill favored, happens to be the former abbot of the T'ien-ning Ssu. He originally entered the sangha because of eye trouble and was one of the two or three Chinese monks I came to admire most.[60] Appearances are deceptive; and the wise physiognomist limits his practice to his own race, if not to his own home town.

Every culture has different work habits. One nineteenth-century observer noted that some monks "did nothing all day but loll on chairs and stools and gaze upon the ground, or into space, or at the people who were working."[61] In the twentieth century, on the other hand, Boerschmann had the following to say about the officers of a monastery on P'u-t'o Shan, who emerged from time to time to sit in chairs outside the door: "It

29   Monks stare at a European visitor.

is exactly the same as with us, only that these monks, like the Chinese in general, get through such voluminous business in a relaxed way that it looks like an avocation. They seldom appear to be busy, are always friendly, and give the impression of having only a small amount of business to handle. But they work through-

30   Monks arrive on pilgrimage at P'u-t'o Shan.

out the entire day: they take no long periods for rest or diversion, and therefore they get no less done than we do."[62] I am not trying to argue that there was no idleness in Chinese monasteries, but only that outsiders unfamiliar with local work habits tended to underestimate the monks' industriousness.

There were other reasons why they tended to underestimate the amount of serious religious practice. The Chinese tradition is that the best things should not be put on display. Lao-tzu said: "The sage wears haircloth on top and carries the jade next to his heart." We have all heard about the curio dealers in Peking who, after the customer had proven his eligibility in the course of tea and conversation, let him see the *really* good pieces in an inner room. It was the same way with the inner rooms of the monastery, where serious religious practice was carried on. The casual visitor was not allowed to enter.[63] We noted earlier that the least exemplary types were the monks most often seen in the streets. Conversely, the most exemplary were seen least often—especially by foreigners. There was a specific geographical reason for this. Most of the foreigners who lived in central China

31 Cheng-lien, retired abbot of the T'ien-ning Ssu, the largest monastery in China. This picture, taken during a period of sealed confinement three years before his death, shows him seated by the wicket through which he carried on all communication with the outside world. Taiwan, 1963.

were businessmen who had little interest in Buddhism or in anything else Chinese. The Sinophiles preferred to live in Peking.
But Buddhist monasticism in Peking, indeed throughout the
north, had been in a state of decline for decades. The existence
of regional differences is one of the most important facts to be
grasped in appraising the state of Chinese Buddhism.

REGIONAL DIFFERENCES

Perhaps the first Western observer to report this was J. B. Pratt,
professor of philosophy at Williams College, who had an open
mind and a very sharp eye. He toured China in 1923-24, visiting
monastery after monastery in many parts of the country. In the
lower Yangtze Valley from Kiukiang to Ningpo, he found a "very
living Buddhism. New temples are being constructed, old ones
repaired and pilgrimages carried on, young monks are studying
and old monks meditating, throughout all this region."[64] But in
Peking, in the northern provinces of Shensi and Chihli, in Szechwan to the west, and in Kwangtung to the south, he found
abandoned monasteries and ignorant monks.

> One sees in Peking but little of the fervent worship so common
> in the lower Yangtze valley.[65]
> In Shantung the dominant religion is not Buddhism, but Taoism . . .
> There are a few Buddhist monasteries in secluded spots, but many
> of these are in a condition that is at least somnolent . . .
> All over central Shansi, in short, Buddhist temples and the Buddhist
> faith are quietly decaying . . . Conditions in Shensi do not differ
> greatly from those in Shansi.[66]
> In and all about Chungking things continue to be almost as bad . . .
> Most Buddhist temples of the region are in a deplorable condition.
> There is hardly one which has not as many Taoist as Buddhist images;
> nearly all of them are deserted and filthy; and a very large percentage
> have been quite handed over to non-religious uses—one, I remember,
> made into a place for the sorting of pig's bristles, another (dedicated
> to Kuan-yin!) used as a military store house for the drying of hams . . .
> In the city of Canton it is difficult to discover any traces of Bud-
> dhism. All the temples have been taken over by Dr. Sun and his
> followers; a few have been left to the monks, while the majority have
> been sold or given up to the military. The principle temple of the
> town, the Wa Lum Ssu [Hua-lin Ssu], is in a state of dirt and decay
> remarkable even for China. Its central shrine is closed, the place is in

32   Johannes Prip-Møller, the outstanding authority on Chinese Buddhist monasteries.

the hands of caretakers, no monks are visible, and the former dormitory and main court are now used for barracks. There is hardly a monk left in Canton. This may in part be owing to the continued state of war from which Canton so long suffered.[67]

All of this contrasted with the vitality of Buddhism in central China. Five years later Prip-Møller found the same thing. His investigations had of necessity to be carried on in "central China and the Yangtze Valley. Buddhism is in a more flourishing condition here today than in any other part of China and consequently the mutual relationship between the monastic frames and the life within them, the representation of which is the aim of this work, could be studied in no other place, not even in the often more beautiful but also better known and much more empty monasteries of the North."[68]

The reader can confirm this with his own eyes by leafing

33 The dilapidated drum tower of the Shao-lin Ssu, one of the most famous monasteries of north China, at Sung Shan in 1920.

34   The great shrine-hall of the Lung-hsing Ssu, Hopei, in 1920.

through the nine hundred folio plates in *Buddhist Monuments in China*.[69] Those magnificent photographs, taken between 1906 and 1929, show us one deserted monastery after another in the north, the northwest, and the south: grass on the roofs, purlins askew, rubble in the courtyards, and seldom a monk in sight. These are the very Chinese monasteries whose art and history made them the most visited and photographed, especially by Japanese but also by Western students of Buddhism. Occasionally one comes to scenes of Kiangsu and Chekiang. What a contrast there is! The monastery buildings look as if the tilers and plasterers had just taken down their scaffolding. Every brick is plumb, every paving stone immaculate. Monks in clean gowns stand in well-tended gardens.

One measure of the vitality of Buddhism in central China was that almost every large monastery there had been looted and burned to the ground by the Taiping rebels in the middle of the nineteenth century. Yet between 1864 and 1912—the last fifty years of the Ch'ing dynasty, when so much in China was on the decline—many of these same monasteries were rebuilt on a lavish

35   The outer buildings of the Asoka Monastery near Ningpo, Chekiang, in 1922, seen across the pond for the release of living creatures.

36 Chin Shan, about 1870 (compare Fig. 4).

scale, some larger than before, and they were soon filled with monks.[70] In Figure 36 the reader will find an interesting photograph of Chin Shan, taken about 1870. This was less than a decade after the Taipings had left its vast buildings in rubble; yet, as the original caption stated, they were "now in better condition than they had been for years."[71] Such rapid reconstruction required massive financial support from Buddhist devotees and protection from government officials. It is unlikely that their support and protection would have been forthcoming unless the religious practice of the monks had retained the respect of the community. This is one reason why in China wealth was an index of religious vitality. The largest and richest monasteries were "highest in moral strength and seriousness of purpose."[72] Such monasteries were found above all in Kiangsu and Chekiang.

Perhaps the most impressive evidence of regional differences can be found in Buddhist population figures. Here is a comparison, as of 1930, between six central provinces and six provinces of the north and south, listed according to the number of monks.[73]

	Monks	Devotees		Monks	Devotees
Kiangsu	91,400	1,139,540	Shantung	2,890	5,730
Chekiang	64,300	1,367,800	Honan	2,450	4,070
Hupeh	54,400	286,900	Hopei	1,780	12,120
Hunan	44,600	64,100	Shensi	780	3,490
Fukien	28,900	96,870	Kweichow	480	2,730
Anhwei	22,100	105,300	Kwangsi	350	15,070

These regional differences in the condition of Buddhism go back for decades or for centuries. It is important to remember that the early Protestant missionaries, based in Macao, Hong Kong, and Canton, became initially most familiar with the state of Buddhism in Kwangtung province, where regional decay—qualitative if not quantitative—had almost certainly begun.[74] Their reports of wine, women, and opium, which they undoubtedly saw, fixed the outlines of a stereotype that later observations in other parts of China were predisposed to confirm—predisposed by the distorting factors already mentioned and by the prejudices absorbed from Confucian conservatives and radical modernizers. As to Europeans outside the missionary community, we come back to where we started: Buddhism was a subject that interested only the Sinophiles and Sinologues in Peking, and what they could see about them there led them to think that it was virtually dead, its monasteries empty and available for rent to all corners by the day or the month.[75] Down in central China, where they could have found flourishing monasteries aplenty, the Europeans were mainly businessmen in the treaty ports, who were suspicious of people that claimed to admire things Chinese and were liable to regard them as soft-headed—perhaps in danger of "going native." They smiled knowingly at the writings of Reginald Johnston (who had indeed gone native) and kept their distance from the unfortunate monks whose temples they rented for summer holidays.

While it is easy to demonstrate that our picture of Chinese Buddhism has been distorted, it is very difficult to show what the degree of distortion has been. If, for example, we define a "good" monk as one who was serious about religious study or practice and followed the pure rules, then we might say that the stereotype includes almost no "good" monks at all. Now what am I trying to claim—that in actuality 5 percent were "good"? or 50 percent?

It is probably true that about 5 percent resided in reputable public monasteries, but there were many others—wanderers, teachers, students, hermits, ascetics, living in one or another kind of hereditary temple—who were certainly no less serious about what they were doing. In all I would guess that "good" monks amounted to at least 10 percent of the Chinese sangha.

I do not believe that this percentage was very different before and after the Buddhist revival. I think that it had long remained fairly constant, so that there was no more immorality and violation of the rules in 1840 than there had been in 840 or would be in 1940. Their incidence tended to be kept at about the same level by the operation of the monastic cycle. If anything, the Buddhist revival was accompanied by a slight drop in ascetic rigor. At any rate, in comparison to the late Ch'ing I have encountered fewer modern reports of such heroically ascetic practices as sealed confinement, wall gazing, vows of silence, writing sutras with blood, burning off fingers, and self-immolation.[76]

In other words, the Buddhist revival does not appear to have been a process of self-purification. What was it then? That is the question to which the final chapter will be addressed.

Chapter XII

THE MEANING
OF THE REVIVAL

T HE concept of a "Buddhist revival in China" was broached in Western literature as early as 1913 and was popularized by missionaries like Reichelt and Hodous before the end of the ensuing decade.[1] By 1924, when J. B. Pratt made his tour, the concept had become well enough accepted so that he used it as the title for one chapter of the resulting book.[2] Reichelt's major work on Chinese Buddhism, published in 1927, contained passages like the following:

When Professor Hodous and the author undertook not long since a rather extensive tour of a number of the leading monasteries, they found everywhere a feverish activity in restoring temple halls and enlarging guest rooms. This was partly due to the steadily increasing number of visits from bands of pilgrims and the growing habit of many educated and seriously minded Confucian scholars and teachers of withdrawing for shorter or longer periods of quiet contemplation and meditation in the monasteries . . . The leading monk in the new Buddhist movement is the famous T'ai-hsü. Besides him may be mentioned Yüan-yin.[3]

From 1920 onward we find far fewer firsthand accounts that dwell on the ignorance of monks. Was this because monks had begun to get a better education in the new seminaries? Similarly, we find fewer accounts that dwell on the immorality of monks and on their addiction to opium.[4] Was this because monastic morals were improving and the opium traffic was being suppressed? Or was it because those who wrote about Chinese Buddhism were now more interested in its merits than in its failings? Are we confronted with a change in the observers or in the observed?

The point of the preceding chapter was obviously that the observed changed less than the observers, and that much of what is called "the Buddhist revival" was simply a reduction in the distorting effect of Christian bias. But what about the contrary effect of Buddhist bias? If corrections are being made to arrive at a balanced assessment, surely this must be taken into account as well. What about my own bias? I have written at length on the condition of modern Chinese Buddhism, which has become, in effect, the "hero" of two large books. I have come to feel that it was wronged by earlier writers and that the wrong should be righted. Thus, quite aside from the fact that I am as incapable of perfect objectivity as the next person, I have a special reason for special pleading. Is it not possible, therefore, that I have amplified rather than corrected for the pro-Buddhist bias of Chinese informants? In China, more than in other countries, the truth is like a Dance of the Seven Veils—always one more layer underneath. That is why one often hears from Chinese friends: "Ah! You Americans are so naive." They mean that we take things at face value rather than looking, as they do, for "something in the background."

In Chapter Ten, for example, I quoted from an interview with a monk who specialized in lecturing. He concluded, as the reader may recall, with a contemptuous reference to a monk who specialized in rites for the dead. This I interpreted to exemplify the split between the two kinds of monks (see p. 210). Later I found out that my informant had been eased out of an abbotship in Taiwan by the maneuvers of the monk for whom he had expressed contempt: there was a long-standing personal feud between them. This did not invalidate my initial interpretation, but it added a new dimension to it. The same applies to the remarks of the monk from Hunan about the "great abbots of

Kiangsu and Chekiang" (p. 217). Some Kiangsu monks had also eased *him* out of an abbotship.

Over and over again I have discovered that informants were involved in personal enmity, either directly or as the heirs to the enmity of their predecessors. It may seem inappropriate for Buddhist monks to have such feelings, but, like most of the world's religious, they are only too human. In the old days on the Mainland, even the learned and devout could be petty or snobbish and get embroiled in factional jealousies and disputes about property and succession. Sometimes in the course of such disputes the long repressed desire for material recompense got the better of the belief that everything material was illusory; and the faith that greater hardship in this life meant greater reward in the next sometimes turned sour—a failure of motivation that is not without parallels on the American university campus. In such a case the monk might become really preoccupied with the acquisition of wealth and power—not unlike some of the famous eunuchs of the Chinese imperial court whose acquisitiveness represented the sublimation of their desire for progeny.

Today the only Mainland monks one can interview are refugees, and factionalism is always more acute among refugees, insecure and short of money, than it is among people back on their native soil. Correction must be made for all this in assessing what they have to say.

Correction must also be made in reading documentary materials on modern Chinese Buddhism. History belongs to those who write it, and the person who wrote more history than any one else was T'ai-hsü, the catalogue of whose works—merely the listing of titles—runs to 138 pages. He and his supporters published no less than eight Buddhist journals. Among them was the only one for which long runs may be found today in Western libraries: *Hai-ch'ao yin.*

Moreover, T'ai-hsü was the only Chinese monk who made a special point of developing relations with foreigners. By spinning off "world" Buddhist organizations, by welcoming foreign visitors at his various establishments, and by making tours abroad during which he portrayed himself as the founder and leader of the revival, his version of the Buddhist past and present came to be accepted by the outside world. Indeed, it was the only version that most foreigners had access to, aside from what they could read in books by Christian missionaries. For example, it is hard to tell where Radhakrishnan heard that "the monasteries are largely recruited from orphans who are left uncared for. Naturally the Buddhist clergy are not strong in intellect, piety, or energy." But it seems quite possible that he heard it from T'ai-hsü, of whom he wrote on the next page: "The most outstanding representative of Buddhism in China is abbot T'ai-hsü, who is learned, religious, and energetic . . . In the few hours that I was privileged to spend with him at his monastery, he made me realize his feeling of the urgency of reform and the need to get back to the inspiring example of the Founder of Buddhism."[5]

When I asked a disciple of T'ai-hsü what had caused the Buddhist revival, he said:

Buddhism had been going constantly downhill before the 1912 revolution, principally because of the lack of persons talented in spreading the dharma and lecturing on the sutras. The reason for this was the deep influence of the Ch'an school, which does not emphasize the written word. Therefore many Buddhists did not understand anything of the doctrines Sakymuni preached. Non-Buddhists, seeing that Buddhists did not know their own doctrines, looked down on them. It was to rectify this situation that eminent Buddhists began to take measures for the training of monks. It was also to some extent a reflection of educational reforms that were sweeping China even before the 1912 revolution.

Now there is much truth in this analysis, just as there is much truth in the opposite view. Precisely the opposite view, for example, was expressed by the three informants who began their monastic career in the 1890's (see p. 135). They remembered Buddhism in the late Ch'ing as flourishing. Those were the good old days, when monks really practiced and studied the doctrine. They themselves had traveled through many provinces in the period 1894-1911, lecturing on the sutras. As one of them put it: "The Ch'ing government protected Buddhism. There was food to eat. But once the Republican period began, monasteries were turned into schools, barracks, and government offices. They were not protected. The monks no longer had food to eat. They were helpless."

Both sides were telling part of the truth. The reformers emphasized how few monks had been lecturing on the sutras under the Ch'ing; yet the nonagenarians had then been lecturing on the sutras themselves. But the reformers meant lecturing to the laity, whereas the nonagenarians were lecturing mainly to brother monks. The reformers exaggerated the decay of Buddhism in order to magnify the need for their reforms. The nonagenarians exaggerated the prosperity of Buddhism because the golden age is always in the past and because, I think, they enjoyed telling me what we youngsters had missed. They flatly denied that government protection had ended and that confiscation of monastic property had begun at least seven years before the coming of the Republic.[6] They probably had very different ideas from the reformers about what constituted prosperity and decay.

Even if we turn to apparently unbiased outside observers, we find that they were prisoners of their language, their standard of living, and the bias of their Chinese friends, who were eager to show them what was modern and Western in China, not its Buddhist monks. Two experiences of J. B. Pratt's are revealing:

In Chungking, I was treated to one of those surprises which turn up every now and then in the study of Chinese Buddhism and which make one question the worth of all second-hand information concerning this elusive subject. We spent three weeks in or near this interesting city and one of my first undertakings was to visit the Buddhist temples and to question everyone I could find as to the local condition of the religion. The unmistakably moribund condition of Buddhism in Chungking is the first impression one gets, and I was assured by a number of resident Americans and Englishmen that nothing further was to be said about the matter. I particularly inquired as to preaching services in Buddhist temples or signs of a revival of Buddhism. An English businessman who had spent several years in the city and was much interested in the religious situation assured me that there was no attempt at Buddhist revival in Chungking and never a preaching service in any of the temples. Two American missionaries of many years' residence told me the same thing. Then, one morning, as I was strolling through the town, I dropped in for a second or third visit to the chief Buddhist temple, and found the place crowded with men and women, listening with great attention to a sermon by a monk. There must have been about three hundred in the audience. One of them told me that preaching services of this sort had been held in that temple every day, except in case of rain, for over three months.

Something similar happened to Pratt in Peking. The week before he left, he was asked to dinner by a Chinese admiral, who introduced him to the pupils at a Buddhist girls' school, founded three years earlier by the admiral and some of his friends. The pupils were vegetarians, dressed simply, and studied the sutras. Pratt concludes: "It was to me rather significant and rather typical of the Buddhist dislike for publicity that I had spent five months in Peking seeking for just this sort of thing before I happened upon the school, and that the best informed resident Europeans I met—men deeply interested in Buddhism—had never heard of it."[7]

Foolish is the man who declares that in China such-and-such does not exist, and rash is the author of handy generalizations. This is the concluding chapter, in which my task is to assess and interpret. Yet, let me repeat, even the simplest facts about Chinese Buddhism are sometimes difficult to establish; and they are always difficult to assess because they are incomplete. Until much more investigation has been carried out, every interpretation must be very, very tentative.

The Buddhist revival began, I believe, as an effort by laymen to reprint the scriptures destroyed in the Taiping Rebellion. It gathered momentum as the discovery of Western Buddhist scholarship stimulated the need for Chinese Buddhist scholarship, and as the invasion of China by Christian evangelists and missionaries led to the idea of training Buddhist evangelists and sending missionaries to India and the West. Up to this point only laymen were involved. The monks, isolated and secure in their monasteries, carried on as usual. But in the last decade of the Ch'ing dynasty, when moves were made to confiscate their property for use in secular education, the monks began to organize schools and social-welfare enterprises as a means of self-defense. They too began to be aware of the need to counter the denigration of Buddhism, to which Christian missionaries had added a new dimension.

The fall of the Ch'ing in 1911 removed the checks both on confiscation and on private organization. Parties, lobbies, and clubs were springing up everywhere. It was logical for the monks to form a lobby to protect their property and for laymen to start clubs that could serve as centers for studying and spreading the dharma and provide members with what Christian laymen could get at the YMCA. All these efforts, clerical and lay, expanded and interacted over the next forty years, reaching a peak that was cut off by the Japanese invasion of 1937.

What are the threads that run through this pattern of events? In the case of laymen one thread was the need for religious identity. John Blofeld tells the following anecdote.

Towards the end of 1943 a Chinese goodwill mission composed of five members and a secretary was sent to England. Upon entering each of the countries they passed *en route,* they had, like all war time travelers, to fill up forms giving brief particulars about themselves. At first, all except the one Christian member of the party left blanks in the spaces provided for religion, but later they became a little self-conscious about this and thought that something more was expected of such eminent representatives of their country, so they began writing "Confucian."[8]

The Western impact on China exacerbated the sense of intellectual insecurity that was common near the end of a dynasty. (It was during such a time of troubles that Buddhism had first taken hold.) In particular, the contact with Western religion made some Chinese dissatisfied with the latitude and fuzziness of their own religious tradition, in which most people were partly Confucian, partly Buddhist, and partly Taoist. The average Westerner had a specific religion. Why should a Chinese not be as well equipped or, like the most progressive Westerners, decide that he was an agnostic or an atheist? So during the Republican period thousands of people in China became atheists; thousands became Christians; and thousands became Buddhists. The lay Buddhist movement burgeoned.

Those who became Buddhists generally had one thing in common. Again it is relevant to quote an observation by John Blofeld: "The *chü-shih* [devotee] is usually a cultured person. He prefers to wear the dignified Chinese gown of blue, grey, or bronze-colored silk, and by his habits and gestures, exhibits his fondness for and understanding of the traditional culture of his country. He is often a poet or painter as well as a philosopher and metaphysician and may be something of a historian or possess knowledge of Chinese herbal medicine in addition. One can appreciate how essentially Chinese the Indian religion has become when one sees its devotees cling to the Chinese past more than almost any other group of educated people."[9] All that Mr. Blofeld says here I can confirm from personal observation.

To choose Buddhism in the search for religious identity meant that one was choosing to be Chinese. It was an expression of cultural loyalism, a denial that things Chinese were inferior.[10] Many of those who chose Buddhism were content to take it as it was. Others felt a need to change it into something that would command greater respect, both from foreigners and from their own countrymen. This brought cultural loyalism into conflict with the need for status—another thread that runs through the Buddhist revival. The need for status—intellectual status—led to the necessity of meeting the challenges of science and Western philosophy, of Marxism, and of Christianity. It helped to bring about the revival of interest in Dharmalaksana, the birth of Buddhist scientism, and participation in modern, Western forms of social welfare. It accentuated the fear of superstition and accelerated the shift from practice to study and from religion to philosophy.

Monks did not have the same problem of religious identity as laymen. They certainly knew they were Buddhists. Most of them became involved in the revival by the need for economic self-preservation, as we have seen. But some of them—whether because of personal insecurity or because they had closer contacts with the new secular currents than their brethren—also felt the need for status. T'ai-hsü is the outstanding example. He advocated whatever changes might be necessary to make Chinese Buddhism into something that no one—Confucian, Christian, or Communist—could look down upon. The irony is that he misread the situation. He thought that Westerners would be impressed by a Buddhism that featured science, scholarship, and welfare. He did not realize that the West already had an adequate supply of these commodities and that, in the long run, it would be far more impressed by just the things he was throwing away— China's unique forms of religious practice.

WAS IT A REVIVAL?

Strictly speaking, the term "revival" should mean that what has declined or expired is restored to the form it originally had, like the resurrection of the dead on the Day of Judgment. But in this sense nothing in history has ever been revived; rebirth has always to some extent been a new birth. Therefore the term "revitalization" may be more useful in describing a complex phenomenon like Vedanta or Neo-Confucianism or the Renaissance, in which only certain features are restored intact from the historic originals.

What elements of early Chinese Buddhism were restored in the period 1850-1950? Do we find, for example, the religious élan of the T'ang dynasty, with its doctrinal ferment, strong State support, and enthusiastic popular participation? We do not. Since the twelfth century, popular participation in Buddhist rites and festivals had been a matter of custom; State support had been limited and intermittent; and doctrines had been in a process of mutual integration rather than innovative change. Thus Chinese Buddhism had long since entered the state of equilibrium that is characteristic of mature religions. This does not mean it was dead or dying. It had simply passed through its initial, exciting, creative phase and now went on performing the functions required of it by Chinese society, which was itself fairly static.

Was there between 1850 and 1950 a renewal of Buddhist creativity in the arts? There was not. Buildings and images continued to be produced by skilled craftsmen, but their products were conventional and pietistic. The links that may once have connected Buddhism with painting and poetry had dissolved.[11]

Was there significant physical growth either in the number of buildings or in the size of the sangha? There was not. The widespread construction work in central China did not signify growth, but simply replacement of what had been destroyed in the Taiping Rebellion. In the outlying provinces, far more monasteries fell into decay than were founded or restored. As for the clergy, it seems likely that the number of monks did rise during the Republican period, but this signified the onset of political disorder rather than an increase in the vitality of Buddhism.

Was there a purification of monastic life, a return to the moral and administrative standards of the T'ang and Sung dynasties? There was not. Where the elite of the sangha was still strong and pure (as in central China), it simply remained so. Study, preaching, and meditation were carried on as before, subject to the monastic cycle of restoration and decay. Furthermore, there is reason to question the idea that a return to the standards of the T'ang and the Sung would have meant purification. In those dynasties the monastic system was more commercialized and secularly involved than it was between 1850 and 1950. For example, between 1850 and 1950 individual monks did not receive land from the State, as they did in the T'ang, when some became rich landowners and busy usurers. Abbots did not make it a practice, as they did in the Sung, of looting monastic property when they retired from office. Monasteries did not operate pawnshops and lotteries, or act as fronts for tax evasion by rich laymen. Monastery landholdings were not worked with temple slaves who were beaten to death by the monks so often that penalties had to be put into law. Ecclesiastical titles and ordination certificates were not sold by the State to fill its treasury at the expense of the quality of the sangha, so that hundreds of thousands of "monks" were laymen in every respect except liability to conscription and taxes. Yet all these practices were common during the T'ang and Sung.

With respect to immorality, scandal can be found throughout the history of Buddhism in China. As early as 389 C.E. monks were being castigated for their addiction to women and wine. In 446 C.E. subterranean apartments were found in one monastery in Ch'ang-an, where monks debauched with women of good family. The relationship between the Empress Wu Tse-t'ien and the politically ambitious monk who was her lover violated every moral principle, Confucian as well as Buddhist. Of course it is difficult to make quantitative comparisons, but if it is true that wealth and power corrupt, then there should have been a higher incidence of corruption under the T'ang and Sung than under the Ch'ing and the Republic. In this respect, at least, it makes no sense for historians of Chinese Buddhism to sigh for the past. It was for better as well as for worse that very little of the past was revived in the course of the so-called Buddhist revival. Except for Dharmalaksana and Tantrism, most elements of the revival were new.

These elements included the clubhouses where laymen met and lectured to one another on the sutras; the clinics, orphanages, and schools; the radio station in Shanghai; the work in prisons; and the efforts to start an ecumenical movement with Buddhists abroad. For the sangha, the new elements included the seminaries, the national Buddhist associations, and the interest shown by some monks in changing the rules—eating no food after noon, observing the summer retreat, and ordaining according to a different chronology—in order to conform with Theravada practice in a spirit of ecumenism.

Thus it is trebly misleading to speak of "the Buddhist revival in China." First, most of what occurred was not a restoration of the past, but a series of innovations; not a religious revival, but a redirection from the religious to the secular. Second, it never affected the Chinese population as a whole. The "occasional Buddhists" who made up the great majority of the laity and the "call monks" who made up the great majority of the sangha did not take part in it. Third, I believe, it concealed certain trends which, if they had continued, would have meant not a growing vitality for Buddhism but its eventual demise as a living religion.

If the Communists had not been victorious, what would Chinese Buddhism have become? Its fate would have been determined, I think, by the continuation of three trends: the decline in lay support; the deterioration of the monastic economy; and the shift away from religious practice.

The proliferation of lay Buddhist societies during the first three decades of the Republican period appeared to mean a rise in support for the sangha. But, as we have seen, it was offset by the growing strength of the enemies of Buddhism. Christians,

Marxists, and modernizers were taking over more positions in government and education as the elderly, conservative patrons of Buddhism died off. Many teachers in middle schools and universities were antireligious. Men like Wu Chih-hui and Hu Shih made Buddhism their specific target. Given these influences, little could come of efforts to interest the youth in the lay Buddhist movement. Almost every young Chinese who sojourned abroad, particularly as a student, returned to China religiously sterilized. To receive a Western education, even in Shanghai, was to lose some of the sense of awe a man had felt as a child when he was taken to the monastery by his grandmother and saw its enormous images and impressive rites. Scientism had far wider appeal than the philosophies of Dharmalaksana, Avatamsaka, and T'ien-t'ai.[12] The Buddhists' efforts to develop their own brand of scientism were more successful in providing comfort for themselves than in winning support from the intelligentsia at large. Although for members of the older generation—the diehard cultural loyalists—Buddhism could serve as a personal and national savior, most of the young saw salvation only in beating the West at its own game. In their eyes Buddhism had nothing to contribute to the anti-imperialist struggle. It did not even offer an ideological vehicle for their hatred of those who had humiliated China.

Equally hollow were most of the administrative feats that appeared to augur well for the monastic economy. It is true that monasteries were sometimes successful in defending their property against encroachment, in recovering property that had already been lost, and in buying more land with surplus income—often with help from the central government and particularly from conservative senior officials.[13] It is not accurate to say that the Kuomintang took "the most draconian measures against temples and clergy."[14] The Nationalist regulations of 1929, to the extent that they had any effect, were more protective than repressive. But after 1926, pressure for land reform was on the rise. Its advocates made no distinction between the individual landlord, whose rents provided luxury for himself and his family, and the landowning monastery, whose rents made it possible for hundreds of persons to live an ascetic life and practice their religion. Therefore no such distinction was made in the laws. In 1942 a law was passed calling for the redistribution of land. Although it was not implemented, it was an omen for the future. Even if the monasteries had continued to be legally protected against confiscation, they would not have been protected against redistribution, and it seems probable that they would eventually have been forced to surrender their land in exchange for bonds of doubtful value.

Already their income from land was being reduced by the unrest in the countryside.[15] Their income from rites for the dead was declining as the family system weakened and care of the dead became less important and more old-fashioned. Their income from donations was dropping as rich devotees died off or diverted part of their religious expenditure to lay clubs and charities. This economic squeeze became appreciable in 1927 and was greatly exacerbated by the Japanese invasion a decade later. By the late 1930's it was clear that other sources of income for monasteries or other means of livelihood for monks would have to be developed. A rich monastery in Changchow started trading in rice. Another in T'ai-chou opened a "work-study center" where monks were taught how to support themselves by manual labor.[16] One of the goals of the Chinese Buddhist Association, mentioned in its successive charters, was "to promote productive labor by the sangha."[17]

Even in central China, then, the facade of monastic prosperity, which lasted until 1950, was being undermined. If the process had continued after 1950, more and more monks would have had to devote more and more of their time to the hotel and restaurant business (which had heretofore been only a sideline at the better monasteries), to other commercial activities, and to industrial and agricultural production. Just as happened, in fact, after the Communist land reforms, they would have had to concentrate on feeding themselves rather than on meditation, study, and religious exercises. The monastic social contract—merit in exchange for rice—would have lapsed.

The third critical trend I have mentioned was the shift away from religious practice. Even if monastic revenues had held up after 1950, there is reason to doubt that they would still have been used to support the work of the meditation hall. For forty years an increasing number of monks had spent an increasing portion of their time on study of the sutras and spreading the dharma as lecturers; or, as "social monks" (*chiao-chi ho-shang*), helping to operate Buddhist associations and periodicals, schools, orphanages, and homes for the aged. Spreading the dharma and aid to the distressed were compassionate activities, consonant with the traditions of Mahayana Buddhism. But many lecturers and social monks, then as now, lived in the city, maintained a large correspondence, sat on committees, attended receptions and dedication ceremonies, and spent much of their time in travel. It was natural for them to give less and less time to religious practice. The more secularized their lives became, the less qualified they were to serve as religious models for laymen.

If the sangha had ceased to exemplify religious practice, what would have been the result? I think it would have been to destroy what was probably the most vital and auspicious element of the Buddhist revival: joint meditation by monks and laymen as carried on, for example, at the Mi-le Yüan in Peking. If such activities had proliferated, it is possible to imagine the enlargement of monasticism into a system that gave laymen a regular role in the religious work of monasteries. That is, laymen who did not feel in a position to commit themselves permanently to monastic life could have entered and re-entered it as circumstances allowed. The distance between the devotee and the ordained monk would have narrowed. Much of this has actually happened in Japan. Possibly it would have happened in China too, so that a Shanghai textile firm, for example, would have subsidized a well-known monastery in order to provide for the spiritual welfare of its employees. But it does not seem probable; and without help in resolving their deepening economic crisis, the large monasteries could have provided neither the venue nor the model for lay-monastic joint practice.

The most probable end result of the process of secularization is that the sangha would have ceased to exist. I doubt whether Buddhism as a living religion could have survived the loss of the third of its Three Jewels. It may be significant that I have never heard a Chinese Buddhist monk speak of a revival of Buddhism in China. One finds the term occasionally in documents, especially those for foreign consumption[18] or those connected with T'ai-hsü, but usually when I have talked to monks whose lives spanned the Republican period, they have shaken their heads sadly and said: "Young monks today know nothing about *ts'ung-lin* and the rules of the meditation hall. Today there are no more meditation halls." In their view, although there might have been an imbalance in favor of intramural religious practice before the revival began, now there was a much more serious imbalance in favor of extramural lecturing and academic research. "In the old days," as one of them put it, "the common people did not approve of monks coming out of the monastery and they would not have been able to understand lectures anyway. They wanted the monks to stay in the monastery, to be good at meditation, and to be learned. Now people want Buddhism to be like Christianity, with monks coming out in public."

I recall a monk in Hong Kong who had copied an important manuscript, which he allowed me to photograph. I suppose that I made quite a fuss over it, since it seemed to be the only copy extant. He himself was impressed neither by the manuscript nor by my enthusiasm for it. He kept urging me to join his group for a year's intensive meditation in a makeshift meditation hall. Shortly after my departure he wrote a letter to say: "You should not go to Treasure Mountain and then come home empty-handed." My suitcases were full of material on Chinese Buddhism, but I knew what he meant.[19]

It has been said that the Buddhist revival was "abortive" because it represented a "failure of drive, of vision, of vitality."[20] My own view is that it never had time to abort, since it was destroyed by the Communists first, and that so long as it lasted it did not succumb to any over-all failure of vitality. It would have succumbed, I believe, to the misdirection of its vitality. That is, even without the Communist victory, it would have been reduced in the end partly to an imitation of the YMCA and partly to an object of sterile philosophizing and academic study in libraries and museums. This does not mean that Buddhist ideas and attitudes, intangible and often anonymous, would have sunk without trace from a culture they had permeated so long. It means simply that most of the identifiably Buddhist, specifically religious institutions and practices would have faded away, as an increasing number of people found them embarrassing and irrelevant.

This assumes that the trends of the Republican period were irreversible. Yet such an assumption is not supported by the history of human religiosity. Repeatedly, religious practices have seemed to fade away only to rise again, perhaps in new forms. Even now in some Christian denominations there is a liturgical revival, a trend from ethics to mystery, a search for myth and symbol. One cannot be sure that a similar reaction would not have developed in China. The Chinese are no less religious than other peoples (though much of what is religious for them may seem profane in Western eyes) and, after their long, stormy reception of science and modernity, one would not have been surprised to see a swing of the pendulum, a new desire to preserve or restore elements of the national culture. Even today, despite the years under Communism, this kind of restoration is not altogether impossible. If the program to eliminate religion on the Mainland were suddenly abandoned, Buddhist institutions that now seem certain to become extinct might turn out to have a future after all. The chances for this would depend, I think, on whether the people of China have now been introduced to alternative institutions that better satisfy their human needs and more closely suit their characteristic ways of thinking. That fundamental question remains to be explored.

37 The race course at Happy Valley, Hong Kong. Several urban temples are installed in the flats overlooking it. A procession of nearly three hundred monks and nuns files down the track, reciting prayers for rain, in May 1963.

POSTSCRIPT

I REMEMBER a monk whom I used to visit at his urban temple in Hong Kong. It was installed in a spacious flat overlooking Happy Valley, complete with every modern convenience. He had a good following among the laity, so that he enjoyed both status and an adequate income. Yet he looked back on his youth as a menial in a Mainland monastery with nostalgia. "It was a bitter life," he said, "but I would rather have it a hundred times more than what I have here. One had no money, no clothes, and it was very hard, but that collective life was really good—you can't imagine how good it was!"

What he meant, I think, was that the monastery was a cohesive, smoothly functioning community that was good to be a part of and made sense of life. It showed a way for the rest of the world to follow, as did Brook Farm or a Shaker village, but, unlike these Western utopias, it had proved its practicability in the course of centuries of successful transmission.

Monks are not alone in having reason to mourn the eclipse of monasticism in China. It is true that most monasteries did not engage in social-welfare work, were not repositories of learning that had some secular use, and did not provide moral leadership for the community. But they served other functions, which benefited the people not only from a Buddhist point of view, in terms of karma and enlightenment, but also from a humanistic point of view, in terms of everyday needs. That is, they offered the benefits provided in the West by three very secular institutions: the park, the hostel, and the sanatorium.

The reader has already seen how Chinese city dwellers, when they had a holiday, would go out to temples in the neighboring hills for amusement and recreation. Monasteries at a greater distance served them on their travels. The accommodations were far superior to what could be found in a village inn, and the setting was idyllic. Robert Fortune, the Victorian botanist who spent years traveling through China in search of tea plants for the plantations of Assam, became almost lyrical when he recollected this:

> All the temples, both large and small, are built in the most romantic situations among the hills, and the neighbouring woods are always preserved and encouraged. What would indicate the residence of a country gentleman in England, is in China the sign of a Buddhist temple, and this holds good all over the country. When the weary traveler, therefore, who has been exposed for hours to the fierce rays of an eastern sun, sees a large clean house showing itself among the trees on a distant hillside, he can be almost sure that it is one of Buddha's temples, where the priests will treat him not only with courtesy, but with kindness.[1]

Many other travelers have shared Fortune's enthusiasm.[2]

Yet the monastery's most important role—at any rate the one of greatest interest to the West, which already abounds in parks and hostels—lay in its unique brand of mental therapy. Imagine the tired citydweller who has decided to spend a few weeks at a mountain monastery. Traveling by various conveyances, he has reached at last the foot of the path that leads up to it. He has only to go a few furlongs before the therapy begins. Suddenly he senses that the noise of wheels and men is growing fainter. The world has been left at the foot of the path. Soon he is in the landscape of the poet's imagination—sheer cliffs and twisted trees, boulders in fantastical shapes, here a waterfall, there a cave. Some caves a thousand years ago were the shelter of monks who figure in legends of enlightenment and the supernatural. The visitor may smile when he recalls the legends, but he prefers to half-believe them.

As he climbs higher, he must pass through one or more gatehouses that bridge streams or block the way in narrow valleys, so as to reinforce the sense of demarcation with the outer world.

Finally he emerges on the sunlit terrace of the monastery itself. He stops to catch his breath, letting his eyes follow the sweep of ancient roofs and listening for the occasional tinkle of the wind-bells on the eaves. The exercise has been invigorating. Now he will be greeted by the guest prefect on duty, have some tea, and choose a room.

During the first few days he becomes gradually aware of the good order around him—the regular processions of the monks to observances, meals, and the meditation hall. Everything is different from what it is at home—the silence, the mountain air, the wafted odors of incense and beancurd, the smell of ancient stones and beams. Sometimes in the middle of the night he is awakened by the booming of the great drum and slips down to the shrine-hall to watch. In the dimness of a few oil lamps he sees the ranks of robed figures facing the immense images, whose beckoning hands are all that can be descried. To the persistent *tok-tok-tok* of the wooden fish the chanting rises and falls, sometimes hypnotically repetitive, sometimes otherworldly. Perhaps it will remind him of happy temple visits as a child with his grandmother. Is this the reason he finds it a comfort to be there, or is it something more elusive?

During the day he may talk with the older monks, visiting them in their cozy apartments or in the library as they bend over a sacred text. It is years since they have turned their backs on life. Perhaps they explain to him the "emptiness of all the dharmas" and remind him that everything is created by the mind. If, as is sometimes the case, he has come there exhausted by worry about some personal problem, it will suddenly seem of less consequence.

On other days he may wander about the mountain enjoying the natural beauty and observing the birds and the animals that live there under the protection of the monastery. Probably he will find some eccentric hermits living nearby in huts or caves. To chat with them offers the citydweller like himself a vicarious taste of the pleasures of escapism. Even from the farthest hermit's hut he can hear the monastery bell, struck every minute or so by a pious monk who hopes that the reverberations will penetrate not merely to nearby valleys but through the earth to hell, so

38   Lung-wang Tung, Hupeh, one of several such cave temples in China.

39   A hermit's stone hut beckons the strolling mountain visitor.

that all sentient beings, men and ghosts alike, are reminded of the Buddha's message of salvation.

After several weeks of this slow life, during which he may be allowed to join the monks briefly in the meditation hall, he will say goodbye to his hosts and return to the metropolis, feeling released and relieved. He has been released not only from the cares of home and office, but from the tedium of Confucian orthodoxy. He has been relieved by a form of therapy—physical and metaphysical—that has none of the stigma of the sanatorium in the West.

What other institution, anywhere in the world, has done this quite so well?

APPENDICES

NOTES

BIBLIOGRAPHY

GLOSSARY INDEX

Appendix 1

BUDDHIST
PERIODICALS

According to the *Chinese Year Book, 1935-1936*, p. 1514, some 44 Chinese Buddhist periodicals were being published in 1934, the most popular being *Hai-ch'ao yin, Wei-yin, Nei-hsüeh,* and *Fo-hsüeh pan-yüeh k'an.* According to another source, a total of 58 Buddhist periodicals was published between 1920 and 1935 in one part of China or another (17 in Kiangsu province): see *Hai-ch'ao yin* 14.1:180-197 (January 1935), cited by Wing-tsit Chan, p. 61. Since at least 12 of the 57 listed below fall on either side of the period 1920-1935, it seems safe to estimate a minimum of 70 periodicals for the whole Republican period.

A few copies of some of them are scattered through Western libraries, but almost no complete runs exist. Below are listed the titles I have come across. The italicized dates are the years in which a periodical began or ceased publication. Other dates could be at any point in the life of a periodical. The purpose of the list is to show how scattered and sporadic the periodical publishing was. It is not, of course, complete. For example, the *Chinese Year Book, 1942-1943*, p. 64, mentions five periodicals for which it gives no characters and which are therefore excluded (*Golden Swastika* in Canton, *Jen-chien fo-chiao* in Chekiang, *Buddhism Critic* in Chengtu, *Chüeh-pao* in Shensi, and *Keng-huang* in Rangoon).

Title	Place of Publication	Dates	Affiliation or remarks
Buddhist China	Shanghai	*1943–1944*	In English and Chinese; edited by a Ceylonese
Ch'ang-sha chü-shih lin-k'an (Changsha Buddhist Devotees Club)	Changsha	1935	
Cheng-hsin chou-k'an (Right Faith weekly)	Hankow	1930–1939	Right Faith Society
Chinese Buddhist	Shanghai	*1930–1932*	Edited by Wong Mou Lam, Pure Karma Society
Ching-tsung yüeh-k'an (Pure Land monthly)	Szechwan	1949 (?)	
Ching-t'u-tsung yüeh-k'an (Pure Land monthly)	Wuchang	1934	
Ching-yeh yüeh-k'an (Pure karma monthly)	Shanghai	1930–1939	Pure Karma Society
Chung-kuo fo-chiao hui-pao (Chinese Buddhist Association newsletter)	Shanghai	1930	Official organ of the CBA
Chung-liu tsa-chih (Midstream miscellany)	Chen-chiang	1943	Published by the Chiao Shan Seminary
Chüeh-chin yüeh-k'an (Chüeh-chin monthly)	Kiangsu	*1936*	Edited by Ta-hsing at Chüeh-chin Ssu
Chüeh-ch'ün chou-pao (Masses enlightenment weekly)	Shanghai	1946	Published by T'ai-hsü at Yü-fo Ssu
Chüeh-hsün yüeh-k'an (Enlightenment monthly)	Shanghai	pre-1949–1955	Organ of Young Men's Buddhist Association, Shanghai

Title	Place of Publication	Dates	Affiliation or remarks
Chüeh-she ts'ung-shu (Bodhi Society miscellany)	Shanghai	*1918–1919* (quarterly)	Edited by T'ai-hsü
Chüeh-sheng jih-pao (Enlightenment daily)	?	?	
Chüeh-wu (Enlightenment)	Shanghai	1919–1926	Occasional supplement in *Min-kuo jih-pao*
Chüeh-yin (Voice of enlightenment)	Macao	1940 (monthly)	T'ai-hsü's group
Chüeh yu-ch'ing (Enlightenment of sentient creatures)	Shanghai	1939–1955	
Fo-chiao hsin-wen (Buddhist news)	Shanghai	1937 (every three days)	Published by Shanghai Buddhist Bookshop
Fo-chiao jih-pao (Buddhist daily)	?	?	
Fo-chiao kung-lun (Buddhist review)	Amoy (?)	1931 (?)– 1939	T'ai-hsü's group
Fo-chiao p'ing-lun (Buddhist critic)	Peking	*1931* (a quarterly)	Published at Po-lin Ssu, apparently by T'ai-hsü's group
Fo-chiao t'e-k'an (Buddhist special)	Shanghai	*1932–1934* (daily)	Published as supplement to *Shih-min pao*
Fo-chiao tsa-chih (Buddhist magazine)	Shansi	1935	
Fo-chiao yüeh-k'an (Buddhist monthly)	Szechwan	1935	
Fo-chiao yüeh-k'an (Buddhist monthly)	Peking	1935	

Title	Place of Publication	Dates	Affiliation or remarks
Fo-chiao yüeh-pao (Buddhist monthly)	Shanghai	*1913* (monthly)	Organ of Chinese General Buddhist Association (Shanghai, 1912)
Fo-chiao yüeh-pao	Tientsin	*1936*	T'ai-hsü's group
Fo-hsin ts'ung-k'an (Buddha mind)	Peking	*1922* (bimonthly)	Published at Kuang-chi Ssu
Fo-hsüeh pan-yüeh k'an (Buddhist semimonthly)	Shanghai	*1930–1943*	Newsletter of Shanghai Buddhist Bookshop
Fo-hsüeh ts'ung-pao (Buddhist miscellany)	Shanghai	*1912–1914* (monthly)	
Fo-hsüeh yüeh-k'an (Buddhist studies monthly)	Peking	*1921–1943*	Edited first at Kuang-chi Ssu; later by Chinese Buddhist Institute
Fo-hua chi-k'an (Buddhist quarterly)	Canton	1925	
Fo-hua hsin ch'ing-nien (New Buddhist youth)	Hankow, Peking	*1923–1924* (monthly)	T'ai-hsü's group
Fo-hua yüeh-k'an (Buddhist monthly)	Peking	1935	
Fo-kuang (Buddha's radiance)	Wuchang	1915	
Hai-ch'ao yin	Hangchow, Hankow, etc.	*1920–* (monthly)	Published by T'ai-hsü
Hsien-tai fo-chiao (Modern Buddhism)	?	?	
Hsien-shih hsün-k'an (Reality)	Amoy	1936	
Hsien-tai seng-chia (Modern sangha)	Amoy	1927–1939 (quarterly)	T'ai-hsü's group

Title	Place of Publication	Dates	Affiliation or remarks
Hsin-teng (Mind's light)	Nanking (?)	c.1926 (ten-day publication)	Published by T'ai-hsü's Chinese Buddhist Education Association
Hu-sheng pao (Protecting life)	Shanghai	1932	
Hua-nan chüeh-yin (South China voice of enlightenment)	Hong Kong	1939	
Hui-teng (Torch of wisdom)	Nantung	1943	
Hung-fa she-k'an (Spreading the dharma)	Ningpo	1932–1935	Published at Kuan-tsung Ssu
Hung-hua yüeh-k'an (Propaganda monthly)	Shanghai	1922(?)–1957	Published by Shanghai Buddist Association
Jen-chien chüeh (Enlightenment for the world)	Amoy	1936 (semimonthly)	
Jen hai-teng yüeh-k'an (Altar lamp for man)	Hong Kong	1935–1939	T'ai-hsü's group
Miao-fa lun (Wheel of the law)	Shanghai	1943	Edited by Chen-hua at Jade Buddha Monastery, Shanghai
Nei-hsüeh (Buddhist metaphysics)	Nanking	1924–1931	Ou-yang Ching-wu's journal
Shang-hai fo-chiao chü-shih-lin lin-k'an (Organ of the Shanghai Buddhist Devotees' Club)	Shanghai	1924–1935	
Shih-tzu hou (Lion's roar)	Kweilin	1940 (?)	

Title	Place of Publication	Dates	Affiliation or remarks
Ta-ch'eng yüeh-k'an (Mahayana monthly)	Amoy	1943	Published by Mahayana Buddhist Society at Miao-shih Ssu
Tz'u-hang hua-pao (Tz'u-hang pictorial)	Shanghai	1933–1934	Pure Land orientation
T'ung-yüan yüeh-k'an (Common vow monthly)	Peking	1943	Published at Sung-chu Ssu, Peking
Wei-miao sheng (Marvelous Voice)	Peking	1936	Published by the Bodhi Society
Wei-yin	Shanghai	1929–1935 (monthly)	Focus on Tantrism
Yin-hsien fo-chiao hui-k'an (Organ of the Yin-hsien Buddhist Association)	Yin-hsien	1936	

Appendix 2

BUDDHIST
SEMINARIES

The following is a list of all seminaries that I have read of or heard mentioned as operating in China between 1912 and 1950. The dates given after each are usually the earliest and/or the last dates on which it was said to be in operation. It may actually have started operating much earlier and continued much later. Only if a date is italicized can it be reliably taken as the year in which a seminary was first established or closed down. The figure in parenthesis is the approximate number of monks enrolled when operation was fully underway. Some of these figures come from only one source and are not reliable. Nonetheless, I believe Wing-tsit Chan is mistaken in stating (p. 83) that "no enrollment ever exceeded sixty."

Anhwei, Anking: Anhwei Fo-hsüeh-hsiao (or Ying-chiang Fo-hsüeh-yüan) 1922-23 (20)
Anhwei, Chiu-hua Shan: Hua-ch'eng Fo-hsüeh-yüan, *1927*-1930 (20)
Chekiang, Hangchow: Fo-chiao Chuan-k'e Lin
Chekiang, Hangchow: Che-chiang Seng Hsüeh-yüan, 1929-1939 (40)
Chekiang, Hangchow: Ming-chiao Hsüeh-yüan
Chekiang, Hangchow: Wu-lin Fo-hsüeh-yüan, 1946-47
Chekiang, Ningpo: Hung-fa Hsüeh-yüan, 1918-1939 (200)
Chekiang, Ningpo: Pai-hu Chiang-t'ang, 1939
Chekiang, P'u-t'o Shan: P'u-t'o Hsüeh-yüan
Chekiang, Sung-p'u: Kuan-yin-ssu Fo-hsüeh-yüan, *1941-1945*
Fukien, Foochow: Ku-shan Fo-hsüeh-yüan, *1931*-1939
Fukien, Amoy: Min-nan Fo-hsüeh-yüan, 1925-1939 (80)

Heilungkiang, Harbin: Chi-le-ssu Fo-hsüeh-yüan, *1924-1943*
Heilungkiang, Suihua: Fa-hua-ssu Fo-hsüeh-yüan, *1930-1945*
Honan, Chu-hsi: Chi-le Fo-hsüeh-yüan, 1925
Honan, Kaifeng: Ho-nan Sheng Fo-hsüeh-yüan
Hopei, Tientsin: Ta-pei-yüan Fo-hsüeh-yüan, 1947-48
Hunan, Nan-yüeh: Chu-sheng Fo-hsüeh-yüan
Hupeh, Wuchang: Wu-ch'ang Fo-hsüeh-yüan, *1922-1937* (70)
Kiangsu, Changchow: Ch'ing-liang Hsüeh-yüan
Kiangsu, Changchow: T'ien-ning Fo-hsüeh-yüan, *1931-1949* (200)
Kiangsu, Changshu: Fa-chieh Hsüeh-yüan, 1919-1934 (40)
Kiangsu, Chen-chiang: Chiao-shan Fo-hsüeh-yüan, *1934*-1946 (80)
Kiangsu, Ju-kao: Fo-hua Hsüeh-yüan
Kiangsu, Kao-yu: Fang-sheng Fo-hsüeh-yüan, *1922*-1924
Kiangsu, Nanking: Ch'i-hsia Fo-hsüeh-yüan, *1940*-1949 (30)
Kiangsu, Nanking: Chin-ling Fo-hsüeh-yüan, 1935-1937 (20)
Kiangsu, Nanking: P'u-te Fo-hsüeh-yüan
Kiangsu, Nanking: Nei-hsüeh-yüan, *1919*-1949 (40)
Kiangsu, Soochow: Ling-yen Fo-hsüeh-yüan (30)
Kiangsu, T'ai-hsien: Fo-hsüeh Yen-chiu-she
Kiangsu, Yangchow: Chüeh-hai Hsüeh-yüan
Kirin, Changchun: Po-jo-ssu Fo-hsüeh-yüan, *1935-1948*
Kirin, Kirin: Kuan-yin Ku-ch'a Fo-hsüeh-yüan, *1943-1945*
Kwangtung, Chaochow: Ling-tung Fo-hsüeh-yüan
Kwangtung, Shiukwan: Nan-hua Chieh-lü Hsüeh-yüan, 1943-1949
Kweichow, Kweiyang: Su-ch'eng Leng-yen Hsüeh-hsiao
Kweichow, Kuei-chou Fo-hsüeh-yüan
Liaoning, Shenyang: Wan-shou-ssu Fo-hsüeh-yüan, *1921-1923*
Liaoning, Shenyang: Po-jo-ssu Fo-hsüeh-yüan, *1929-1931*
Liaoning, Shenyang: Tz'u-en Fo-hsüeh-yüan, 1944-1948 (40)
Liaoning, Yingkow: Leng-yen Fo-hsüeh-yüan, *1943-1945* (40)
Shantung, Tsinan: Hsüeh-fo She
Shantung, Tsingtao: Chan-shan Fo-hsüeh-yüan, *1935-1949* (40)
Shansi: P'u-t'ung Seng Hsüeh-hsiao
Shensi, Sian: Pa-li San-tsang Yüan, 1939-1945
Shensi, Sian: Ta-hsing-ssu Fo-hsüeh-yüan, *1922-23*
Szechwan, Chengtu: Wen-shu Fo-hsüeh-yüan
Szechwan, Chengtu: Ssu-ch'uan Fo-hsüeh-yüan, 1925
Szechwan, Chengtu: Lin-tsung Fo-hsüeh-yüan
Szechwan, Hsintu: Pao-kuang Fo-hsüeh-yüan
Szechwan, Hokiang: Fa-wang Hsüeh-yüan
Szechwan, Chungking: Han-tsang Chiao-li Yüan, *1931-1949* (60-100)
Peking: Chung-kuo Fo-chiao Hsüeh-yüan, 1941 (200)
Peking: Fa-yüan Fo-hsüeh-yüan, 1937
Peking: Hung-tz'u Fo-hsüeh-yüan, 1924-1934
Peking: Mi-le Yüan, 1925-1930

Peking: Nien-hua-ssu Fo-hsüeh-yüan, 1930?
Peking: Po-lin Fo-hsüeh-yüan, *1930-31*
Peking: P'u-t'i Hsüeh-she
Peking: San-shih Fo-hsüeh-yüan
Peking: Tsang-wen Hsüeh-yüan
Shanghai (later Hangchow): Hua-yen Ta-hsüeh, *1912-1916* (60)
Shanghai: Ching-an-ssu Fo-hsüeh-yüan, 1946-47?
Shanghai: Yü-fo-ssu Fo-hsüeh-yüan, 1946-47?
Shanghai: Yüan-ming Chiang-t'ang

Location unknown
    Chüeh-lü Hsüeh-yüan
    Fa-ch'ang Hsüeh-yüan
    Chiang-nan Fo-hsüeh-yüan
    T'ai-tsung Hsüeh-yüan
    San-fo Chiang-t'ang

At the 18 seminaries for which we have figures on enrollment, the average was 72. Let us assume that for the remaining 53 the average was half this, or 35. For 36 seminaries we have at least a partial period of operation, which averaged eight years. Let us assume that for the other 35 seminaries the average was six years. Since the usual course lasted three years, one third of the total number of students enrolled should have graduated annually. This would mean 3456 graduates from the 18 seminaries (graduating 24 a year for eight years) and 3816 graduates from 53 seminaries (graduating 12 a year for six years).

The result would be a total of about 7,500 seminarians graduating in China between 1912 and 1950, most of them between 1920 and 1940. It is a small quantity compared to the total number of monks (about 500,000), but large if compared to the number of seminaries, Buddhist associations, and public monasteries where many of the more able graduates hoped to make their careers.

This sort of estimate on the basis of inadequate data gives at least an idea of the order of magnitude. It seems safe to say that not hundreds of monks were trained during the Republican period, but several thousand.

Appendix 3

MONASTIC
POPULATION FIGURES

T'IEN-T'UNG SSU

The T'ien-t'ung Ssu was visited by Robert Fortune in May 1844. He was told that about 100 priests were connected with the institution, "but that many were always absent on missions to various parts of the country" (*Three Years,* p. 173). Bishop Smith, who visited T'ien-t'ung twice in 1845, states that it had over a 100 monks (George Smith, p. 184). When Mrs. Gordon Cumming visited T'ien-t'ung in 1879, she saw about a 100 monks taking part in afternoon devotions, whereas Bishop Smith had only seen 30 in 1845 (Cumming, p. 292). Hackmann, who spent two days there in March 1902, states that it had 200 monks living there regularly ("Das Buddhistischen-Kloster Tien-dong," p. 174). When Sekino and Tokiwa visited it in 1922, they found that it had "not less than" 250 monks (*Shina Bukkyō shiseki,* V, 163). In 1930, when Yüan-ying was elected abbot, it had over 300 monks (*Yüan-ying,* p. 13). Informants who lived there then have told me that after Yüan-ying enlarged the premises in 1932, the number of resident monks went up to 400 or even to 500—which was the population that T'ien-t'ung had had seven centuries earlier when visited by Dogen (H. Dumoulin, *History of Zen Buddhism,* New York, 1963, p. 154). A figure of 400 had already been recorded in 1929 by Mrs. F. R. Millican (letter to J. B. Pratt, June 12, 1929, Pratt Collection, Williams College).

KU SHAN

The first two figures on Ku Shan also come from Bishop Smith and Robert Fortune. Smith visited it in 1845 and reported that it had about 100 monks, of whom 60 were generally resident (George Smith, p. 369). Fortune visited it in 1848 and saw over a 100 monks at lunch. He also noted that there were "upwards of a hundred cushions" for kneeling in the great shrine-hall (*Journey to the Tea Countries,* p. 137). J. Doolittle, who lived in Foochow during the 1850's and 1860's, states (p. 182) that it had 100-200 monks. J. Thomson, who visited it about 1872, states (p. 157) that it had 200 monks. Mrs. Gordon Cumming noted down the figure 300 in 1879, but said that "rarely are more than half that number on the spot" (Cumming, p. 182). Before 1920 it had "a dining room for three hundred monks" (Hodous, pp. 19ff). Tokiwa who visited it in 1929, states that there were then 400 monks in residence (Tokiwa Daijō, *Shina Bukkyō shiseki kinen-shū,* p. 253). Informants who lived there in the 1930's have told me that there were 400 to 500 monks in residence.

P'U-T'O SHAN

When Bishop Smith visited P'u-t'o Shan in 1845, he was told that 600 monks resided on the island and 300 others were generally absent in neighboring provinces (George Smith, p. 313). Lieutenant F. E. Forbes of the Royal Navy, who was there at about the same time, was given the same figure: 600-700 (*Five Years in China, 1842-1847,* London, 1848, p. 168). About a half century later the number was placed at 1,000 (H. C. Du Bose, *Dragon, Image, and Demon,* London, 1886, p. 277). As of 1908 a careful investigator said there were about 1,500 (Boerschmann, p. 12). About 1920 the number had reportedly increased to 2,000 (Hodous, p. 44; also *Official Guide to Eastern Asia,* Tokyo, 1915, IV, 268). More specifically, the Fa-yü Ssu, one of P'u-t'o's three principal monasteries, which had 80 monks in 1845 according to George Smith (p. 314), had 200 monks in 1908 according to Boerschmann (p. 12).

There are also figures inconsistent with the above. In 1844 Robert Fortune was told that P'u-t'o Shan had 2,000 monks, although many of them were "constantly absent on begging expeditions" (*Three Years,* p. 185). About 1872 its "ecclesiastical population" was again said to be 2,000 (Thomson, III, 15). On the other hand, there is the statement of Abbé Huc, who was in Chekiang in 1849, that "the vast monasteries of Pou-t'ou . . . are now entirely abandoned" (II, 197).

HAI-CH'UANG SSU, CANTON

This was said to have 160 monks in residence in 1845 (George Smith, p. 34) and 200-250 in 1879 (Cumming, p. 62; William C. Hunter, *Bits of Old China,* Taipei, 1966, p. 176).

No single figure in this appendix can be wholly relied on, since none represents a physical head count, but taken together they fit in better with the picture of a growing sangha than that of a dwindling one, particularly since they are not offset by figures showing declines in other monasteries, with the single exception of the Kuo-ch'ing Ssu on T'ien-t'ai Shan. There the monastic population apparently declined from 200 in 1856 (Edkins, p. 38) to 160 monks in 1895 (Richard, *Forty-Five Years in China,* p. 274) to perhaps 150 monks in the 1930's (according to one of these 150). This was the same population it had had in the Sung dynasty (Kenneth K. S. Ch'en, p. 274).

Appendix 4

REGIONAL DECAY

Although this book does not attempt to deal with the history of Buddhism in China before the end of the Ch'ing dynasty, it may be useful to point out historical questions that need to be answered. One of the most interesting concerns regional decay. When did an exceptionally high proportion of monasteries in provinces away from the Yangtze Valley begin to decline?

The ruinous state into which some of them had fallen by the 1920's did not necessarily mean many years of neglect. It does not take long for Chinese temple buildings to deteriorate. To maintain its roofs alone, Chin Shan kept ten tilers steadily employed. Also, it was natural for the decline of monasteries, once started, to accelerate geometrically (see Chapter V). This might explain why, for example, Pratt in 1924 found Buddhism in Szechwan in a state of decay, whereas A. J. Little, who toured the province in 1897, had found it flowering: Szechwan was "to Buddhism what Bavaria is to Catholicism." See Little, pp. 45, 75-81, 239-240. The pitiful dilapidation of the Lung-hsing Ssu, Cheng-ting, Hopei, because of the loss of income-producing property, was said to have taken place "in recent years" (Sekino Tei and Tokiwa Daijō, *Shina Bukkyō shiseki*, IV, 175-178, and plates 133-145; see Fig. 34 in this volume).

Yet, according to one investigator, "it is generally known that Buddhism reached its present sorry state in North China about the beginning of the Ming dynasty, around 1400" (see W. A. Grootaers, "Rural Temples around Hsüan-hua," *Folklore Studies*, 10.1:74, 1957), whereas already in the Sung dynasty the provinces of Kiangsu, Chekiang, and Fukien were noted for their number of Buddhists (see W. Eberhard, "Chinese Regional Stereotypes," *Asian Survey*, 5.12:604-605, December 1965).

Decay in Kwangtung province seems to have begun at least as early as the second half of the nineteenth century. Some confirmation of this may be seen in the incidence of monastic construction, although, as pointed out earlier (Chapter V, note 20), the information on this topic is inadequate. Figures gathered by W. Eberhard from 15 Kwangtung district gazeteers show that whereas in 28 districts of Fukien, Chekiang, Kiangsu, Anhwei, Hunan, and Hupei the construction of new Buddhist temples in 1850-1899 was more than double what it had been in 1800-1849, in the Kwangtung districts it *decreased* to a sixth of what it had been in the earlier half century ("Temple Building," p. 298). Parallel evidence is given by C. K. Yang concerning the founding and restoration of monastic institutions (Buddhist *and* Taoist) in two districts of Kiangsu, one district of Kwangtung, and one district of Hopei. In the Kiangsu districts seven temples were restored in 1850-1911 whereas only one had been restored in the preceding two centuries; and eleven new ones were founded whereas only one had been founded in the previous two hundred years. In the districts of Kwangtung and Hopei, on the other hand, the picture was the reverse. Few monastic institutions had been either restored or founded and almost all of them in the first two hundred years, not in the last fifty years of the Ch'ing dynasty. See C. K. Yang, pp. 343-349.

It would be interesting to learn when it became customary in Kwangtung (as it was in no other Chinese province) for monks and nuns to live in the same institution (although in separate dormitories). It would also be interesting to learn when the dietary rules began to be more flagrantly violated than elsewhere. There are many accounts like J. H. Gray's (I, 115) of a supper party given by the abbot of the Hai-ch'uang Ssu, Canton, in 1861: "The viands consisted of roast pork, boiled fowl, fish, rice, and vegetables . . . Supper being ended, the abbot together with his cousin, who was one of the guests, retired to an opium couch in the same apartment and enjoyed four or five pipes of the obnoxious drug." It is suggestive that Giles speaks of the "loathsome dens which serve as the sleeping apartments of the monks" in Canton, whereas Hackmann describes their rooms at a Chekiang monastery as neat and cheerful (see Giles, p. 285, and Hackmann, "Buddhist Monastery Life," pp. 247-248).

Even if it could be established *when* monasteries began to decay throughout certain regions, it would not explain *why*. Was it because of the impoverishment of the populace, which no longer had the surplus income to support as many monks as before? This answer might apply to north China, where productivity had been lowered by centuries of deforestation and dessication. Or was it that in some regions Buddhism did not have such deep psychological roots and hence withered there first? That is, since the sangha was economically dependent on lay piety as much as lay prosperity, was it a drop in piety rather than wealth that brought about the monasteries' decline? Pratt (pp. 354, 370) writes that he saw very few domestic shrines in north China and was convinced that "the number of earnest Buddhists outside the lower Yangtse valley is very small indeed." We know that there were thirty to sixty times as many devotees in central China as in the north. But why?

Notes

I. THE BEGINNINGS OF THE REVIVAL

1. See, for example, Yin-shun, *T'ai-hsü ta-shih nien-p'u* (Chronological biography of the Venerable T'ai-hsü; Hong Kong, 1950), p. 37; Wing-tsit Chan, *Religious Trends in Modern China* (New York, 1953), pp. 59-60; Karl Ludwig Reichelt, *The Transformed Abbot* (London, 1954), pp. 59-61; Kuan Chiung, "Buddhism," in *Chinese Year Book, 1935-1936* (Shanghai, 1935), p. 1512; Kenneth K. S. Ch'en, *Buddhism in China: A Historical Survey* (Princeton, 1964), pp. 448, 449, 454.

2. Here and below, age is given by Chinese reckoning. By ours Yang was only one or two years old when he became engaged. He was given, incidentally, the courtesy name of Jen-shan (ideograms identical with those of Jen-shan, the monk mentioned in Chapter II).

3. See Buwei Yang Chao, *Autobiography of a Chinese Woman* (New York, 1947), pp. 82-88; also her "Hsien-tsu Jen-shan-kung chih sheng-p'ing" (The life of my grandfather Jen-shan), *P'u-t'i shu* (Bodhedrum), Taichung, 8.11:6-9 (October 1960), and "Wo-ti tsu-fu" (My grandfather), *Chuan-chi wen-hsüeh* (Biographical literature), Taipei, 3.3:17-20 (September 1963). Mrs. Chao is Yang's grand-daughter and spent much of her childhood with him. There are discrepancies in ages and dates among her three accounts and between her accounts and others in Chinese. One of the latter states that Yang's interest in Buddhism dated from 1864 after, not before, his father's death and began not in Hangchow, but in Anking, where he is said to have bought first the Diamond Sutra, then *The Awakening of Faith,* and to have begun his intercourse with monks. See "Yang Jen-shan chü-shih shih-lüeh" (Brief biography of Yang Jen-shan) in *Yang Jen-shan chü-shih i-chu* (Peking, 1923), p. 2. I have generally followed the last of the three accounts written by Mrs. Chao, who would surely have the fullest knowledge of such intimate family problems as Yang's disillusionment. At least one point in Mrs. Chao's version is confirmed by Timothy Richard, to whom Yang said that the book which converted him from Confucianism to Buddhism was *The Awakening of Faith.* See Timothy Richard, tr., *The Awakening of Faith in the Mahayana Doctrine* (Shanghai, 1907), p. x.

4. "Yang Jen-shan chü-shih shih-lüeh," p. 2b. The "age of the dharma in decay" refers to the present period of the final decline of Buddhism as foretold by the Buddha. On the Lung-tsang Tripitaka, see p. 228. Shuang-ching evidently refers to the Wan-shou Ssu on Ching Shan, Yü-hang, Chekiang, which was burned by the Taiping rebels.

5. At any rate "Yang Jen-shan chü-shih shih-lüeh," p. 2b, places this along with events occurring in 1866.

6. I have not been able to find out in what year the press began to use the name Chin-ling K'o-ching Ch'u, but this name is given as the publisher of a copy of the *Leng-yen ching*, dated 1869, now in the Chinese-Japanese library at Harvard University. In 1961 a Japanese delegation visiting the Press was told that it had been established in 1868, but Kuan Chiung gives the year as 1865—see *Chinese Year Book, 1935-1936*, p. 1512. Kuan Chiung's articles in successive English editions of Commercial Press yearbooks are authoritative and will often be cited below. Oddly enough they do not appear in the Chinese editions. Kuan was a founder and leader of the Pure Karma Society and a member of the Standing Committee of the Chinese Buddhist Association (founded in Shanghai, 1929). From 1903 to 1927 he served as a magistrate of the Mixed Court of the International Settlement of Shanghai.

7. I capitalize the word "buddha" only when it refers to *the* Buddha, Sakyamuni. To recite buddha's name usually meant to repeat continuously the phrase "Homage to the buddha Amitabha," but the names of one or more other buddhas might be substituted.

8. Chou Hsiang-kuang, *A History of Chinese Buddhism* (Allahabad, 1955), p. 219. Chou is not a wholly reliable source. He confuses Liu Chih-t'ien with Tseng Chi-tse and gives the year of Yang's appointment to London as 1875, not 1878.

9. Richard, *The Awakening of Faith*, p. ix. I have not read elsewhere of these other presses, but Mrs. Chao recalls that woodblocks from Soochow and Hangchow, as well as from Yangchow and from two presses in Nanking itself, in all of which her grandfather was active, were gradually collected at the Chinling Scriptural Press to a value of $400,000 (Chinese currency).

10. Most Chinese sources do not mention a trip to Japan by Yang himself, and Mrs. Chao has stated categorically in a letter to me that he never went there. Yet, according to T'ai-hsü's biographer, Yang served in the Chinese embassy in Japan and traveled about there with Nanjio: see Yin-shun, *T'ai-hsü*, p. 37. Wing-tsit Chan says (p. 60) that he "brought back" many texts from Japan. The discrepancy is an important one because, as we shall see, Japan influenced the Buddhist revival in many ways.

11. He advertised terrestrial and celestial globes in Chinese newspapers "manufactured by himself," at £2.10 the pair. The well-known missionary, Arthur E. Moule, bought a pair and had an interesting conversation with Yang, whom he found to be "a well educated and well read man . . . ready also with real eloquence and lucid arrangement of thought to defend Buddhism." See Arthur E. Moule, *New China and Old* (London, 1891), pp. 163-166.

12. *Ssu* is the commonest word for a Buddhist monastery or nunnery. See Holmes Welch, *The Practice of Chinese Buddhism* (Cambridge, Mass., 1967), p. 465, n. 4. Many Chinese and Sanskrit terms are defined below in the index.

13. Otto Franke, "Eine neue Buddhistische Propaganda," *T'oung Pao*, 5:302-303 (1894); see also Lewis Hodous, *Buddhism and Buddhists in China* (New York, 1924), p. 63; J.J.M. DeGroot, *Sectarianism and Religious Persecution in China* (Amsterdam, 1903), I, 257. Flogging and banishment were the penalty for ordinary membership in a society; only the leaders were strangled.

14. "Yang Jen-shan chü-shih shih-lüeh," p. 4b.

15. Otto Franke, "Eine neue Buddhistische Propaganda," p. 306.

16. Yin-shun, *T'ai-hsü*, p. 37.

17. "Yang Jen-shan chü-shih shih-lüeh," p. 4b. What Yang did not realize was that Richard regarded the *Ch'i-hsin lun* as "a Christian book," which attested to the possibility of spreading the gospel among Chinese Buddhists. When Yang found out that the English text was "full of Christian terms which were diametrically opposed to the fundamental teaching of the Buddha dharma," he felt that he had been tricked, and he therefore refused to help other Europeans with Buddhist translation projects. See *Chinese Buddhist* (Shanghai), 1.1:4 (April 1930).

18. This textbook, the *Shih-chiao san-tzu ching* (Buddhist three-character classic), had been composed during the Ming dynasty in the same three-character phrases as the Confucian *San-tzu ching* that served as a primer for most Chinese schoolchildren. Yang changed its title to *Fo-chiao ch'u-hsüeh k'o-pen* (Buddhist primer), after thoroughly revising a recent revision by Yin-kuang.

19. According to a later account, Yang started the school "at the suggestion of Ven. Anagarika Dharmapala to send Chinese pupils to study Pali and Sanskrit in India" (*Chinese Buddhist*, 1.1:4, April 1930). According to Yang's biography, it was his meeting with Dharmapala in 1893 that caused him to advocate education for monks and to compile the textbook just mentioned ("Yang Jen-shan chü-shih shih-lüeh," p. 4b). Hodous, on the other hand, states that the school was established "under Japanese influence . . . The students were to go to Japan for further training and the more promising ones were to go to study in India" (Hodous, p. 64).

20. Yang was lecturing on the *Surangama Sutra* in the spring of 1909, when T'ai-hsü was enrolled. Su Man-shu, who taught English there, was living as a layman at the time. Yin-shun, *T'ai-hsü*, p. 37.

21. It is interesting to note that early publications of the Chin-ling Press in the Harvard library are standard sutras (*Leng-yen ching*, 1869; *Vimalakirti-nirdesa Sutra*, 1870; *Lotus Sutra*, 1871) and that the first Dharmalaksana text in its collection was published in 1896. This suggests that Yang Wen-hui's interest in Idealist philosophy came later in his career, apparently after his wife's kinsman brought back Dharmalaksana texts from Japan.

22. Different sources give different dates, indicating, for example, that the school operated in 1907-08 rather than 1908-09 or that it operated for two years rather than one. When Franke visited it in November 1908, he found it still in a formative state. He gives the text of its house rules and an appeal for financial support signed by Yang's Buddhist friends like Ts'en Tseng-chih and Mei Kuang-hsi. See Otto Franke, "Ein Buddhistischer Reformversuch in China," *T'oung Pao*, Ser. 2 (1909), pp. 567-602.

23. "Yang Jen-shan chü-shih shih-lüeh," p, 2b; Min Erh-ch'ang, *Pei-chuan Chi-pu* (Supplement to Stele Biographies), 27:17b. Cheng was a follower of the Pure Land school, which emphasizes devotional practice more than study of the sutras; yet in a sense the reprinting of sutras was itself a devotional practice (see Chapter Five). I think Wing-tsit Chan (p. 60) is mistaken in saying that Yang Wen-hui "published the Chinese Tripitaka, the Buddhist Canon, for the first time since 1738." Yang never published it in full; nor was he the first person of his time to publish it in part.

24. Yüeh-hsia ran the Anhwei Buddhist Association (An-hui Sheng Fo-chiao Hui) at the Ying-chiang Ssu in Anking for three years starting in 1900. It is not

clear what the work of the association comprised, but students were enrolled
for study. Possibly, then, it was actually a Buddhist school that antedated the
Hunan Sangha School set up in 1904. See Cheng-lien, *Ch'ang-chou T'ien-ning
ssu-chih* (History of the T'ien-ning Ssu in Changchow; Shanghai, 1948), 7:103.
There is also a statement that in 1906 Hsü-yün went to Peking with Eight Fingers
to present a petition "as representative of the Buddhist Association" (meaning,
perhaps, the "Buddhist community"): see Ts'en Hsüeh-lü, *Hsü-yün ho-shang
nien-p'u* (Chronological biography of the Venerable Hsü-yün), 3rd ed. (Hong
Kong, 1962), p. 43. Finally there is a statement that in 1909 Yüan-ying held
office as the chief councillor of the Chinese Buddhist Association (Chung-kuo
Fo-chiao Hui): see *Yüan-ying fa-shih chi-nien k'an* (Memorial volume for the
Reverend Yüan-ying; Singapore, 1954), p. 18. I have seen no other references to
these early associations—if in fact they really were associations.

25. *Ming-i tai-fang lu*, quoted by Wolfgang Franke in *The Reform and Abolition of the Traditional Chinese Examination System* (Cambridge, Mass., 1963),
pp. 22, 78. It is significant that the *Ming-i tai-fang lu* "was popularized by Liang
Ch'i-eh'ao and his followers at the close of the Manchu dynasty as revolutionary
literature": see Arthur W. Hummel, ed., *Eminent Chinese of the Ch'ing Period,
1644-1912* (Washington, D.C., 1943), p. 354.

26. Here and below I have relied mainly on Wolfgang Franke, pp. 43-46, although he fails to point out a certain ambiguity in the edict of July 10, 1898.
This edict did not speak of making schools out of Buddhist monasteries (*ssu*),
but only out of temples of ancestral and popular worship (*tz'u-miao*). Temples of
popular worship (*miao*) might have been taken to include the smaller Buddhist
temples but hardly the large monasteries, which therefore should not have been
affected by the edict. Yet here and there it seems to have been interpreted in the
light of Chang Chih-tung's *Ch'üan-hsüeh p'ien*. Chang had proposed that seven
out of ten Buddhist and Taoist monasteries (*ssu, kuan*) in each hsien should be
turned into schools (*hsüeh-t'ang*) and that seven tenths of their agricultural
property (49 percent of all such monastic property) should be used to provide
income to defray the operating expenses of the schools. The monks would be
left with three tenths of their monasteries and all the landed income thereof, in
addition to the income of three tenths of the land of the temples that had been
turned into schools. Furthermore, they would receive compensation for the value
of the agricultural land they had lost—altogether not so harsh an approach as
was eventually adopted by the enemies of Buddhism, but harsher than what
would seem to have been authorized by the edict of July 10, 1898. See Jérôme
Tobar, *K'iuen-hio p'ien, Exhortation à l'étude par S. Exc. Tchang Tche-tong*
(Variétés Sinologiques, no. 26; Shanghai, 1909), pp. 95-96.

27. The decree that ancestral halls and temples were to remain as they were
was issued on September 26, 1898, four days after the Dowager Empress resumed
power. See Chu Shou-p'eng, *Kuang-hsü ch'ao tung-hua-lu* (Tung-hua records of
the Kuang-hsü reign; Peking, 1958), p. 4204.

28. C. K. Yang, *Religion in Chinese Society* (Berkeley, 1961), pp. 325-326.
Although Yang gives the date of the decree as 1904, Hodous (p. 64) gives it as
1902. I have been unable to locate the original text, but I am confident that
something to this effect existed since it is referred to in so many sources. Arthur
H. Smith, writing in 1906 or earlier, says: "Under the exigencies of the present
poverty of national resources all Chinese temples not officially listed are liable to

have their lands confiscated for the support of local schools and academies": see *The Uplift of China* (New York, 1912), pp. 107-108. See also P. W. Kuo, *The Chinese System of Public Education* (New York, 1915), p. 147; F.L.H. Pott, "Modern Education," in H. F. McNair, ed., *China* (Berkeley, 1946), pp. 430-431. Although its dates are unreliable, Hsü-yün's autobiography refers to a wave of confiscation in the winter of 1905-06: see Ts'en Hsüeh-lü, *Hsü-yün ho-shang nien-p'u*, p. 42; cf. Yin-shun, *T'ai-hsü*, p. 35. Makita Tairyō cites examples of confiscation of temples for schools in the years 1901-1906—see *Chugoku kinsei Bukkyōshi kenkyū* (Studies in the history of modern Chinese Buddhism; Kyoto, 1957), pp. 261-262. More investigation is needed.

29. Cyrus H. Peake, *Nationalism and Education in Modern China* (New York, 1932), p. 46. In Hunan, according to Peake, temples were borrowed rather than confiscated.

30. Yin-shun, *T'ai-hsü*, p. 25. Cf. Mizuno Baigyō, *Shina Bukkyō no genjo ni tsuite* (The present state of Chinese Buddhism; Tokyo, 1926), pp. 2, 23. Mizuno states that, as soon as these schools were registered, they got government protection.

31. See Welch, *Practice*, appendix 1; and appendix 3 in the present volume.

32. See Otto Franke, "Die Propaganda des japanischen Buddhismus in China," in *Ostasiatische Neubildungen* (Hamburg, 1911), pp. 160-161; and Yin-shun, *T'ai-hsü*, pp. 35-36. This episode will be discussed at greater length in Chapter IX.

33. Eight Fingers was an abbreviation for his sobriquet, "the Eight-Fingered Ascetic" (Pa-chih T'ou-t'o). On finger burning, see Welch, *Practice*, p. 324.

34. See Ts'en, Hsüeh-lü, *Hsü-yün ho-shang nien-p'u*, p. 43. Ts'en gives an erroneous date (1906) and text for this decree, which may be found in the *Ch'ing shih-lu;* see *Ta-ch'ing te-tsung ching (Kuang-hsü) huang-ti shih-lu* (Veritable records of the Ch'ing emperor Kuang-hsü; Taipei, 1964), 543:6b-7. The date is given in Kuo T'ing-i, *Chin-tai Chung-kuo shih-shih jih-chih* (Daily chronology of historical events in modern China; Taipei, 1963), II, 1225. Curiously enough, Hodous (p. 64) also gives the date as 1906.

35. Chou Hsiang-kuang, p. 214.

36. A Buddhist Primary School (Fo-chiao Hsiao-hsüeh T'ang) was started at the Kuan-yin Ssu, Peking, by its abbot, Chüeh-hsien. A Buddhist Lecture Training Center (Fo-chiao Chiang-hsi So) was operating at the Chieh-tai Ssu, Ningpo, in 1909. The abbot of this monastery, Yüan-ying, had studied meditation under Eight Fingers in 1903 and was to be another leading figure in the Buddhist revival. In 1909 there was also a Hua-yü Primary School on P'u-t'o Shan, which was probably set up under the aegis of Yin-kuang, the leader of the Pure Land revival who had first edited Yang's Buddhist primer. One of the many questions that deserves further study is the relationship of these schools to the monastic "educational associations" that were set up in accordance with a government order of 1906. At least two such associations came into existence in 1908: the Kiangsu Sangha Educational Association (Chiang-su Seng Chiao-yü Hui) and the Ningpo Sangha Educational Association. The latter was founded by Eight Fingers. Presumably the work of these associations was parallel to that of their lay counterparts set up the same year: that is, they were supposed to establish schools. However, despite conferences and cooperation, they are said to have had little success. The necessary money was available (from rich monasteries), but it was difficult to find good teachers and administrators. (See Yin-shun, *T'ai-hsü,*

pp. 35-36.) At any rate, none of the early schools is connected to any of the associations' efforts in the sources I have seen.

37. Concern for endowment meant that not all visitors to the big monasteries were received in the same way (just as there are gradations in the treatment of prospective donors when they visit a university campus). This is illustrated by a popular anecdote. One day a young man with neither money nor position came to offer incense at a large Kiangsu monastery. When he had finished his offering, the guest prefect looked him over and said "Sit down." Then, turning to one of his subordinates, he said "Tea." A few years later, having attained official rank and salary, the young man returned. This time the prefect greeted him more warmly with "Please sit down" and gave the order "Let tea be prepared." When the man returned for the third time as a high official, the prefect was a model of deference and courtesy: "Please take the seat of honor. Let the best tea be prepared."

38. Yin-shun, *T'ai-hsü*, p. 24.

39. For a discussion of *hua-t'ou*, see Welch, *Practice*, p. 69.

40. Yin-shun, *T'ai-hsü*, p. 33.

41. Yin-shun, *T'ai-hsü*, p. 34.

42. *Ko-ming chün* (Revolutionary army) was part of an extremely inflammatory anti-Manchu book published by the journal *Su-pao*.

43. The revolutionaries with whom he is said to have had the most contact were P'an Ta-wei, Mo Chi-p'eng, and Liang Shang-t'ung (see Yin-shun, *T'ai-hsü*, p. 42). Mo Chi-p'eng was a well-known anarchist of this period who was associated with the "assassination teams" that specialized in killing government officials in south China.

44. On transmission of the dharma (that is, of the right to abbotship), see Welch, *Practice*, pp. 156-168.

45. On this first lay initiation, termed "taking Refuge in the Three Jewels," see *ibid.*, pp. 359-361.

46. On the events of 1902-03, see Li Chien-nung, *The Political History of China 1840-1928*, tr. Ssu Yu Teng and Jeremy Ingalls (Princeton, 1956), p. 191, and Feng Tzu-yu, *Chung-hua min-kuo k'ai-kuo-ch'ien ko-ming shih* (History of China's prerevolutionary period; Chungking, 1943), I, 118ff. According to one source, Tsung-yang was editor-in-chief of *Su-pao*: see Chu Chieh-hsien, ed., *Ch'i-hsia shan-chih* (History of Ch'i-hsia Shan; Hong Kong, 1962), p. 67. Tsung-yang's contributions to the revolutionary movement are confirmed by a biographical notice that appears in *K'ai-kuo ming-jen mo-chi* (Holographs of the nation's founders), published by the Kuomintang History Bureau (Taipei, 1961), 1:9-10; and by Feng Tzu-yu, *Ko-ming i-shih* (Vignettes of the Revolution; Chungking, 1944), III, 170ff. My statements about Tsung-yang that do not come from these sources or from Chu Chieh-hsien, pp. 66-71, are based on interviews with monks connected to him.

47. Mrs. Hardoon's religious name was Chia-ling, that is, Kalavinka, a beautiful song-bird of the Himalayas. The full transliteration of Kalavinka in Chinese is *chia-ling p'in-chia*, the last two characters of which provided the name of the edition of the Tripitaka that she financed, as well as the name of the Pin-chia Ching-she, a retreat house in the grounds of Hardoon Gardens (at the corner of Avenue Foch and Seymour Road). The estate also included a nunnery and the building where Yüeh-hsia started the Avatamsaka University (see Chapter

X, note 5). There was also a dormitory in which monks properly introduced could stay for as long as they liked and get money for books and travel. Although devotions were held twice a day, the focus was on meditation and study. This, at any rate, was what one monk recalled who stayed there in 1937.

48. See note 20. An interesting though brief biography (51 pages) is to be found in Henry McAleavy, *Su Man-shu, a Sino-Japanese Genius* (London, 1960).

49. Liang Ch'i-ch'ao, *Intellectual Trends in the Ch'ing Period*, tr. Immanuel C. Y. Hsü (Cambridge, Mass., 1959), p. 108.

50. *Ibid.*, p. 112. Maitreya and Vasubandhu were founders of the Yogacara school of Buddhist philosophy in fifth-century India.

51. Tu Ch'eng-hsiang, *Tsou Jung* (Nanking, 1946), p. 82.

52. Early in 1922 Tai had been among those who supported the Federation of Antireligionists. In October, depressed about political turmoil in Szechwan, he attempted suicide by jumping into the Yangtze; after this traumatic experience he became a devout Buddhist. In the 1930's he was a leading patron of the Ch'i-hsia Ssu, an important monastery near Nanking, where he had a memorial pagoda built for his old friend, Tsung-yang. See Ch'en T'ien-hsi, *Tai Chi-t'ao hsien-sheng pien-nien chuan-chi* (Chronological biography of Tai Chi-t'ao; Hong Kong, 1958), p. 33; Chu Chieh-hsien, p. 97; *Hsiang-kang fo-chiao* (Buddhism in Hong Kong), 50:32 (July 1964).

53. Yin-shun, *T'ai-hsü*, p. 48, supplemented by the recollections of an elderly Kiangsu monk. However, an even older informant said that the story of monks taking part in the battle of Nanking is a fabrication.

54. Cheng-lien, 7:102.

55. Richard, *The Awakening of Faith*, p. ix.

II. THE STRUGGLE FOR NATIONAL LEADERSHIP

1. Ts'en Hsüeh-lü, *Hsü-yün ho-shang nien-p'u*, p. 59.

2. Reichelt, *The Transformed Abbot*, p. 80.

3. James Bissett Pratt, *The Pilgrimage of Buddhism and a Buddhist Pilgrimage* (New York, 1928), pp. 385-386. For more information on this group, which Pratt calls "the Young Men's Buddhist Association," see Chapter IV, note 35.

4. Yin-shun, *T'ai-hsü*, p. 47.

5. A detailed description of the administration and daily life at Chin Shan is given in Welch, *Practice*, pp. 10-80.

6. Chin Shan meant either the hillock or the principal monastery on it. If one wished to refer to the monastery specifically, in contradistinction to anything else there, one spoke of the "Chiang-t'ien Ssu" or, less formally, the "Chin-shan Ssu." On this synecdochic use of *shan and ssu*, see *ibid.*, p. 467, n. 4.

7. On the differences between hereditary temples like the Kuan-yin Ko and public monasteries like the Chiang-t'ien Ssu, see *ibid.*, p. 137.

8. The Socialist Party had been founded by Chiang K'ang-hu in November 1911. Within a year it had eighty branches, many of them in Kiangsu, some with 500-600 members. It was dissolved by Yüan Shih-k'ai in August 1913.

9. Chi-shan was a tonsure disciple of Ch'an-ching, former abbot of Chin Shan, and his monastery in Yangchow had Chin Shan's help in collecting its rents. See *ibid.*, p. 406.

10. Yin-shun, *T'ai-hsü*, pp. 49-50. A disciple of Shuang-t'ing recalled that the

latter stayed in jail longer than Ch'ing-ch'üan, but that both were released in a general amnesty proclaimed by Sun Yat-sen, who also dissolved the Association for the Advancement of Buddhism.

11. Some sources omit the "Chung-kuo" and refer to it simply as the Buddhist Association.

12. It is interesting that, although the charter claimed the right to government protection, it also claimed "absolute independence" of government control. See Wei-huan, "Buddhism in Modern China," *T'ien Hsia Monthly*, 9.2:153 (September 1939). I have not found the original Chinese text of the charter.

13. Yin-shun, *T'ai-hsü*, p. 52. Wing-tsit Chan (p. 57) says that their "pronouncements bitterly criticized the inability of the Buddhist clergy to uphold their religion."

14. Mizuno Baigyō, *Shina Bukkyo kinseishi no kenkyū* (Studies in the history of modern Chinese Buddhism; Tokyo, 1925), pp. 64-66.

15. Ts'en Hsüeh-lü, *Hsü-yün ho-shang nien-p'u*, pp. 60-61. The text states: "In the winter (1911-12) the Buddhist Great Harmony Association (Fo-chiao Ta-t'ung Hui) and the Buddhist Association (Fo-chiao Hui) had a dispute. A telegram was sent to Yünnan asking me to come. When I got to Shanghai, I went to see P'u-ch'ang, T'ai-hsü, Jen-shan, and Ti-hsien and got things straightened out; then the General Buddhist Association was set up at the Ching-an Ssu." Drawing on unspecified sources, the editor notes: "In Shanghai the Buddhist Association (Fo-chiao Hui) got into conflict with all quarters because of its new charter. Hsü-yün went north to Shanghai and talked it over with Chi-ch'an [Eight Fingers] and Yeh-k'ai [the abbot of the T'ien-ning Ssu]. In Nanking they went to see Sun Yat-sen and discussed revision of the charter. When this was over, he went to Peking with Chi-ch'an to see Yüan Shih-k'ai." These passages need further elucidation.

16. Yin-shun, *T'ai-hsü*, p. 52. Wing-tsit Chan (p. 57) states that Ou-yang's association was organized "for the sole purpose" of fighting the proposal before Parliament to make Confucianism the state religion. But Professor Chan also tells us that this proposal was not brought before Parliament until 1913 (pp. 7-8). Perhaps he has found evidence of continued activities by the association. His definition, incidentally, of its "sole purpose" is belied by the ambitious clauses of the charter quoted above.

17. Yin-shun, *T'ai-hsü*, p. 52. This statement may be anachronistic. The association charter, as published in October 1912, is stated to have been approved by the ministries of the Interior and Education in Nanking on February 12, 1912: see *Fo-hsüeh ts'ung-pao* (Buddhist miscellany), no. 1. If the invasion of Chin Shan took place on February 7, it would have been difficult to draw up this charter and get it approved within five days. Further investigation is needed.

18. Yin-shun, *T'ai-hsü*, p. 52. This may be a reference to an effort made independently by several of the patriotic leaders of the association to set up a Buddhist Defense Society (Fo-chiao Chiu-meng Hui) that would help the government to resist foreign encroachment and partition by means of voluntary contribution of monastic property for military expenses. This was reported in the autumn of 1912. See *Fo-hsüeh ts'ung-pao*, no. 3 (December 1913).

19. His monastic name was Ching-an, and his style was Chi-ch'an. Born in Hunan in 1852, he was ordained at Nan-yüeh in 1868. Since 1875 he had served as abbot of a series of well-known monasteries. See Pa-chih t'ou-t'o, *Pa-chih t'ou-t'o shih-chi* (Collected poems of the Eight-Fingered Ascetic; Taipei, 1956); and

R. F. Johnston, "A Poet Monk of Modern China," *Journal of the North China Branch of the Royal Asiatic Society*, 43:14-30 (1932).

20. The Chinese text of the charter is given in *Fo-hsüeh ts'ung-pao*, no. 1 (October 1912). What appears to be an English summary is given by Yu-yue Tsu in "Present Tendencies in Chinese Buddhism," *Journal of Religion*, 1.5:500 (September 1921). Bishop Tsu, however, includes two provisions that are not found in the Chinese. First, no one was to be ordained under the age of twenty and without three years' training. Second, it was stated that "for monks to hire themselves out for the performance of funeral services, especially appearing in funeral processions, is considered derogatory to the dignity of the monastic order, and so the practice is to be strictly prohibited." I can find nothing of this sort either in the pages of *Fo-hsüeh ts'ung-pao* cited or in the amended version of the charter printed in *Fo-chiao yüeh-pao* (The Buddhist monthly), no. 1 (May 1913). Although he was often inaccurate, it seems hard to believe that Bishop Tsu would be guilty of pure invention. Since he states that what he was summarizing was the "program" adopted at the inaugural meeting in Shanghai, it may not have been the charter but some other document. If so, this might be the only surviving record of an extremely significant move (the prohibition of mortuary professionalism), far more radical than anything else that we know to have been contemplated by the association. Was it the handiwork of T'ai-hsü or Jen-shan? More investigation is needed.

21. This account comes from *Fo-hsüeh ts'ung-pao*, no. 3 (December 1912). The date of death is given erroneously in several sources as January 8, 1913 (see, for example, Yin-shun, *T'ai-hsü*, p. 54, and Tao-an's introduction to Pa-chih t'ou-t'o, p. 2).

22. Yin-shun, *T'ai-hsü*, p. 55. The cabinet promulgated the amended version of the charter (see note 20).

23. The Ching-an Ssu was the official headquarters, although the staff lived and did some of the work at the Ch'ing-liang Ssu. The national conference, however, was held at the Liu-yün Ssu, as the inaugural conference had been a year earlier. The Peking headquarters were in the Fa-yüan Ssu under the Venerable Tao-chieh. Although it is not clear which ones were stationed permanently in Shanghai, among the staff members were many able and well-known monks: Wen-hsi, Yüan-ying, Pen-chung, Ying-ch'ien, Yüeh-hsia, T'ai-hsü, and Ti-hsien.

24. *Fo-chiao yüeh-pao* was published from May through September 1913. Its editorial offices were at the Ch'ing-liang Ssu. Ch'ing-hai was general manager and T'ai-hsü was one of the editors. Contributing editors included Yüan-ying, Jen-shan, Wen-hsi, Tsung-yang.

25. In Ningpo, for example, the leading monks of the Yen-ch'ing Ssu had been openly drinking wine and smoking opium. Troops had occupied part of the premises for five or six years. In the autumn of 1912 the authorities expelled some of the leading monks and imprisoned others, then requested that the local branch of the Buddhist Association send a reliable monk to take over. Accordingly, Ti-hsien, "the leading exponent of the T'ien-t'ai school," became the new abbot on January 21, 1913. He changed the name of the monastery to the Kuan-tsung Ssu and announced the plan to start a Buddhist Research Center (Fo-chiao Yen-chiu She). See *Fo-hsüeh ts'ung-pao*, no. 5 (February 1913).

26. Another reason may have been the dispersal of staff. Yüeh-hsia moved to Hangchow, T'ai-hsü to P'u-t'o Shan, and Ti-hsien to Ningpo.

27. For more on these regulations, see pp. 137-138.

28. "Chang-chia" was his title, not his name. Properly speaking, one should refer to him as "the Chang-chia Living Buddha" or "the Chang-chia Hutukhtu." On his historical role, see p. 174.

29. Yeh Kung-cho may have been one of them. He was both a member of the clique and a prominent lay Buddhist.

30. Yin-shun, *T'ai-hsü*, pp. 76, 102-103. Yu-yue Tsu places these events two years earlier. See "Present Tendencies in Chinese Buddhism," p. 502.

31. Yin-shun, *T'ai-hsü*, p. 76.

32. T'ai-hsü's Association for the Advancement of Buddhism, Ou-yang's Chinese Buddhist Association, the Chinese General Buddhist Association (Shanghai, 1912), and the Chinese Buddhist Association (Peking, 1917).

33. The charters of the Buddhist Society of the Great Vow (Fo-chiao Hung-shih Hui), the League for the Support of Buddhism (Wei-ch'ih Fo-chiao T'ung-meng hui), the Young Buddhist Study Association (Fo-chiao Ch'ing-nien Hsüeh-hui), and the Buddhist Research Society (Fo-hsüeh Yen-chiu Hui) are printed in *Fo-chiao yüeh-pao*, no. 1 (May 1913), but it is not clear to what extent they remained active. The same applies to another group, the Central Buddhist Confederation (Chung-yang Fo-chiao Kung-hui) discussed in *Fo-hsüeh ts'ung-pao*, no. 6 (March 1913). With headquarters in Peking, it claimed branches in seven northern provinces. A Buddhist Federation (Fo-chiao Lien-ho-hui) is also said to have been in existence at this time: see *Chung-kuo fo-chiao hui wu-shih-i nien-tu nien-chien* (Year book of the fifty-first year of the Chinese Buddhist Association; Taipei, n.d.), p. 1. But this may be identical with the Chinese Buddhist Federation that was not founded until 1925 in Peking (see Chapter III, note 22). Yu-yue Tsu mentions the following among organizations that appeared in the early years of the Republic: the Buddhist Confederation (Fo-chiao Kung-hui), the Chinese Yellow Swastika Society (Chung-hua Huang-wan-tzu Hui), the Buddhist Moral Endeavor Society (Fo-chiao Chin-te Hui), and the Buddhist Research Society (Fo-hsüeh Yen-chiu She). See Yu-yue Tsu, "Present Tendencies in Chinese Buddhism," pp. 500-501. Finally, a Buddhist Great Harmony Society (Fo-chiao Ta-t'ung Hui) was in existence about April 1912 (Yin-shun, *T'ai-hsü*, p. 52; see also above, note 15). There may be some duplication among the groups with similar names.

34. *Yüan-ying*, p. 13.

35. One source tells us that eminent monks held meetings in Shanghai and sent deputations to argue against the proposal with the ministries of the Interior and Education, but that what really turned the tide was Feng Yü-hsiang's visit to Ch'i-hsia Shan in July 1928. Feng, the famous "Christian general," stopped for a meal there with several dozen of his followers, among whom was Minister of the Interior Hsüeh Tu-pi. While Feng was chatting with the monks beforehand, one of them voiced his fears about the confiscation plan. The general made no comment, but when the meal was over he asked to be shown to the great shrine-hall. There he reverently placed incense in the bronze burner and prostrated himself before the buddha image. His followers were astonished, and Hsüeh Tu-pi (who owed his position to Feng) changed his mind. See Chu Chieh-hsien, pp. 78-79. I have also heard this anecdote from Ming-ch'ang, the monk with whom Feng chatted and who led him to the great shrine-hall. Robert Payne recounts seeing Feng lecture to student monks (followers of T'ai-hsü) at a monastery near Chung-king in 1942, and adds that Feng's father was a devout Buddhist layman. See Robert Payne, *Forever China* (New York, 1945), p. 274.

36. *Yüan-ying*, p. 13.

37. On January 25, 1929, the Ministry of the Interior had promulgated "Regulations for the Control of Monasteries and Temples" (*Ssu-miao kuan-li t'iao-li*) in twenty-one articles, some of which seriously infringed on monks' control over monastic property. See Makita Tairyō, *Chūgoku kinsei Bukkyōshi kenkyū* (Studies in the history of modern Chinese Buddhism; Kyoto, 1957), p. 269, and *Hai-ch'ao yin wen-k'u* (Hai-ch'ao yin collections), pt. 1, vol. 2, pp. 76-79. I have not had an opportunity to check the original text of these regulations, but several authorities confirm that to repeal them was one of the main purposes in setting up the Chinese Buddhist Association (Shanghai, 1929). See Yin-shun, *T'ai-hsü*, p. 289, and *Yüan-ying*, p. 13.

38. Yin-shun, *T'ai-hsü*, p. 258. Some sources credit T'ai-hsü with a leading role in the establishment of this new Chinese Buddhist Association—for example, Chou Hsiang-kuang, p. 17; and *Chung-kuo fo-chiao hui*, p. 2, which does not mention Yüan-ying at all, perhaps because he later became an "un-person" by accepting the presidency of the Communist-sponsored Chinese Buddhist Association. Yin-shun, from whom we could expect to hear any claim that T'ai-hsü had a role in the establishment of the new association, states merely that the members of his Buddhist Study Association in Nanking had joined with Yüan-ying's Kiangsu-Chekiang Buddhist Association in calling the inaugural conference (*T'ai-hsü*, p. 289).

39. This charter was published in *Chinese Buddhism*, 1.2:59-63 (July 1930). It is a simple document that provides for three administrative bodies, annual elections, several levels or branches, and such unexceptionable aims as social-welfare work, the propagation of Buddhism, and research. One of its weaknesses is the failure to require annual dues which, it was decided in 1930, were to be voluntary contributions fixed by the provincial representatives.

40. These four are the branches mentioned in *Chung-kuo fo-chiao hui*, p. 2, but since the regulations of December 7, 1929, gave wide powers to branches of the association, including the right to ratify the sale of property, it seems probable that other branches were soon established—or had survived from the days of earlier Buddhist associations. For example, a branch of the Chinese General Buddhist Association (Shanghai, 1912), established in Canton in 1912, still existed as such in 1928: see Tokiwa Daijō, *Shina Bukkyō shiseki kinen-shū* (Buddhist monuments in China, memorial collection; Tokyo, 1931), pp. 34-35. In 1922, when no national association appears to have been active, there was a hsien branch in Huang-mei, Hupeh: see Sekimo Tei and Tokiwa Daijō, *Shina Bukkyō shiseki* (Buddhist monuments in China; Tokyo, 1925-1929), vol. 4, plate 126.

41. *Hsien-tai seng-chia*, 4.2:180 (June 1931).

42. Yin-shun, *T'ai-hsü*, p. 326.

43. *Hai-ch'ao yin*, 16.3:28 (March 1935).

44. Yin-shun, *T'ai-hsü*, p. 339.

45. *Yüan-ying*, p. 13; Makita Tairyō, *Chūgoku kinsei Bukkyōshi*, p. 270. There is a significant parallel with the course of efforts to limit the activities of another component of traditional culture: Chinese medicine. In February 1929 (less than a year after the National Education Conference that resolved to confiscate monastic property), the Ministry of Health convened a conference that resolved to ban schools of Chinese medicine and to prohibit advertising or propaganda by its practitioners. The practitioners responded by forming a national association

that lobbied and protested (especially through conservative politicians and overseas Chinese) until the Ministry of Health had to abandon its plans. In the 1930's this national association kept calling for government support of its members' research, hospitals, and schools, and in 1935 it petitioned the Fifth Kuomintang Congress for equality at law with Western doctors—a petition that was finally granted in 1943. I am indebted for this information to Ralph Croizier.

46. Makita mentions that in 1933 a group of Hupeh educators discussed the possibility of trying to get an income from monastic property; and in 1935 the heads of the education departments of seven provinces unsuccessfully (and halfheartedly) asked the Ministry of Education for permission to take over monastic buildings and income. See Makita Tairyō, *Chugoku kinsei Bukkyōshi*, pp. 277-279.

47. *Yüan-ying*, p. 13. Yin-shun states that the association had applied for the Kuomintang's approval (*p'i-chun*) when it was first established in 1929 (*T'ai-hsü*, p. 292), but did not receive it until 1931 (p. 324).

48. *Yüan-ying*, p. 13. The report on the fifth national conference that appears in *Hai-ch'ao yin*, 14.7:93-94 (July 15, 1933), does not cast any clear light on the nature of the crisis.

49. Perhaps he has the year wrong, for elsewhere we read that in 1934 the association "changed from a system of three levels to two. There was opposition to this from the provinces." See *Chung-kuo fo-chiao hui*, p. 2.

50. For the details of the new charter, see p. 141 ff. It was drawn up partly because of a new effort by the reformers to take over the association. Earlier in 1936 the People's Training Bureau of the Kuomintang, apparently at the instigation of T'ai-hsü, had proposed a revision of the charter that provided for control of the internal operation of monasteries (including their finances, rules, and daily life) and for other reforms pleasing to "monk intellectuals." The rest of the sangha "erupted like a volcano" in protest and the proposal was dropped. See Fa-fang, "Nijūgo-nen-do Min-koku Bukkyokai no kaiko" (Review of Chinese Buddhist circles during 1936), in *Nikka Bukkyō kenkyukai nempō daininen* (Second annual report of the Japanese-Chinese Buddhist Research Society; Kyoto, 1937), pp. 230-232. The charter that was actually passed in November 1936, by tightening government control, undercut one of the arguments that could be advanced by the reformers to justify any future effort to take over the association. Furthermore, conservative dominance was probably fortified by article 22, which reserved to the sangha (with its majority of conservatives) at least two thirds of the seats on the standing committee and at least half the seats on the executive and supervisory committees.

51. See *Chinese Year Book, 1937* (Shanghai, 1937), p. 73. The 1935-36 edition of this yearbook (p. 1516) gave the figure as 435, and the 1936-37 edition as 476; there was evidently an annual increase of thirty to forty branches in this period.

52. For example, Wing-tsit Chan, p. 58. Professor Chan is probably confusing the Chinese Buddhist Association (Shanghai, 1929) with the Chinese Buddhist Study Association (Nanking, 1928), which did move to Chungking.

53. Yin-shun, *T'ai-hsü*, p. 448; *Yüan-ying*, p. 13.

54. In 1943, for example, he lectured widely in central and north China. In Peking he was received by the mayor, who suspended the slaughter of animals throughout the city on the day of his lecture in order to end a drought. See *Buddhist China*, 1.2:10 (Winter 1943).

55. Yin-shun, *T'ai-hsü*, p. 488.

56. Chung-kuo Tsung-chiao-t'u Lien-i-hui. Yin-shun, *T'ai-hsü*, pp. 498, 501.

57. Yin-shun, *T'ai-hsü*, p. 518. The full committee consisted of T'ai-hsü, Chang-chia, Hsü-yün, Yüan-ying, Ch'ang-yüan, Ch'üan-lang, Li Tzu-k'uan, Ch'ü Wen-liu, and Huang Ch'ing-lan.

58. The text of this charter is given in Lin Chin-tung, *Chung-kuo fo-chiao fa-ling hui-pien* (Classified collection of laws and decrees on Chinese Buddhism; Taipei, 1958), pp. 233-239. In accordance with article 7, by-laws passed at the same time provided for close control by the association over tonsure, ordination, and the selection of abbots (pp. 241-245)—types of control that do not appear to have been provided for since 1912-13.

59. This is the first of eight obligations printed on individual membership cards in 1946.

60. According to the 1936 charter, article 35, monks and nuns paid dues of $1 a year, while lay devotees paid $5. According to the 1947 charter, article 36, both paid the same ($5,000 in the rapidly inflating currency of the day). A reliable informant, however, recalled that there was still a differential between sangha and laity, and said that they paid the equivalent of $2 and $10 respectively.

61. See *Kuang-hui-ti pa-nien* (Eight glorious years; Hong Kong, 1958), p. 176.

62. One officer of a district chapter has told me that "sometimes it succeeded in helping and sometimes it did not." Most of the information given above on the gap between paper and practice comes from a reliable lay informant who played a leading role in the work of the association after 1945.

III.   T'AI-HSÜ

1. On sealed confinement, see Welch, *Practice*, pp. 321-322.

2. *Cheng-li seng-chia chih-tu lun*, first published in 1919, later included in the complete works (see note 3).

3. See *T'ai-hsü ta-shih ch'üan-shu* (Complete works of the Venerable T'ai-hsü; Hong Kong, 1953), p'ien 9, pt. 1.

4. This scheme, although the figures differ, appears to be the final version of earlier schemes prepared in 1930 and 1935. It is described by Fa-fang, a disciple of T'ai-hsü's, in "Chūgoku Bukkyō no genjō" (The present state of Chinese Buddhism), in *Nikka Bukkyō kenkyukai nempō daiichinen* (First annual report of the Japanese-Chinese Research Society; Kyoto, 1936), pp. 38-45.

5. In 1924 and again in 1928 he contemplated returning to lay life. At one time he considered that if it was of more benefit to Buddhism to be a layman, then one should be a layman. See Yin-shun, *T'ai-hsü*, pp. 247-248. At other times he advised people against entering the sangha and even said that it was better to seek enlightenment as a layman than as a monk. See Yu-yue Tsu, "Present Tendencies in Chinese Buddhism," p. 510.

6. This plan was presented in the first issue of *Hai-ch'ao yin* (1920), of which I have been unable to find a copy. It is described by Yu-yue Tsu in "Present Tendencies in Chinese Buddhism," p. 506.

7. "A Statement to Asiatic Buddhists," *Young East*, 1.6:179-180 (Nov. 8, 1925).

8. The charter of the Bodhi Society called for religious cultivation to be carried on by members, who were obliged to take the Three Refuges, to observe

certain prohibitions, to hold a week of buddha recitation and a week of meditation in winter, to release living creatures on the Buddha's birthday, and so on.
See Frank Millican, "T'ai-hsü and Modern Buddhism," *Chinese Recorder*, 54.6:329-
330 (June 1923); and Yu-yue Tsu, "Present Tendencies in Chinese Buddhism,"
pp. 504-505. T'ai-hsü's biographer reveals the real purpose of the society when
he states that T'ai-hsü and his friends, "seeing that the European War was not
yet over, felt that the first Buddhist study group should be established and then
gradually schemes could be made for moving ahead [to reorganize the sangha].
Such was the origin of the Bodhi Society whose program was: publication of
writing in special fields, editing collections, lecturing on Buddhism, and carrying
on religious cultivation (*hsiu-hsing*)." Yin-shun, *T'ai-hsü*, pp. 94-95.

This had no connection with the Bodhi societies founded in Peking and
Shanghai (see p. 179). Millican alludes to a Buddhist association (*fo-hsüeh hui*)
that T'ai-hsü apparently organized in Shanghai in 1918, a separate entity from
the Bodhi Society, and that seems to have still been active there in 1923. I have
found no reference to this in Chinese sources.

9. This account of the World Buddhist Federation is based mainly on the
following sources: Yin-shun, *T'ai-hsü*, pp. 158-162, 176-178, 217; Mizuno Baigyō,
Shina Bukkyō no genjo, pp. 90-95; *Eastern Buddhist*, 3.2:190 (July-September
1924), 3.3:247-278 (October-December 1924); *Young East*, 1.6:179-182 (Nov.
8, 1925); Karl Ludwig Reichelt, "A Conference of Chinese Buddhist Leaders,"
Chinese Recorder, 54.11:667-669 (November 1923).

10. Professor Takakusu Junjiro had originally been among those recommended
for the delegation by the Japanese Buddhist Federation, but he was too busy
editing the Taishō Tripitaka.

11. Mizuno gives the text of the constitution and says that it represented a
revision of an existing constitution. He calls 1924 the third year of the conference and implies that T'ai-hsü began his lectures in 1922, a statement for which
I can find no confirmation. See Mizuno Baigyō, *Shina Bukkyō no genjo*, pp. 93-94.

12. Yin-shun, *T'ai-hsü*, pp. 199, 217.

13. Wing-tsit Chan, p. 58.

14. Yin-shun, *T'ai-hsü*, pp. 160, 178.

15. Reichelt, "A Conference of Chinese Buddhist Leaders," p. 668. Yin-shun,
(*T'ai-hsü*, p. 160) states that he attended in 1924. Perhaps he did so in both years,
which would help to explain the discrepancies between the two accounts.

16. *Chung-kuo fo-chiao hui*, pp. 1-2; Mizuno Baigyō, *Shina Bukkyō no genjo*,
pp. 94-95.

17. *Buddhist China* (London, 1913).

18. Reichelt, "A Conference of Chinese Buddhist Leaders," p. 669. The italics
are Reichelt's. Cf. John Blofeld, *The Wheel of Life* (London, 1959), p. 179.

19. See pp. 27-28 and Chapter IV, note 35.

20. Pratt, p. 387.

21. This is clearly stated by Yin-shun in *T'ai-hsü*, pp. 194-195.

22. Mizuno Baigyō, *Shina Bukkyō kinseishi*, pp. 66-67; *Shina Bukkyō no genjo*,
pp. 72-87. There are some problems of chronology here. According to the second
citation, at least one of the branches (Hunan) had been set up prior to the Lu
Shan Conference of 1924. If so, unless it was the relic of an earlier group, the
purpose of its parent organization cannot have been merely to legitimize the
dispatch of delegates to the Tokyo conference, which had not yet been proposed.

According to another source, the branches included Hupei, not Hunan, and the headquarters were in Wuchang, not Peking (see Makita Tairyō, *Chūgoku kinsei Bukkyōshi*, p. 264). Perhaps the headquarters were only moved to Peking after the formal inauguration on April 6, 1925.

23. Mizuno Baigyō, *Shina Bukkyō no genjo*, pp. 97-98.

24. It relinquished its international claims when it was renamed the Chinese Buddhist Education Center. It served for a time as the editorial office for *Hai-ch'ao yin* and *Hsin-teng*. See Yin-shun, *T'ai-hsü*, pp. 215, 217.

25. Yin-shun, *T'ai-hsü*, pp. 208-209.

26. *Buddhism in England*, 3.7:162 (January 1929).

27. Yin-shun, *T'ai-hsü*, p. 266.

28. This is taken from a review of T'ai-hsü, *Lectures in Buddhism* (Paris, 1928), which appeared in the *Bulletin de l'Association française des amis de l'orient*, no. 7, pp. 93-94. This association, of which Sylvain Lévi was a vice-president, sponsored (jointly with the Association Franco-Chinoise) T'ai-hsü's October 14 lecture at the Musée Guimet on the subject, "Buddhism in History and Its Recent Tendencies," printed in *Lectures in Buddhism*, pp. 15-29.

29. *Chinese Buddhist*, 1.4:156-158 (January 1931). This letter was dated November 11, 1929.

The task of reconciling the differing versions of T'ai-hsü's world tour would not be an easy one. Among the difficulties is the fact that his biographer gives only the Chinese transliterations for the names of the people and organizations with whom T'ai-hsü came in contact. Thus it is fairly clear that Lung-shu-pei-le is Grace Constant Lounsberry, but not so clear whether Ko-la-nai is Barnett Conlan, the Irish art critic who is said to have interested Miss Lounsberry in T'ai-hsü's visit to begin with: see *Maha Bodhi*, 73.3-4:83-84 (March-April 1965). Since Conlan was the translator (from French to English?) of T'ai-hsü's *Lectures in Buddhism*, he must also be the mysterious "Kuen-lun" who wrote the foreword. In T'ai-hsü's biography, his name is given as Pai-nai-neng (see Yin-shun, *T'ai-hsü*, p. 267).

Doubt may be cast on my Chinese informant's account by the fact that, while the lectures at the Musée Guimet started on October 14, the founding meeting of the World Buddhist Institute took place on October 20, and among the founders were Sylvain Lévi (Hsi-erh-fa Le-fei) and Professor Laloy (La-erh-hua): see Yin-shun, *T'ai-hsü*, pp. 265, 267. But T'ai-hsü seems simply to have been up to his old trick of borrowing prestigious names without authorization from their owners. The text does not state that Lévi and Laloy were actually present. The reviewer quoted above, who may well have been Lévi himself, remarked of the list of founders: "The names of several orientalists are cited, not without confusing the names of those who have joined with those whom they hope to have join." At the inaugural meeting of the Paris chapter, held January 3, 1929 (when T'ai-hsü was still in Berlin), quite a different group took part: "Mr. and Mrs. Humphreys, Mr. Hou Yong Ling [Hu Yung-lin], Mlle. Politour, the first European pupil of His Eminence, who is going to China to study Buddhism, Mr. Kniazeff, a Russian Chinese scholar, Mon. de Maratray, the French poet and writer, and Mon. de Malan" (*Maha Bodhi*, 37.3:157 [March 1929]). Mlle. Politour, who was indeed T'ai-hsü's first European pupil (having taken the Refuges with him on September 28), apparently did not go to China. But the fifteen to twenty members of Les Amis du Bouddhisme continued to meet every week or two at Miss Lounsberry's house and became the principal Buddhist group in France.

30. "His two attendants admirably filled the role of interpreter," according to *Buddhism in England*, 3.7:127 (January 1929).

31. *Maha Bodhi*, 37.1:46-47 (January 1929).

32. Shih-chieh Fo-hsüeh-yüan T'u-shu-kuan. According to some sources, the library and seminary together were now considered to be the library. See Wei-huan, p. 148. A hundred thousand volumes (*chüan*) in Chinese might be equivalent to less than ten thousand in a Western language.

33. *Ibid*. Cf. Yin-shun, *T'ai-hsü*, p. 321; Fa-fang, "Chūgoku Bukkyō," pp. 10ff. In 1950, when T'ai-hsü's follower Fa-fang represented China at the first conference of the World Fellowship of Buddhists, he listed his affiliation as "the World Buddhist Institute, Wuchang," so that the imaginary existence of this organization was prolonged for two decades.

34. In March 1937, for example, he joined with Japanese Buddhists at the Higashi Honganji temple in Shanghai in trying to set up an International Buddhist Peace Society—not a very promising venture at that time.

35. Yin-shun, *T'ai-hsü*, p. 257.

36. T'ai-hsü, *Lectures in Buddhism*, pp. 38, 43-45, 49. Cf. similar statements of T'ai-hsü quoted from his *Lu-shan hsüeh* by Yu-yue Tsu, "Trends of Thought and Religion in China," *The New Orient* (Chicago, 1933), pp. 322-323. Here he points out that Buddhism offers what science cannot, "a direct insight into the realities of the universe, an intuitive experience only acquired by oneself where all logic, analogy, or scientific hypothesis are of no avail."

37. Wing-tsit Chan, pp. 124-125. For an exposition of T'ai-hsü's version of Dharmalaksana—a subject that lies outside the scope of this book—see *ibid.*, pp. 118-126.

38. In 1945 a former abbot of the T'ien-t'ung Ssu, when expatiating on the relationship of Buddhism and science, told a student: "Now, isn't this the space age we are living in? In twenty years scientists are going to start visiting other planets. And how will they talk to the people who live there? Obviously they will have to use Sanskrit [the language of the gods, who inhabit the heavens] and *we* will have to teach them. So study your Sanskrit well." A more sophisticated example can be found in Chu Pao-ch'ang, "Wei-shih hsin-chieh" (A new explanation of Idealism), *Yen-ching hsüeh-pao*, no. 23 (June 1938), in which the concepts of the Wei-shih school are compared with those of Alfred North Whitehead.

39. See T'ai-hsü, "The Meaning of Buddhism," trans. F. R. Millican, *Chinese Recorder*, 65.11:690 (November 1934).

40. All of this is as recounted by the head of the Chengtu YMCA to J. B. Pratt. See Pratt, pp. 383-384.

41. On sarira relics, see Welch, *Practice*, p. 345.

42. Reichelt, *The Transformed Abbot*, pp. 80-81.

43. This information on the troubles at T'ai-hsü's seminaries comes from *ibid.*, pp. 91-93, 97. Reichelt obviously got the information from Miao-chi, a Buddhist convert to Christianity. All the dates are questionable (the seminary at the Nan P'u-t'o Ssu in Amoy, for example, did not open until 1925), and some of the touches (like visiting brothels) were probably added to make it a better story. But its substance may well be accurate.

44. Wei-huan, p. 147.

45. *Maha Bodhi*, 37.1:46-47 (January 1929).

46. *Buddhism in England*, 3.6:129-130 (December 1928).

47. Payne, p. 274.

48. The preparatory committee of the Chinese Buddhist Study Association was established on July 28, 1928, but the inaugural meeting of the Association was held on November 29, 1929. See Yin-shun, *T'ai-hsü*, pp. 257, 299.

49. *Chinese Year Book, 1942-1943* (n.p., n.d.), p. 63. T'ai-hsü also took this opportunity to let it be known that his own periodical, *Hai-ch'ao yin*, "held the unique position of being the most influential of all Buddhist publications in China"—a characterization that was probably true (if one was speaking of influence on non-Buddhists as well) but that gave the casual reader no idea of the large volume of other Buddhist periodicals, some of which were more popular with devout and conservative Buddhists than the reform-oriented *Hai-ch'ao yin*. Later yearbooks claimed that membership in the Chinese Buddhist Study Association had been 9,000 before the move to Chungking and reached 2,000 even after it, including the members of twelve branches in Szechwan, Chekiang, Fukien, Kansu, and Shanghai: see *China Handbook, 1937-1943* (New York, 1943), p. 843, and *China Handbook, 1945* (New York, 1947), p. 600. These figures have been contradicted by an informant who was a prominent member of the organization during that period. It is possible that T'ai-hsü was playing a "numbers game" by including the membership of other groups, particularly the existing branches of the Chinese Buddhist Association (Shanghai, 1929).

50. Fa-fang's report is filled with errors: "In 1912 a Central Chinese Buddhist Federation was founded in Nanking [wrong] by the famous Pa-tze-to-tas (eight-fingered) poet-monk, Chi-chan. His disciple, Tai-hsü, founded in 1915 [wrong] the Buddhist Progressive Society in the famous Zen temple, King San Su [Chin-shan Ssu] near Nanking where he introduced many reforms and trained young monks to learn the doctrine thoroughly and go out into the world [wrong] . . . The Central Buddhist Federation gradually took over all the temples and assumed control of their well-being and upkeep [wrong]. When Tai-hsü became its President in 1928 [wrong], he reorganized it . . . During the Japanese invasion the Buddhist Federation, under the direction of Tai-hsü [wrong], concentrated its attention on works of mercy . . . At the end of the war Tai-hsü was again [wrong] elected head of the Buddhist Federation, but he passed away in 1947." *Report of the Inaugural Conference of the World Fellowship of Buddhists* (Colombo, n.d.), pp. 56-57. Cf. Chapter II, note 38. With T'ai-hsü's own disciples making such claims, his European followers may perhaps be pardoned for announcing that "during the first year of the Republic when T'ai-hsü was twenty-three years old, he founded the Chinese Buddhist Association with its headquarters in Nanking and its branches in many big cities"—an idea they obviously got from T'ai-hsü himself (see T'ai-hsü, *Lectures in Buddhism*, p. 12).

51. A slightly different explanation is given by Mizuno, who collaborated with T'ai-hsü on the World Buddhist Federation. Mizuno says that, for a Chinese, "world" means China, since China includes different races and people from different areas—an explanation that is reminiscent of the old concept that the Middle Kingdom included all under heaven (Mizuno Baigyō, *Shina Bukkyō no genjo*, p. 88).

52. Blofeld, *Wheel of Life*, p. 180.

53. See, for example, the letter from Tai Chi-t'ao to T'ai-hsü of June 16, 1935,

reprinted in Ch'en T'ien-hsi, ed., *Tai Chi-t'ao hsien-sheng wen-ts'un* (Writings of Tai Chi-t'ao; Taipei, 1959), pp. 1245-1246.

IV. THE LAY BUDDHIST MOVEMENT

1. On the wealth of the sangha, see Welch, *Practice*, pp. 240-241.

2. Somewhat arbitrarily, I translate *hui* as "association" when it occurs in the name of a group that was national in scope or pretensions, and as "society" when it occurs in the name of a local group.

3. On the history of these societies, see Kenneth K. S. Ch'en, pp. 290-295, 402.

4. In 1724, for example, women were ordered to cease forming societies for offering incense at temples or for celebrating the festival days of divinities. See *Ch'in-ting ta-Ch'ing hui-tien shih-li* (Collected statutes and precedents of the Ch'ing dynasty; Shanghai, 1899), 501:8. There was always the danger that a Buddhist society might be mistaken for a branch of one of the heretical sects, against which the law provided the most stringent penalties.

5. See Hummel for information on the following: P'eng Shao-sheng (p. 615), Lo Yu-kao (p. 614), Wang Wen-chih (p. 840). P'eng Shao-sheng was a devout Pure Land ascetic who in 1784 "retired to a temple where he remained for more than ten years, practicing silence and keeping the precepts strictly." Wang Wen-chih, who was also engaged in devout and ascetic practices, became a monk at the age of fifty in 1778.

6. Liang Ch'i-ch'ao, p. 116.

7. Hodous, p. 66. This may partly explain why the few figures available on the age of men who became monks between 1915 and 1949 show that two thirds of them did so between twenty and fifty (see Welch, *Practice*, pp. 251-252).

8. For example, Kenneth J. Saunders wrote at this time: "Buddhism in China, decadent though it is in many places, is reviving itself . . . Many men, indeed, disillusioned at the failure of the revolution, are seeking the quiet, other worldly retreats of Buddhism and others of scholarly bent delight in the classical scriptures which the early missionaries from India translated into Chinese" (*Buddhism in the Modern World*, London, 1922, pp. 66-67). Also J. Prip-Møller: "Quite a few military men, growing weary of their blood-thirsty metier, have entered the monasteries" (*Chinese Buddhist Monasteries*, Copenhagen, 1937, p. 299).

9. See Ernst Boerschmann, *P'u-t'o Shan* (Berlin, 1911), p. 30: "Such examples of well educated men of high standing are not frequent, but also not terribly rare."

10. See Welch, *Practice*, pp. 389-390.

11. See *Maha Bodhi*, 41.12:531-532 (December 1933). Marshal Sun was reportedly killed by the daughter of a man whose death he was believed to have caused. Another convert was General Wang Jui-hua, who served as Harbin's first chief of police under the Japanese and then, because of the difficulties he encountered, entered a Buddhist temple (see *New York Times*, Feb. 12, 1928, pt. 4, p. 8).

12. He eventually became Hsü-yün's biographer. The quotation comes from an interview with a member of his family.

13. One source speaks of a statistical report that showed 422 in the Yangtze Valley area, 67 in Kwangtung, 52 in the north, and 30 in Manchuria (note the

absence of a figure for western China). Most of them were "organized and managed solely by Buddhist laymen." See *Chinese Buddhist*, 1.2:42 (July 1930).

14. I do not mean that vegetarian restaurants were operated only by merit clubs or that merit clubs operated only vegetarian restaurants. The by-laws of the Fukien Merit Club, for example, called for it to promote study, lectures, distribution of sutras, reciting buddha's name, and charitable activities. See Tokiwa Daijō, *Shina Bukkyō shiseki kinen-shū*, p. 155.

15. The name meant "the society for study of the third period," i.e., the third in the three periods of the Buddha's preaching as divided by the Dharmalaksana school: (1) Agama, (2) Prajna, (3) Dharmalaksana. See *Chinese Buddhist*, 1.1:7 (April 1930). It was organized about 1924 by Han Ch'ing-ching.

16. For more details of Pure Land practice and its aims, see Welch, *Practice*, pp. 89-100; and pp. 383-384 for the daily religious duties of members of the Buddhist societies.

17. Fo-chiao Ching-yeh She. It is described by Reichelt in *The Transformed Abbot*, pp. 48-51, where for some reason it is romanized as "Chin-nieh She."

18. This was founded in 1918 as the Buddhist Devotees Club (Fo-chiao Chü-shih-lin) and the word "world" (*shih-chieh*) was prefixed when the club was reorganized in 1922. The change of names signified that it welcomed as members people who came to China from all over the world and took as its goal that people all over the world should become enlightened. It was particularly active in publishing. Ting Fu-pao, who had the largest Buddhist bookstore in Shanghai and edited the largest Chinese Buddhist dictionary, was head of its publications department. It had a street chapel, rather like T'ai-hsü's in Wuhan (described on p. 68). It also held private lectures for its members which, during the one short period that we have figures for, were attended by about as many men as women. The administration and control of the club, however, was clearly in the hands of men. One of its sections was charged with releasing animals on festival days. In the years 1923 and 1925 it released the following: 4,078 catties of yellow eels, 488 catties of carp, 18,208 catties of snails, 1,200 catties of clams, 14,790 turtles, 327 catties of edible frogs, 3,634 small birds, 19 cattle, 18 sheep, 505 catties of snake fish, 20 catties of loach fish, 715 catties of black fish, 25 catties of eels, 75 hens. This represented a total outlay of $3,045. Like other expenses it was met by members of the club. See Mizuno Baigyō, *Shina Bukkyō no genjo*, pp. 48-49.

19. Wei-huan, p. 154.

20. Pratt, pp. 386-387.

21. Wei-huan (p. 154) states that when it was founded it was called the Hankow Buddhist Society (Han-k'ou Fo-chiao Hui) and was transformed into the Hupeh Buddhist Association by General T'ang Sheng-chih, who had previously been an active patron of Buddhism in Hunan (cf. C. K. Yang, p. 211). Pratt (pp. 386-387) calls it the Young Men's Buddhist Association, but explains that "its local name was the Hankow Buddhist Society," and later confuses it with the defunct Chinese Buddhist Association (Shanghai, 1912). My informant—its former president—states that it was always called the Right Faith Society and that its first president was Wang Sen-p'u, whereas, according to *Hai-ch'ao yin*, 2.3:1 (March 20, 1921), the president of the Hankow Buddhist Society in 1921 was Li K'ai-shen.

Wei-huan gives a key role in its establishment to the monk Ta-yü, whereas my informant gives a key role to T'ai-hsü. He recalls, on the other hand, that T'ai-hsü had a quarrel with Hupeh Governor Li Yin-ch'en, who had helped to found both the Right Faith Society and the Wuchang Buddhist Seminary—a quarrel so bitter that Governor Li resigned as patron of the seminary and was replaced by Wang Sen-p'u. All this was said to have happened before 1926. The picture is further confused by the reference to a Right Faith Society in Wuchang, not Hankow, that is said to have been established in January 1924 by Yang Hsüan-ch'eng, who like Wang Sen-p'u was a disciple of T'ai-hsü (see Yin-shun, *T'ai-hsü*, p. 165). More investigation is needed.

22. There are contradictory figures on the size of the membership. This one was given by the former president.

23. On devotions, see Welch, *Practice*, pp. 54-58, 71. On the dress worn by lay devotees at devotions, see *ibid.*, p. 114. When Pratt visited the society in October 1923, he observed devotions in progress at 6:00 P.M. A monk and three laymen "in priestly garb" were lined up on one side of the shrine-hall (before an image of Amitabha) while opposite them stood six laywomen and seven boys. All of them were chanting with "a good deal of fervor." Pratt was told that three monks resided there (see Pratt Notebooks, Williams College Library). I was told by the former president that monks did not reside there, but were called in from T'ai-hsü's seminary whenever their expertise was needed for special rites. The former president first joined the society in 1929, and he would probably not have known if, six years earlier, monks had lived on the premises in order to help the lay staff get started performing devotions in the correct way.

24. In Canton the Liu-jung Ssu was said to have been supported for a time by the Canton Devotees Club.

25. On the hall of rebirth (*wang-sheng t'ang*), see Welch, *Practice*, p. 203.

26. See *ibid.*, pp. 384-385. In 1938 Osgood came upon a lay Buddhist club near Kunming, the members of which performed rites for the dead under the leadership of a local monk. They were paid for this, just as if they had been monks themselves. These activities were said to have started early in the Republican era. See Cornelius Osgood, *Village Life in Old China* (New York, 1963), pp. 294-296.

27. A brief history of this monastery is given in Ch'en Tsung-fan, *Yen-tu tsung-k'ao* (Investigations into old Peking; Peking, 1931), 2:180-181, where it is referred to as the Mi-le An and alternatively as the Shih-fang Ch'an-yüan. Another source states that in 1925 it was already in disrepair, without a monk in charge, and partly occupied by neighboring families. In that year T'an-hsü was asked to take it over by two of the devotees who were interested in it, Chang Ching-nan and Ma Chi-p'ing, the latter being private secretary to Tuan Ch'i-jui. T'an-hsü and his followers operated a seminary there until 1930. See T'an-hsü, *Ying-ch'en hui-i lu* (Reminiscences of shadow and dust; Hong Kong, 1955), II, 37-38. It was apparently after this seminary closed that the monastery was taken over by T'ung-yüan, who was abbot when Chen-k'ung arrived. In the *Hua-pei tsung-chiao nien-chien ti-i hao* (North China yearbook of religion, no. 1; Peking, 1941), p. 114, the name of the head monk is given as K'o-kuan (it was he who succeeded the first abbot, T'ung-yüan, shortly after the arrival of Chen-k'ung). The sect is given as Hsien-shou (Avatamsaka), although according to my informant it was Lin-chi (on the nature of sects, see Chapter X). There were at least two other Mi-le Yüan in Peking.

28. On the duties of the rector (*shou-tso*), see Welch, *Practice,* pp. 37, 39, 68. The original Chinese of this and other monastic titles (which have been translated into English in many different ways) is given with my own English translation in the glossary index of *The Practice of Chinese Buddhism.*

29. On the daily schedule at Chin Shan and the Kao-min Ssu, see *ibid.,* appendix 3.

30. The name of the Kao-min rector was Fa-chou. My informant did not know whether Chen-k'ung was his dharma disciple or had ever sat in the meditation hall of the Kao-min Ssu.

31. On signals and patrols, see *ibid.,* appendices 3-4.

32. On the *fang-ts'an* meal served to monks in their seats in the meditation hall, see *ibid.,* p. 73. On private instruction or tutorials (*ch'ing k'ai-shih*), see *ibid.,* p. 70.

33. Mizuno Baigyō, *Shina Bukkyō no genjo,* p. 45. I have found no description of this club in other sources. Mizuno Baigyō, *Shina Bukkyō no genjo,* p. 48, mentions what appears to have been another such hybrid in Hsüan-hua, northwest of Peking. The Hsüan-hua Pure Karma Hall (Ching-yeh T'ang) was established by Hsü Yüan-ming, a lay devotee, in 1920. Pao-i, the abbot of Hung-lo Shan, the famous Pure Land center, was asked to get it properly set up. It had a great shrine-hall, a guest department, refectory, and other sections that would normally be found only in a monastery.

In Taiwan today one finds laymen and even lay women living in monasteries together with monks and officially listed as guest prefect, chef (*tien-tso*), and so on. The only thing that sets them apart is their long hair. Although for centuries in China women have lived like nuns in "vegetarian halls" and men have held office in heterodox sects, this sort of thing appears to be a new development in Chinese Buddhism.

34. Kuan Chiung (see Chapter I, note 6) writes: "It can be stated without fear of contradiction that a revival of Buddhism in China can only come about when Buddhism will return to China from the western world. The young men of today in China, particularly the students and college graduates, will never understand or accept many aspects of Buddhism which is prevalent in China today." *Chinese Year Book, 1935-1936,* p. 1516.

35. An example of this ephemerality was the Buddhist New Youth Society (Fo-hua Hsin-ch'ing-nien Hui). Created in 1922 or early 1923, it had originally been housed in the Hankow Buddhist Association. On July 8, 1923, T'ai-hsü had ordered it to move to the Kuan-yin Ssu in Peking, where it remained for the next few years of sporadic life (Yin-shun, *T'ai-hsü,* p. 160). In 1924 it was said to have been "temporarily disbanded" (Pratt, p. 386). Mizuno tells us that in 1925 it opened a trade school for workmen and that it was spreading Buddhism among students at Peking University. I have come across no mention of it at a later date, unless the Hankow branch survived as the Youth Department (Ch'ing-nien Pu) of the Right Faith Society. See pp. 27-28, 58.

V. BUILDING AND PUBLISHING

1. For example, the T'ai-tzu Pagoda on P'u-t'o Shan was rebuilt shortly before 1923, and the Chen-mang Pagoda at the T'ien-t'ung Ssu was rebuilt between 1918 and 1922 (Sekino Tei and Tokiwa Daijō, *Shina Bukkyō shiseki,* vol. 5,

plates 108, 116). At about the same time extensive repairs were made at the Wan-nien Ssu on T'ien-t'ai Shan (*ibid.*, vol. 4, plates 67-69), and the K'ai-fu Ssu in Changsha (*Hsien-tai fo-hsüeh*, 59.11:28, Nov. 13, 1959). The Pao-t'ung Ssu, Wuchang was repaired in 1923 (*North China Daily News*, Feb. 20, 1924), the Fa-hai Ssu, Foochow was repaired in 1929 (*Yüan-ying*, p. 13), and the Pai-ma Ssu, Loyang, in 1934-35. Another instance of reconstruction was the T'ien-wang Tien of the Ling-yin Ssu in Hangchow, torn down in 1925 and replaced with a new one by 1931: see Robert F. Fitch, *Hangchow Itineraries* (Shanghai, 1929), p. 23, and C. B. Day, *Chinese Peasant Cults* (Shanghai, 1940), p. 35. On the re-building of the Leng-yen Pagoda, Chi-tsu Shan, in 1929, see Ting Sing-wu, *China the Beautiful* (Hong Kong, 1955), p. 82.

2. A decline in popular support not only shrank the monastery's income, but also deprived it of the possibility of periodic reconstruction of buildings. According to my informants, both reconstruction and restoration were usually financed by public subscription. This tends to be confirmed by the inadequate sample in C. K. Yang, pp. 320-321, and by figures on temples in Shanghai, most of which were presumably built during its growth as a treaty port. Of its 73 Buddhist monasteries and temples on which information is available, 8 were built by im-perial decree, 30 by soliciting subscriptions, and 15 by donations from devotees; 13 were the private temples of rich families, and 7 were rest houses. See *Shang-hai shih nien-chien* (Shanghai year book; Shanghai, 1935), p. U4. J. B. Pratt (p. 687) mentions a temple in Ma-chang, Hopei, that was renovated at the cost of $100,000 in gold "collected from among the common people."

3. The Lung-hua Ssu in Shanghai, for example, had been physically destroyed by fire or rebellion three times and wholly or partly rebuilt eleven times between 687 and 1935.

4. The words "heirs" here means not sons by blood, but successive owners ac-cording to religious "family": see Welch, *Practice*, pp. 129-130.

5. Ts'en Hsüeh-lü, *Hsü-yün ho-shang nien-p'u*, pp. 35-38.

6. *Ibid.*, p. 71.

7. Blofeld, *Wheel of Life*, pp. 157, 160.

8. See Tokiwa Daijō, *Shina-Bukkyō shiseki kinen-shū*, pp. 253-256, 273.

9. For a more complete explanation of the abuses at Ku Shan before Hsü-yün took over, see Welch, *Practice*, pp. 139-140.

10. Ts'en Hsüeh-lü, *Hsü-yün ho-shang nien-p'u*, p. 91. Here as elsewhere one cannot help wondering whether Hsü-yün was really as much revered by high officials as his autobiography frequently suggests.

11. Hsü-yün's autobiography states merely that "everything was put into order," perhaps because the sale of ranks was something "not fit to print." (Ts'en Hsüeh-lü, *Hsü-yün ho-shang nien-p'u*, p. 92.) My information about correction of abuses comes from monks who were there at the time.

12. The first attempt at reconstruction had been made fifteen years earlier by General Li Ken-yüan, who was living there at the time. This can be seen by comparing photographs taken in 1918, which show the monastery buildings over-grown with vegetation and apparently abandoned, with photographs taken in 1919 and 1928, which show the jungle cut back and signs of housekeeping and repair. See Tokiwa Daijō, *Shina-Bukkyō shiseki kinen-shū*, plates 31-45.

13. Ts'en Hsüeh-lü, *Hsü-yün ho-shang nien-p'u*, p. 113.

14. Welch, "Dharma Scrolls and the Succession of Abbots in Chinese Monasteries," *T'oung Pao*, 50.1-3:98-101. On Tsung-yang, who restored it, see above, pp. 16-18.

15. On the Ling-yen Ssu see Welch, *Practice*, pp. 90-91. An account of the restoration of the Ch'ung-sheng Ssu is given in Tokiwa Daijō, *Shina-Bukkyō shiseki kinen-shū*, pp. 200-202. Formerly it had been a rich monastery with over 8,000 *mou* of land, but because the quality of its abbots declined, the land had been lost and the buildings had fallen into ruin. During the 1920's Ta-pen, concurrently the abbot of Ku Shan, reconstructed the buildings and recovered much of the land from squatter peasants. At the end of 1928 he handed over the abbotship to Yüan-ying, whom he considered qualified to maintain the restoration. Photographs taken then show the great shrine-hall and dharma hall just rebuilt, with a giant Buddha image and two "jade" Buddhas imported from Burma. See Chapter IX, note 67.

16. See Chapter XI, notes 70-71.

17. The Fa-tsang Ssu in the French Settlement of Shanghai is said to have been founded in the early years of the Republic. In the 1930's it housed about one hundred monks, who were kept busy performing rites for the dead. See Welch, *Practice*, pp. 199-201.

18. The smaller new monasteries were the Fa-hua Ssu in Suihua (1927) and the Ta-ch'eng Ssu in Heilungkiang (1929). The monasteries restored were the Po-jo Ssu, Shenyang (1922), the Kuan-yin Ku-ch'a, Kirin (1938), and the Ta-pei Yüan, Tientsin (1942). See T'an-hsü, II, 222.

19. The leading proponent of this theory was J.J.M. De Groot, for whom it was an *idée fixe* (like his theory that the *Fan-wang ching* is the key to understanding the practice of Buddhism in China). He states flatly that the purpose of monasteries was to "regulate the *feng-shui* . . . It is a fact that at present the people maintain them solely because they are convinced that they regulate the winds and rains . . . Therefore their monks are true priests of *feng-shui,* supported in that capacity by the people." See *Le Code du Mahayana en Chine, son influence sur la vie monacale et sur le monde laïque* (Amsterdam, 1893), p. 100. See also De Groot, *Religion of the Chinese* (New York, 1910), pp. 186-187, and his article "Buddhism in China" in Hasting, *Encyclopedia of Religion and Ethics*, III, 555. De Groot's thesis appears to have been accepted by Joseph Edkins (see, for example, *The Religious Condition of the Chinese*, London, 1859, pp. 39-40) and Lewis Hodous (pp. 23, 28). My informants have said that in general geomancy determined *where* a temple would be built but not *that* it would be built.

20. C. K. Yang's figures will be found in *Religion in Chinese Society*, pp. 343-349. Myers' figures are given in an unpublished article, "Bridge and Temple Construction in Modern China: The Case of Szechwan during the Ch'ing and Republican Periods," which he was kind enough to let me see in manuscript. I am no less grateful to Wolfram Eberhard for sending an early draft of his "Temple Building Activities in Medieval and Modern China," published in *Monumenta Serica*, 23:264-318 (1964).

The figures compiled by Yang and Myers do not distinguish Buddhist from Taoist institutions. Eberhard makes this distinction on the basis of names (such as *ssu* versus *kuan*). Unfortunately, some Buddhist *ssu* have been taken over by Taoists and some Taoist *kuan* have been taken over by Buddhists, so that this is not a wholly reliable criterion. Nor is the name of an institution (which is often the only clue to its nature that a gazetteer provides) a reliable criterion of its size or of the sex and activities of its inmates.

21. See, for examples, Hodous, pp. 65-66; Saunders, pp. 66-67; and Pratt, p. 686. As early as 1911, when Hackmann visited Wu-t'ai Shan, Shansi, one of the four sacred mountains of Chinese Buddhism, he reported that "nowadays there seems to be a revival, for I saw many buildings being restored": see H. Hackmann, *A German Scholar in the East* (London, 1914), p. 18. Similarly in 1920 when Bishop Huntington visited another of the sacred mountains, Chiu-hua Shan, he found that the temples were in excellent repair and the roads had much improved since his last visit five or six years earlier. Some stretches of road were still being worked on. (Letter of November 28, 1920, from Bishop D. T. Huntington to Lewis Hodous, in the Hodous Collection, Hartford Theological Seminary, Hartford, Connecticut.) When C. B. Day went to the Asoka Monastery about 1930, he found that "a magnificent new temple" was being built to house a Buddha relic and a gigantic reclining Buddha (*Chinese Peasant Cults*, pp. 183-184). A fair sample of how the nineteenth-century observer viewed the state of Buddhist construction may be found in M. Huc, *Journey through the Chinese Empire* (New York, 1856), II, 197-198; and Robert Fortune, *Three Years' Wanderings in the Northern Provinces of China, Including a Visit to the Tea, Silk, and Cotton Countries with an Account of the Agriculture and Horticulture of the Chinese, New Plants, etc.* (London, 1847), pp. xiv-xv.

22. The three editions were the P'in-chia, the Commercial Press, and the Sung (Ch'i-sha) Tripitakas.

23. Wing-tsit Chan, p. 61. The largest Buddhist dictionary, *Fo-hsüeh ta tz'u-tien*, contains 3,294 pages.

24. Kuan Chiung in *Chinese Year Book, 1935-1936*, pp. 1512-1513.

25. *Hsien-tai fo-hsüeh*, 1.4:35 (December 1950).

26. The other two publishing houses in Peking were the Keng-shen Scriptural Circulation Center at the Ta-fo Ssu and the San-shih Hsüeh-hui. Beginning about 1933, the Scriptural Circulation Center at the Ta-fo Ssu issued an annual catalogue of thousands of Buddhist books, the *Fo-hsüeh shu-mu*, which gave publisher, author, and price. At the back there were sections offering holy pictures, liturgical instruments, incense, and rosaries—from which one may infer that the interests of prospective buyers were not purely academic. The Shanghai Buddhist Bookshop (Shang-hai Fo-hsüeh Shu-tien), the largest of its kind in that city, published its own newsletter (see Appendix 1).

27. Chen-hua, who was a disciple of Shuang-t'ing, the abbot of Chin Shan, compiled a Chinese Buddhist biographical dictionary of a million and a half words, the manuscript of which had to be left behind when his followers fled the Communists.

28. Harry A. Franck, *Roving through Southern China* (New York, 1925), p. 553. An equally surprising object of worship was an advertisement for the Mellins brand of prepared foods, which was decorated with an Indian or Burmese figure of the Buddha: Graham noticed it hung over an altar to Amitabha on Omei Shan. See David Crockett Graham, *Religion in Szechwan Province, China* (Washington, D.C., 1928), vol. 80, no. 4 of Smithsonian Miscellaneous Collections, pp. 57, 68.

VI. BUDDHIST EDUCATION

1. For a description of the training received by novices, see Welch, *Practice*, pp. 282-283.

2. On Pao-hua Shan, see *ibid.*, pp. 286-294.

3. At Pao-hua Shan the Vinaya hall and the board halls were separate and distinct. By many outsiders, however, "Vinaya hall" was used as a collective term to refer to any sort of training before or after ordination.

4. On the summer retreat (*an-chü*), see *ibid.*, pp. 109-110.

5. *Chung-pan t'ang* and *hsi-pan t'ang*. Prip-Møller errs in calling the former "east board hall" (*tung pan-t'ang*): see *Chinese Buddhist Monasteries*, p. 221. *Tung* (east) and *chung* (bell) are easily confused in speech (though not in writing), and it would be natural to assume that a west hall was balanced by an east hall.

6. Prip-Møller (p. 219) provides a floorplan. The lidded benches for sitting in meditation were called *hung-kuei* (red cabinets) whereas in the meditation hall they had no lid and were called *ch'un-teng*. The bell and board hung outside the door, whereas in the meditation hall they hung inside. On the layout of the meditation hall, see Welch, *Practice*, pp. 48-53.

7. The bell and board were struck to signal for the activities of the monks throughout the day, particularly their movement from hall to hall for devotions and meals.

8. On the "release of burning mouths" (*fang-yen k'ou*), see *ibid.*, pp. 185-187.

9. That is, *yin-li shih*. See *ibid.*, p. 289.

10. On the "four great [ranks of] instructors" (*ssu-ta pan-shou*), see *ibid.*, p. 39.

11. The copying work was termed *ch'ao wen-shu*.

12. For a fuller description of the traditional system of lectures, see *ibid.*, pp. 310-314.

13. Students attending a Vinaya school did teach the rules to ordinands and later in their career, if they lived in a small temple, they taught them to the novices who were studying there. But the lecture system affected a much greater percentage of the sangha.

Even at Pao-hua Shan the Vinaya school was not large. According to my informant, there were about a hundred monks enrolled. This is confirmed by the floorplan in Prip-Møller, p. 219, which shows that each board hall had room for about twenty students to sleep and sit in meditation, but for about sixteen more to sit at the tables and write.

I have asked many informants about the existence of other Vinaya or board halls before 1911. Some knew so little about these institutions that they confused the Vinaya hall (*hsüeh-chieh t'ang*) with the ordinands hall (*hsin-chieh t'ang*—see Welch, *Practice*, p. 287). One or two informants hazarded the opinion that Chiao Shan in Chen-chiang had a Vinaya hall, but I have heard of none elsewhere. The board halls at Pao-hua Shan are said to have been started by its second abbot, Chien-yüeh Tu-t'i, who built its ordination platform in 1663 (see Prip-Møller, pp. 284-285). One might have expected other ordination centers to follow suit, especially since the following adage was current: "For the first five years specialize in learning the Vinaya rules: only then may you study doctrine and take part in meditation." But even if the only Vinaya school in China was the one at Pao-hua Shan, it was still a significant element in the traditional system of monastic education, for which this monastery served as a model.

14. The claim that this was the first *fo-hsüeh-yüan* is made in Yin-shun, *T'ai-hsü*, p. 140, where its opening date is given as September 1, 1922. Mizuno Baigyō, *Shina Bukkyō kinseishi*, p. 74, gives the date as July 17, 1921, and Reichelt has Miao-chi enrolled there in January 1921, apparently a full year before the idea of the school was broached (*The Transformed Abbot*, p. 80).

15. *Chinese Year Book, 1937*, p. 1445.

16. See T'an-hsü, pp. 64-65. On the start of this seminary, see Chapter II, note 25.

17. The treatises they read were, for example, the *Chiao-kuan kang-tsung* (Taisho, 1939), *T'ien-t'ai ssu-chiao i* (Taisho, 1931), *Mo-ho chih-kuan* (Taisho, 1911), *Hsiao chih-kuan* (Taisho, 1915)—all T'ien-t'ai texts.

18. On the date, see Yin-shun, *T'ai-hsü*, p. 199. Reichelt states that the seminary was visited by Miao-chi on his way to Taiwan, where he arrived July 29, 1923 (*The Transformed Abbot*, p. 97). Possibly what he visited was a predecessor institution. In the first decade of this century, Nan P'u-t'o was described as "a kind of training school for priests of this order. There are usually some twenty candidates in attendance": see Philip W. Pitcher, *In and About Amoy* (Shanghai, 1909), p. 78.

19. Yin-shun, *T'ai-hsü*, pp. 233-234. This source gives the name of the retiring abbot as Hui-ch'üan, but other sources state that he was Chuan-feng, who along with Ch'ang-hsing went to invite T'ai-hsü to take over.

20. Students had to pass examinations every month and every semester. Those who failed the latter were not promoted.

21. The Tibetan component outside Chungking was founded in 1931 as the Sino-Tibetan Buddhist Institute (Han-tsang Chiao-li Yüan). It will be discussed in Chapters IX and X. The Peking component was the Po-lin Seminary, set up under Ch'ang-hsing in 1930 at the Po-lin Ssu as the Chinese-English Department of the World Buddhist Institute. It closed after a year because of financial difficulties. The Pali Tripitaka Institute (Pa-li San-tsang Yüan) was set up during the 1930's at the Hsing-shan Ssu in Sian, and it was still in operation in 1945. At least one other school, the Ling-tung Seminary in Chaochow, Kwangtung province, was being operated by a disciple of T'ai-hsü in the late 1930's. The Japanese invasion closed the Wuchang Seminary in 1937 and the South Fukien Seminary in 1939, as already stated.

22. Yin-shun, *T'ai-hsü*, p. 140; Mizuno Baigyō, *Shina Bukkyō kinseishi*, p. 74; *Shina Bukkyō no genjo*, pp. 11-12.

23. What most of them offered was traditional Chinese literature, Chinese history and geography, arithmetic, and perhaps English or Japanese. Generally it was a three-year course, sometimes with an additional two or three years of graduate work. The program usually included a meditation period in the evening, so that there was less of a shift of emphasis from practice to theory than at T'ai-hsü's schools. There was also a tendency to moderate the strictness of monastic discipline. T'an-hsü, the monk who set up six new monasteries in north China, also set up thirteen new seminaries (T'an-hsü, pp. 224-225). He himself had been a student at the Kuan-tsung Ssu, where even minor offenses were punished by beating. He did not perpetuate this tradition. At his seminaries the

usual punishment was to chant a sutra or to make a prostration to the buddha image or to the person offended. Beating was considered old-fashioned.

24. For example, in the seminary at the Ying-chiang Ssu, Anking, the lecturer was already using a blackboard in 1922; the students took notes; there were monthly and semestral examinations; and diplomas were given to those who passed the three-year course. The name of this seminary was the An-hui Fo-chiao Hsüeh-hsiao (Anhwei Buddhist Religious School), and the principal was Ch'ang-hsing, who later set up the South Fukien Seminary. He had begun his teaching career at the Hsing-fu Ssu in Chang-shu, Kiangsu, in 1919.

25. In his recension of the monastery's history, the abbot states that it was initially established by Yeh-k'ai as a private school (ssu-shu) inside the monastery in 1901; and was turned into the T'ien-ning Primary School (T'ien-ning Ch'u-chi Hsiao-hsüeh) in 1912. See Cheng-lien, 1:19.

26. The conservative prejudice against new-fangled educational terminology still existed in 1943, when Hsü-yün set up a seminary at the Nan-hua Ssu and called it a chieh-lü hsüeh-yüan (Vinaya study institute) instead of hsüeh-t'ang or fo-hsüeh-yüan. See Ts'en Hsüeh-lü, Hsü-yün ho-shang nien-p'u, p. 124. The curriculum, according to an informant who was connected with it, consisted entirely of Buddhist texts. There is some uncertainty whether the Vinaya study institute which Hsü-yün set up at Ku Shan in 1931 changed its name to fo-hsüeh-yüan when Tz'u-chou became head of it in 1934, or after Hsü-yün left for good in 1935. Ibid., pp. 93, 94, 102.

27. "Dean" (chiao-wu chu-jen) was the term for the director of studies at progressive seminaries like T'ai-hsü's, whereas at the Kuan-tsung Ssu he was termed the chien-hsüeh.

28. This information largely comes from Yang Wen-hui's descendants, who had a long and bitter dispute with Ou-yang over the disposition of their family real estate in Nanking. Yang had willed it to the Chin-ling Scriptural Press on the condition that his descendants could live indefinitely in two of the four main courtyards; and in return he enjoined them to subsidize the press from their own incomes as soon as they could afford to. This gave rise to misunderstandings that were not settled until 1936. See Buwei Yang Chao, Autobiography, pp. 47, 90-91. One of Ou-yang's disciples told me that the persons left in charge of the press by Yang's testamentary instructions were Li I-cho, Ou-yang Ching-wu, and Mei Kuang-hsi.

29. Wing-tsit Chan and others translate the name more literally as "Institute of Inner Studies." But according to Ou-yang's disciple, nei-hsüeh (inner studies) meant metaphysics (hsing-erh-shang hsüeh) as opposed to wai-hsüeh (science). The more usual meaning was simply Buddhist as opposed to non-Buddhist studies. "Chih-na" was the standard Japanese name for China. Its use caused much resentment as anti-Japanese feeling mounted. According to his disciple, Ou-yang explained it as an abbreviation for Chih-na Ni-she, the transliteration of a Sanskrit term meaning "sacred country" (shen-chou). One cannot help wondering whether this explanation was an afterthought.

30. Tsung-yang presumably got the money from Mrs. Hardoon. More money was raised by Ou-yang on a trip to Kunming in 1919 or 1920. According to one source, he also drew freely on the funds originally donated to Yang Wen-hui by forty-eight lay devotees for reprinting the Tripitaka.

31. Mizuno Baigyō, *Shina Bukkyō kinseishi*, p. 84; *Shina Bukkyō no genjo*, pp. 13-19.

32. Ou-yang's contributions are explained at length in Wing-tsit Chan, pp. 93-135.

33. Mizuno states that in the mid-1920's the institute was receiving regular donations of $4,000 a year from Yeh Kung-cho (*Shina Bukkyō no genjo*, p. 16); later a subvention of $2,000 a year from the Academia Sinica was said to have been arranged by Ts'ai Yüan-p'ei.

34. It moved to the town of Kiangtsin about twenty miles southwest of Chungking. This happened because among Ou-yang's disciples was Hsiung Hsün-ch'i, professor of foreign languages at Peking University, who had studied at the Metaphysical Institute in the early 1930's at the suggestion of his teacher, Liang Sou-ming. Hsiung came from a rich Kiangtsin family and therefore was able to provide a home for the institute after the Japanese attack in 1937. Many of the books and woodblocks of the Chin-ling Scriptural Press were also moved to Kiangtsin, where publishing continued. The premises there were called the "Szechwan Branch of the Metaphysical Institute" (Chih-na Nei-hsüeh Yüan Shu-yüan). Ou-yang died there February 23, 1943, after which his work was carried on by Lü Ch'eng (Lü Ch'iu-i).

35. Paul Demiéville, after examining the Japanese studies on the authenticity of this work, reached the conclusion that it had indeed been translated from Sanskrit (by Paramartha in 550 c.e.) but that it had been originally written by someone later than Asvagosha, to whom it was traditionally attributed. See Demiéville,, "Sur l'authenticité du ta tch'eng k'i sin louen," *Bulletin de la Maison Franco-Japonaise* (Tokyo, 1929), 2.1:74-76. The same conclusion is supported by the most recent translator: see Yoshita S. Hakeda, *The Awakening of Faith, Attributed to Asvagosha* (New York, 1967). Ou-yang's theoretical objection to the *Awakening* was in regard to its assertion that "Thusness can be 'perfumed.'" See Wing-tsit Chan, p. 114, which states that for years Ou-yang and T'ai-hsü's institutes "rivaled each other, primarily on the issue of the nature of Thusness." Ou-yang could not accept "the *Awakening* position that Thusness involved Ignorance, that it can be aroused, and that it can create. To the Wei-shih School Thusness transcends Ignorance, is not aroused, and does not create" (pp. 117, 123). It would be interesting to see such discussions subjected to ordinary-language analysis in the manner of Wittgenstein or Moore.

36. *Chinese Buddhist*, 1.1:7 (April 1930), mentions an enrollment of twenty advanced students, apparently meaning that there was a total of twenty students, all advanced. The same enrollment—"about twenty advanced students"—is given for the school in 1936 (*Chinese Year Book, 1936-1937*, p. 1445).

37. Yin-shun, *T'ai-hsü*, p. 108. An assistant of Ou-yang's proposed emending this to read: "We are opposed to fostering those who selfishly pursue nirvana." It is not clear whether the proposal was followed. T'ai-hsü also took exception to Ou-yang's rejection of the *Awakening of Faith* as a forgery.

VII.   SOCIAL ACTION BY THE SANGHA

1. When J. H. Gray was visiting Pai-yün Shan, he was asked for help by a monk suffering "from a loathsome disease . . . I urged him to return with me to Canton so that I might place him under the care of Dr. Kerr of the Medical

Missionary Hospital. On hearing of my intentions the abbot took me aside and begged me not to show any kindness to a man who had doubtless been guilty in a former state of existence of some very heinous sin, for which the gods were then making him pay the well-merited penalty" (*China*, II, 47). Regardless of Gray's anti-Buddhist bias and his possible confusion of "the gods" with karma, the main point of this story is entirely credible.

2. Gray gives examples of sheltering flood victims (II, 34), distribution of clothing (II, 56), and coffins for the poor (II, 58), all paid for by lay donors. Presumably lay donors were also paying for a "soup kitchen" at which three thousand persons a day were reportedly fed at a Buddhist temple in about 1926: see *Atlantic Monthly*, 139:281 (February 1927).

3. Mizuno Baigyō, *Shina Bukkyō no genjo*, p. 65.

4. A monk who was manager in 1925 stated that the primary school was part of the orphanage, but that the boys went outside to middle school at thirteen and at eighteen to university.

5. According to a report on the orphanage, prepared by its management in 1917, but not printed until 1921, the annual operating expenses were $6,000 a year. See *Hai-ch'ao yin*, vol. 2, no. 3 (March 20, 1921). The 1925 manager mentioned an additional source of income: two temple fairs, one in the fourth month and one in the eighth, with Chinese opera, puppet shows, and other kinds of entertainment. The proceeds from the sale of tickets at 30 cents apiece went to support the orphanage. On the other hand, the income that the monastery derived from the rites for the dead did *not* go to support it. Fiscally the orphanage was separate, although the monastery was financially responsible for it.

6. Sidney D. Gamble, *Peking, a Social Survey* (New York, 1921), pp. 289-290. By 1917, the year before the Princeton survey, more than 400 orphans had completed their training and left the orphanage with jobs: see *Hai-ch'ao Yin*, vol. 2, no. 3 (Mar. 20, 1921).

7. Pratt, p. 380. Pratt's travel diaries provide additional information. After the boys at the Lung-ch'üan orphanage finished primary school, they spent half of each day on academic work and half on learning a trade. Their study of Buddhism (especially Pure Land doctrine and the operation of karma) was tested in examinations given twice a year. There were four laymen teaching academic subjects as well as instructors in the crafts. Whereas the former manager spoke of 300 inmates in 1925, Pratt reports 100 as of 1924—the only major inconsistency in the accounts I have collected. As to the two orphanages in Ningpo, one was located behind a temple, had 120 boys, five to fifteen years old, all fatherless, all going to school, where they studied not only academic subjects but also carpentry, shoemaking, sewing, and printing. The two senior classes went to school at night and worked by day. The money necessary to operate the orphanage was raised among lay Buddhists, including overseas Chinese. See Pratt Notebooks, Williams College Library.

8. The abbot's name was Hsin-hsüeh. The Chamber of Commerce continued to play a role. In 1917 it was custodian of the deed to the 27 *mou* of land that the monastery had donated to the orphanage for the main set of buildings.

9. The information in these two paragraphs comes from *Hai-ch'ao yin*, vol. 2, no. 3 (Mar. 20, 1921).

10. *Yüan-ying*, p. 12; cf. Yin-shun, *T'ai-hsü*, p. 94. This orphanage was probably identical with one of those described by Pratt.

11. Mizuno Baigyō, *Shina Bukkyō no genjo*, pp. 20, 65.

12. Monks set up temporary hospitals to treat disaster victims in Hunan and Szechwan, according to Mizuno, *ibid.*, p. 69. In 1948 the Chih-te Buddhist Hospital was started in Canton according to Ts'en Hsüeh-lü, *Hsü-yün ho-shang nien-p'u*, p. 156. But I have been unable to get details of any long-term hospital operation.

13. See Chapter V. Another free primary school for poor children was started by Hsü-yün in Kükiang in 1943 (see Ts'en Hsüeh-lü, *Hsü yün ho-shang nien-p'u*, p. 124), and yet another was started at the monastery Hsü-yün restored in Kunming, the Hua-t'ing Ssu (see Osgood, p. 84).

14. This information came from a former prior of the Liu-yün Ssu. The lay school at the Pao-kuang Ssu had several monks on its teaching staff (see Prip-Møller, p. 143).

15. Primary schools were connected with the Po-jo Ssu Seminary in Changchun and the Chan-shan Ssu Seminary in Tsingtao. A middle school was connected with the seminary at the Chi-le Ssu in Harbin. See T'an-hsü, p. 224. Rather impressive figures on the number of Buddhist primary schools in north China (300 schools with 11,000 pupils in Hopei, Shantung, Peking, and Tientsin) are given in *Hua-pei tsung-chiao nien-chien ti-i hao* (North China yearbook of religion, No. 1; Peking, 1941), pp. 185-188. Confirmation is needed.

16. Even to serve in the ambulance corps violated the Pratimoksa rules that forbade a monk to witness military engagements: see S. Beal, *Catena of Buddhist Scriptures* (London, 1871), pp. 225-226. But it did not violate the more important vow not to bear weapons (the tenth vow of the *Fan-wang ching;* see De Groot, *Le Code du Mahayana*, pp. 46-47).

17. *Yüan-ying*, p. 13; cf. Clarence H. Hamilton, "Buddhism," in H. F. McNair, ed., *China* (Berkeley, 1946), p. 299. More information on these teams and on other first-aid corps can be found in *Chinese Year Book, 1942-1943*, p. 63.

18. Ts'en Hsüeh-lü, *Hsü-yün ho-shang nien-p'u*, p. 146.

19. See Chu Chieh-hsien, p. 83. Another source states that Ch'i-hsia Shan and the Kuang-hsiao Ssu (in T'ai-hsien) sheltered and fed over 100,000 refugees (see *Chinese Year Book, 1942-1943*, p. 63).

20. Chu Chieh-hsien, p. 83, supplemented by the recollections of the prior of Ch'i-hsia Shan at that time.

21. See Reichelt, *The Transformed Abbot*, p. 83. Although this makes it sound as if no Buddhists had thought of the idea before then, prison visiting was an activity called for by the charter of the Chinese Buddhist Association, adopted in Shanghai in 1912. Just as the Buddhists tended to minimize the force of Christian example, missionaries like Reichelt tended to maximize it.

22. Day, p. 198; *Chinese Year Book, 1936-1937*, p. 1449.

23. Reichelt, *Truth and Tradition in Chinese Buddhism* (Shanghai, 1927), p. 232.

24. An exception was the primary-middle school operated by the Pao-kuang Ssu, Chengtu, at which "a few" of the teachers are said to have been ordained monks. The school was housed in the columbarium (*p'u-t'ung ta*). See Prip-Møller, p. 143.

25. Mizuno Baigyō, *Shina Bukkyō no genjo*, pp. 65-66.

26. On the 1929 regulations, see p. 139. Makita Tairyō, *Chūgoku kinsei Bukkyōshi* (p. 277), states that under regulations issued on January 14, 1935, monasteries were to spend 1 to 5 percent of their total income (depending on size) for

public education, refugee relief, and public health, either independently or in cooperation with other monasteries.

VIII. SANGHA AND STATE

1. Prostration to the ruler was forbidden by the fortieth vow of the *Fan-wang Ching* (see De Groot, *Le Code du Mahayana,* pp. 74-75). They were exempted from it in south China during the fifth and sixth centuries. Although the exemption was revoked by Sui Yang-ti in 607 and again under the T'ang, it continued to be intermittently given. See Kenneth K. S. Ch'en, pp. 105, 202, 214.

2. These exemptions are all mentioned in the Ch'ing Code: see *Ta-ch'ing lü-li hsin-tseng t'ung-tsuan chi-ch'eng* (Newly enlarged comprehensive edition of the Ch'ing legal code; Shao-chou, 1898), 8:23. "Police investigation" is *wu chi-ch'a.* C. K. Yang (p. 189) translates it "exempt from . . . police surveillance." Perhaps it refers to surveillance under the *pao-chia* system.

3. Justus Doolittle, *Social Life of the Chinese,* ed. Paxton Hood (London, 1868), p. 189. Many missionaries speak of the large number of criminals in the sangha. See George Smith, *A Narrative of an Exploratory Visit to Each of the Consular Cities of China and to the Islands of Hong Kong and Chusan, in Behalf of the Church Missionary Society in the Years 1844, 1845, 1846,* rev. ed. (London, 1847), p. 184; John Henry Gray, *China, a History of the Laws, Manners, and Customs of the People* (London, 1878), I, 119; Reichelt, *Truth and Tradition,* p. 232.

4. The text of this imperial edict of 1705 was engraved on stone and erected at the P'u-chi Ssu. A translation is given in Reginald F. Johnston, *Buddhist China* (London, 1913), pp. 351-353. The emperor explains that his studies of Confucianism and duties as a ruler have left him no leisure to become familiar with Buddhist sutras, but he is satisfied that in both systems virtue is the essential thing. On his anti-Buddhist edicts, see De Groot, *Sectarianism,* pp. 107-108, 113, 115-116.

5. The K'ang-hsi Emperor stayed at the famous ordination center of Pao-hua Shan and gave it a new name. He also stayed at the T'ien-t'ung Ssu near Ningpo and the Kao-min Ssu near Yangchow. He presented imperial holographs to both Kao-min and Chin Shan. T'ien-t'ung received them from the emperors who preceded and followed him.

6. Prip-Møller, pp. 218, 221, 285, 295.

7. Such ambivalent imperial treatment of Buddhism was not a new phenomenon. For example, the Chin Emperor, Shih-tsung (1161-1189), prohibited the construction of temples and the exemption of monks from civic duties, but personally encouraged temple construction, to which he donated land and money, and was on good terms with many of the eminent monks of the time. See Kenneth K. S. Ch'en, p. 412.

8. Ts'en Hsüeh-lü, *Hsü-yün ho-shang nien-p'u,* p. 44.

9. *Ta-ch'ing lü-li,* 8:15; translated by De Groot in *Sectarianism,* I, 99; and (less exactly) by C. K. Yang, pp. 188-189.

10. *Ta-ch'ing lü-li,* 8:17-18; De Groot, *Sectarianism,* I, 97; C. K. Yang, pp. 187-188.

11. *Ta-ch'ing lü-li,* 8:23; De Groot, *Sectarianism,* I, 111-112; see also Welch, *Practice,* p. 504.

12. One student of the Chinese legal tradition has written that the "law was regarded only as punishment for violations of the social and political order. The need of such punishment was an admission of the inadequacy of the moral code [*li*] and a sign that education and the example of virtue had failed. This attitude remained throughout imperial history . . . 'One does not read the codes' became a known quotation, indicating the view that the law was vulgar, and for vulgar people only." See Franz Michael, "The Role of Law in Traditionalist, Nationalist, and Communist China," *China Quarterly*, 9:128 (January-March 1962).

13. I am indebted to Professor Derk Bodde for his kindness in letting me see the manuscript of his forthcoming book, "Law in Imperial China," in which he translates and comments on a representative sample of the 6,000-odd cases in the *Hsing-an hui-lan*. In this sample, monks are tried for common lay offenses—theft, assault, adultery, sedition, and extortion—but not for violating the laws for the control of the sangha. The only case in which one of these laws was cited involved a monk who had beaten his disciple to death. The Board of Punishments ruled that, since the monk was under forty years old, he had taken the disciple illegally. Hence the latter was not really a disciple, and the monk could be sentenced under the statute on layman killing layman in a quarrel rather than under the statute that covered master killing disciple. There was no question of punishment for violation of the age limitation itself. The reference is to *Hsing-an hui-lan*, 17.38:146.

Some readers will be skeptical about the claim that during the late Ch'ing dynasty the laws directed at the sangha were "empty." They will recall that J.J.M. De Groot, who spent many years in China studying Chinese Buddhism and observing it in practice, presents thirty pages of translations from the code to show that Buddhists had been severely restricted, if not persecuted, throughout the Ming and the Ch'ing. It is true that he qualifies his position by saying: "The probability remains, of course, that some of the resolutions and ordinances have fallen into disuse." But his thesis is clearly that most of them were enforced. See *Sectarianism*, I, 101, and cf. C. K. Yang, pp. 187-190, where Professor Yang also qualifies himself by pointing out that it was uncertain how effectively the laws were enforced, but seems to be arguing that most of the laws were enforced most of the time. I can only say that I have not found evidence to contradict the testimony of the Ch'ing dynasty monks I have mentioned. Buddhist documentary sources either do not allude to the enforcement of the laws on the sangha or indicate that they were not enforced. Where De Groot gives illustrations of their enforcement, the culprits are members of heterodox sects, not orthodox Buddhist monks.

An interesting case of the so-called emptiness of the law is the prohibition of the issuance of ordination certificates except by the government. Several of my informants have said that this prohibition was canceled by the Yung-cheng Emperor (1723-1735). A sentence to that effect is included in the text of the 1949 ordination certificates of the Nan-hua Ssu: "Ch'ing Shih-tsung abolished the system of ordination certificates and let the monks and nuns of the empire be tonsured and ordained without restriction." Kuan Chiung makes the same statement in the *Chinese Year Book, 1935-1936*, pp. 151-152, as does Wei-huan, p. 146. However, De Groot quotes a Ch'ien-lung decree of 1737, and Professor Ch'en quotes one of 1739 to the effect that the system of ordination certificates was again to be practiced (De Groot, *Sectarianism*, I, 111, and Kenneth K. S.

Ch'en, p. 454). De Groot states unequivocally that control over the issuance of ordination certificates "still prevails in our days" (*Sectarianism,* I, 112). It is clearly provided for in nineteenth-century editions of the Ch'ing Code. Yet those who were ordained in the nineteenth century say that they both received and issued private certificates.

Perhaps the best evidence of the emptiness of the law is to be found in the more repressive measures cited by De Groot himself. In 1632 it was decreed that ordination certificates should be given only to those who understood the sutras; in 1635 that no male over the age of sixteen could join the sangha; in the same year that no monastery in Peking could house more than ten monks; and in 1677 that no scaffoldings could be erected at monasteries and no theatrical performances could take place there. According to the decrees of 1723 and 1812, no female was permitted to offer incense in a Buddhist temple (*ibid.,* pp. 107-117, and cf. *Ch'in-ting ta-Ch'ing hui-tien shih-li, chüan* 501). In terms of actual practice toward the end of the nineteenth century, such laws were indeed "nonsense," and they call into question enforcement of other laws for the control of the sangha.

A lawyer in Hong Kong once told me (with some indignation): "The Ch'ing laws were enforced just like your laws in the United States. Whoever has been telling you otherwise is talking nonsense." It may be that national pride is now at stake here. Further investigation is needed.

14. H. Hackmann, *Buddhism as a Religion* (London, 1910), p. 233; D. J. MacGowan, "Self-Immolation by Fire," *Chinese Recorder,* 19.11:515 (November 1888). MacGowan states that the *seng-kang ssu* at Mount T'ien-t'ai was appointed by the provincial treasurer and was "archbishop of Chehkiang." Cf. George Smith, p. 314. When Hackmann visited Wu-t'ai Shan in 1911, he found that the Living Buddha Chang-chia had been chosen by the government to head all the monasteries there. Chang-chia was then twenty-two years old and is the same person who, still with government backing, became president of the Chinese Buddhist Association in 1947. Hackmann, *German Scholar in the East,* pp. 118-125.

15. Doolittle, p. 186. Similarly, Soothill states that in the 1880's sangha officials were permitted to have no legal authority over the monks, their powers being limited to moral suasion. See W. E. Soothill, *Timothy Richard of China* (London, 1924), p. 162. I have seen little mention of sangha officials in the biographies of monks active during the late Ch'ing.

16. My source for these regulations (entitled *Ssu-yüan kuan-li chan-hsing kuei-tse*) is Makita Tairyō, *Chūgoku kinsei Bukkyōshi,* p. 262, which cites Hsieh Chen-min, ed., *Chung-hua min-kuo li-fa shih* (History of legislation under the Republic) chap. 3, sec. 10.

17. This measure, originally entitled Regulations for the control of Monasteries and Temples (*Kuan-li ssu-miao t'iao-ling*) is said to have been slightly modified in 1921 and thereafter referred to as the Regulations for the Protection of Monastic and Temple Property (*Ssu-miao ts'ai-ch'an pao-hu t'iao-ling*): see Makita Tairyō, *Chūgoku kinsei Bukkyōshi,* p. 263. Another source summarizes their main features differently: (1) registration of temples and monasteries, monks and nuns; (2) taxation of temple property; (3) nonalienation of temple property; (4) subjection of religious activities and preaching services to police regulations. See Yu-yue Tsu, "Present Tendencies in Chinese Buddhism," p. 502.

18. Yin-shun, *T'ai-hsü,* p. 76.

19. See Lin Chin-tung, pp. 1-16. Lin appears to omit regulations like those of October 29, 1915, and January 25, 1929 (see Chapter II, note 37), which might be used as evidence that the central government had been oppressive to Buddhism. I have not checked Lin's collection of laws against other legal compendia.

20. This provision was annulled by a Ministry of Interior directive of January 3, 1948 (serial number Li 0019), which shifted to the Chinese Buddhist Association the responsibility for undertaking such activities and for assigning them to member groups in the areas of education, culture, public welfare, charity, and production (Lin Chin-tung, p. 191). See also Chapter VII, note 26. On production, see Chapter XII, note 17.

21. This was confirmed in a Ministry of Interior communication of April 1933 (Lin Chin-tung, pp. 171-172). However, a later Ministry of Interior directive (Li 359, April 10, 1936) stated that an abbot who violated the monastic rules could be removed from office by the local authorities at the request of the local Buddhist association or, if there was no local association, then on their own initiative (Lin Chin-tung, p. 190; cf. p. 182).

22. Executive Yüan circular 724, September 26, 1938 (Lin Chin-tung, p. 10). Even in the Ch'ing dynasty there does not appear to have been any law requiring government approval of the election of abbots. Hackmann, however, states that the appointment of the abbot of a small monastery that he happened to visit in Chekiang had to be ratified by the government. It would be natural for the name of the new abbot to be reported to the authorities *post facto;* and in an unusual case the authorities might disapprove of his election and insist that it be canceled. Such a *post facto* report could be easily confused (by an outsider) with a system of securing official approval of candidates before the election took place. See H. Hackmann, "Buddhist Monastery Life in China," *East of Asia Magazine,* 1.3:251-252 (September 1902). For a full discussion of the customs followed at different monasteries in choosing abbots, see Welch, *Practice,* pp. 151-171.

23. Ministry of Interior directive, February 11, 1921; Executive Yüan circulars 637 and 810, 1932 (Lin Chin-tung, pp. 5-6, 191-192). Where a local Buddhist association did exist, it had the initial responsibility for selecting the abbot of an abandoned monastery. Executive Yüan circular 423 (1931) provided that "in case of deserted or ruined temples, the religious association concerned may choose a head monk to take charge of it, so long as their choice does not violate the customs and rules for the transmission of authority in that particular temple and they have consulted the Buddhist or Taoist monks of the area" (Lin Chin-tung, p. 5). But officials had long felt free to choose an abbot where the circumstances seemed to justify their intervention. In 1915, for example, the governor of Shansi appointed a monk to take charge of a half-ruined monastery near Tatung (see Prip-Møller, pp. 381, 385).

24. Near the very end of the Republican period, control over tonsure, ordination, and the selection of abbots was assumed by the Chinese Buddhist Association, but not by the government itself. See Chapter II, note 58.

25. If a monk saved up the money that lay devotees had given him to gain merit or show respect—not because he was soliciting it to build a temple—then presumably the temple he built with it was considered his private property. It seems likely that the great majority of small hereditary temples, which in turn were the great majority of Buddhist monastic institutions, originated in this way.

W. Eberhard has found that 54 percent of the Buddhist temples in a broad sample of districts and centuries were financed by the monks themselves rather than by officials or ordinary laypeople (see "Temple Building," p. 284). R. H. Myers has found that in one Szechwan hsien the building or restoration of the great majority of Buddhist temples had been organized and financed by the monks themselves, presumably with their own savings.

26. A Ministry of Interior circular of March 23, 1933, speaks of "overdue statements" and urges local officials to send out reminders (Lin Chin-tung, pp. 170-171). It seems improbable that tax-wary Chinese monks would have submitted such statements except under pressure.

27. Ministry of Interior directive (Li 359), April 10, 1936 (Lin Chin-tung, p. 190).

28. Lin Chin-tung, pp. 185-186.

29. The text of the amended charter is given in *Chinese Year Book, 1937* (Shanghai, 1937), pp. 71-73.

30. Chapter II, Article 15. The provision for restriction in accordance with the law was dropped in the 1946 Constitution.

31. Serial numbers T'ung 567, 1917; Shang 3191, 1930 (Lin Chin-tung, pp. 7-8).

32. Executive Yüan circular 810, 1932 (Lin Chin-tung, p. 5; cf. 724, p. 9). This distinction between common and government property is often blurred by the translation "public property." Thus C. K. Yang says: "All temple properties under the Ch'ing as well as the Republican governments were required to be registered as public property and were regarded by the officials as such." Therefore, he adds, "there was no legal protection against expropriation by the government" (C. K. Yang, p. 326). This would appear to be a non sequitur.

33. Shang 255, 1916; Shang 3095, 1930; Shang 67, 1931 (Lin Chin-tung, pp. 2, 14, 11).

34. National Government Instruction No. 400, August 1, 1931 (Lin Chin-tung, pp. 167-168). Yin-shun, *T'ai-hsü* (p. 324) gives T'ai-hsü credit for having originated these proposals.

35. Yu-yue Tsu, "Present Tendencies in Chinese Buddhism," p. 503.

36. Tokiwa Daijō, *Shina-bukkyō shiseki kinen-shū*, plates 1-19.

37. C. K. Yang (pp. 369, 370) points out that in the first two decades of the Republican period half the temples in Hunan were converted to schools or other public uses, as were 60 percent of those in Ting-hsien, Hopei. Unfortunately Professor Yang does not give a breakdown as to religion, so it is not clear how many of those confiscated were Buddhist. John Shryrock does give such a breakdown for the temples in Anking from 1915 to 1924: see *The Temples of Anking* (Paris 1931), pp. 142-151. Out of 50 Buddhist temples, only 3 were destroyed and only 2 confiscated. But of 54 temples dedicated to popular divinities and famous men, 22 were destroyed or confiscated. Similarly in 1928, when the Chekiang provincial government instructed its Civil Affairs Bureau to confiscate temples, those that were Buddhist were specifically exempted. Buildings dedicated to the Sun, Moon, Fire, City Gods, Soil Gods, Kitchen God, and other popular divinities "without historical basis or present value" were to be razed or converted (and many were), but other temples would be spared. See Day, pp. 190-194. On the whole, there seems reason to question Ta-hsing's statement, quoted

by Wing-tsit Chan (p. 55) that by 1935 30 percent of Buddhist properties in China had been appropriated for barracks and police stations, and 50 percent for schools.

38. Reichelt, *Truth and Tradition,* p. 299.

39. Edward Bing-shuey Lee, *Modern Canton* (Shanghai, 1936), p. 96. Edward J. M. Rhoads has pointed out to me that the *South China Morning Post,* June 15, 1912, p. 5, carried a dispatch from Fatshan stating that, according to a government order issued in May, nunneries were to be closed and nuns under forty were to be returned to lay life because they "deceive people and get women to give them money and food in return for promised help and protection, which they are unable to provide." About 30 nunneries and 300 nuns in Fatshan alone were said to have been affected.

40. These included the Ch'ang-shou Ssu, Hai-ch'uang Ssu, Hua-lin Ssu, Kuang-hsiao Ssu, Ta-fo Ssu, that is, all the major monasteries except the Liu-jung Ssu. Outside the city, those on White Cloud Mountain were confiscated to make a municipal park, while the lands of the Fei-lai Ssu were sold to meet military expenses. As for small temples, hundreds of them, Buddhist and other, were said to have been sold at auction in the early 1920's by order of the military authorities. Their contents found a good market among curio dealers, and the total proceeds were two million dollars in gold. Temples that were not sold or razed were used as barracks. Firsthand testimony of these developments is offered by Frank G. Carpenter, *China* (New York, 1925), pp. 42-43; Harry A. Franck, pp. 277-279; and Pratt, p. 682. Franck includes (pp. 278-279) an eloquent description of his visit to the Hua-lin Ssu in 1924. "The seven-story pagoda of white marble presented by Ch'ien Lung was still intact inside another of the buildings . . . Nearly all the rest of the great establishment was in full course of destruction. Laughing men were tumbling over the huge iron-heavy pillars, probably of teak; women as well as men were carrying out the blue-black bricks. One old priest wandered disconsolately about the place like an old bird that sees its nest destroyed by some ruthless boy. Hall after hall fell under the picks and crowbars . . . It seemed strange that where people are still so largely superstitious there appeared to be no trouble in getting plenty of workmen to demolish and carry off this once powerful joss-house. No doubt they had no choice in the matter; we noticed that there were plenty of soldiers about to make sure that no one stopped working; besides, Sun had already defied so many gods and evil spirits that even the common people may have begun to lose their belief in the dangers of flouting them." I have not searched Chinese sources for the decree which, according to Franck, confiscated all the monasteries in Canton about 1922, but David Roy has been kind enough to draw my attention to articles in the *Kuang-chou min-kuo jih-pao* (Canton Republican daily), Oct. 18 and 28, 1926 (both p. 7), on a recent decree that confiscated the nunneries in that city.

41. Harry A. Franck, pp. 207, 235, 267, 271. On paper images, see Welch, *Practice,* pp. 191-194.

42. Harry A. Franck, pp. 279, 311. In South China it had long been the custom to wait until the flesh had decayed and reinter the bones in an earthenware jar. The coffin could then be used to make medicine, musical instruments, or even for the construction of bridges and pig-feeding troughs. See J.J.M. De Groot, *The Religious System of China* (Leiden, 1892), I, 328-329. What troubled

the bereaved was not the ultimate use to which the coffin was put, but forced and untimely disinterment.

43. See, for example, Makita Tairyō, *Chūgoku kinsei Bukkyōshi*, p. 267; Day, p. 194.

44. In 1928, for example, when a faith cure took place at a pagoda near Peking, the Bureau of Public Safety "banned pilgrimages and put a cordon of police around the pagoda. The Bureaus of Public Safety are a new Nationalist institution doing admirable work of a diversified character. They are especially down on religious superstition and at Hangchow, Chekiang, have ordered that the worship of idols in prisons shall be prohibited because it does not in any way atone for the crimes of the prisoners." See *The Times* (London), Sept. 10, 1928, p. 11. One of the first acts of the Nationalists after they took Kiangsi was to confiscate all the property of the Chang T'ien-shih, the head of one of the principal sects of Taoism. "How," they asked, "could this remnant of wizardry be permitted to survive in the era of the people's revolution?" (*Kuang-chou min-chou jih-pao,* Jan. 7, 1927, p. 4).

45. This is confirmed by census figures. See Welch, *Practice*, appendix 1.

46. See Blofeld, *Jewel in the Lotus*, pp. 23, 48; Makita Tairyō, *Chūgoku kinsei Bukkyōshi*, p. 247; Amano Motonosuke, *Shina nogyo keizai-ron* (The Chinese agricultural economy; Tokyo, 1942), I, 73-74.

47. This time it did not come from President Chiang but from the National Military Council which, in March 1936, at the request of the Bodhi Society in Shanghai, issued a circular order to all army commanders to protect Buddhist temples, books, and works of art (*Chinese Year Book, 1937*, p. 74).

48. The text of the decree is given in Lin Chin-tung, p. 170. One informant recalled seeing similar notices posted at monasteries in the Yangtze region from 1936 onward (possibly the order of March 1936, mentioned in the preceding note), and during the war at monasteries on Omei Shan. In the latter case they were signed by the National Airforce Headquarters in Chungking.

49. For a good example, see Welch, *Practice*, p. 498, n. 40.

50. Makita Tairyō, *Chūgoku kinsei Bukkyōshi*, pp. 263-264.

51. Ministry of Interior directive, July 1931 (Lin Chin-tung, pp. 184-185).

52. Ministry of Interior directive to the police department of the capital, November 12, 1932 (Lin Chin-tung, p. 185).

53. In 1930 there was a presidential order to abolish this tax, wherever it was being levied, within a limited period of time. Nonetheless, it continued to be levied in Chekiang. In March 1935 the Executive Yüan sent an instruction (Hsün-ling 5973) to the Chekiang provincial government, ordering it to remind the authorities of every municipality and hsien that the tax was prohibited and should be abolished promptly (Makita Tairyō, *Chūgoku kinsei Bukkyōshi*, p. 276). Similarly, in 1946 the Ministry of the Interior directed the government of Fukien to order the local authorities to desist from collecting such taxes in that province (Ministry of Interior directive, Li 0724, November 6, 1946; Lin Chin-tung, p. 190). In each case, there was obvious resistance on the part of the local authorities to giving up a convenient source of income, and it is not clear whether all of them did so. Makita gives useful information about these levies in different areas. They included a license fee for each monk and taxes on incense, candles, and tinfoil, as well as on Buddhist services (release of burning mouths,

plenary masses, penances—see Welch, *Practice,* pp. 185-195). In Canton the license fee was $30 a year per monk. In Hangchow the tax on services was 10 percent, payable in advance to the Municipal Finance Bureau. In Ningpo the tax on services brought in nearly $30,000 in 1935. It was collected by the local branch of the Chinese Buddhist Association, which kept $6,000 to cover its expenses and $2,600 as a tax-farming fee. Makita quotes a statement by the Chekiang Department of Civil Affairs to the effect that "the collection of the tax on Buddhist services started in the Ch'ing dynasty" (Makita Tairyō, *Chūgoku kinsei Bukkyōshi,* p. 275). This might be simply an attempt at self-justification. At any rate, elderly informants who were monks under the Ch'ing have spoken as if such a tax did not exist then. More investigation is needed.

54. Makita Tairyō, *Chūgoku kinsei Bukkyōshi,* pp. 267-268.

55. Day, p. 194.

56. Osgood, p. 323.

57. *Ibid.,* p. 319.

58. Chu Chieh-hsien, pp. 79-80, 133-135, supplemented by information from the prior who wrote to Lin Sen. This is, of course, the monastery's version of what happened.

59. See Welch, *Practice,* pp. 228-229. Similarly, as noted in Chapter V, Governor Li Han-hun directed the local authorities to give Nan-hua Ssu 500 *mou* of fruit plantation and forest and to restore to it some farmland that it had originally owned but that had been taken over by the local peasants.

60. See *ibid.,* pp. 226-227.

61. This was a company of 150 soldiers under Major Wang Sun-ying, the commanding officer of the first battalion of the training regiment of the Fukien army. Throughout the night members of this unit stood guard on the surrounding hillocks, which did not prevent the peasants from setting fire to the monastery woods. See Tokiwa Daijō, *Shina Bukkyō shiseki, kinen-shū,* pp. 201-202. Cf. Chapter V, note 15.

62. Tao-chün [Martin Steinkirk], *Buddha und China: Tsi-hia-schan* (Potsdam, 1940); p. 11. Prip-Møller (p. 227) mentions that soldiers were stationed at Pao-hua Shan in 1931 to guard the monks and their guests from attacks by bandits.

63. Ts'en Hsüeh-lü, *Hsü-yün ho-shang nien-p'u,* pp. 63-64. This story may be hard to believe, but it is true that Hsiung Hsi-ling was active as a patron of Buddhism. He helped to secure ratification of the charter of the Chinese Buddhist Association (Shanghai, 1912).

64. Ts'en Hsüeh-lu, *Hsü-yun ho-shang nien-p'u,* pp. 72, 87.

65. Their names were:

Lin Sen, chief of state

Tuan Ch'i-jui, chief of state

Chang Shao-tseng, prime minister

Hsiung Hsi-ling, prime minister

Liang Shih-i, prime minister

P'an Fu, prime minister

Chang Chi, president of Legislative Yüan

Chü Cheng, president of Judicial Yüan

Tai Chi-t'ao, president of Examination Yüan

Lin Hsiang, president of Supreme Court

Chuang Yün-k'uan, president of Administrative Court

Li Ken-yüan, minister of agriculture

Ts'ao Ju-lin, minister of communications

Yeh Kung-cho, minister of communications

Liang Ch'i-ch'ao, minister of finance

Chai Wen-hsüan, governor of Fengtien

Chu Ch'ing-lan, governor of Heilungkiang

Hu Ching-i, governor of Honan

Chao Heng-t'i, governor of Hunan

Ho Chien, governor of Hunan

T'ang Hsiang-ming, governor of Hunan

T'ang Sheng-chih, governor of Hunan

Hsiao Yao-nan, governor of Hupeh

Li Yin-ch'en, governor of Hupeh

Chang Kuang-chien, governor of Kansu

Ch'i Hsieh-yüan, governor of Kiangsu

Ch'i Yao-lin, governor of Kiangsu

Lu Hung-hsiang, governor of Kiangsu

Yang Yu-t'ing, governor of Kiangsu

Ch'en Ming-shu, governor of Kwangtung

Li Han-hun, governor of Kwangtung

Ch'ü Ying-kuang, governor of Shantung

T'ang Chi-yao, governor of Yünnan

In this list "governor" is used indiscriminately for civil and military governors (the latter being known as *tutu* or *tuchün*, that is, warlords) and for chairmen of provincial governments. Most people listed held office before the Northern Expedition (1926-27). Not all were Buddhist to the same degree. There were also some non-Buddhist officials who had connections with Buddhism even at the highest level. For example, Chiang Kai-shek used to stay in a suite of rooms reserved for him at the Ch'i-hsia Ssu (like the Ch'ien-lung Emperor). In 1943 he invited the Venerable Hsü-yün to a vegetarian meal, at which he questioned him about Buddhist doctrine (Ts'en Hsüeh-lü, *Hsü-yün ho-shang nien-p'u*, pp. 115-117). Although he himself was a Methodist convert, his sister Zai-lian (Juilien) was at one time an active Buddhist devotee (*Chinese Year Book, 1936-1937*, p. 1450).

66. One informant, however, recalled that once during the 1920's the municipal government of Peking proclaimed a day of no slaughter in order to hasten the end of a drought. This amounted to at least a nod of recognition to the Buddhist theory of merit.

67. Ministry of Interior directive (Li 2617), October 13, 1947 (Lin Chin-tung, p. 191). Under the Ch'ing dynasty many monasteries had enjoyed tax exemption on all their property.

68. A single informant stated that, when he was a student at the seminary of the Chin-ling Ssu near Nanking, the curriculum included a course in Kuomintang "party doctrine" (*tang-i*), instituted by the monastery, not by the government. All other informants have stated that at the seminaries they knew (and none had been at Chin-ling), there was never a course in party doctrine or any other formal political study.

69. Arthur F. Wright, *Buddhism in Chinese History* (Stanford, 1959), p. 117.

70. Quoted by Kenneth K. S. Ch'en, p. 105. See also E. Zürcher, *The Buddhist Conquest of China: The Spread and Adaptation of Buddhism in Early Medieval China* (Leiden, 1959), p. 211.

71. Prip-Møller, p. 366.

72. See the quotation referenced in Chapter III, note 7.

73. *Fo-hua hsin ch'ing-nien*, 2.2:26 (May or June 1924). I am indebted to Stephen Hay for this clipping.

74. Ts'en Hsüeh-lü, *Hsü-yün ho-shang nien-p'u*, pp. 112-113.

75. Admission to the Right Faith Society, for example, was given to anyone sponsored by two members. Members of a secret society could join if they wished, so long as they concealed their background, but few are said to have done so.

IX. FOREIGN CONTACTS

1. See Etō Shinsaku, *Nanpaku Etō Shimpei Ikō* (Tokyo, 1900) 2:45b-47b.

2. Satō Saburō, "Chūgoku ni okeru Nihon Bukkyō no fukyo ken o megutte" (Japanese Buddhist missionary rights in China), in *Chūgoku kankei ronsetsu shiryō* (Collected articles on China; Tokyo, 1966), vol. 3, pt. 1, pp. 208-213.

3. James Troup, "On the tenets of the Shinshiu or 'True Sect' of Buddhists," *Transactions of the Asiatic Society of Japan*, 16:14-16 (June 1886).

4. Takada Gikō, ed., *Chūshi shūkyo daidō renmei nenkan* (Yearbook of the Central China League of Religious Federations; Shanghai, 1943), p. 10. I am obliged to Ho Kuang-chung for making this book available to me.

5. Satō Saburō, pp. 210-211.

6. *Ibid.*

7. See *Higashi Honganji Shanhai kaikyō rokujūnen shi* (Sixty years of the Higashi Honganji in Shanghai; Shanghai, 1937), pp. 86-88. These schools (*hsüeh-t'ang*) were opened in Nanking, Hangchow, Chüanchow, and Amoy.

8. See Otto Franke, "Die Propaganda," p. 159; and Marius B. Jansen, *The Japanese and Sun Yat-sen* (Cambridge, 1954), pp. 100-102.

9. Cf. p. 12 above, and see Otto Franke, "Die Propaganda," p. 159ff, and Yin-shun, *T'ai-hsü*, pp. 35-36. The latter states that thirteen monasteries in Hangchow alone became affiliated with the Honganji.

10. Takada Gikō, p. 14.

11. Many of the temples that were established were simply the residences of Chinese converts, whose chief interest was in getting Japanese business or protection.

12. The Fifth Buddhist Council, held in Mandalay in 1871, was almost entirely a Burmese affair and its purpose was textual recension, not ecumenical cooperation. The Maha Bodhi Society in India is said to have held an international Buddhist conference in 1891, attended by delegates from Ceylon, Burma, China, and Japan, but its nature and significance cannot be assessed without more details, which, thus far, I have been unable to obtain.

13. The number of Chinese delegates is sometimes given as 26 (for example, by Yin-shun, *T'ai-hsü*, p. 203). According to the official conference report (see note 17), there were 20 regular members in the Chinese delegation, assisted by a staff of 7 interpreters, acolytes, and so on. In addition there were 6 persons who joined the delegation on their own initiative, 3 of them from Shensi. Presumably their travel expenses were not paid by the Chinese government as were the expenses of the regular delegates, some of whom had been selected by Tuan Ch'i-jui, then Chinese chief of state, and his private secretary, Ma Chi-p'ing, both Buddhists themselves (T'an-hsü, II, 37).

14. Among the delegates, I can only identify a few, like Tao-chieh and T'an-hsü, who were as firmly committed to religious practice as to doctrinal study and toward whom the modernizers at the conference were therefore aloof and "terribly cold" (T'an-hsü, II, 39).

15. The official head of the Chinese delegation and Chinese vice-chairman of

the conference was Tao-chieh, under whom T'ai-hsü had studied twenty years before (Yin-shun, *T'ai-hsü*, p. 26ff). T'ai-hsü may be pardoned, perhaps, for giving people the impression that he was himself the chief of the delegation. See, for example, *Young East*, 1.6:177 (Nov. 8, 1925); T'ai-hsü, *Lectures in Buddhism*, p. 14.

16. *Young East*, 1.6:179-180. On Mizuno, see pp. 11-12. The impression is unavoidable that he had long been cooperating with various agencies of the Japanese government.

17. Officially the conference host was the Japanese Buddhist Federation, which published a complete report on it the following year: see Bukkyō Rengō-kai, ed., *Tōa Bukkyō takai kiyō* (Summary of the East Asian Buddhist conference; Tokyo, 1926). This report explains that, before deciding to hold the conference, the federation had consulted the Ministry of Education and the Bureau for Chinese Cultural Activities (Taishi Bunka Jigōbu—see p. 3 of the report). This bureau had been set up under the Foreign Ministry to use Boxer Indemnity funds for various purposes, such as the creation of research institutes in Peking and Shanghai, financial aid to Chinese students in Japan, and the exchange of specialists between the two countries (p. 661). In 1924 it had sent Saeki Teien and Kimura Taiken to the Lu Shan conference, and now it was providing 13,000 of the 37,740 yen for the Tokyo conference (pp. 784-785). Its head, Count Okabe Nagakage, attended the conference, as did Kimura Eiichi of the Foreign Ministry's Asiatic Bureau. Also present was Shiraiwa Ryūhei, chairman of the East Asia Common Culture Association, which was another organ for promoting Japanese cultural penetration of China. Okabe's and Shiraiwa's presence is mentioned on p. 755, and Kimura's in *Young East*, 1.6:173.

18. T'an-hsü, II, 41-43.

19. Tokiwa Daijō, *Shina Bukkyō shiseki kinen-shū*, p. 203. Both Tokyo and Kyoto had chairs of Buddhist studies.

20. Yin-shun, *T'ai-hsü*, p. 213.

21. *Eastern Buddhist*, 3.2:190 (July-September 1924).

22. Chinese lay devotees went to Japan to learn Tantric Buddhism from Shingon masters. Chinese monks went for academic study (two in 1936 and two more in early 1937). See *Chinese Year Book, 1937*, p. 73, and Fa-fang, "Nijūgo-nen-do," pp. 224-225.

23. The Sino-Japanese Buddhist Association (Chung-jih Fo-chiao Hui) was probably formed in 1936, but in any case before the Japanese invasion. At about the same time the Sino-Japanese Tantric Association (Chung-jih Mi-chiao Hui) was established (*Chinese Year Book, 1937*, p. 73). There was also a Japanese-Chinese Buddhist Research Association (Jih-hua Yen-chiu Fo-chiao Hui), based in Kyoto, which published annual volumes of scholarly papers in 1936-37.

24. Takada Gikō, p. 14.

25. Takada Gikō, pp. 24-36, lists a total of 11 temples established between 1876 and 1937, but on p. 14 he speaks of 10 temples having been set up before 1937 and of 49 (not 46) being in operation as of December 1942. It seems clear that he does not include temples that had gone out of operation, like some in Nanking, Changsha, and Fukien. The only temple outside Shanghai that survived from the era before 1937 was the Honganji temple in Hankow, established in 1906, which in 1942 had 1,200 Japanese and 150 Chinese parishioners.

26. For example, in 1942 at the original Honganji temple in Shanghai the

number of Japanese parishioners was 4,930 and the number of Chinese was zero.

27. Two officers of the Ching-an Ssu in Shanghai are said to have been arrested, and in Canton the abbot of the Liu-jung Ssu, T'ieh-ch'an, was executed.

28. Takada Gikō, p. 1, states that the league was set up in April 1937 in accordance with a policy formulated by the Military Intelligence Bureau in October 1938 (sic). According to another Japanese source, the *China Annual* (Shanghai, 1944), p. 529, it was set up by "Japanese religious bodies" in February 1939 with headquarters in Shanghai and the following purposes: (1) to create Sino-Japanese Buddhist associations in different parts of central China; (2) to sponsor the exchange of Chinese and Japanese students of religion; (3) to restore Chinese temples; (4) to promote educational and social-welfare work; and (5) to encourage "Japanese religionists to advance into China in support of the league's cause." It was obligatory for Japanese Shinto, Buddhist, and Christian groups in China to join. The president (in 1943) was Prince Konoye Fumimaro, and the vice-president was Count Otani, head of the Higashi-Honganji sect.

29. Takada Gikō, pp. 1, 4, 5. The changes in the bureaucratic status of the Central China League of Religious Federations appear to have been as follows. After being set up under the military authorities, it was transferred to the liaison office of the Central China Liaison Office (sic) of the Office for the Resurgence of Asia (Kōain), which had been created in December 1938 directly under the Cabinet in order to formulate policy on and handle relations with China. In April 1942 the league was placed under the supervision of the Foreign Ministry through its representatives in Shanghai. In November 1942 it seems to have been returned to the Office for the Resurgence of Asia, when the latter was integrated into the Ministry for Great East Asian Co-Prosperity.

Quaritch Wales, writing at about this time, gives a slightly different organizational history: "Buddhist propaganda has for several years been carried on by the New Asia Bureau of the Dai Nippon Buddhist Association, which is under the joint control of the Japanese Education and War Ministries. It is responsible for all missionary work in East Asia and long before Pearl Harbor was already deeply entrenched in north China. There [sic], the more systematically to further its ends, the New Asia Bureau had established Sino-Japanese Buddhist associations at Hangchow, Amoy, and Nanking, subsidized by the Special Service Section of the Army, naturally not with purely religious motives." See *Free World*, 5.5:248 (May 1943).

30. Takada Gikō, pp. 24-36.

31. The most significant absentee was Yüan-ying, the national head of the Chinese Buddhist Association (Shanghai, 1929).

32. Bombardment damaged the Liu-yün Ssu in Shanghai and Chiao Shan in Chen-chiang; the Chu-lin Ssu, also in Chen-chiang, is said to have been wholly destroyed by marauding Japanese troops.

33. John Blofeld, who visited Wu-t'ai Shan in 1937, describes a monastery with several hundred monks where "the main pavilion . . . was arranged in the Chinese way, but many services were held in a smaller building where purely Thibetan rites were performed" (*Jewel in the Lotus*, p. 97). A visitor to Wu-t'ai Shan in 1911 wrote: "The most curious feature of Buddhism on the Wutaishan is the amalgamating of Chinese Buddhism and Lamaism . . . Both doctrines borrow from one another in habits and arrangements . . . The structure of the temple is, for the greater part, Chinese, but the form of the pagodas is mostly Indo-Tibetan.

The interior, too, forms a mixture of Chinese and Tibetan. Chinese and Tibetan idols stand side by side, Tibeto-Mongolian inscriptions are next to Chinese ones, Tibetan butter lamps, praying cylinders, also boards on which the monks throw themselves for prayers, all such things are seen here in Chinese temples. In their services, too, one style blends with another." Hackmann, *German Scholar in the East,* pp. 118-119.

34. On the Chang-chia Hutukhtu, see H. S. Brunnert and V. V. Hagelstrom, *Present Day Political Organization of China,* trans. A. Beltchenko and E. E. Moran (Shanghai, 1921), p. 476; the discussion of *lCan-skya Rol-pa'i-rdo-r'je* (*lCan-skya* being the Tibetan spelling of *Chang-chia*) in L. Petech, *China and Tibet in the Early 18th Century* (Leiden, 1950), pp. 2, 91, 157-159, 162, 189, 241, 242; and Robert James Miller, *Monasteries and Culture Change in Inner Mongolia* (Wiesbaden, 1959), pp. 70-72. Chang-chia eventually held a series of high government and party posts. He was a member of the Mongolian and Tibetan Affairs Commission from 1930 until his death and a member of the Kuomintang Supervisory Committee, 1935-1950. He was elected to the National Assembly in 1947 —the same year that he became chairman of the newly reconstituted Chinese Buddhist Association.

35. See *Fo-hsüeh ts'ung-pao,* no. 3 (December 1912).

36. Some converts believed that not only could they make progress toward enlightenment but also that, through the right mudra or mantra, almost anything —from a winning lottery ticket to greater sexual vigor—could be obtained with minimal effort (see Welch, *Practice,* pp. 385-387). Many of them were intrigued by the mystification of Tantric rites, and one Chinese Buddhist monk was prompted to complain scornfully that "from high officials of the government down to the old ladies who frequent temples to burn incense . . . all feel honored when a few drops of holy water from an antique bronze jar are sprinkled on their bent heads with a peacock feather by a Tibetan lama." See Wei-huan, p. 144.

37. In the order of their arrival in China (and in Chinese orthography), the lamas on whom I have collected information—not all of it confirmed by documentary sources—were as follows: (1) An-ch'in, a living buddha who left Tibet with the Panchen Lama in 1923 and went back in 1933 to negotiate with the Dalai for the Panchen's peaceful return; (2) To-chieh, a *geshe* who came from Sikang but had spent many years in Lhasa, Mongolia, and Wu-t'ai Shan before going to teach at T'ai-hsü's Tibetan school in Peking in 1925; (3) Kung-ka, a living buddha from a monastery near Minya Kongka (hence his name) in Sikang; (4) Ken-sang, a living buddha from a monastery near Kung-ka's, who taught at T'ai-hsü's Tibetan school in Szechwan but also won many disciples in Hunan and Hupeh; (5) A-wang, an abbot of Sera, who spent a year or two in Chengtu during the early 1930's, lecturing and raising money for his monastery, then returned to Lhasa; (6) Sheng-lou, a living buddha from the Yünnan borderland who toured China in the early 1930's (and whose powers reputedly included the ability to make small holes open up in the crania of people who heard him lecture); (7) Tung-pen, a *geshe* from Drebung, who came to teach at T'ai-hsü's Szechwan school about 1937 and died there next year; (8) Jung-tseng, who passed through south China in 1937; (9) A-wang, (Sermay Khenpo Nga-wang Namgyal, as distinct from the aforementioned A-wang, i.e., Gyurmay Yundrung Khenpo Ngawang Namgyal) who "went to China purely for propagating Buddhism, [but] did many good services for the Tibetan government [and]

on his return to Tibet was rewarded by the Tibetan government" (Tibetan source).

The Mongolian and Tibetan Affairs Commission conferred religious titles on Ken-sang and To-chieh, among others. The To-chieh listed above may be identical with the Dorje Rimpoche, also from Sikang, who initiated John Blofeld in 1935. But such an identification is not supported by comparison of the photograph in Blofeld, *Wheel of Life,* facing p. 64, and the frontispiece of *Ch'eng-tu hsi-nan ho-p'ing fa-hui t'e-k'an* (The Chengtu religious meeting for peace in the southwest; Chengtu, 1932). The latter includes a biography of To-chieh (pp. 25-28), which makes him, rather than the Panchen or No-na, the reviver of Chinese interest in Tantrism when he arrived in Peking at about the same time as they did.

38. Two members of the Panchen's entourage also received government posts. His principal adviser, Lo-sang Lang-chia, became a member of the Mongolian and Tibetan Affairs Commission in 1929, as did Lo-sang Chien-tsang. The latter headed the Panchen's office in Nanking from 1931 onwards, and in 1935 became a member of the Central Executive Committee of the Kuomintang.

39. Paul Demiéville, *Le Concile de Lhasa* (Paris, 1952), gives a complete account of how the Ch'an monk Ta-ch'eng lost a written debate carried on with Indian monks about 792-794 C.E. Ta-ch'eng advocated the theory that sudden enlightenment could be won by transcending differentiated ideas; his adversaries favored a gradual, analytical approach to enlightenment. This debate decided the outcome of the competition between Chinese and Indians for influence over Tibetan Buddhism, which thereafter was Indian-oriented.

40. *Chinese Year Book, 1937* (Shanghai, 1937), p. 73. Shirob left Lhasa in mid-January 1937 and arrived in Shanghai (via Calcutta and Colombo) on March 22. He was received almost immediately by the Minister of Education in Nanking, who thanked him for coming to speak at Peiping, Tsinghua, National Central, Chung-shan, and Wuhan universities, and asked for his help in improving the ministry's program of Tibetan translation. This program was centered on a large Chinese-Tibetan dictionary, the purpose of which, like the purpose of inviting Shirob, was said to be "greater cultural understanding between Tibetans and Hans." See *Fo-chiao pan-yüeh k'an* (Buddhist semimonthly), 7.8:16-17 (Apr. 16, 1937). Since Shirob did not speak Chinese, he lectured through an interpreter. Most of the other lamas in China learned to speak well enough to be able to handle the exposition of practice, though not always of doctrine.

41. Shirob served as a member of the People's Political Council (1938-1949); an alternate member of the Kuomintang Sixth Supervisory Committee (1945-1949); and a vice-chairman of the Mongolian and Tibetan Affairs Commission (1947-1949).

42. The office of the Dalai Lama states that many of the Tibetan lamas in China "persistently remained loyal to the Tibetan government and did many good services for their country." This statement was part of a commentary on an early draft of this chapter, which I had sent them asking if it contained errors of fact. In it I had written, among other things, that the Panchen Lama "was *persona non grata* in Lhasa." They informed me that this was "a serious mistake. Throughout his life, far from declaring him *persona non grata,* he [the Panchen Lama] was revered by the Government and the people of Tibet in a measure that equaled only second to the Dalai Lama." I was also told that

Shirob Jaltso (properly spelled Sherab Gyaltsho—I use the Chinese Communist spelling because it is better known) was "never listed as *persona non grata.*" I myself have heard the Dalai Lama express deep respect for Shirob as an eminent scholar whose only fault was the pride that had led him to make rash emendations in the Tripitaka, thus incurring the censure of the previous Dalai Lama. Despite Shirob's collaboration with the Nationalists and later with the Communists, "one had no right to say he was pro-Chinese." Tibetans do not like to air their dirty linen in public, and Tibetan lamas in particular observe the rule that no monk should speak ill of another. Therefore, even more than in the case of Chinese Buddhism, it is difficult for the outsider to get an accurate picture of factional struggles.

43. *Taisho,* 246. See also M. W. de Visser, *Ancient Buddhism in Japan* (Paris, 1928), pp. 517, 532, 612.

44. On religious names, see Welch, *Practice,* pp. 279-281.

45. The guiding spirit of the society was Ch'ü Ying-kuang, formerly governor of Shantung and Chekiang and Minister of the Interior. He was a committed Tantrist, but the society also counted among its members exoteric monks like Yin-kuang and Yüan-ying and lay devotees like Wang I-t'ing. This Bodhi Society (P'u-t'i Hsüeh-hui), formally inaugurated in November 1935, had no connection with the Bodhi Society (Chüeh-she) established by T'ai-hsü in 1918. Another esoteric group in Shanghai was the Mi-ch'eng Ching-she.

46. *Chinese Buddhist,* 1.1:1 (April 1930).

47. Wong will be remembered by some readers for his translation of the Platform Sutra, *The Sutra of Wei Lang* (London, 1947). He was not the first Chinese to study Theravada in Ceylon. The monk Wan-hui preceded him by several years—see *Eastern Buddhist,* 3.3:274 (October-December 1924).

48. It was a common practice for Chinese monks to take their ordination vows a second or third time in order to strengthen their commitment or in order to draw inspiration from an eminent ordaining monk. Hence, from the Chinese point of view, receiving the Theravada ordination meant supplementing, not replacing, the Mahayana ordination. See Welch, *Practice,* pp. 334-335.

49. Their names were Pei-kuan, Teng-tz'u, Hsing-chiao, and Chüeh-yüan. Financed by leading devotees, they were supposed to remain in Thailand four years. Pei-kuan withdrew by 1937. See *Chinese Year Book, 1936-1937,* p. 1446; and Fa-fang, "Nijugo-nen-do," p. 222.

50. Their Chinese religious names, followed by their Theravada names, were Hsiu-lu (Kondanna), Wei-chih (Bhaddiya), Hui-sung (Vappa), Fa-chou (Mahanama), and Wei-huan (Assaji). Their later histories would make an interesting study in acculturation. Wei-huan left the monkhood within a few months and returned to China, where he married. Eventually he became the principal English interpreter for the Chinese Buddhist Association established in Peking in 1953. Fa-chou married a girl of Dutch descent and eventually became a lecturer at the University of Ceylon. Hui-sung, who stayed longest, became mentally deranged. Wei-chih, after disrobing, went to Singapore where he died during the war. Hsiu-lu, after disrobing, went to India where he pursued his studies at Santiniketan or Nalanda. Only the information about the first two men is reliable. Another unsettled question is who sent them to Ceylon in the first place. Their Sinhalese hosts believed that they had been selected and sent by T'ai-hsü; and it is true that he acted as their guarantor (see Yin-shun, *T'ai-hsü,* p. 404). But

another Chinese source states that their group was "formed by the Chinese Buddhist Association in accordance with the proposal made by the Pure Karma Buddhist Association," both of which were housed in the same building in Shanghai. See *Chinese Year Book, 1936-1937*, p. 1446.

51. Liao-ts'an (Dhammakitti), who went to Ceylon in 1945, returned to China about 1953 with Fa-fang's ashes, disrobed, and became an instructor in Pali at the Chinese Buddhist Institute in Peking.

52. Today many Theravada Buddhists have a very different attitude and publicly advocate tolerance and respect for Mahayana Buddhism. In 1956 the fourth Conference of the World Fellowship of Buddhists voted to abolish even the use of the terms "Theravada" and "Mahayana": see *Report of the 4th World Buddhist Conference* (Kathmandu, n.d.), p. 2. There are some Theravadins, however, who still believe that the world would be a better place if Mahayana were removed from it.

53. He received the information at first hand from Liao-ts'an (Dhammakitti), who had heard the complaints of members of the 1936 group. The latter are stated to have been novices (*sha-mi*) when they left China, and the Theravada ordination they received on May 6, 1936, was also apparently the novices' ordination. Hence there would have been more justification for withholding the respect due to bhikkhus than in the case of the Liao-ts'an and his fellow monk, who came in 1945. More information is needed.

54. I have heard this from many informants. See also Reichelt, *The Transformed Abbot*, p. 156, and "A Conference of Chinese Buddhist Leaders," p. 668; Pratt, p. 311. A Buddhist monk once explained to me that, although it was true that Jesus had risen after three days, no one should think he had done this "just by becoming a Christian." He had performed religious exercises (*hsiu-hsing*) and that was how he had achieved resurrection. There was no attempt on the part of this monk to deny the miracle of resurrection, only to fit it into the Buddhist scheme. Nor did monks deny the efficacy of Christian rites. The head of a small temple near Ningpo allowed one missionary to teach his disciple "prayers to the true God and sacred words about Jesus Christ," perhaps in the hope that it would procure for him some of the advantages it had won for the missionary. See Moule, p. 167.

55. Edkins, p. 75. Buddhist tolerance is attested to by many sources. In 1875 Timothy Richard, when he was baptizing converts in Shantung, found that he had no building convenient to the river where they could change their clothes. He explained his problem to the monk in charge of a Buddhist temple there, who "readily consented" to lend some of its rooms for this purpose. See Timothy Richard, *Forty-Five Years in China* (New York, 1916), p. 95. In 1879 the largest lama temple in Peking allowed a colporteur of the National Bible Society of Scotland to run a bookstore within the temple, where on several days a week Christian books were sold. See C. F. Gordon Cumming, *Wanderings in China* (Edinburgh and London, 1888), pp. 4-9.

56. Harry A. Franck, pp. 575-576.

57. In the early 1890's De Groot reported: "It has often happened to the author of these lines that when he was taking his meal in one of the monasteries where he was staying, he was visited by monks who were curious to see how he ate and what he ate; but it was enough for them to smell the odour of his roast of pork or his leg of mutton and they would be forced to make a hasty exit from

the room; they felt overcome by nausea. With such strict vegetarianism, it goes without saying that when non-vegetarian lay people come to stay sometimes in a monastery they are not allowed to have their food prepared in the monks' kitchen. There are small separate kitchens for them, where their own servants can stew things up for them" (*Le Code du Mahayana*, p. 103). In 1908, when Boerschmann stayed on P'u-t'o Shan, he grew tired of vegetarian fare and sent his cook to smuggle in some chickens (Boerschmann, p. 166). In this and some other instances the monks are portrayed as tacitly or even gleefully cooperating in getting meat to the foreigners. It seems more likely that their cooperation, when it was forthcoming (and often it was refused), was reluctant and indignant. There was a compelling practical reason for this. If Chinese pilgrims saw meat being eaten at a monastery, many of them would take their patronage elsewhere. This was understood by early Western travelers like Archibald John Little: see his *Mt. Omi and Beyond* (London, 1901), pp. 75, 81, and 83. Little also provides an example of the Westerner's tendency to haggle over charges for food (pp. 68, 83). The meanest bit of haggling was probably perpetrated by Mrs. C. F. Gordon Cumming. In 1879 she visited the T'ien-t'ung Ssu, one of the model monasteries of China. After she and her party had enjoyed an "excellent dinner," they were asked to give the equivalent of English tenpence. Mrs. Cumming offered eight pence. When the offer was accepted, she tipped the waiter tuppence halfpenny and noted that he "grinned with delight. Can I give you a better proof that we have reached a spot where foreigners are almost unknown?" (Cumming, p. 291.) Mrs. Cumming was quite mistaken, of course, about foreigners being unknown: probably more had stayed at T'ien-t'ung than at any other monastery in that area. Even today Westerners with plenty of dollars in their pockets take pride in doing the poor Chinese shopkeeper out of a few cents, partly to show their *savoir faire* and partly out of fear of being cheated themselves. But the monastery was not a shop, and this sort of behavior was regarded as most inappropriate there.

58. Soothill, *Timothy Richard of China*, pp. 162-163.

59. Mizuno Baigyō, *Shina Bukkyō kinseishi*, p. 58.

60. Reichelt quotes a warning by the late Ming monk, Hsi-ming, against "being deceived into joining the Catholic church or some other outside sect," and states that it was often reprinted (*Truth and Tradition*, pp. 157-158).

61. On this abjuration, see Welch, *Practice*, pp. 359-360. Buddhists rejected Taoism as heterodoxy but tolerated it as another approach to the truth. Taoist monks could expect to be put up at Buddhist monasteries (see Welch, *Practice*, p. 401). Yet one gets the impression that many Buddhists became less tolerant of Taoism during the Republican period. This may be partly because it was more scathingly condemned as superstition by foreigners and partly because of the example of sectarian distinctiveness provided by the Christian missionaries.

62. It was in 1920 that Reichelt first proposed an "institute for special work among the Buddhists." He wanted to make contact with monks whose hearts were filled with bitterness toward Christianity because, as he wrote, some Christians were "so fatally lacking in a sympathetic and gentle attitude towards others." It was to be "a half-way house" with many of the features of a Buddhist monastery, including a wandering-monks hall, a meditation hall, a belltower, a crematorium, and a hall for the aged. See Karl Ludwig Reichelt, "Special Work among Chinese Buddhists," *Chinese Recorder*, 51.7:491-497 (July 1920). When

it finally started operating, under the name of the Christian Mission to the Buddhists, in the autumn of 1922, it had only a "very small, semi-foreign house." After a year and a half it moved to somewhat larger quarters, which included a dining room, where vegetarian meals were served, and the all-important "pilgrims hall" where monks were allowed to put up for three days (as they would be at a Buddhist temple) and to stay longer if they were interested in serious study. The layout was "just as in monasteries, with two long platforms where they can spread their bedding, and, above them, shelves where they can place their things. Between the two platforms there is an altar with an incense burner and two candlesticks and above all an impressive crucifix." Even more significant was the arrangement of the chapel, to which they were summoned for worship twice a day (as they would be in a monastery) by "a Chinese bell with deep tones." The altar was of red lacquer "in a true Chinese style," adorned with gilt designs that included "the lotus lily, symbolizing the purity, the fire, and the water of the cleansing spirit" (but also, of course, symbolizing the Buddha Amitabha and his Pure Land), "the swastica of peace and cosmic union" (but also one of the Buddha's sacred marks and a general symbol for Buddhism), and the cross over a lotus, which was the mission's emblem.

Just as in a Chinese temple, plaques with parallel inscriptions were hung on the walls. One bore a quotation from the Gospel according to St. John: "The true light that enlightens every man has come into the world." The other legend was more Buddhist in flavor than Christian: "[Join in] the great vow compassionately to help people across to the other shore" (ta-yüan tz'u-hang).

These efforts to make Buddhist monks feel at home attracted a large number of them as visitors (about a thousand annually), but in the first four and a half years of operation only seventeen male Chinese were converted and baptized. See Notto Normann Thelle, "The Christian Mission to the Buddhists," *Chinese Recorder,* 58.9:571-575 (September 1927). A photograph of four of the Buddhist and Taoist novices, whom Thelle says were enrolled in the boys' school opened by the mission, appears in the *Chinese Recorder,* 54.11 (November 1923), facing p. 671. When the permanent headquarters of the mission were contructed at Tao-fung Shan in the New Territories of Hong Kong during the 1930's, the similarity to a Buddhist monastery became almost as close as Reichelt had originally envisaged it. Some missionaries were afraid that he was being too broad-minded in his use of Buddhist motifs and even that he might be fostering a kind of Buddhist-Christian syncretism. He and his colleagues maintained, however, that their only purpose was to "lead these people into a living faith in Jesus Christ" (Thelle, p. 571.)

63. *Maha Bodhi,* 41.3.4:133 (March-April 1933).

64. Most of the information on Chao-k'ung up to this point is taken from David Lampe and Laszlo Szenasi, *The Self-Made Villain* (London, 1961).

65. Victor Purcell, *The Chinese in Southeast Asia* (London, 1951), p. 47.

66. Ts'en Hsüeh-lü, *Hsü-yün ho-shang nien-p'u* (Hong Kong, 1962), pp. 21-22, 40-43, 47-48. I have been unable to get confirmation of this story in Thailand; nor have I been able to confirm the related episode, in which Hsü-yün on his way to Bangkok that year met an Englishman who had been British consul in T'eng-yüeh and Kunming and who allegedly gave Hsü-yün three thousand pounds sterling toward the expense of transporting a set of the Tripitaka back to Yünnan. The records of the Foreign Office in London do not appear to reveal who this may have been.

67. White marble images from Burma and Thailand, termed in Chinese "jade buddhas" (*yü-fo*), have been popular in China over the past century. In the late 1890's a set of such images was made in India for a Chinese monk from P'u-t'o Shan, who spent the better part of three years at Oudh overseeing the work. So popular were these particular images that when they arrived in Shanghai, they were kept on exhibit in nearby Woosung at the request of the authorities: "a large number of Chinese visit them daily, which is quite profitable for the railway." See *Journal of the North China Branch of the Royal Asiatic Society*, 31:203 (1896-1897). These may well have been the jade buddhas installed during the reconstruction of the Fa-yü Ssu on P'u-t'o Shan.

68. Ts'en Hsüeh-lü, *Hsü-yün ho-shang nien-p'u*, p. 66. I have not had an opportunity to check on this account in the records of the Singapore police.

69. Cheng-lien, 7:102. Cf. Chou Hsiang-kuang, p. 214.

70. For example, in 1916 the head of the Chi-le Ssu, Pen-chung, led a group of his Refuges disciples to Ku Shan to receive the lay ordination: they made up 5 out of the 6 upasakas that year and 40 out of the 114 upasikas. This information comes from the 1916 ordination yearbook.

71. See *Yüan-ying*, pp. 13-14.

72. However, they came from around Amoy rather than from Foochow, where Ku Shan was located. So did many Ku Shan monks.

73. See *Chüeh-shih*, 336:4 (Sept. 11, 1966).

74. *Chinese Year Book, 1937*, p. 74.

X. SECTS AND DISSENSION

1. For a fuller explanation of the nature of sects in Chinese Buddhism, see Welch, *Practice*, pp. 395-400. Liturgy, rules, dress, diet, calendar, and mode of organization were virtually the same at all the large monasteries in China regardless of sect. On the doctrines of the different sects, many summaries are available in English. Among the best is Junjirō Takakusu, *The Essentials of Buddhist Philosophy*, ed. Wing-tsit Chan and Charles A. Moore (Hawaii, 1956).

2. See *ibid.*, pp. 90-91, 100.

3. Kuan Chiung in *Chinese Year Book, 1935-1936*, p. 1513. "Disciples" means, of course, mostly Refuges disciples, not monks.

4. In Chinese it was termed Fa-hsiang Tsung (Dharmalaksana) or Wei-shih Tsung (Vijnaptamatrata) or Tz'u-en Tsung (after its founder). Some authorities would prefer to speak of the Dharmalaksana "school," but I find it less confusing to translate *tsung* consistently as "sect," except in cases that do not involve the Chinese system of religious lineage.

5. Yüeh-hsia first set up the Avatamsaka University (Hua-yen Ta-hsüeh) in Hardoon Gardens (see Chapter I, note 47), where he went just after the 1911 revolution. He enrolled sixty students for a three-year course, built a meditation hall and a lecture hall, and held meditation every day (presumably modeled on the practice at the T'ien-ning Ssu, of which he was a dharma disciple—see Welch, *Practice*, p. 450). Three years later, just as the preparatory course was finishing, some kind of religious dispute forced Yüeh-hsia to move the university to the Hai-ch'ao Ssu in Hangchow, where those who had finished the preparatory course now took the regular course of another three years. Sixty were said to have graduated. Yüeh-hsia then went to lecture in Peking, got into political trouble, became abbot of the Hsing-fu Ssu, and died at the end of 1917. See Cheng-lien, 7:102. Since

Yüeh-hsia had also run a school in Anhwei in 1900 and a school in Nanking in 1910, he must be considered one of the leaders of monastic education in modern China.

6. Kuan Chiung in *Chinese Year Book, 1935-1936*, p. 1513. On Kuan's authority in these matters, see Chapter I, note 6.

7. Ts'en Hsüeh-lü, *Hsü-yün ho-shang fa-hui*, p. 263.

8. This date comes from Yin-shun, *T'ai-hsü*, p. 183, where the name of the school is given as the College for the Study of Tibetan (Tsang-wen Hsüeh-yüan). My informant, who lived at the school for about a year, serving part of the time as private secretary to T'ai-hsü, recalls clearly that this was prefixed by the word "Buddhist" (Fo-chiao).

9. Especially Yang Ming-ch'en and Hu Jui-lin. The latter was a director of the ephemeral Chinese Buddhist Federation (see p. 58) and a member of the Chinese delegation to the East Asian Buddhist Conference in Tokyo in 1925 (see p. 169).

10. In 1933-1935 about half of its hundred-odd students were laymen. As at the school in Peking, they attended classes and devotions along with the monks. Although the school premises consisted of a monastery (the Chin-yün Ssu in Pei-p'ei), monastic terminology was avoided in all titles and many activities. For example, the proctor was called *she-chien* rather than *seng-chih*, and chores were called *lao-tso* rather than *ch'u-p'o*.

11. For an eloquent Buddhist statement of the case against lineal succession to the abbotship, see Welch, *Practice*, pp. 173-176.

12. Prip-Møller, p. 304. I was told that it belonged to no sect.

13. Similarly Chiao Shan, which had belonged to the Ts'ao-tung sect of Ch'an at the end of the Ch'ing dynasty, came to be thought of as multisectarian during the Republican period, despite the fact that the abbotship remained in the Ts'ao-tung lineage. Under Abbot Ta-hsü it began to give greater emphasis to Pure Land practice (see Welch, *Practice*, p. 399), and in 1935 a Buddhist seminary was established there.

14. See *ibid.*, pp. 255-257.

15. On their rights to the abbotship, see *ibid.*, pp. 450-452.

16. Liang Ch'i-ch'ao, p. 117. C. K. Yang points out that Liang was among the first to maintain that Chinese society was built on a rationalistic basis and that religion, if it existed at all in China, was unimportant. For a striking quotation from Liang to this effect, see Yang, "Confucian Thought and Chinese Religion," in John K. Fairbank, ed., *Chinese Thought and Institutions* (Chicago, 1957), p. 270; and cf. *Religion in Chinese Society*, pp. 244-277. Rereading these passages from Yang, I am impressed by the degree to which our views coincide (with regard to modern Confucian defensiveness and the antireligious facade it created); and it may be worth noting that when I was writing this chapter, I had completely forgotten what he had written, so that (if my judgment is worth anything) my conclusions confirm his rather than merely repeat them.

17. *Ibid.* This is actually a quotation from Chiang Fang-chen with which Liang says he very much agrees.

18. His daughter died at seventeen, and his younger son drowned at nineteen. His elder son, who had abandoned his post at Ma-tang in the face of the Japanese attack, was executed for treason in 1940—the same year that Ou-yang's wife died. Three of his favorite pupils also died at early ages. Pious Buddhists could

point to all of this as evidence of karmic retribution for Ou-yang's arrogance toward monks and his rejection of religious practice.

19. The progress of the bodhisattva was divided into ten stages. Monks maintained that a person could not get beyond the third stage unless in at least one of his lives he had entered the sangha. See Welch, *Practice*, p. 85.

20. A lay informant from Kao-pi, thirty miles north of Chaochow in northeastern Kwangtung, has told me that there, where Hakkas predominated and one found no proper monks or monasteries, the local village temples were operated by pseudo-monks. They were still called *ho-shang* and on occasion would gather from different temples to perform Buddhist mortuary rites, dressed in yellow *chia-sa* and wearing Vairocana hats. Ordinarily, after being on duty at their temples during the day, they would return at night to wife, children, and a menu from which meat was by no means excluded. They were apparently unordained, used lay names, and did not shave their heads. The images in their temples were usually of Sakyamuni and Kuan-yin, whose birthdays they celebrated every year. They were distinct from the geomancers and from Taoist priests, the latter being uncommon in the area. This sort of pseudo-sangha sounds very much like what De Groot describes in neighboring Amoy and like the *na-mo lao* in other areas, that is, the "fellows who recite *na-mo*" (homage to some deity). On the lay Buddhist club in Yünnan, see Chapter IV, note 26.

21. In 1928 some young monks unsuccessfully petitioned the Bureau of Social Welfare in Nanking to forbid monastic celibacy, so that monks might be like Protestant ministers or Buddhist priests in Japan: see *The Times* (London), October 5, 1928, p. 13. In 1936 the monk Chih-feng took part in a symposium in which he argued that for the future development of Buddhism it was necessary for the sangha to lead a married life. Later he himself disrobed and married. See Makita Tairyō, "Gendai chugoku Bukkyō no seikatsu kihan" (The norms of Buddhist life in contemporary China), *Bukkyō Daigaku kenkyū kiyō* (The memorial of records, Bukkyō University), 35:240 (Oct. 23, 1958).

22. Even well-educated devotees believed in their efficacy. On November 11, 1934, Tai Chi-t'ao wrote the abbot of Pao-hua Shan to thank him for having its monks perform a penance service for the benefit of orphaned souls who had been victims of calamity. He enclosed twenty silver dollars to cover the incense, flowers, and paper money used in the ceremony and fifty dollars for the monks and lay workmen who had performed it. See *Tai Chi-t'ao hsien-sheng wen-ts'un*, p. 1239. The opposite extreme is best exemplified by Hu Shih, who was so much opposed to rites for the dead that, even when his own mother died (and she had been a devout Buddhist), he refused to allow Buddhist monks to conduct a service for her. See E. T. C. Werner, "Reform in Chinese Mourning Rites," *The New China Review*, 2.3:228 (June 1920).

23. On volunteer plenary masses, see Welch, *Practice*, p. 198.

24. See Edward Bing-shuey Lee, *Modern Canton*, p. 97. These figures seem to bear some relationship to those quoted by Tsukamoto from a "Canton municipal survey of 1932," which listed the following:

	Male	Female
Buddhists	5,212	8,376
Taoists	299	197
Moslems	1,047	1,109
Protestants	2,951	3,201

See Tsukamoto Zenryu, "Chukaminkoku no Bukkyu," in Bukkyo Daigaku, ed., *Toyo gaku ronso* (Kyoto, 1952), p. 23.

25. Hackmann, *Buddhism as a Religion*, p. 256.

26. W. E. Soothill, *A Mission in China* (London, 1907), p. 280. It is quite possible that the reason why Wenchow officials paid respects to the Tripitaka was that it had been bestowed by the emperor. Nonetheless, Soothill's comment must reflect exasperating experiences that he had had as a missionary trying to penetrate the true religious feelings of educated Chinese.

27. Louis Lecompte, *Journey through the Empire of China* (London, 1697), p. 331; J. J. M. De Groot, "Buddhist Masses for the Dead at Amoy," *Actes du sixième congrès international des orientalistes* (Leiden, 1885), pt. 4, sec. 4, p. 31; Carl F. Kupfer, *Sacred Places in China* (Cincinnati, 1911), p. 108; K. L. Reichelt, *Religion in Chinese Garment* (London, 1951), p. 149. Some of this testimony must be interpreted in the light of the observers' obvious desire "to take the mandarins down a peg." But at least it shows the need to question whether, as one authority asserts, the concepts of ghosts and spirits held by Chinese intellectuals were "entirely different from the concepts of spirits roaming the universe as understood by the ignorant masses" (Wing-tsit Chan, p. 258).

28. See Ch'en Ch'i-t'ien, *Chi-yüan hui-i lu* (Reminiscences of Ch'en Ch'i-t'ien; Taipei, 1965), pp. 16, 21, 38, 39, 77, 78. I am indebted to David Roy for bringing this book to my attention.

29. See Welch, *Practice*, pp. 14-15, 62-63, 79, 107-108, 119.

30. Yin-shun, *T'ai-hsü*, p. 40. Cf. Chapter III, note 5.

31. Letters from Mrs. F. R. Millican to J. B. Pratt, January 12 and March 4, 1929, Pratt Collection, Williams College Library. In one of Pratt's own notebooks he mentions the opposition to T'ai-hsü expressed by the chief magistrate of Ningpo, a very rich and intelligent person, who had written a book on Pure Land.

XI. CHRISTIAN STEREOTYPES AND BUDDHIST REALITIES

1. De Groot, *Sectarianism*. The five missionaries were Samuel Beal, Joseph Edkins, E. J. Eitel, H. Hackmann, and Timothy Richard.

2. Perhaps the most favorable view of Buddhist doctrine was taken by Timothy Richard, who believed that Mahayana Buddhism was an Asian form of Christianity which Asvagosha had learned from a Christian missionary, perhaps the Apostle Thomas. Only the terminology was Buddhist (hence Richard translated the word "Buddha" as "God"). This being so, Christianity was the fundamental component of the single world religion that, in Richard's opinion, was soon to emerge. On the other hand, the fact that he looked on Chinese Buddhists as separated brethren did not mean that he approved of the errors into which they had fallen. He disapproved of monasticism and ascetic practices, and he deplored the "low state of Buddhism in China today." In general his attitude toward the actual Chinese Buddhist system and establishment was almost as negative as that of missionaries who did not share his interfaith enthusiasm. See Timothy Richard, *The New Testament of Higher Buddhism* (Edinburgh, 1910), pp. 1-52, 127-145. The *locus classicus* for missionary description of Chinese Buddhist monasteries is probably in Matteo Ricci, especially his description of the Nan-hua Ssu in 1589, where "the monks lived in great licentiousness." See Pasquale M. d'Elia, ed., *Fonti Ricciane:*

Documenti originali concernenti Matteo Ricci e la storia delle prime relazioni tra l'Europa e la Cina (1579-1615), 3 vols. (Rome, 1942, 1949), I, NN340.

3. George Smith, pp. 229-231.

4. *Ibid.*, pp. 184-185. Bishop Smith was by no means the most intolerant of Christian observers. His Roman Catholic contemporary, Abbé Huc, traveled much more extensively through China but appears to have learned even less about the condition of Chinese Buddhism, as can be seen in the following: "There do not exist any monasteries, properly so-called, where bonzes live in community . . . In each house there is indeed a chief, but he is rather an administrator of temporal goods than a spiritual superior. He does not exercise any authority over his brethren, who live without any rule, just as their caprice dictates . . . To make yourself a bonze, you have only to shave your head and put on a robe with long, wide sleeves." Huc, pp. 202-203.

5. Arthur H. Smith, pp. 107-108. Smith (p. 84) quotes the following from the pen of J. Dyer Ball: "It [Buddhism] excites but little enthusiasm at the present day in China; its priests are ignorant, low, and immoral; addicted to opium; despised by the people; held up to contempt and ridicule; and the gibe and joke of the populace" (no reference given).

6. Ernest J. Eitel, *Buddhism, Its Historical, Theoretical, and Popular Aspects*, 3rd ed. (Hong Kong, 1884), p. 33.

7. Hackmann, *Buddhism as a Religion*, pp. 247-248. In 1902-03 Hackmann visited over a hundred monasteries in eleven provinces, living in some for weeks at a time; see *T'oung Pao*, series II, 2:652 (1908).

8. De Groot, *Sectarianism*, I, 132.

9. On the 1667 census, see *Ch'in-ting ta-Ch'ing hui-tien shih-li*, 501:4. On the 1930 figures, see Welch, *Practice*, pp. 412-419, based on *Shen-pao nien-chien* (*Shen-pao* year book; Shanghai, 1936), p. 1278. According to these same sources, the number of nuns rose in 250 years from 8,615 to 225,200, and the number of temples rose from 79,622 (apparently including Taoist temples) to 232,900 (excluding Taoist temples).

10. On these figures, see Appendix 3.

11. Timothy Richard, "The Influence of Buddhism in China," *Chinese Recorder*, 21.2:60 (February 1890).

12. Richard, *Forty-Five Years in China*, p. 159-160.

13. *Ibid.*, pp. 272, 281.

14. Soothill, *Mission in China*, p. 280.

15. They were acquired in 1893 by the Fa-yü Ssu on P'u-t'o Shan; in 1904 by the T'ou-t'o Ssu in Wenchow (apparently not the Tripitaka mentioned by Soothill, which seems to have arrived about 1895); in 1906 by the Ying-chiang Ssu, Chi-tsu Shan, Yünnan; and in 1908 by the Fo-ting Ssu on P'u-t'o Shan. The source for the first two examples is *Bodhedrum* (Taichung), 9.1:8 (December 1960); for the third, see Ts'en Hsüeh-lü, *Hsü-yün ho-shang nien-p'u*, p. 44; the Tripitaka for the Fo-ting Ssu had not yet actually been bought, but collection of the necessary 11,000 taels (about U.S. $8,500) was 80 percent completed in 1908, according to Boerschmann, p. 174.

16. George Smith, p. 234.

17. Wei-huan, p. 141. Compare the scripture perusal chamber at the Liu-yün Ssu, Shanghai (see Welch, *Practice*, pp. 102-103). On the literacy of monks, see Welch, *Practice*, pp. 257-258.

18. Cumming, p. 332.

19. On the form of these lectures see above, p. 106.

20. Richard, "The Influence of Buddhism in China," pp. 60-61.

21. De Groot, *Le Code du Mahayana*, p. 141; cf. *ibid.*, pp. 136, 142.

22. Richard, *Forty-Five Years in China*, p. 278.

23. Hodous, p. 67.

24. Herbert A. Giles, *Historic China and Other Sketches* (London, 1882), p. 115. Lan Ting-yüan (1680-1733) took an active interest in suppressing heterodox religion. Once when he was a magistrate in Kwangtung, he personally arrested and executed the leaders of a syncretist sect. Giles was not himself a missionary. An illustration of the missionaries' acceptance of the Confucian view is provided by the Reverend Arthur H. Smith who "particularly objected to [monks] withdrawing large tracts of land from the use of the community 'in order to support in idleness, gambling, opium-smoking, and vice social vampires who added nothing to the common weal, but sucked the life blood of China.'" This is quoted (without a citation) by Paul A. Varg, *Missionaries, Chinese, and Diplomats* (Princeton, 1958), p. 109.

25. On the background and motivation of monks, see Welch, *Practice*, pp. 248-269.

26. Fortune, *Three Years*, pp. 186-187.

27. De Groot, for example, states that during devotions monks had to "keep the eyes ever downcast without permitting oneself a single glance upwards or to the side . . . This is also certainly the reason for the motionlessness of the entire assembly during the recitation of liturgy. The spectator detects no movement among all those heads, those arms, those hands. It appears to him that talking statues are standing or kneeling before the holy images" (*Le Code du Mahayana*, pp. 164-165). On P'u-t'o Shan Boerschmann found that the elderly monks in the buddha recitation hall "were so absorbed in their work and so oblivious to the world that they did not let their concentration be disturbed by my presence," whereas the younger monks in the meditation hall could not "control their curiosity to look at outsiders who came into the room and at whom they glanced, to a greater or lesser extent, from between their eyelids" (Boerschmann, pp. 136, 141). My own observation has been that most monks try to avoid distraction when they chant the sutras, but are not immune to it.

28. H. Hackmann, "Das Buddhisten-Kloster Tien-dong in der Chinesischen Provinz Chekiang," *Zeitschrift für Missionskunde und Religionswissenschaft*, 17:173-178 (Heidelberg, 1902).

29. Hackmann, *Buddhism as a Religion*, pp. 222-223.

30. For example, the Hu-shan Ssu near Huchow, where Fortune saw silkworms being raised and killed—a very serious violation of the Vinaya in Chinese eyes— was "in a most dilapidated condition"—Robert Fortune, *A Residence among the Chinese* (London, 1857), p. 367. Where the rules were violated, money for repairs was less likely to be forthcoming from lay devotees. This was one of the reasons for the monastic cycle (see Chapter V).

31. MacGowan, p. 515.

32. Hackmann, *Buddhism as a Religion*, p. 247.

33. Giles, p. 284.

34. See C. R. Boxer, *South China in the Sixteenth Century* (London, 1953),

pp. 118, 217, 310. Galeote Pereira, Peter Mundy, and others make similar statements.

35. The clergy seems to have enjoyed a particularly poor reputation, for example, in Kwangtung, whereas just the reverse was true in northern Kiangsu. There most fathers were glad to have one of their sons become a monk, not only because it might secure for them a more favorable rebirth but also because it was an approved career (see Welch, *Practice*, pp. 255-257).

36. For more information on call monks (*ying-fu seng*), see Welch, *Practice*, chap. 7, n. 24. The movement against performing funerary rites for money may go back to 1912 (see Chapter II above, note 20). It is interesting that a set of rules enforced at the Pao-kuang Ssu in the 1930's included the following: "Whoever goes out to recite or chant sutras in order to make money for himself will be punished" (Prip-Møller, p. 366).

37. I have not collected information that could be used to estimate what proportions of the uneducated populace held what attitudes toward call monks. But I do not see why there should have been a widespread attitude of contempt. After all, providing help for the spirits of the deceased was, in terms of filial piety, an estimable profession. I would venture the opinion that the Chinese do not feel the same degree of defilement by death that many other peoples do, perhaps because the revered spirit of the deceased is supposed to cling to the body for quite a time after death.

38. This does not quite fit the Weberian concept of "heroic or virtuoso religiosity" as opposed to "mass religiosity": see Max Weber, *Essays in Sociology*, tr. Hans Garth and C. Wright Mills (New York, 1946), p. 287. Weber's categories seem inappropriate to the Chinese sangha, in which the distinction between elite and mass does not correspond to the distinction between monastery and parish church. Many large public monasteries in China provided religious services for the laity of their district, while many small temples were places of study and retreat.

39. For example, in 1897 "Reverend T'ung-chih expounded the *Surangama Sutra* at Chiao Shan; there were one thousand people in the audience" (Ts'en Hsüeh-lü, *Hsü-yün ho-shang nien-p'u*, p. 26). According to Prip-Møller (pp. 380-381) T'ung-chih lectured on the *Surangama Sutra* at Chiao Shan in the summer of 1898. For other examples, see Welch, *Practice*, p. 313.

40. Ts'en Hsüeh-lü, *Hsü-yün ho-shang nien-p'u*, pp. 35, 42.

41. Although it is difficult to make quantitative comparisons, lecturing in the late Ch'ing appears to have been qualitatively the same as in the T'ang dynasty, when, according to one authority, "the audience listening to such lectures consisted primarily of monks residing within the monastery—about 250 to 400 in the case of the important temples" (Kenneth K. S. Ch'en, p. 287).

42. De Groot and Yang quote the *Ta-ch'ing hui-tien* to the effect that "the Buddhist and Taoist clergy shall not go to public places to chant the sutras, beg, explain the operation of karma, or collect money"; this was reinforced by a decree of 1646 that called for the punishment of abbots and closure of monasteries whose monks violated these provisions. By the late Ch'ing they were probably as much of a dead letter as other legal provisions regarding the sangha, but it could be argued that earlier they inhibited the start of evangelistic practices. See De Groot, *Sectarianism*, I, 113, 115, and C. K. Yang, p. 205. These authorities cite *Ta-ch'ing*

hui-tien, 55:18, but I have been unable to find the passage in the editions available to me.

43. Hodous, p. 67. On p. 55 he mentions that recently a monk had spent a few months lecturing on Buddhism at the Kuan-yin Ssu in Peking "to members of Parliament and scholars from various parts of China."

44. Hackmann writes as if he had visited Pao-hua Shan, but there is reason to question this (see Welch, *Practice,* chap. 4, n 15). The T'ien-t'ung Ssu was the only model monastery frequented by Westerners, who usually described it in favorable terms. Two visitors during the 1930's told me that they never saw a richer monastery, better maintained, and with more learned monks: it was "one of the few places that made an impression of scholarship and good order." Its good order can be seen in photographs taken about 1920; see Sekino Tei and Tokiwa Daijō, *Shina Bukkyō shiseki,* vol. 5, plates 103-108.

45. John L. Nevius, *China and the Chinese* (New York, 1869), p. 164.

46. Boerschmann, pp. 146-147, 162, 164.

47. *Ibid.,* pp. 162-163.

48. Johnston (*Buddhist China,* pp. 261-262) offers some pungent quotations from the pens of Gutzlaff and Medhurst. He ridicules the "noxious libel" that "Chinese monasteries are the habitual resort of the vicious and depraved" and offers the opinion, based on "personal observation and enquiry during frequent residence in many of the principal monasteries of China," that "the reputation of such monasteries as those of Chiu-hua and Puto, which are far from the demoralizing influences of the great towns, is in most cases deservedly high" (p. 319). I have seen no earlier counterattack on the missionaries in defense of Buddhism, but their obloquies on Chinese ways in general drew fire as early as 1864, when Sir Frederick Bruce, British minister in Peking, wrote to his sister about the "missionaries who systematically falsify the moral condition of China." See *Ch'ing-shih wen-t'i,* 1.5:14 (April 1967).

49. Reichelt, "Special Work among Chinese Buddhists," pp. 491-497.

50. Reichelt, *Truth and Tradition,* p. 154. Reichelt (see *ibid.,* p. 23) was apparently the first Westerner to get far enough behind the scenes to appreciate the role of Chin Shan as a model monastery and training ground for superior monks. The existence of good monks and bad—dragons and snakes mixed together, as Buddhists say—probably explains the almost schizophrenic contradictions in some testimony. For example, on one page we are told by W. J. Clennell, formerly of the British consular service: "I have seen this religion [Buddhism] in many provinces, in Fukien, in Chekiang, in Anhwei, in Hupei, in Kiangsi, in Shantung, in Manchuria, on the hills behind Peking. I have breathed the air of it in scores of villages, among a rustic simple people, where thirty miles is reckoned a long day's journey, and I know that in such surrounding it is a beautiful and real faith, supplying human needs. I have also seen it in great popular pilgrim centers, in the environs of great cities, real still to many of the folk who come, yet mixed and tainted with mendicancy, impudence, tawdriness, and sham, for the true delicacy of it all is stifled in the bustle of the crowded, active world. It is not to be learned from books . . . but in the shadows of its own sanctuaries, in the silence of the hills" (*The Historical Development of Religion in China,* London, 1917, p. 101). Yet a few pages later he calls Buddhist monks "lazy, sensual, vicious, cruel, ignorant, greedy, cunning, murderous, harbourers of robbers and prosti-

tutes, deluders of the ignorant, jugglers, grinders of the faces of the poor, beasts of darkness, hypocrites, and parasites" (*ibid.*, p. 124).

51. For example, John Shryock, who had lived eight years in Anking when he published his book about its temples, wrote: "It is frequently said by foreigners that the monks are ignorant and have little or no education. This is true, perhaps, of the majority, but at the Yin Chiang Tzi and Ti Tsang An monasteries, there are very well-read and cultivated men" (*The Temples of Anking*, Paris, 1931, p. 72).

Testimony on the state of the sangha in the 1930's comes from John Blofeld: "Generally speaking, however, the majority of monks and nuns in well-run monasteries lead severely simple lives, and discipline for the younger members of the community is strict" (*Jewel in the Lotus*, pp. 165-166).

Observations in the 1930's and 1940's were the basis for the following in a personal communication from D. L. Phelps, who translated the *Omei Illustrated Guide Book* (Chengtu, 1936): "I had great admiration for the abbots of the large monasteries. Many had been menial workers who rose by their intelligence and strength of character. They were great administrators, tough and strong. Some were real Zen masters."

52. Kenneth K. S. Ch'en, p. 452.

53. *Ibid.*, p. 546.

54. Wing-tsit Chan, p. 54.

55. See *ibid.*, pp. 65, 68-69, 70, 80-81. See also Welch, *Practice*, p. 325.

56. See, for example, Chapter IV, note 17; Chapter XII, note 3; Welch, *Practice*, chap. 1, n. 34. Nor did Reichelt always get his facts straight. He wrote the following about the "father" of the Buddhist revival: "One of China's scholars, Yang Wen-hui, who had long served in the country's diplomatic service and who had spent many years in America and Europe, was sent in 1875 to Japan as Chinese ambassador. He was deeply interested in religious matters and used all his leisure to study Japanese Buddhism. Yang Wen-hui belonged to a family of officials noted for Buddhist interests and he too found his spiritual home in that religion . . . When he returned to his ancestral home in Nanking . . . he set aside a large part of his home, with its park and pavilions for . . . the first Buddhist layman's academy in China . . . In the autumn of 1880 it was officially opened. The first course had twelve students, seven scholars and five monks . . . When he died in 1912 . . . Yang had appointed as his successor Ou-yang Ching-wu, one of his dearest and most promising disciples" (Reichelt, *The Transformed Abbot*, pp. 59-61).

Actually Yang Wen-hui was never sent to Japan as Chinese ambassador. His only diplomatic service was in London as a counselor of the embassy and began in 1878, not 1875. He never visited Japan or America at all. His family, far from being "noted for Buddhist interests," was Confucian: he was the first to become interested in Buddhism. He did not set aside a large part of his home for a Buddhist academy in 1880, but a small part for a Buddhist press in 1874. It was not his "ancestral home," but a property he had acquired himself. When the academy finally did open (in 1907), it had not twelve students, but twenty-four. Before Yang died (in 1911, not 1912) he appointed Ch'en Kao-an as his principal successor. Ou-yang Ching-wu was merely left in charge of the collation of texts.

No doubt my own book contains many of the same kind of errors.

57. Even the seasoned traveler was sometimes overwhelmed. Harry A. Franck, after he stayed at a hotel near Canton, wrote (pp. 305-306) about the "haphazard cooking going on in what we reserve as the hotel lobby, miserable narrow stairways unswept since Confucius first left home, gambling and the fondling of prostitutes going on openly in most of the rooms, everything under the sun that has no place in a hotel crowded into it, with no attention to guests or prospective clients from any one until they won it by creating some form of uproar, the miserable rooms containing little, of a desirable nature, except mosquito-nets black with age and lack of laundering sagging about wooden-floored bed-steads covered only with a straw mat bearing the imprint of a thousand previous unbathed guests. Those who wanted it were furnished one unmentionable quilt, the blackened cotton oozing out of it in places like coagulated blood from gaping wounds." Equally indignant is Franck's description of a West River steamer, where the kitchen was "closely flanked by two conveniences [toilets] outdoing in filthiness anything that mere words can express. Of the habits of the half-dozen discards from the human garbage-heap who worked there, how they dipped water from the river in the same buckets they used for slops and even filth, of the unutterable condition of their few utensils and of the cooking style in general, I shall only say that I have nothing to gain by nauseating the reader" (*ibid.*, p. 376).

58. Robert Fortune, *A Journey to the Tea Countries of China* (London, 1852), pp. 137-138. He is describing the monks at Ku Shan in 1848.

59. Letter from Mrs. F. R. Millican to J. B. Pratt, June 12, 1929, Pratt Collection, Williams College Library.

60. Tao-an (312-385), one of the most eminent monks in Chinese history, was famous for his ugliness. Some entered the sangha precisely because they were ugly and hence had been rejected by the girls they loved or by society at large; or, as in the case of the abbot of the T'ien-ning Ssu, because of a disease that affected their appearance.

61. Fortune, *Residence,* pp. 268-269.

62. Boerschmann, p. 158.

63. Even the special visitor was often excluded. In 1923, for example, when Pratt visited Chieh-chuang Ssu in Soochow, he discovered that 110 of the 200 resident monks were enrolled in the meditation hall. When he asked if he might look in on them, he was told that, because of the danger of disturbing them, this was not allowed. (Many casual visitors, of course, would not have even known that the monastery *had* a meditation hall.) See Pratt Notebooks, Williams College Library.

64. Pratt, p. 686. Cf. pp. 312-313, 354, 683.

65. *Ibid.,* p. 687. Not only worship, but study lacked fervor in Peking. In 1918, when the illustrious Ti-hsien went there to expound the sutras, he found that not one of the temples was in the habit of holding lectures and not one of their monks came to hear his. All they did was to perform rites for the dead, which provided them with a "comfortable living." See T'an-hsü, I, 91-92.

66. Pratt, pp. 686, 688. Pratt did not visit Wu-t'ai Shan, the one place in north China where Buddhism (albeit more in its Lamaistic than its Chinese form) was still flourishing during the Republican period; nor had he heard about Hung-lo Shan where, at least until the last years of the Ch'ing dynasty, Pure Land practice was being carried on with great vigor and devotion (see Welch, *Practice,* p. 100).

67. Pratt, pp. 685, 682. On Canton, see also above, pp. 147-148.

68. Prip-Møller, preface, n.p. Cf. p. 139.

69. Sekino Tei and Tokiwa Daijō, *Shina Bukkyō shiseki*, has five volumes of text and five folios of plates; Tokiwa Daijō, *Shina Bukkyō shiseki kinen shū* has one volume of text and one folio of plates. The latter is entirely devoted to the monasteries of central, southeast, and south China and contains most of the photographs of prosperous monasteries to which I refer. Many of the same photographs and others like them may be found in the ten folios of Sekino Tei and Tokiwa Daijō, *Shina bunka shiseki* (Cultural monuments of China; Tokyo, 1939-1940).

70. For example, Chin Shan, Chiao Shan, Pao-hua Shan, and the T'ien-ning Ssu in Kiangsu; the Hua-ch'eng Ssu, Kan-lu Ssu, Pai-sui Kung, and Ying-chiang Ssu in Anhwei; the Ch'an-yüan Ssu, Chao-ch'ing Ssu, Ching-shan Ssu, Ling-yin Ssu, and the Liu-ho T'a in Chekiang; the Pao-t'ung Ssu in Hupeh. The T'ien-ning Ssu was one of those rebuilt on a larger scale than before.

71. John Thomson, *Illustrations of China and Its People*, 2nd ed. (London, 1874), vol. 3, plate 17. Pao-hua Shan was in full operation again by 1885 (see Prip-Møller, p. 296). The reconstruction of the great shrine-hall of the Ling-yin Ssu, the largest monastery in Hangchow, was completed in 1911 at a cost of 150,000 taels: see Fitch, *Hangchow Itineraries* (Shanghai, 1929), p. 29. Ting-hu Shan, the largest monastery in Kwangtung province, was rebuilt by 1878 (Gray, I, 129). Another striking case was the Ch'an-yüan Ssu at West T'ien-mu Shan. It was handsomely rebuilt within five years despite the fact that "the whole neighbourhood had been so ravaged by the T'ai-p'ing devastation that even then, in 1896, after nearly forty years, all the surrounding villages were in ruins, the roads mostly choked with jungle, and so infested with robbers that innkeepers kept spears lashed to the bedstead in their guest rooms for the use of travellers." See Clennell, p. 100, and Chuang Yü, *T'ien-mu Shan* (Shanghai, 1923), p. 3 and plates 8-9. R. F. Johnston found this monastery in a "very flourishing condition" when he visited it about 1913 ("A Poet Monk of Modern China," p. 15).

72. Reichelt, *Religion in Chinese Garment*, p. 131. I have attempted to explain why this was so in *Practice*, pp. 4, 14, 128, and in my article "Changing Attitudes toward Religion in Modern China," in *China in Perspective* (Wellesley College, 1967), pp. 79-97, where I apply the phrase "monastic social contract" to the exchange of merit for rice. Lay people supplied monks with the means of livelihood; and in return monks supplied lay people with the merit needed to prevent unfavorable rebirth and natural disasters. More merit meant more rice, so that the strictest monasteries were the richest.

73. See, Welch, *Practice*, appendix 1; also above, Chapter IV, note 13. in 1965 a committee established in Taiwan to compile biographies of the most eminent monks of the Republican period drew up a preliminary list of the names to be included. There were seventy-six names from Kiangsu, Hunan, Hupei, Fukien, and Chekiang; only eighteen from the other sixteen provinces. Another important piece of evidence for the greater prosperity of Buddhism in central China is the greater length of ordinations there (see *ibid.*, p. 295). Reichelt noted that ordination was something dispensed with altogether "in northern China, where the Buddhist society is in a rather disorganized condition" (*Truth and Tradition*, p. 234).

74. For some speculations on the history of regional differences, see Appendix 4.

75. Monastic practice was called "dead" by Walter Liebenthal, an eminent scholar of Buddhism and long-time resident of Peking, in "The Problem of Chinese Buddhism," *Visvabharati Quarterly*, 18.3:237 (November 1952-January 1953).

76. See, for example, Fortune, *Residence*, pp. 186-187, 348-349, 362; Edkins, pp. 38-39, 188-189; Gray, I, 111; Hodous, p. 21; MacGowan, pp. 445 ff; Ts'en Hsüeh-lü, *Hsü-yün ho-shang nien-p'u*, p. 11. For a description of these ascetic practices, see Welch, *Practice*, pp. 318-328.

XII. THE MEANING OF THE REVIVAL

1. Johnston, *Buddhist China* (1913), p. viii: "We are about to witness . . . a partial revival in Buddhism" in China. Johnston based this prediction on the recent establishment of Buddhist associations and periodicals. In an article published in 1921, "Present Tendencies in Chinese Buddhism," Bishop Tsu refers to the associations and periodicals of 1912-1913 as "the first wave of the Buddhist revival" (p. 501) and to T'ai-hsü's efforts of 1918-1921 as the second wave (pp. 504-511). Mention, though not affirmation, of a "Buddhistic revival" is found two years earlier in *The China Mission Year Book, 1919* (No. 10, pp. 85-86). That number, incidentally, was the first to include an article on the state of non-Christian religions in China. Many later numbers contained similar articles, indicating that missionaries were coming to look on such religions with greater interest. In 1926 there was a change of title to *The China Christian Year Book* in token of a broader role envisaged by the editors. I did not discover this series until the present volume had gone to the printer and have therefore been unable to utilize it for the confirmation (and sometimes new information) that it provides. Particularly useful are the articles in the yearbooks for 1924 (pp. 50-77), 1926 (pp. 71-79, 449-469), 1929 (pp. 122-141), and 1936-1957 (pp. 98-111).

2. Pratt, chap. 19. See also Franck's contemporaneous but independent observations of a "renaissance in Chinese Buddhism . . . There is much repairing and repainting of the gaudy colors, constructing of new altars, even of brand new temples" (Harry A. Franck, pp. 29, 44).

3. Reichelt, *Truth and Tradition*, pp. 299-301; Cf. Hodous, *Buddhism and Buddhists*, p. 66. Yüan-yin is, of course, Yüan-ying. Reichelt gives the wrong Chinese character as well as the wrong romanization.

4. The only reference to their opium addiction that I have noted after 1920 is in Blofeld, *Jewel in the Lotus*, p. 26.

5. S. Radhakrishnan, *India and China* (Bombay, 1944), pp. 123-124.

6. When asked about the late Ch'ing decree permitting the conversion of temples into schools, one of them said: "Utter nonsense! Unthinkable! If there had been anything like that, I would be the one to know."

7. Pratt, pp. 382-383, 391. The Europeans in Peking often went for outings to the temples in the Western Hills, most of which were moribund, but never (so far as I know) to the few small temples in the city where Buddhism was still alive.

After B. L. Broughton, an English Buddhist, visited China in 1932, he wrote: "I made Shanghai my center for six weeks and then made excursions to Ningpo, Puto Shan, Suchow [presumably Soochow], and Hangchow . . . Everywhere I found Buddhist activity and fine social work in the form of schools, clinics and hospitals, and orphanages. You do not hear these things from the ordinary

European travelers, but I have seen them." See *Maha Bodi,* 41.3-4:133-134 (March-April 1933).

8. Blofeld, *Jewel in the Lotus,* p. 17.

9. *Ibid.,* pp. 58-59. One might add that not only did many devotees possess some theoretical knowledge of Chinese herbal medicine, but in case of illness they often preferred the Chinese practitioner to the M.D. Similarly, they preferred to write with a brush and used the lunar calendar to a greater extent than other educated Chinese.

10. The defense of Buddhism by cultural loyalists can be traced back to the beginning of the Republican era. In 1912, for example, Ts'ai O had decided to attach 70 percent of the revenue of Buddhist monasteries in Yünnan for the support of government schools, but he had to abandon his plan because of the opposition of a society dedicated to preserve everything purely Yünnanese in the economy, literature, and art. See Albert Maybon, *La République chinoise* (Paris, 1914), p. 130.

11. Some, but not all, art historians consider that Ch'an (Zen) Buddhism inspired certain characteristics of Southern Sung painting, as for example the spontaneity and "suddenness" of technique, the preoccupation with mist and clouds (equated to *sunya,* the void), and the contemplative ideal as exemplified by the monks and hermits portrayed.

12. For an interesting discussion of the popularity of scientism, see D.W.Y. Kwok, *Scientism in Chinese Thought, 1900-1950* (New Haven, 1965).

13. See above, pp. 153-154, and Welch, *Practice,* pp. 222, 228-229, 233. A case not yet mentioned was the Ch'i-t'a Ssu, one of the principal monasteries of Ningpo. In 1876 it had only 13 *mou* of farmland. By 1937, through skillful management of surplus income, it had built up its holdings to 613 *mou.* See Makita Tairyō, *Chūgoku kinsei Bukkyōshi,* pp. 254-255.

14. Wright, p. 117.

15. See Welch, *Practice,* pp. 227-228, 237-239, 241-243.

16. On the rice trade of the T'ien-ning Ssu, Changchow, see Welch, *Practice,* pp. 235-239. The Fu-t'ien Work-Study Center in T'ai-chou was set up in 1938 by the Venerable Chih-kuang because he believed that in the future monasteries would no longer be able to depend on landed income for their support. He borrowed ten looms from a lay patron and used his own money to buy the necessary materials, yarn, and hemp. The working force was composed of the twenty monks enrolled in the seminary of the Kuang-hsiao Ssu plus about ten nuns from the nearby nunnery. It was at this nunnery that the looms were set up and the work was actually carried on. There was no regular schedule for attendance. Seminary classes were held at 9-11 A.M. and 2-4 P.M. Then up to ten students might go over to work on the looms instead of attending evening devotions (everybody attended morning devotions). The cloth and towels produced were partly sold to devotees and local people and partly given away as presents. They were of poor quality because there was no one to teach the monks how to operate the looms. The total income was small—certainly not enough to support those engaged in the work. When the land rents of the Kuang-hsiao Ssu were cut off by rural unrest, the work center as well as the seminary had to close down. The monks returned to their own small temples. No one disapproved of the work center, I was told; there was nothing specifically against it in the Vinaya. This information came from a monk who was himself involved in its operation.

17. The charter of the Chinese Buddhist Association (Shanghai, 1912) stated that "in order to benefit the people's livelihood . . . monasteries must report their holdings of woods and fields to the parent Association, so that the parent Association in concert with its branches may organize agricultural and forestry companies (*kung-ssu*) to carry on reclamation and afforestation work" (*Fo-hsüeh ts'ung-pao*, no. 1, October 1912). The original charter of the Chinese Buddhist Association (Shanghai, 1929) spoke of "promoting agricultural enterprises" (*Chinese Buddhism,* 1.2:61-62, July 1930). The revised charter of 1936 called for the "encouragement of productive labor by monks (so far as this does not conflict with the principles of Buddhism and its teachings)" (*Chinese Year Book, 1937*, p. 71). The 1947 charter dropped the parenthetical proviso and, in listing types of group members of the association, included "Buddhist farms and factories"—as if these were already or about to be a common phenomenon (Lin Chin-tung, pp. 234-235). All this represents a shift of thinking, if not of practice, away from the Vinaya rules, according to which monks were not allowed to engage in agricultural labor.

18. An article entitled "The Revival of Buddhism in China" appeared in the English-language *Chinese Buddhist,* 1.1:4 (April 1930).

19. The full statement was: "You should not go to Treasure Mountain and then come home empty-handed. You must bring back a little of the nonarising, absolute dharma (*wu-sheng fa*) to Harvard University. What is this dharma of the absolute? It can make you happy in body and mind, lengthen your life, eliminate all illness, and only through it can your research colleagues at Harvard obtain release by getting the sweet dew that you may bring them."

20. Wright, p. 116.

POSTSCRIPT

1. Fortune, *Three Years,* p. 180. Cf. *Journey to the Tea Countries,* p. 226.

2. A few years later Nevius (p. 86) wrote that monasteries "are found in the most beautiful and romantic situations which the country affords." In the twentieth century Prip-Møller, who spent four years living in one monastery after another, wrote (p. 138) of "the unfailing hospitality of their inhabitants. Even though this is in conformity with the foremost rules of the faith, still the practice of the precept is so wholehearted and genuine that no matter what kind of accommodation is available, the spirit in which it is offered is incapable of betterment . . . This atmosphere of human friendliness pervaded practically all the monasteries visited by the writer."

Bibliography

Especially useful works are marked with an asterisk.

Amano Motonosuke 天野元之助. *Shina nōgyo keizai-ron* 支那農業經濟論 (The Chinese agricultural economy), Vol. 1. 2nd ed.; Tokyo, 1942.

*Blofeld, John Eaton Calthorpe. *The Jewel in the Lotus*. London, 1948; 193 pp.

———*The Wheel of Life*. London, 1959; 263 pp.

*Boerschmann, Ernst. *P'u-t'o Shan* (*Die Baukunst und religiöse Kultur der Chinesen*, Band I). Berlin, 1911; 203 pp.

Boulais, Guy. *Manuel du Code Chinois* (Varietés Sinologiques, No. 55). Shanghai, 1924; 740 pp. +6 +7.

Bukkyō Rengo-kai 佛教聯合會, ed. *Tōa Bukkyō taikai kiyō* 東亞佛教大會記要 (Summary of the East Asian Buddhist conference.) Tokyo, 1926.

Callahan, Paul E. "T'ai Hsü and the New Buddhist Movement," *Papers on China*, 6:149–188. Harvard University, East Asian Research Center, 1952.

*Chan, Wing-tsit. *Religious Trends in Modern China*. New York, 1953; 327 pp.

Chao, Buwei Yang 趙楊步偉. "Hsien-tsu Jen-shan-kung chih sheng-p'ing" 先祖仁山公之生平 (The life of my grandfather Jen-shan), *P'u-t'i shu* (Bodhedrum) 菩提樹, 8.11:6–9 (Taichung, October 1960).

*———"Wo-ti tsu-fu" 我的祖父 (My grandfather), *Chuan-chi wen-hsüeh* 傳記文學 (Biographical literature), 3.3:17–20 (Taipei, September 1963).

Ch'en Ch'i-t'ien 陳啓天. *Chi-yüan hui-i lu* 寄園回憶錄 (Reminiscences of Ch'en Ch'i-t'ien). Taipei, 1965.

*Ch'en, Kenneth K.S. *Buddhism in China: A Historical Survey*. Princeton, 1964; 560 pp.

Ch'en T'ien-hsi 陳天錫. *Tai Chi-t'ao hsien-sheng pien-nien chuan-chi* 戴季陶先生編年傳記 (Chronological biography of Tai Chi-t'ao). Hong Kong, 1958.

———ed. *Tai Chi-t'ao hsien-sheng wen-ts'un* 戴季陶先生文存 (Writings of Tai Chi-t'ao). Taipei, 1959.

Ch'en Tsung-fan 陳宗藩. *Yen-tu ts'ung-k'ao* 燕都叢考 (Investigations into old Peking). Peiping, 1931.

*Cheng-lien 證蓮. *Ch'ang-chou T'ien-ning-ssu chih* 常州天寧寺志 (History of the T'ien-ning Ssu in Changchow). 11 *chüan;* Shanghai, 1948.

Ch'eng-tu hsi-nan ho-p'ing fa-hui t'e-k'an 成都西南和平法會特刊 (The Chengtu religious meeting for peace in the southwest). Chengtu, 1932.

Ch'in-ting ta-Ch'ing hui-tien shih-li 欽定大清會典事例 (Collected statutes and precedents of the Ch'ing dynasty). Shanghai, 1899.

Chou Hsiang-kuang. *A History of Chinese Buddhism.* Allahabad, 1955; 264 pp.

*Chu Chieh-hsüan 朱潔軒, ed. *Ch'i-hsia-shan chih* 棲霞山志 (History of Ch'i-hsia Shan). Hong Kong, 1962.

Chu Pao-ch'ang 朱寶昌. "Wei-shih hsin-chieh" 唯識新解 (A new explanation of Idealism), *Yen-ching hsüeh-pao* 燕京學報, 23: 93-127 (June 1938).

Chu Shou-p'eng 朱壽朋, ed. *Kuang-hsü-ch'ao tung-hua-lu* 光緒朝東華錄 (Tung-hua records of the Kuang-hsü reign). Peking, 1958.

Chuang Yü 莊兪. *T'ien-mu Shan* 天目山. Shanghai, 1923.

Chung-kuo fo-chiao hui wu-shih-i nien-tu nien-chien 中國佛教會五十一年度年鑑 (Yearbook of the fifty-first year of the Chinese Buddhist Association). Taiwan, n.d.

Clennell, W.J. *The Historical Development of Religion in China.* London, 1917; 260 pp.

Cumming, C.F. Gordon. *Wanderings in China.* Edinburgh and London, 1888; 528 pp.

Day, C.B. *Chinese Peasant Cults.* Shanghai, 1940; 243 pp.

De Groot, see Groot.

Doolittle, Justus. *Social Life of the Chinese,* ed. Paxton Hood. London, 1868; 633 pp.

Eberhard, Wolfram. "Temple Building Activities in Medieval and Modern China," *Monumenta Serica,* 23:264-318 (1964).

———"Chinese Regional Stereotypes," *Asian Survey,* 5.12:604-605 (December 1965).

———"Religious Activities and Religious Books in Modern China," *Zeitschrift für Missionswissenschaft und Religionswissenschaft,* 49.4: 260-269 (Münster, October 1968).

Edkins, Joseph. *The Religious Condition of the Chinese.* London, 1859; 288 pp.

Eitel, Ernest J. *Buddhism, Its Historical, Theoretical, and Popular Aspects.* 3rd ed.; Hong Kong, 1884; 145 pp.

Etō Shinsaku 江藤新作. *Nampaku Etō Shimpei Ikō* 南白江藤新平遺稿. Tokyo, 1900.

Fa-fang 法舫. "Chugoku Bukkyō no genjō" 中國佛教の現狀 (The present state of Chinese Buddhism); in *Nikka bukkyō kenkyukai nempō daiichinen* 日華佛教研究會年報第一年 (Annual of the Japanese-Chinese Buddhist Research Society, first year), pp. 28-47. Kyoto, 1936.

———"Nijūgo-nen-do Min-koku Bukkyokai no kaiko" 二十五年度民國佛教界の回顧 (Review of Chinese Buddhist circles during 1936); in *Nikka Bukkyō kenkyukai nempō daininen* 日華佛教研究會年報第二年 (Annual of the Japanese-Chinese Buddhist Research Society, second year), pp. 222-234. Kyoto, 1937.

Feng Tzu-yu 馮自由. *Chung-hua min-kuo k'ai-kuo-ch'ien ko-ming shih* 中華民國開國前革命史 (History of China's prerevolutionary period). Chungking, 1943.

———*Ko-ming i-shih* 革命逸史 (Vignettes of the Revolution). Chungking, 1944.

Fitch, Robert F. *Hangchow Itineraries.* Shanghai, 1929; 94 pp.

———*Pootoo Itineraries.* Shanghai, 1929; 90 pp.

Fo-chiao pan-yüeh k'an 佛教半月刊 (Buddhist semi-monthly).

Fo-chiao yüeh-pao 佛教月報 (Buddhist monthly).

Fo-hsüeh ts'ung-pao 佛學叢報 (Buddhist miscellany).

Fortune, Robert. *Three Years' Wanderings in the Northern Provinces of China, Including a Visit to the Tea, Silk and Cotton Countries, with an Account of the Agriculture and Horticulture of the Chinese, New Plants, etc.* London, 1847; 406 pp. +xiv.

———*A Journey to the Tea Countries of China, including Sung-lo and the Bohea Hills with a Short Notice of the East India Company's Tea Plantations in the Himalaya Mountains.* London, 1852; 398 pp.

———*A Residence Among the Chinese Inland, on the Coast and at Sea: Being a Narrative of Scenes and Adventures During a Third Visit to China, from 1853 to 1856, including Notices of Many Natural Productions and Works of Art, the Culture of Silk, etc., with Suggestions on the Present War.* London, 1857; 440 pp.

*Franck, Harry A. *Roving through Southern China.* New York, 1925; 649 pp.

*Franke, Otto. "Eine neue Buddistische propaganda," *T'oung Pao*, 5:299–310 (1894).

———"Ein Buddhistischer Reformversuch in China," *T'oung Pao*, Ser. 2 (1909).

Franke, Wolfgang. *The Reform and Abolition of the Traditional Chinese Examination System.* Cambridge, Mass., 1963; 100 pp.

Gamble, Sidney D. *Peking, a Social Survey.* New York, 1921; 521 pp.

Giles, Herbert A. *Historic China and Other Sketches.* London, 1882; 405 pp.

Graham, David Crockett. *Religion in Szechwan Province, China* (Washington, D.C., 1928), Vol. 80, No. 4 of Smithsonian Miscellaneous Collections; 83 pp.

Gray, John Henry. *China, a History of the Laws, Manners and Customs of the People.* 2 vols.; London, 1878; Vol. 1, 397 pp.; Vol. 2, 374 pp.

Groot, J.J.M. de. "Buddhist Masses for the Dead at Amoy," *Actes du sixième Congrés International des Orientalistes.* Pt. 4, Sec. 4, pp. 1–120. Leiden, 1885.

———*Le Code du Mahayana en Chine, son influence sur la vie monacal et sur le monde laïque.* Amsterdam, 1893; 271 pp.

*———*Sectarianism and Religious Persecution in China.* Amsterdam; Vol. 1 (1903), Vol. 2 (1904); 595 pp.

———*Religion of the Chinese.* New York, 1910; 230 pp.

Hackmann, H. "Buddhist Monastery Life in China," *East of Asia Magazine*, 1.3:239–261 (September 1902).

———"Das Buddhisten-Kloster Tien-dong in der Chinesischen Provinz Chekiang," *Zeitschrift für Missionskunde und Religionswissenschaft*, 17:173–178 (Heidelberg, 1902).

———*Buddhism as a Religion.* London, 1910; 315 pp.

———*A German Scholar in the East.* London, 1914; 223 pp.

Hai-ch'ao yin wen-k'u 海潮音文庫 (Hai-ch'ao yin collections). Shanghai, 1931.

Higashi Honganji Shanhai kaikyō rokujūnen shi 東本願寺上海開教六十年史 (Sixty years of the Higashi Honganji in Shanghai). Shanghai, 1937.

*Hodous, Lewis. *Buddhism and Buddhists in China.* New York, 1924; 84 pp.

Hsiang-kang fo-chiao 香港佛教 (Buddhism in Hong Kong).

Hsieh Chen-min 謝振民, ed. *Chung-hua min-kuo li-fa shih* 中華民國立法史 (History of legislation under the Republic). 1948.

Hsien-tai fo-hsüeh 現代佛學 (Modern Buddhism).

*Hsien-tai seng-chia*現代僧伽 (Modern sangha).

Hsin-teng 心燈 (Torch for the mind).

*_Hua-pei tsung-chiao nien-chien, ti-i hao_ 華北宗教年鑑, 第一號 (North China year-book of religion, No. 1). Peking, 1941.

Huc, M. *Journey Through the Chinese Empire*. New York, 1856. 2 vols.; Vol. 1, 421 pp.; Vol. 2, 399 pp.

Hummel, Arthur W., ed. *Eminent Chinese of the Ch'ing Period, 1644-1912*. 2 vols.; Washington, D.C., 1943; 1103 pp.

*Johnston, Reginald F. *Buddhist China*. London, 1913; 403 pp.

———"A Poet Monk of Modern China," *Journal of the North China Branch of the Royal Asiatic Society*, 43:14-30 (1932).

K'ai-kuo ming-jen mo-chi 開國名人墨蹟 (Holographs of the nation's founders). Taipei: Kuomintang History Bureau, 1961.

*Kuan Chiung.."Buddhism," in *The Chinese Year Book, 1935-1936*, pp. 1510-1516. Shanghai, 1935.

*———"Buddhism," in *The Chinese Year Book, 1936-1937*, pp. 1445-1450. Shanghai, 1936.

*———"Buddhism," in *The Chinese Year Book, 1937*, pp. 70-75. Shanghai, 1937.

Kuang-chou min-kuo jih-pao 廣州民國日報 (Canton Republican daily).

Kuang-hui-ti pa-nien 光輝的八年 (Eight glorious years). Hong Kong, 1958.

Kuo T'ing-i 郭廷以. *Chin-tai Chung-kuo shih-shih jih-chih* 近代中國史事日誌 (Daily chronology of historical events in modern China). 2 vols.; Taipei, 1963.

Lampe, David and Laszlo Szenasi. *The Self-made Villain*. London, 1961; 215 pp.

Liang Ch'i-ch'ao. *Intellectual Trends in the Ch'ing Period*, tr. Immanuel C.Y. Hsü. Cambridge, Mass., 1959; 147+53 pp.

*Lin Chin-tung 林錦東, ed. *Chung-kuo fo-chiao fa-ling hui-pien* 中國佛教法令彙編 (Classified collection of laws and decrees on Chinese Buddhism). Taipei, 1958.

Little, Archibald John. *Mount Omi and Beyond*. London, 1901; 272 pp.

*Makita Tairyō 牧田諦亮. *Chugoku kinsei Bukkyōshi kenkyū* 中國近世佛教史研究 (Studies in the history of modern Chinese Buddhism). Kyoto, 1957.

———"Gendai Chugoku Bukkyō no seikatsu kihan" 現代中國佛教の生活規範 (The norms of Buddhist life in contemporary China); in *Bukkyō Daigaku kenkyū kiyo*, 佛教大學研究紀要 (Research bulletins of Bukkyō University), No. 35 (Oct. 23, 1958).

Millican, Frank R. "T'ai-hsü and Modern Buddhism," *Chinese Recorder*, 54.6:326-334 (June 1923).

*Mizuno Baigyō 水野梅曉. *Shina Bukkyō kinseishi no kenkyū* 支那佛教近世史の研究 (Studies in the history of modern Chinese Buddhism). Tokyo, 1925.

*———Shina Bukkyō no genjō ni tsuite 支那佛教の現狀に就て (The present state of Chinese Buddhism). Tokyo, 1926.

MacGowan, D.J. "Self-Immolation by Fire," *Chinese Recorder*, 19.10:445-451; 19.11: 508-521 (October and November 1888).

McAleavy, Henry. *Su Man-shu, A Sino-Japanese Genius*. London, 1960; 51 pp.

McDaniel, C. Yates. "Buddhism Makes Its Peace with the New Order," *Asia*, 35.9: 536-541 (September 1935).

Min Erh-ch'ang 閔爾昌, ed. *Pei-chuan chi pu* 碑傳集補 (Supplement to Stele Biographies). Peiping, 1931.

Nevius, John L. *China and the Chinese*. New York, 1869; 456 pp.

Osgood, Cornelius. *Village Life in Old China*. New York, 1963; 401 pp.

Pa-chih t'ou-t'o 八指頭陀. *Pa-chih t'ou-t'o shih-chi* 八指頭陀詩集 (Collected poems of the Eight-fingered Ascetic). Taipei, 1956.

Payne, Robert. *Forever China*. New York, 1945; 573 pp.

*Pratt, James Bissett. *The Pilgrimage of Buddhism and a Buddhist Pilgrimage*. New York, 1928; 758 pp.

*Prip-Møller, J. *Chinese Buddhist Monasteries*. Copenhagen, 1937; 369 pp.

Reichelt, Karl Ludwig. "Special Work among Chinese Buddhists," *Chinese Recorder*, 51.7:491–497 (July 1920).

———"A Conference of Chinese Buddhist Leaders," *Chinese Recorder*, 54.11:667–669 (November 1923).

*———*Truth and Tradition in Chinese Buddhism*. Shanghai, 1927; 330 pp.

———*Religion in Chinese Garment*. London, 1951; 180 pp.

*———*The Transformed Abbot*. London, 1954; 157 pp.

Richard, Timothy. "The Influence of Buddhism in China," *Chinese Recorder*, 21.2:60 (February 1890).

———, tr. *The Awakening of Faith in the Mahayana Doctrine: The New Buddhism*, by Patriarch Ashvagosha. Shanghai, 1907; xxv+45 pp. English text+46 pp. Chinese text.

———*The New Testament of Higher Buddhism*. Edinburgh, 1910; 275 pp. (an expanded version of his *Awakening of Faith*).

———*Forty-Five Years in China*. New York, 1916; 384 pp.

Satō Saburō 佐藤三郎. "Chūgoku ni okeru Nihon Bukkyō no fukyo ken o megutte" 中國における日本佛教の布教權をめぐつて (Japanese Buddhist missionary rights in China); in *Chūgoku kankei ronsetsu shiryō* 中國關係論說資料 (Collected articles on China), Vol. 3, Pt. 1, pp. 208–234. Tokyo, 1966.

*Sekino Tei 關野貞 and Tokiwa Daijō 常盤大定. *Shina Bukkyō shiseki* 支那佛教史蹟 (Buddhist monuments in China). Tokyo, 1925–1929. 5 folios of plates, with 150 plates each; 5 vols. annotations.

———*Shina bunka shiseki* 支那文化史蹟 (Cultural monuments in China). 10 vols.; 10 folios plates; Tokyo, 1939–1940.

Shang-hai shih nien-chien 上海市年鑑 (Shanghai yearbook). Shanghai, 1935.

Shryock, John. *The Temples of Anking*. Paris, 1931; 206 pp.

Smith, Arthur H. *The Uplift of China*. 2nd ed.; New York, 1921; 282 pp.

Smith, George. *A Narrative of an Exploratory Visit to Each of the Consular Cities of China and to the Islands of Hong Kong and Chusan in Behalf of the Church Missionary Society in the Years 1844, 1845, 1846*. 2nd ed.; London, 1847; 467 pp.

Soothill, W.E. *A Mission in China*. London, 1907; 293 pp.

———*Timothy Richard of China*. London, 1924; 230 pp.

Ta-Ch'ing lü-li hsin-tseng t'ung-tsuan chi-ch'eng 大清律例新增統纂集成 (Newly enlarged comprehensive edition of the Ch'ing legal code). Shao-chou, 1898.

Ta-Ch'ing Te-tsung Ching (Kuang-hsü) huang-ti shih-lu 大清德宗景 (光緒) 皇帝實錄 (Veritable records of the Kuang-hsü emperor). Taipei, 1964.

T'ai-hsü. *Lectures in Buddhism*. Paris, 1928; 92 pp.

T'ai-hsü ta-shih ch'üan-shu 太虛大師全書 (Complete works of the Venerable T'ai-hsü). Hong Kong, 1953.

Taisho shinshū daizokyo 大正新修大藏經 (Taisho Tripitaka), ed. Takakusu Junjirō 高楠順次郎 and Watanabe Kaigyoku 渡邊海旭. Tokyo, 1924–1929.

Takada Gikō 高田儀光, ed. *Chūshi Shūkyō Daidō remmei nenkan* 中支宗教大同聯盟年鑑 (Yearbook of the Central China League of Religious Federations). Shanghai, 1943.

*T'an-hsü 倓虛. *Ying-ch'en hui-i lu* 影塵回憶錄 (Reminiscences of shadows and dust). 2 vols.; Hong Kong, 1955. Vol. 1, 246 pp.; Vol. 2, 304 pp.

Tao-chün [Martin Steinkirk]. *Buddha und China : Tsi-hia-schan*. Potsdam, 1940; 30 pp.

*Tokiwa Daijō 常盤大定. *Shina Bukkyō shiseki kinen-shū* 支那佛教史蹟, 記念集 (Buddhist monuments in China, memorial collection). Tokyo, 1931.

——— *Shina Bukkyō shiseki tōsaki* 支那佛教史蹟踏查記 (On-the-spot investigations of Chinese Buddhist monuments). Tokyo, 1938.

Ts'en Hsüeh-lü 岑學呂. *Hsü-yün ho-shang fa-hui* 虛雲和尚法彙 (Religious writings of the Venerable Hsü-yün). 2nd ed.; Hong Kong, 1962.

*———*Hsü-yün ho-shang nien-p'u* 虛雲和尚年譜 (Chronological biography of the Venerable Hsü-yün). 3rd ed.; Hong Kong, 1962.

*Tsu Yu-yue. "Present Tendencies in Chinese Buddhism," *Journal of Religion*, 1.5: 497–512 (September 1921).

——— "Trends of Thought and Religion in China," *The New Orient* (Chicago, 1933).

Tu Ch'eng-hsiang 杜呈祥. *Tsou Jung* 鄒容. Nanking, 1946.

Visser, M.W. de. *Ancient Buddhism in Japan*. 2 vols.; Paris, 1928; 763 pp.

Welch, Holmes. "The Buddhist Career," *Journal of the Hong Kong Branch of the Royal Asiatic Society*, 2:37–48 (1962).

——— "Dharma Scrolls and the Succession of Abbots in Chinese Monasteries," *T'oung Pao*, 50.1–3:93–149 (1963).

——— "The Chinese Sangha, the Good and the Bad," *The Buddhist Annual*, 1:23–26 (Colombo, 1964).

——— "The Foreign Relations of Buddhism in Modern China," *Journal of the Hong Kong Branch of the Royal Asiatic Society*, 6:73–99 (1966).

——— "Changing Attitudes toward Religion in Modern China," in *China in Perspective*, pp. 79–97. Wellesley, Mass., 1967.

*———*The Practice of Chinese Buddhism, 1900–1950*. Cambridge, Mass., 1967; 568 pp.

*Wei-huan. "Buddhism in Modern China," *T'ien Hsia Monthly*, 9.2: 140–155 (September 1939).

Wright, Arthur W. *Buddhism in Chinese History*. Stanford, 1959; 144 pp.

*Yang, C.K. *Religion in Chinese Society*. Berkeley, 1961; 473 pp.

*"Yang Jen-shan chü-shih shih-lüeh" 楊仁山居士事略 (Brief biography of Yang Jen-shan); in *Yang Jen-shan chü-shih i-chü* 楊仁山居士遺著 (Collected works of Yang Jen-shan). Peking, 1923.

*Yin-shun 印順. *T'ai-hsü ta-shih nien-p'u* 太虛大師年譜 (Chronological biography of the Venerable T'ai-hsü). Hong Kong, 1950.

* *Yüan-ying fa-shih chi-nien k'an* 圓瑛法師紀念刊 (Memorial volume for the Reverend Yüan-ying). Singapore, 1954.

Glossary Index

Names of Buddhist periodicals and seminaries are listed in Appendices 1 and 2, the contents of which are not duplicated below, except where a name also occurs in the text.

Common names (like Shanghai or Sun Yat-sen) are not indexed or are given without ideograms.

The location of monasteries is approximate, just as it is in Chinese usage. "T'ien-t'ung Ssu (Ningpo)" means simply that the T'ien-t'ung Ssu is in the general area of Ningpo (actually it is about twenty-two kilometers east-southeast of that city).

The names of some important persons are followed by their dates and by biographic tags, which are offered to facilitate identification, not as epitomes of their lives.

A few minor corrections have been incorporated in the entries below, as well as some explanatory cross-references (explaining, for example, that *Chüeh-shu* was the abbreviated form of *Chüeh-she ts'ung-shu*), the need for which was discovered too late for them to be included in the text.

HARVARD EAST ASIAN SERIES

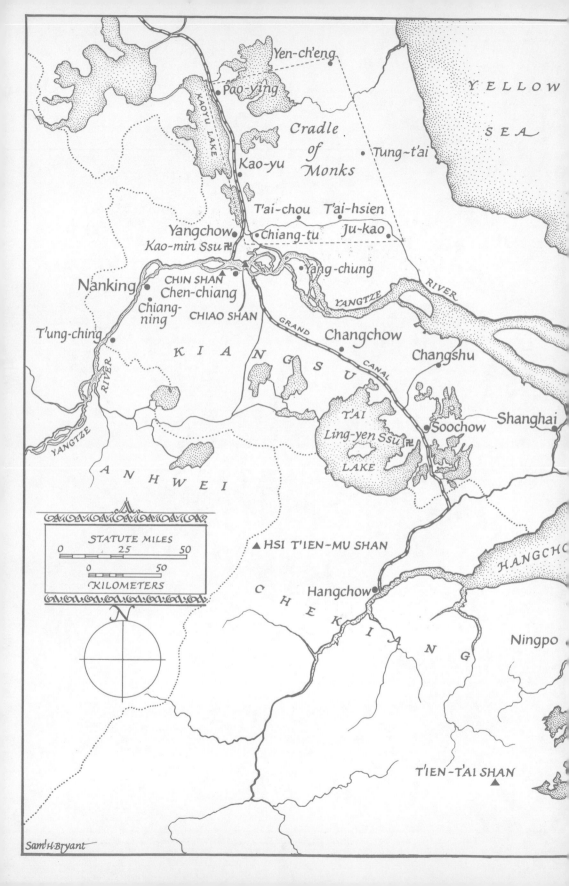

YELLOW

SEA

Yen-ch'eng

Pao-ying

KAOYU LAKE

Cradle
of
Monks

Tung-t'ai

Kao-yu

T'ai-chou   T'ai-hsien

Yangchow   Chiang-tu   Ju-kao

Kao-min Ssu卍

CHIN SHAN   Yang-chung

Nanking   Chen-chiang

Chiang-   CHIAO SHAN   YANGTZE   RIVER
ning

T'ung-ching   K   I   A   N   G   S   U   Changchow   Changshu

RIVER   GRAND   CANAL

YANGTZE   T'AI   Ling-yen Ssu卍   Soochow   Shanghai

LAKE

A   N   H   W   E   I

STATUTE MILES
0   25   50
0   50
KILOMETERS

▲ HSI T'IEN-MU SHAN

N

C   H   E   K   I   A   N   G   HANGCHO

Hangchow

Ningpo

T'IEN-T'AI SHAN ▲

Sam.l H. Bryant